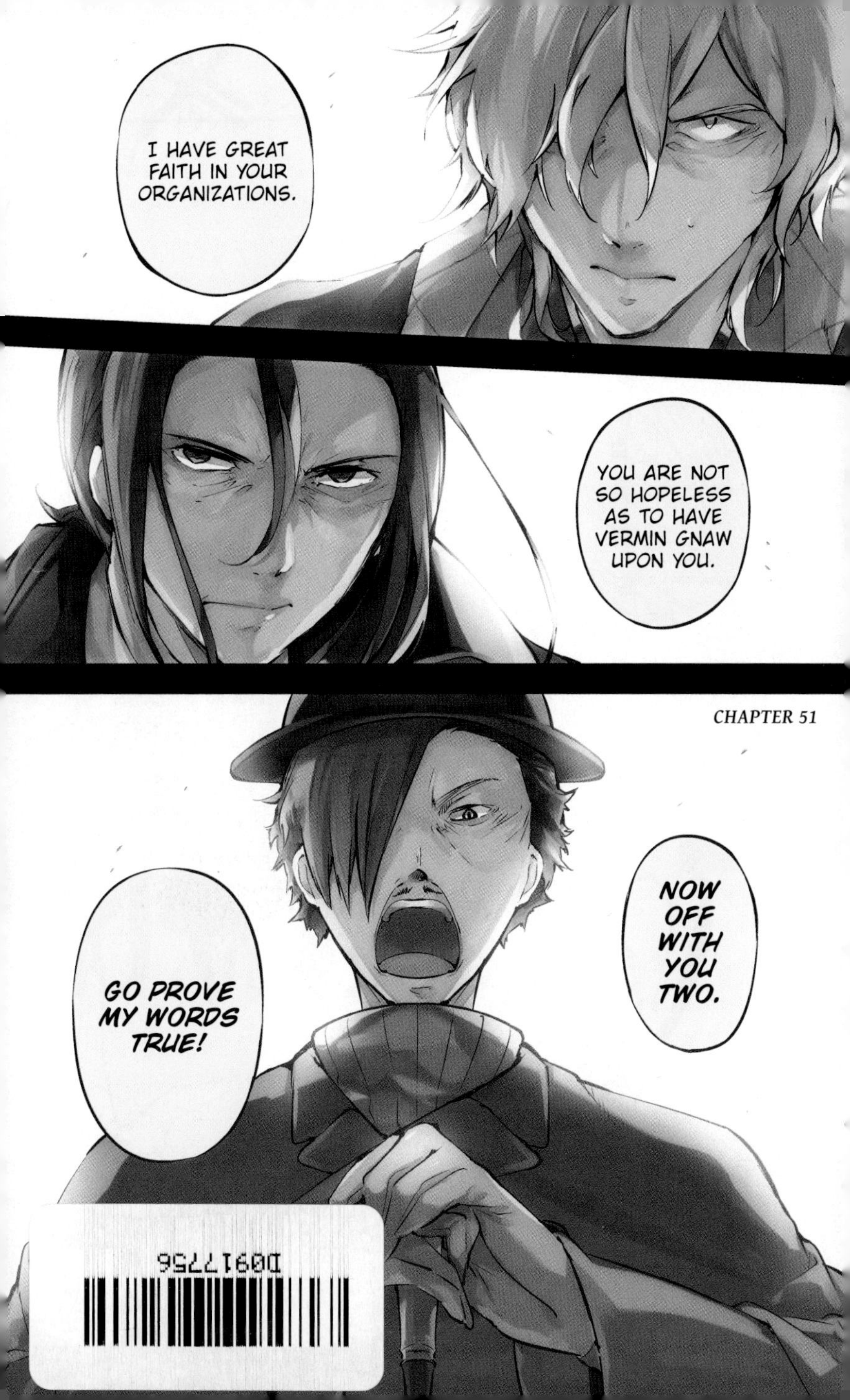
I HAVE GREAT FAITH IN YOUR ORGANIZATIONS.
YOU ARE NOT SO HOPELESS AS TO HAVE VERMIN GNAW UPON YOU.
CHAPTER 51
NOW OFF WITH YOU TWO.
GO PROVE MY WORDS TRUE!

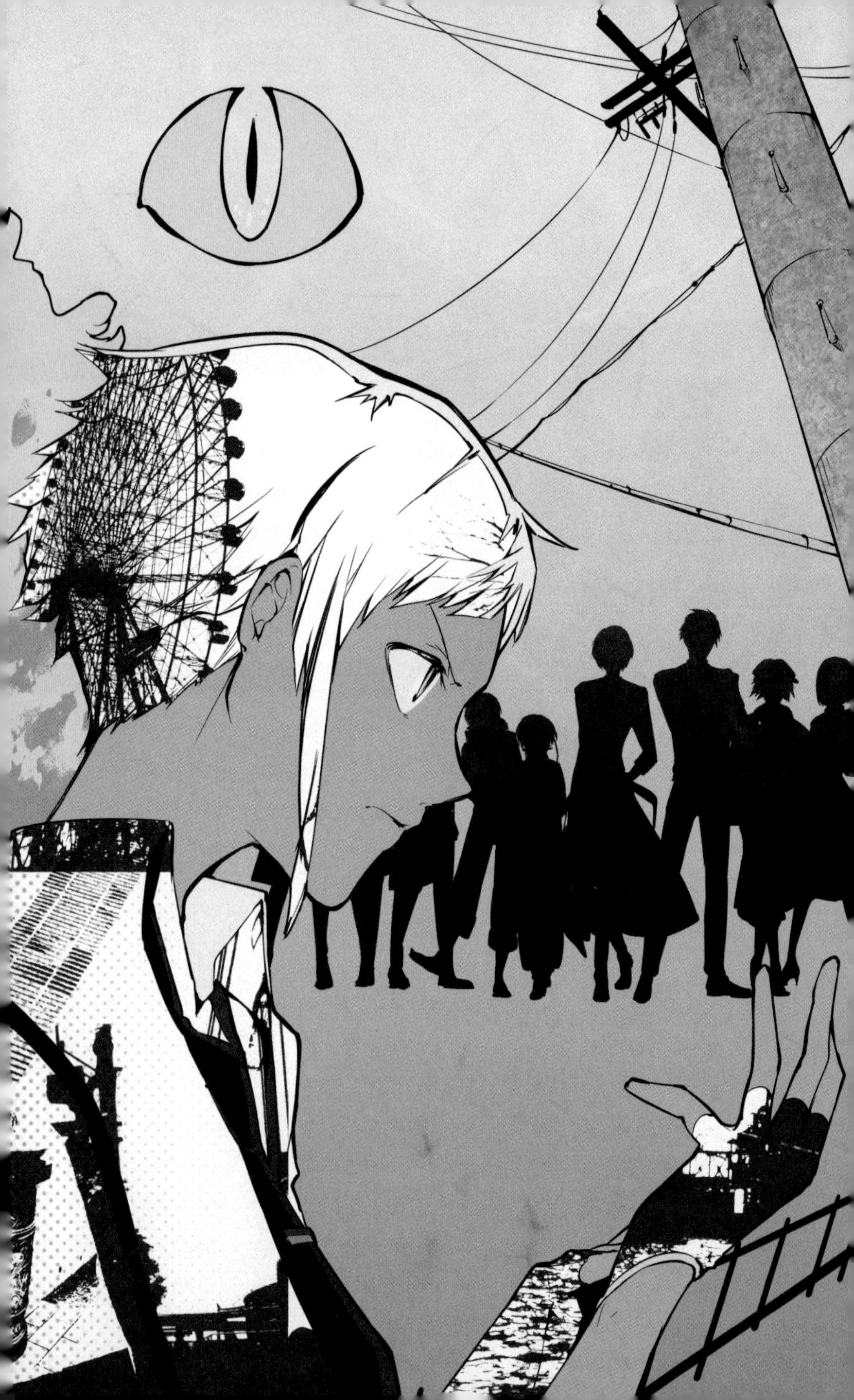

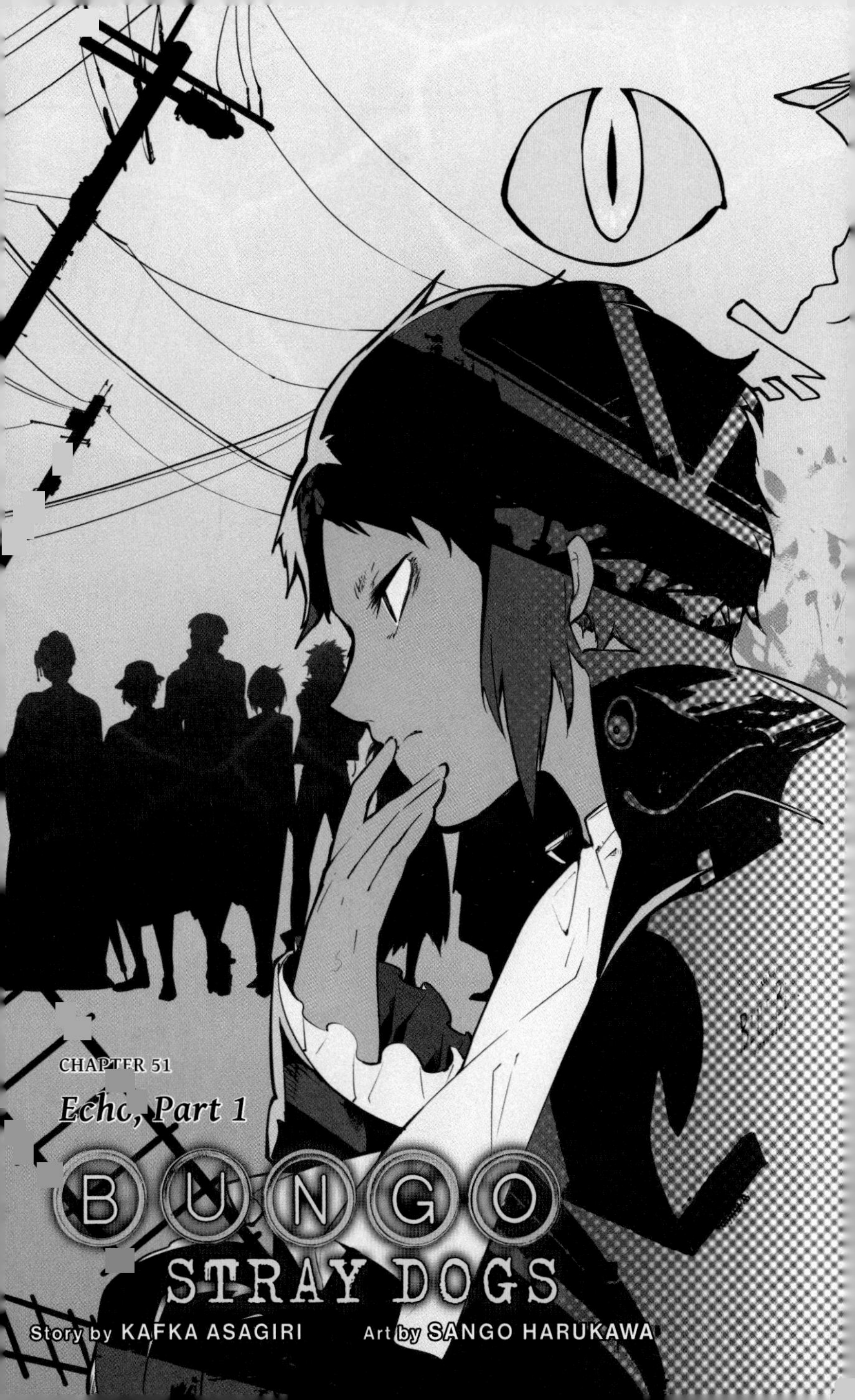
CHAPTER 51
Echo, Part 1
BUNGO
STRAY DOGS
Story by KAFKA ASAGIRI
Art by SANGO HARUKAWA

TABLE of CONTENTS

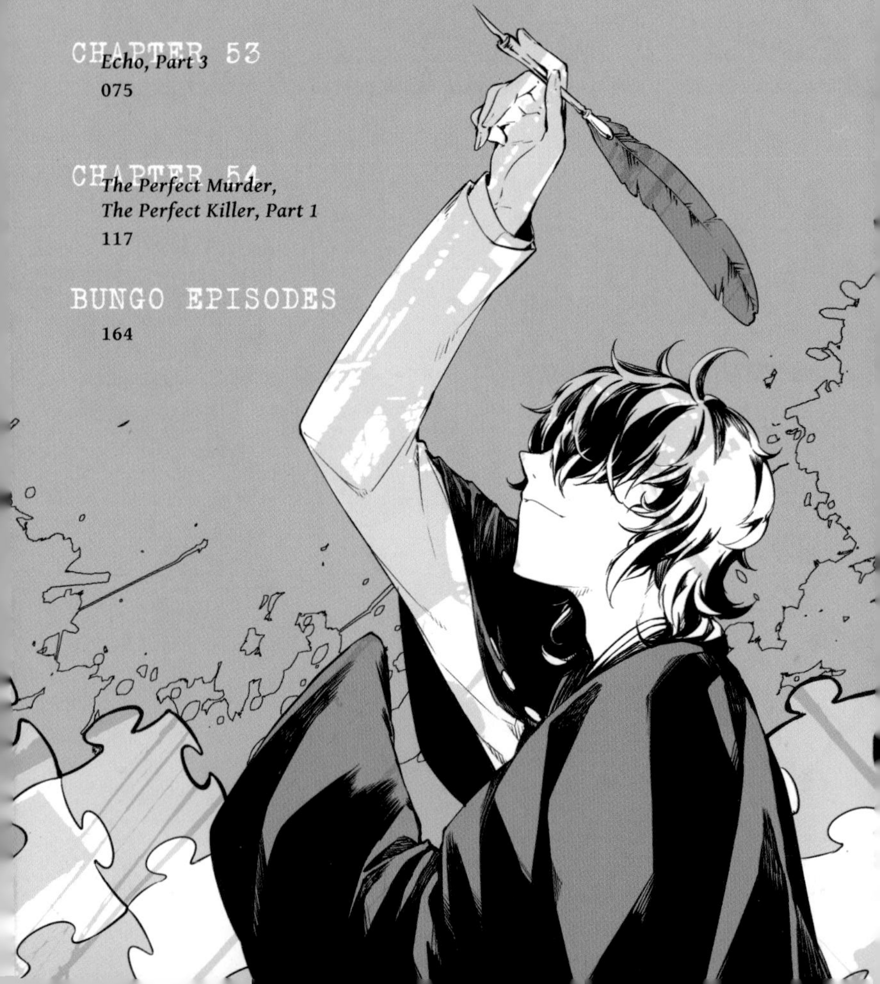

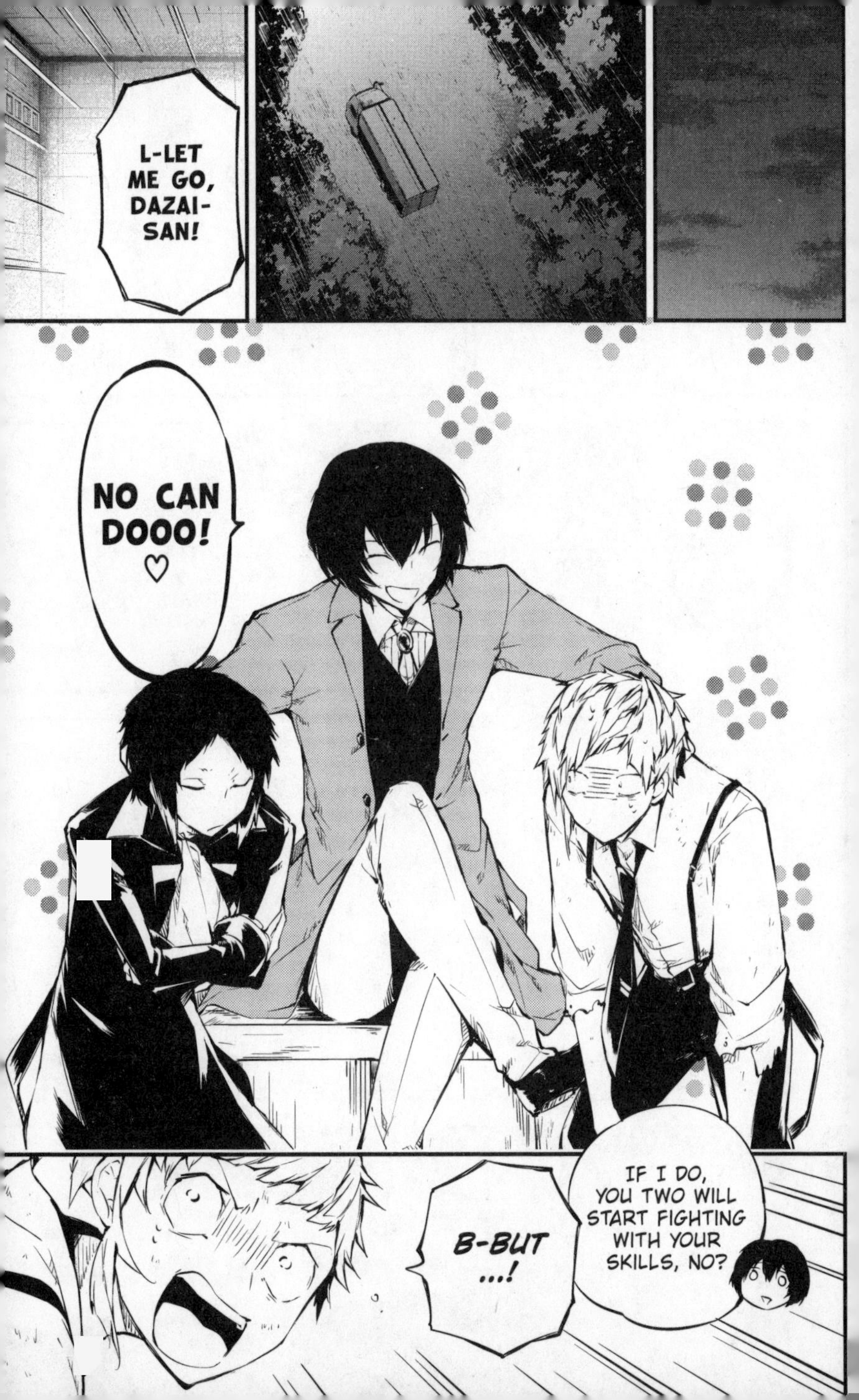
L-LET ME GO, DAZAI-SAN!
NO CAN DOOO! ♡
IF I DO, YOU TWO WILL START FIGHTING WITH YOUR SKILLS, NO?
B-BUT ...!

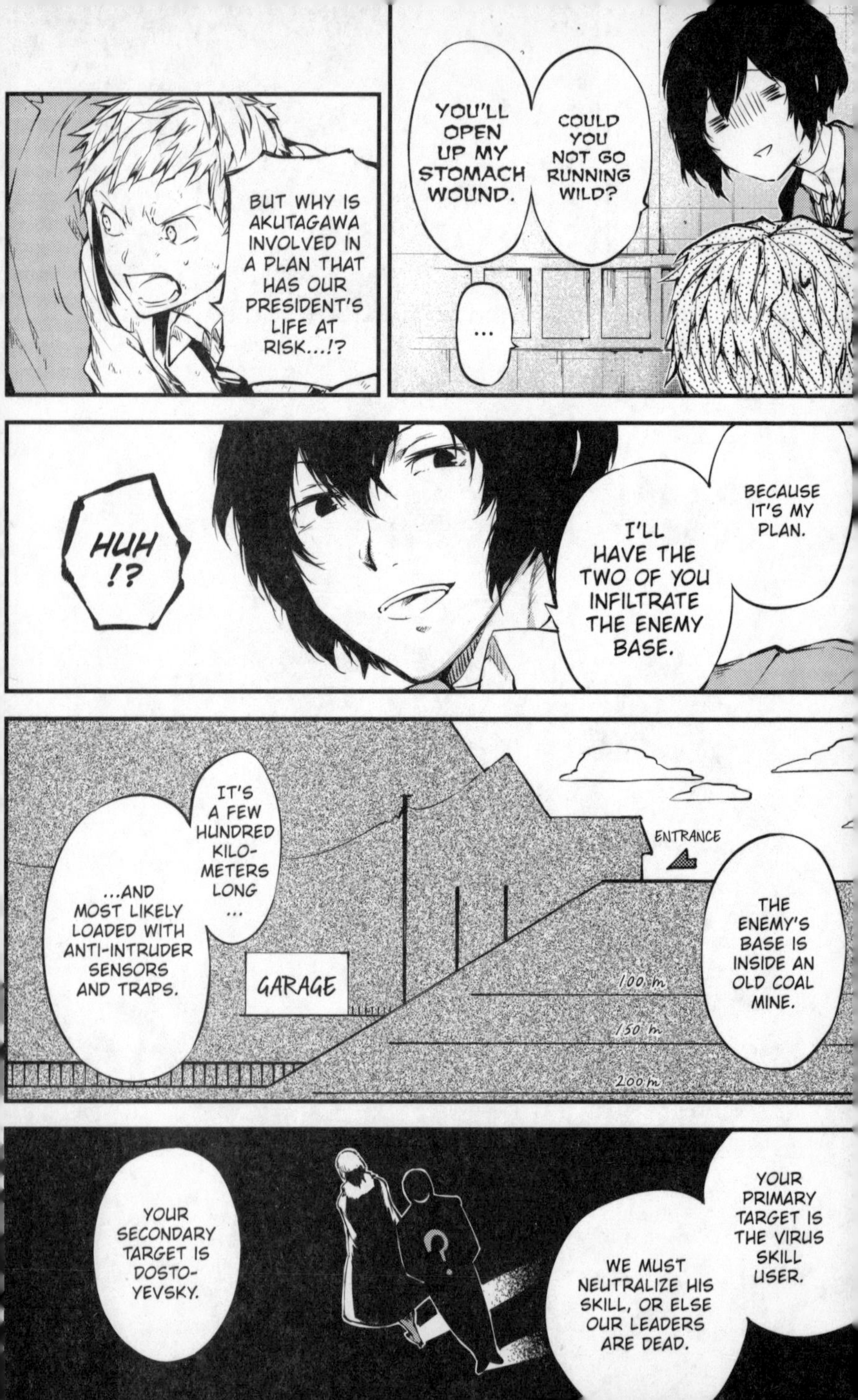
COULD YOU NOT GO RUNNING WILD?
YOU'LL OPEN UP MY STOMACH WOUND.
...
BUT WHY IS AKUTAGAWA INVOLVED IN A PLAN THAT HAS OUR PRESIDENT'S LIFE AT RISK...!?
BECAUSE IT'S MY PLAN.
I'LL HAVE THE TWO OF YOU INFILTRATE THE ENEMY BASE.
HUH!?
THE ENEMY'S BASE IS INSIDE AN OLD COAL MINE.
ENTRANCE
IT'S A FEW HUNDRED KILOMETERS LONG...
...AND MOST LIKELY LOADED WITH ANTI-INTRUDER SENSORS AND TRAPS.
GARAGE
100 m
150 m
200 m
YOUR PRIMARY TARGET IS THE VIRUS SKILL USER.
WE MUST NEUTRALIZE HIS SKILL, OR ELSE OUR LEADERS ARE DEAD.
YOUR SECONDARY TARGET IS DOSTOYEVSKY.

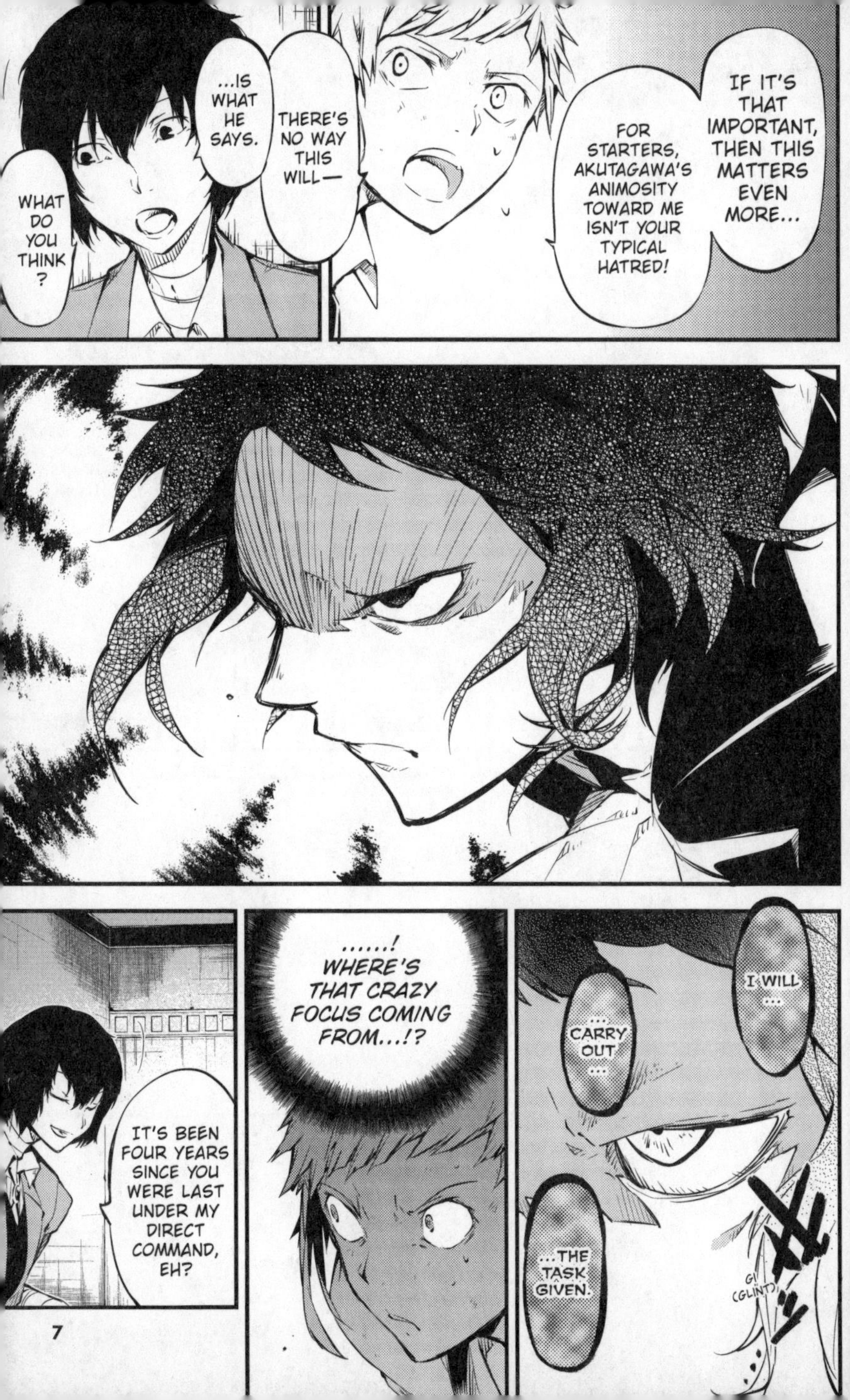
IF IT'S THAT IMPORTANT, THEN THIS MATTERS EVEN MORE...
FOR STARTERS, AKUTAGAWA'S ANIMOSITY TOWARD ME ISN'T YOUR TYPICAL HATRED!
THERE'S NO WAY THIS WILL—
...IS WHAT HE SAYS.
WHAT DO YOU THINK?
I WILL...
...CARRY OUT...
...THE TASK GIVEN.
GI (GLINT)
......! WHERE'S THAT CRAZY FOCUS COMING FROM...!?
IT'S BEEN FOUR YEARS SINCE YOU WERE LAST UNDER MY DIRECT COMMAND, EH?

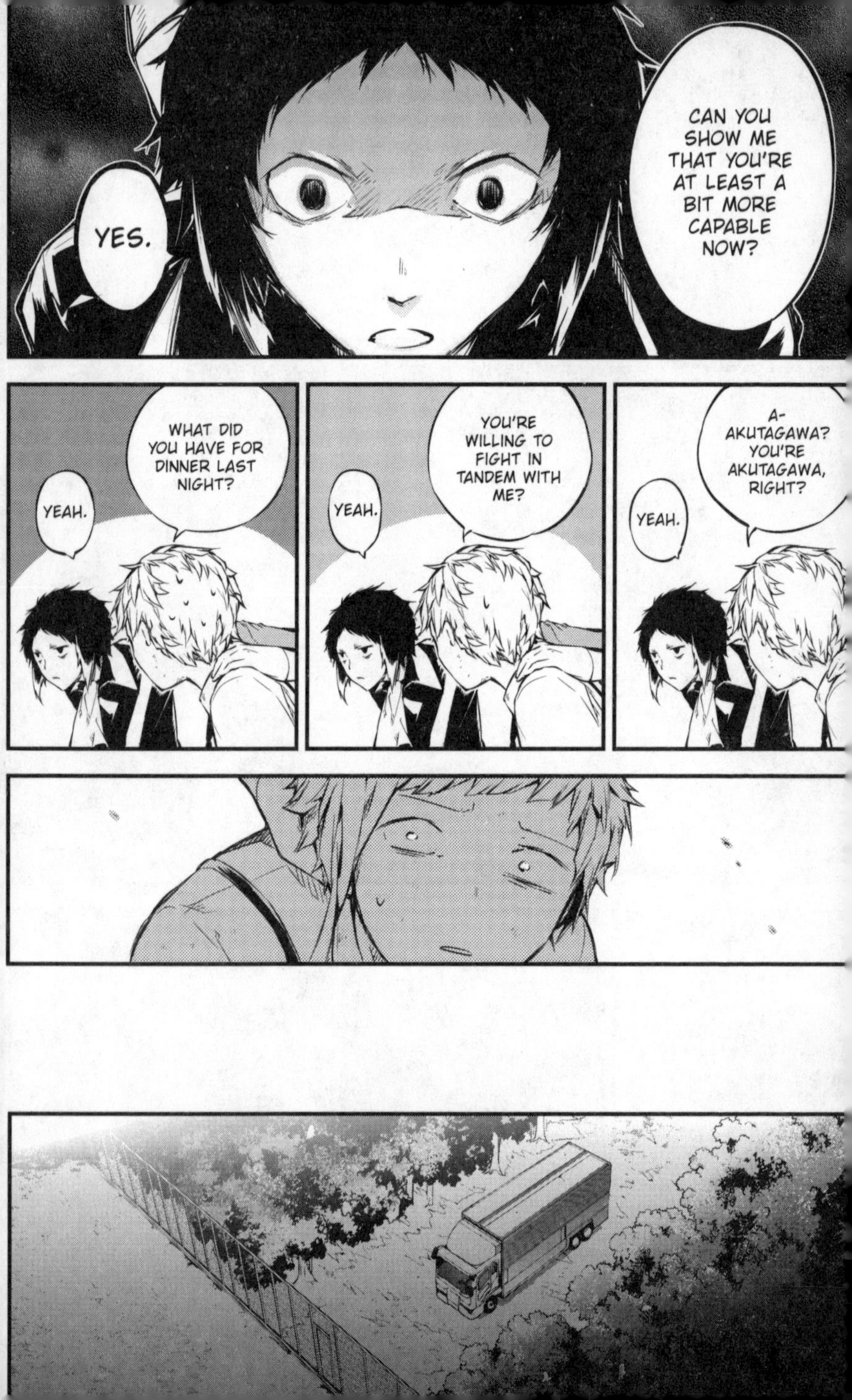
CAN YOU SHOW ME THAT YOU'RE AT LEAST A BIT MORE CAPABLE NOW?
YES.
A- AKUTAGAWA? YOU'RE AKUTAGAWA, RIGHT?
YEAH.
YOU'RE WILLING TO FIGHT IN TANDEM WITH ME?
YEAH.
WHAT DID YOU HAVE FOR DINNER LAST NIGHT?
YEAH.

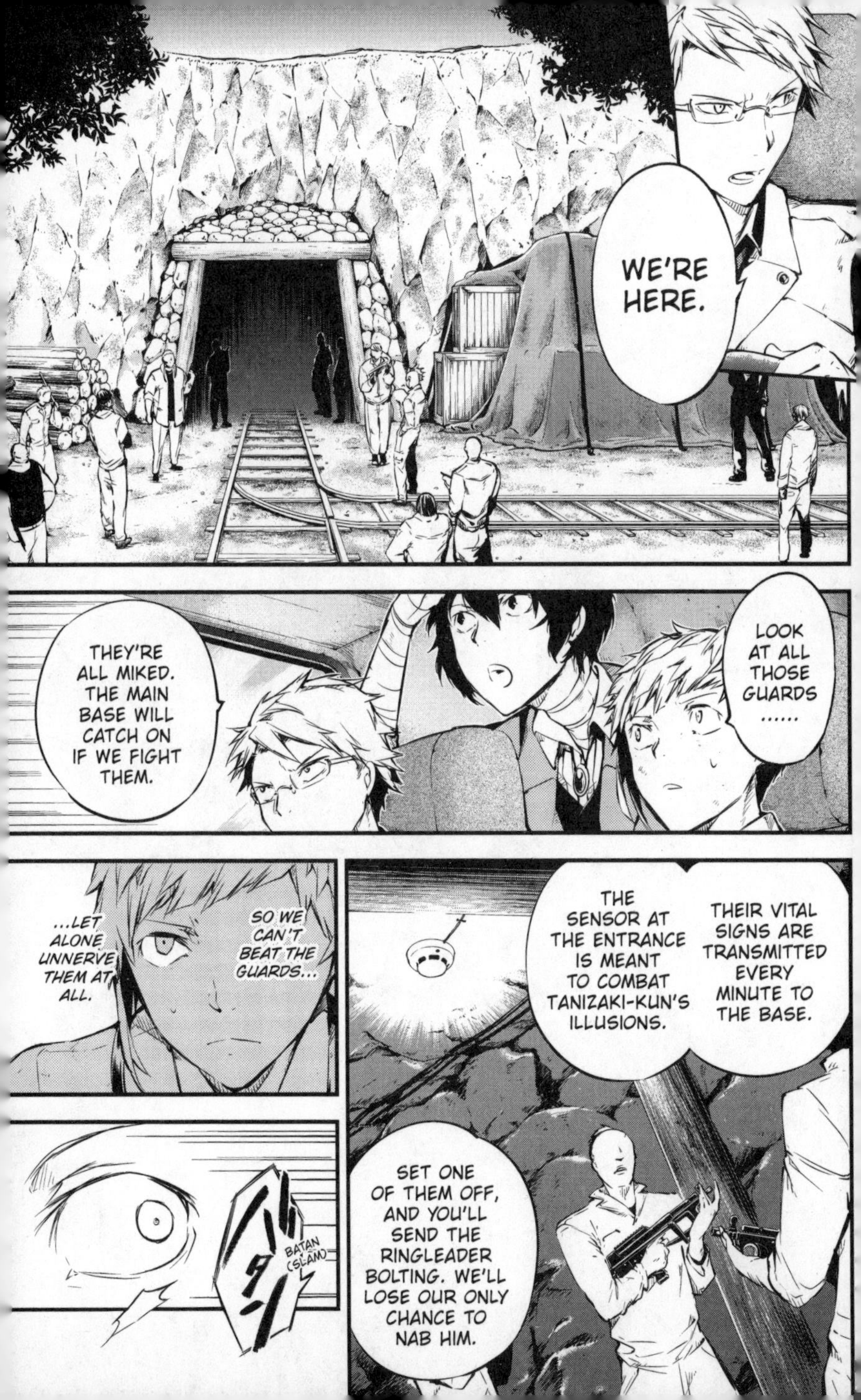
WE'RE HERE.
LOOK AT ALL THOSE GUARDS......
THEY'RE ALL MIKED. THE MAIN BASE WILL CATCH ON IF WE FIGHT THEM.
THEIR VITAL SIGNS ARE TRANSMITTED EVERY MINUTE TO THE BASE.
THE SENSOR AT THE ENTRANCE IS MEANT TO COMBAT TANIZAKI-KUN'S ILLUSIONS.
SET ONE OF THEM OFF, AND YOU'LL SEND THE RINGLEADER BOLTING. WE'LL LOSE OUR ONLY CHANCE TO NAB HIM.
SO WE CAN'T BEAT THE GUARDS...
...LET ALONE UNNERVE THEM AT ALL.
BATAN (SLAM)

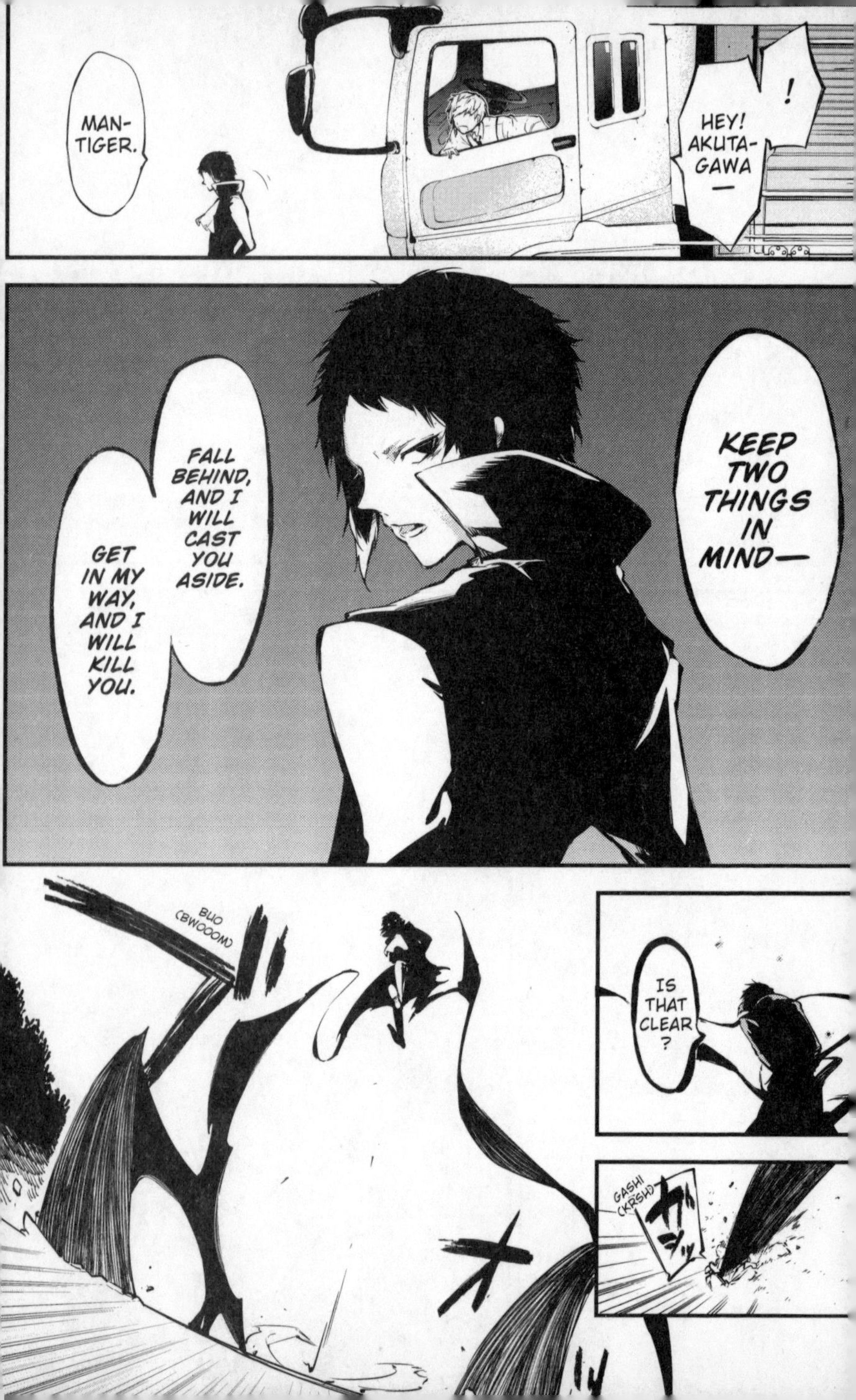
!
HEY! AKUTA-GAWA—
MAN-TIGER.
KEEP TWO THINGS IN MIND—
FALL BEHIND, AND I WILL CAST YOU ASIDE.
GET IN MY WAY, AND I WILL KILL YOU.
IS THAT CLEAR?
GASHI (KRSH)
BUO (BWOOOM)

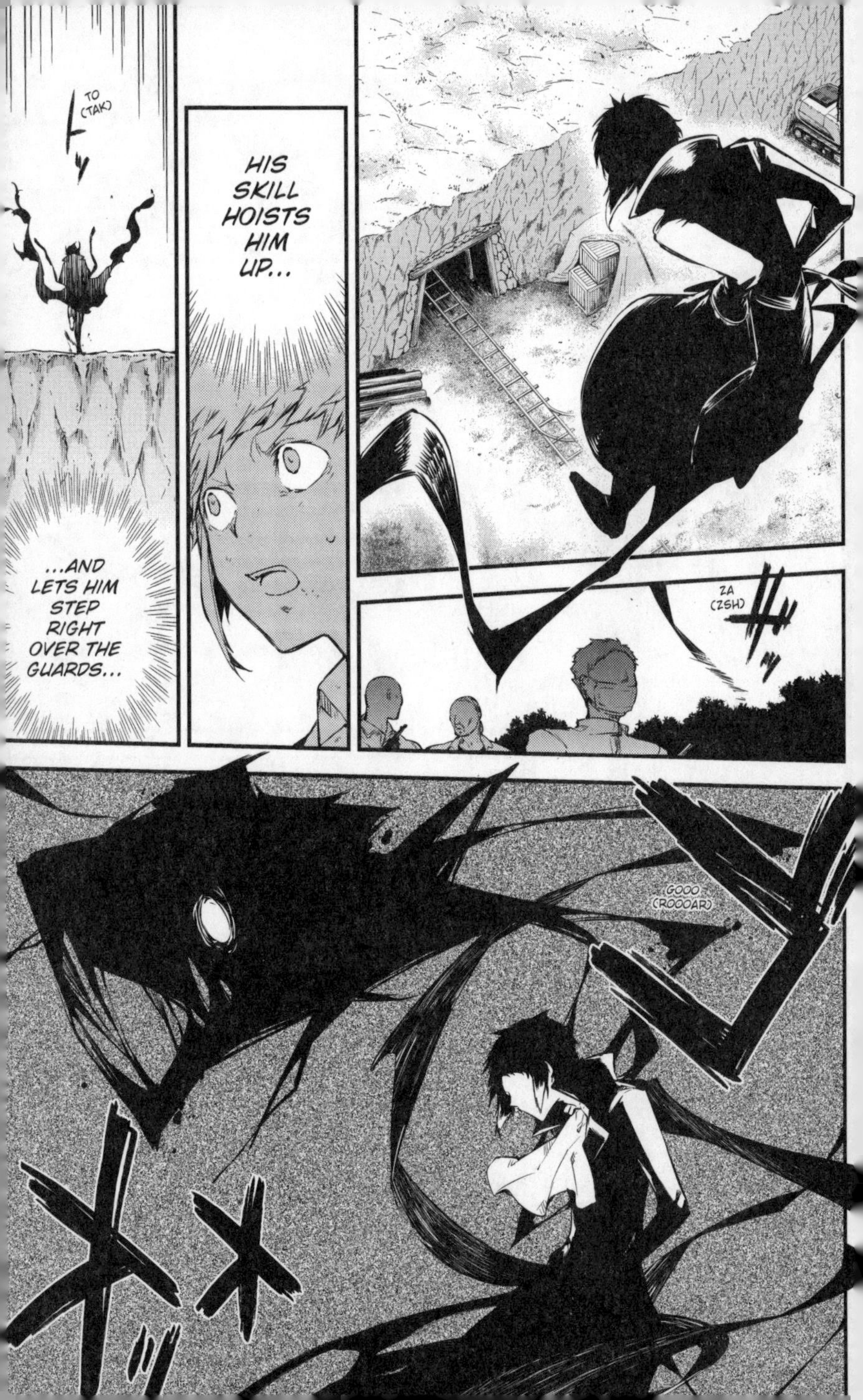
ZA (ZSH)
HIS SKILL HOISTS HIM UP...
TO (TAK)
...AND LETS HIM STEP RIGHT OVER THE GUARDS...
GOOO (ROOOAR)

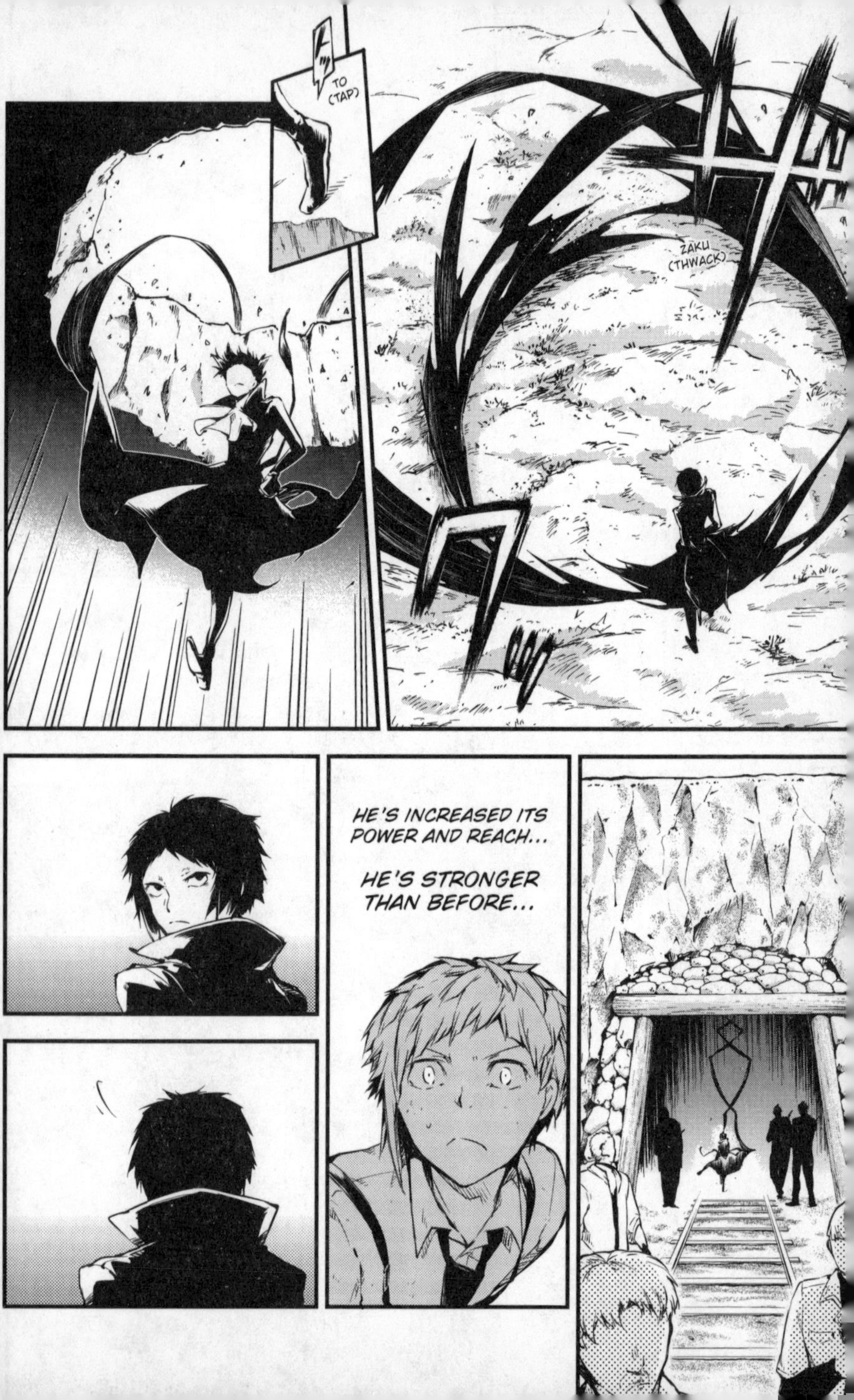
ZAKU (THWACK)
TO (TAP)
HE'S INCREASED ITS POWER AND REACH...
HE'S STRONGER THAN BEFORE...

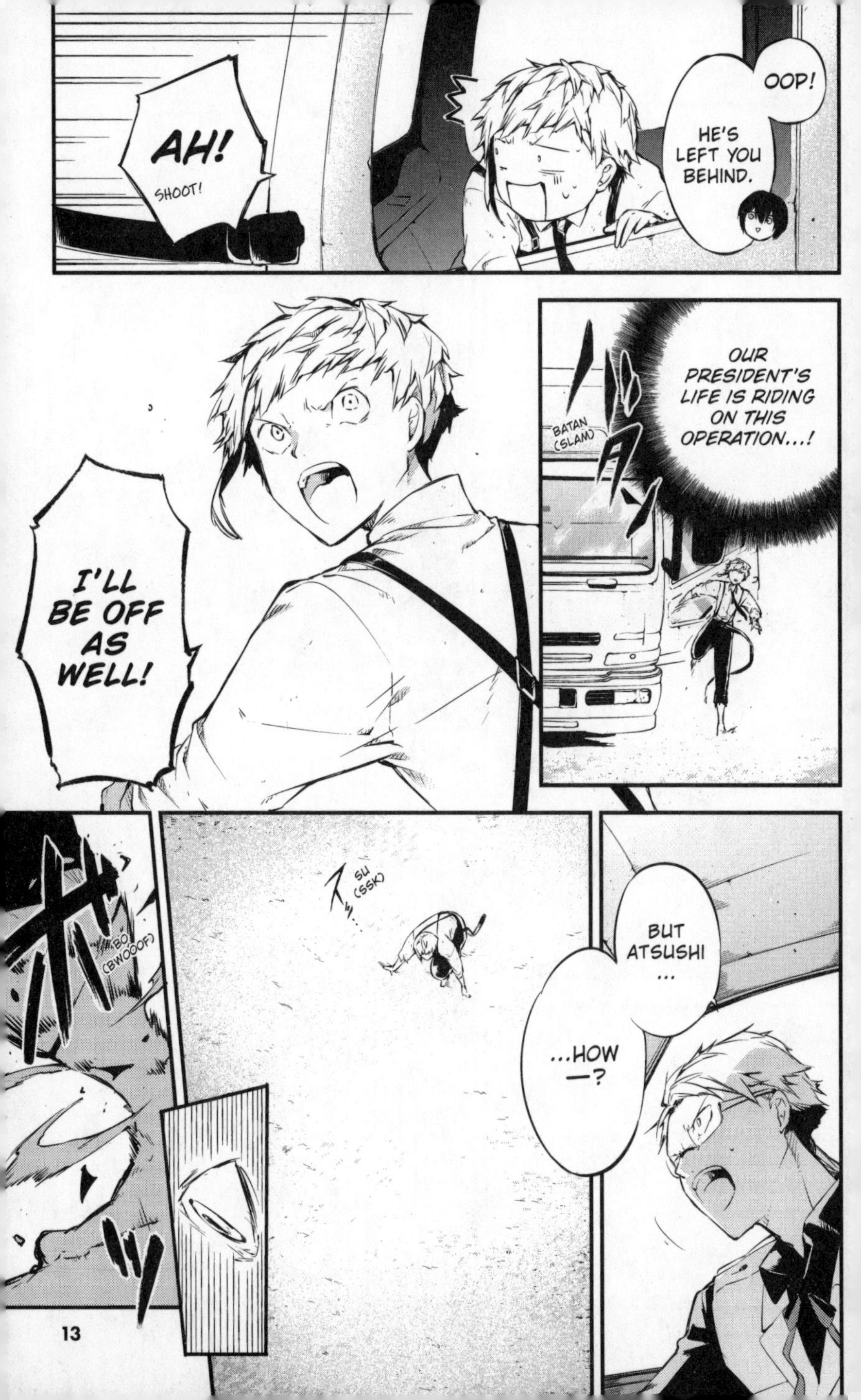
OOP!
HE'S LEFT YOU BEHIND.
AH!
SHOOT!
BATAN (SLAM)
OUR PRESIDENT'S LIFE IS RIDING ON THIS OPERATION...!
I'LL BE OFF AS WELL!
BUT ATSUSHI ...
...HOW—?
SU (SSK)
BO (BWOOOF)

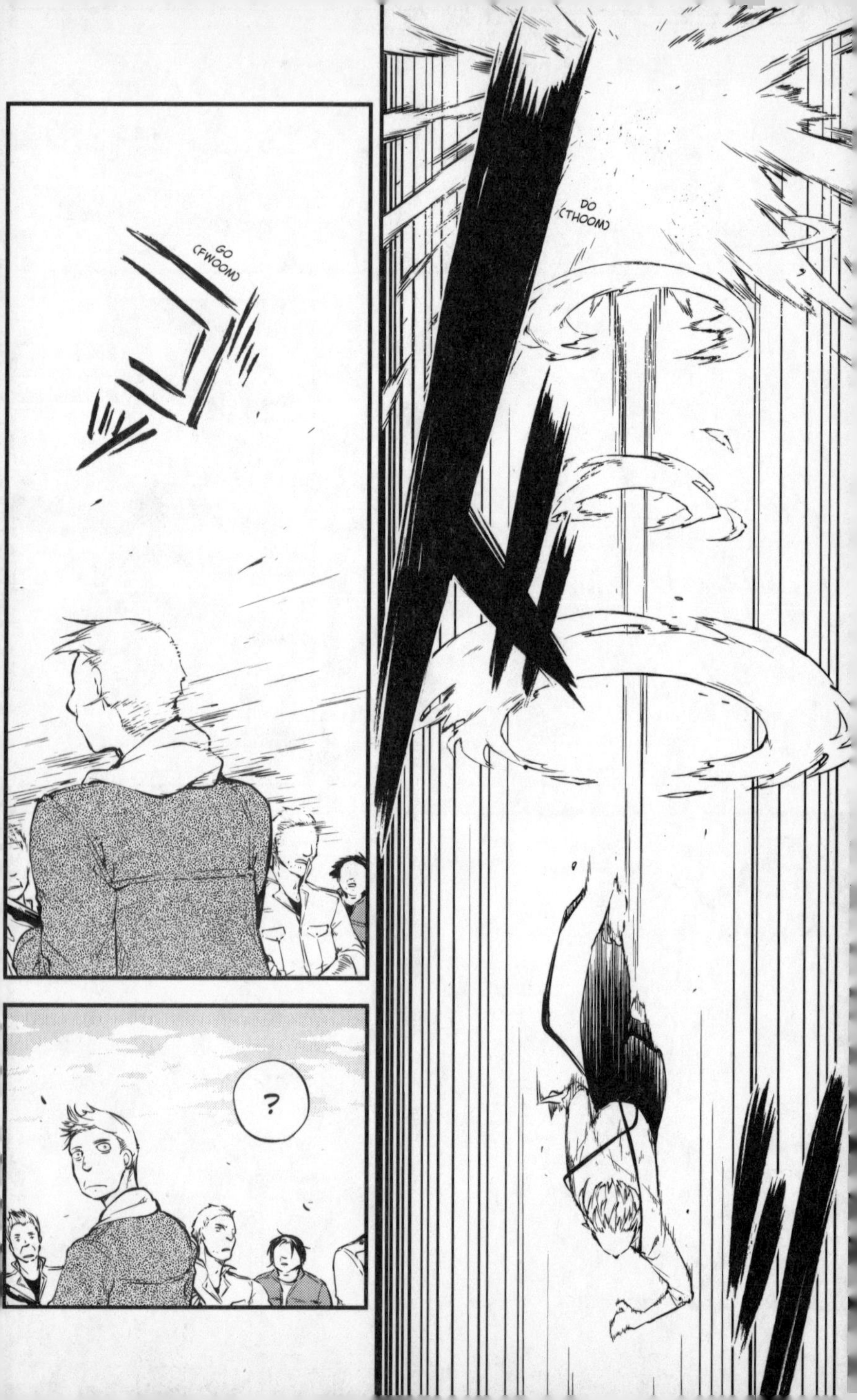
DO (THOOM)
GO (FWOOM)
?

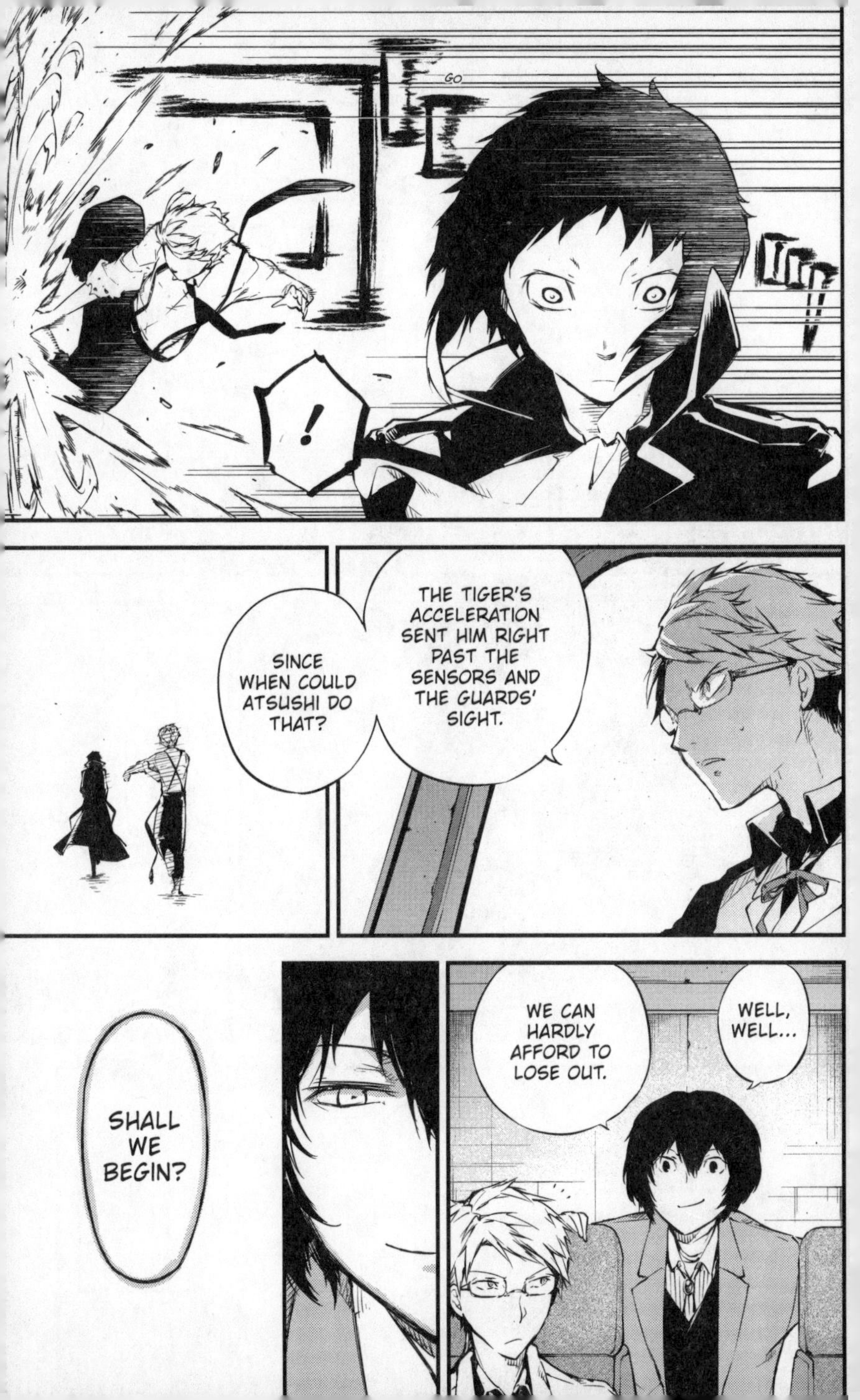
GO
!
THE TIGER'S ACCELERATION SENT HIM RIGHT PAST THE SENSORS AND THE GUARDS' SIGHT.
SINCE WHEN COULD ATSUSHI DO THAT?
WELL, WELL...
WE CAN HARDLY AFFORD TO LOSE OUT.
SHALL WE BEGIN?

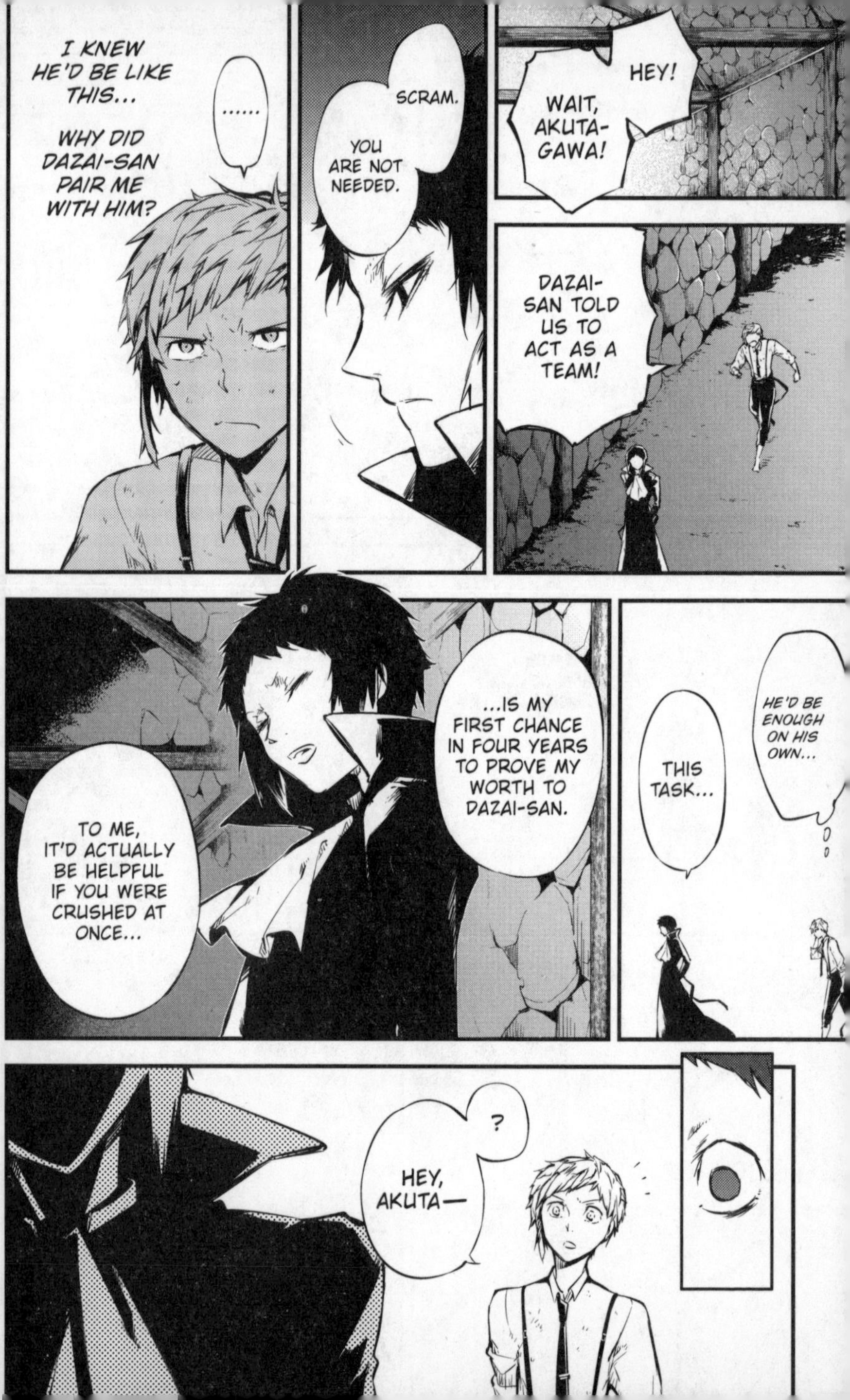
HEY!
WAIT, AKUTA-GAWA!
DAZAI-SAN TOLD US TO ACT AS A TEAM!
SCRAM.
YOU ARE NOT NEEDED.
......
I KNEW HE'D BE LIKE THIS...
WHY DID DAZAI-SAN PAIR ME WITH HIM?
HE'D BE ENOUGH ON HIS OWN...
THIS TASK...
...IS MY FIRST CHANCE IN FOUR YEARS TO PROVE MY WORTH TO DAZAI-SAN.
TO ME, IT'D ACTUALLY BE HELPFUL IF YOU WERE CRUSHED AT ONCE...
?
HEY, AKUTA—

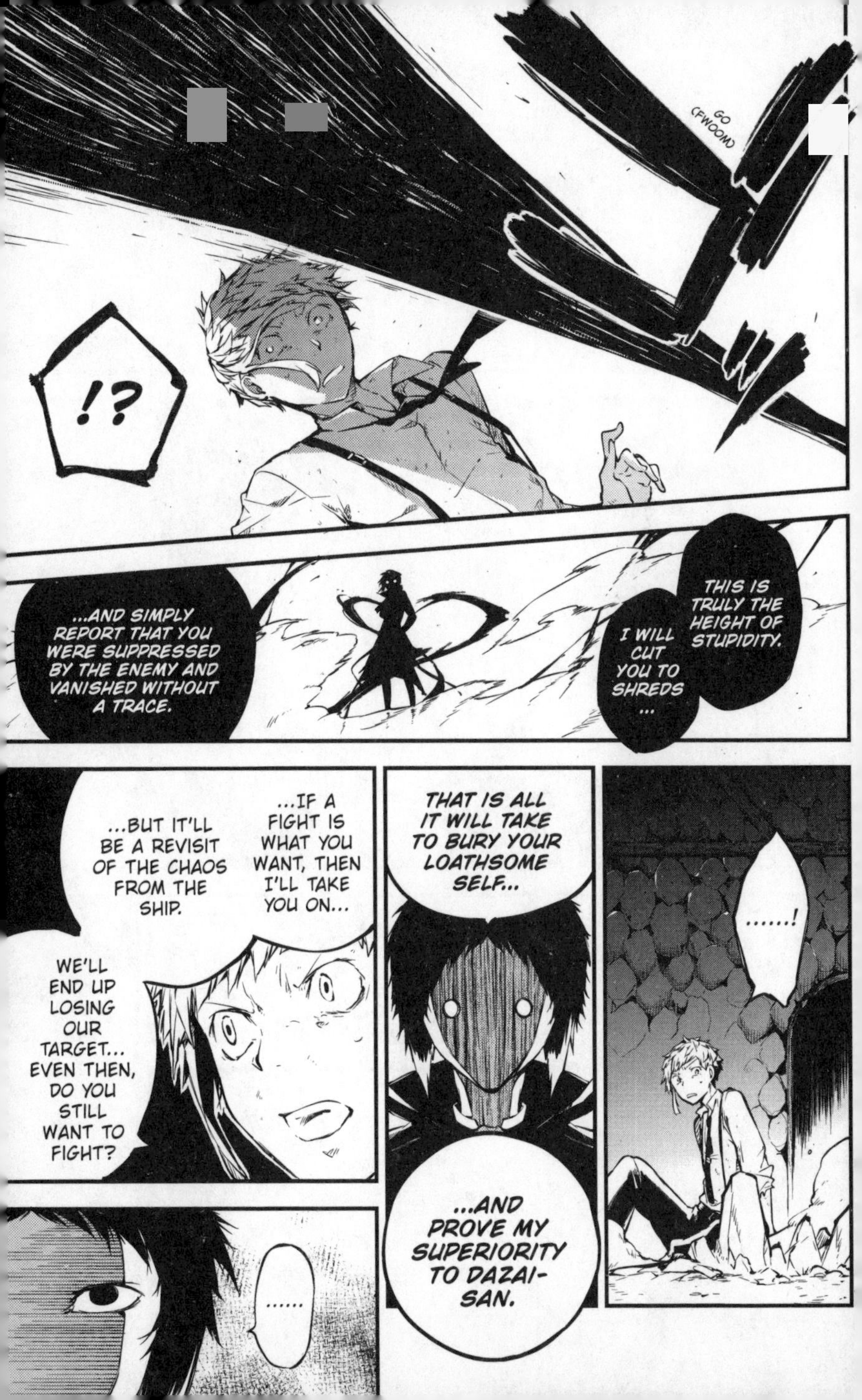
GO (FWOOM)
!?
THIS IS TRULY THE HEIGHT OF STUPIDITY.
I WILL CUT YOU TO SHREDS ...
...AND SIMPLY REPORT THAT YOU WERE SUPPRESSED BY THE ENEMY AND VANISHED WITHOUT A TRACE.
......!
THAT IS ALL IT WILL TAKE TO BURY YOUR LOATHSOME SELF...
...AND PROVE MY SUPERIORITY TO DAZAI-SAN.
...IF A FIGHT IS WHAT YOU WANT, THEN I'LL TAKE YOU ON...
...BUT IT'LL BE A REVISIT OF THE CHAOS FROM THE SHIP.
WE'LL END UP LOSING OUR TARGET... EVEN THEN, DO YOU STILL WANT TO FIGHT?
......

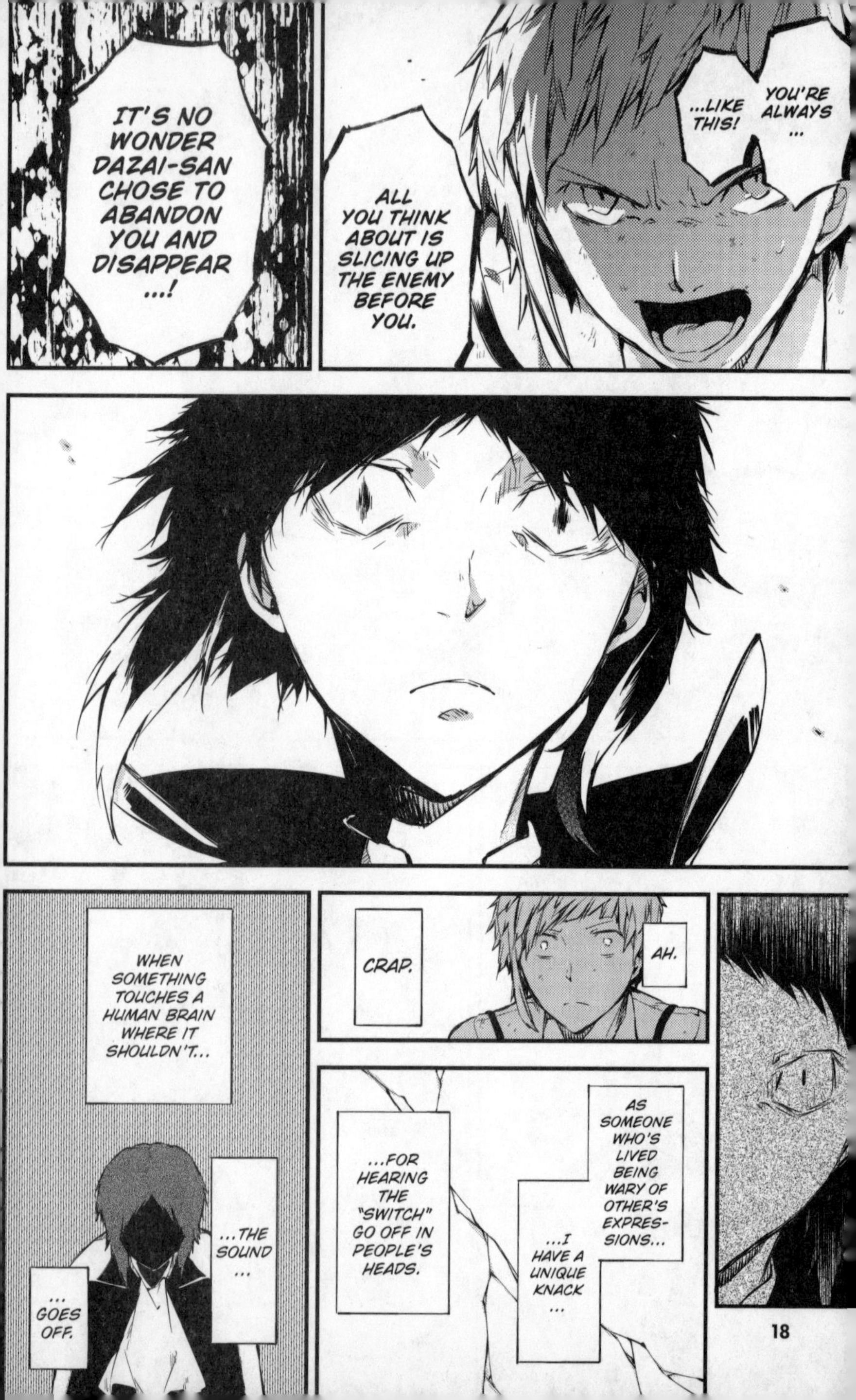
YOU'RE ALWAYS ...
...LIKE THIS!
ALL YOU THINK ABOUT IS SLICING UP THE ENEMY BEFORE YOU.
IT'S NO WONDER DAZAI-SAN CHOSE TO ABANDON YOU AND DISAPPEAR ...!
AH.
CRAP.
AS SOMEONE WHO'S LIVED BEING WARY OF OTHER'S EXPRES-SIONS...
...I HAVE A UNIQUE KNACK ...
...FOR HEARING THE "SWITCH" GO OFF IN PEOPLE'S HEADS.
WHEN SOMETHING TOUCHES A HUMAN BRAIN WHERE IT SHOULDN'T...
...THE SOUND ...
... GOES OFF.

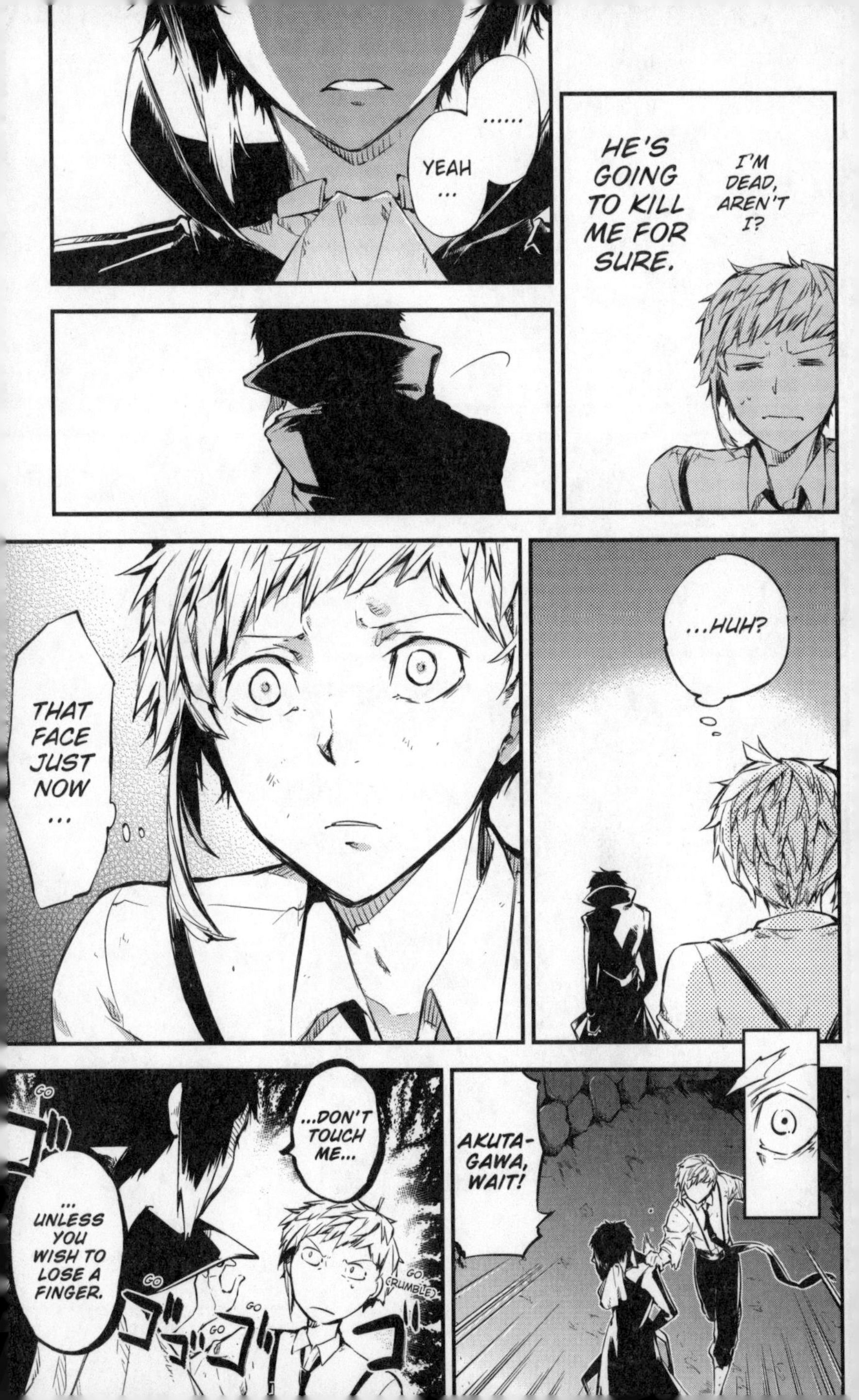
I'M DEAD, AREN'T I?
HE'S GOING TO KILL ME FOR SURE.
...... YEAH ...
...HUH?
THAT FACE JUST NOW ...
AKUTA-GAWA, WAIT!
...DON'T TOUCH ME...
... UNLESS YOU WISH TO LOSE A FINGER.
GO
GO
GO
GO
GO (CRUMBLE)

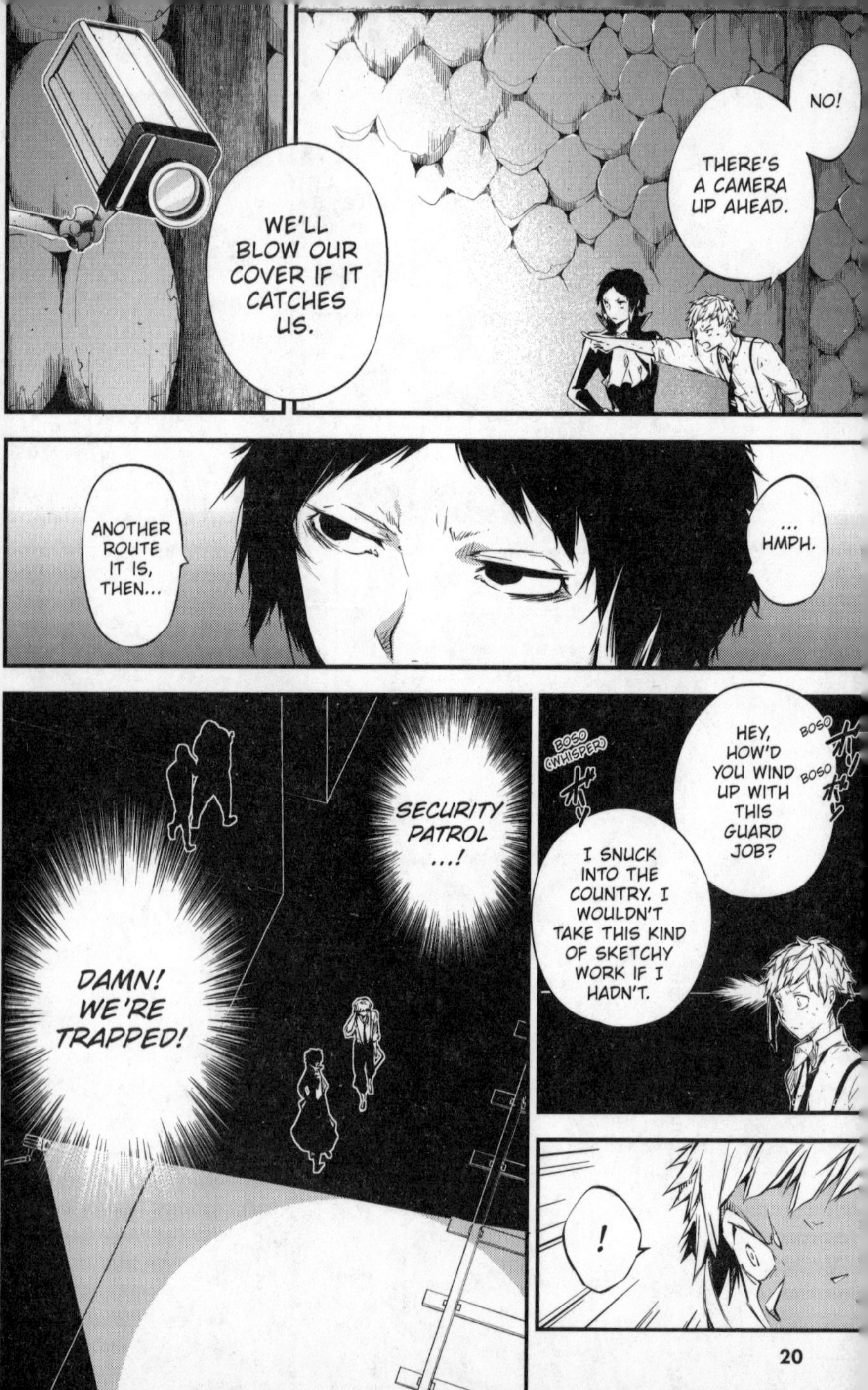
NO!
THERE'S A CAMERA UP AHEAD.
WE'LL BLOW OUR COVER IF IT CATCHES US.
... HMPH.
ANOTHER ROUTE IT IS, THEN...
BOSO
BOSO
HEY, HOW'D YOU WIND UP WITH THIS GUARD JOB?
BOSO (WHISPER)
I SNUCK INTO THE COUNTRY. I WOULDN'T TAKE THIS KIND OF SKETCHY WORK IF I HADN'T.
!
SECURITY PATROL ...!
DAMN! WE'RE TRAPPED!

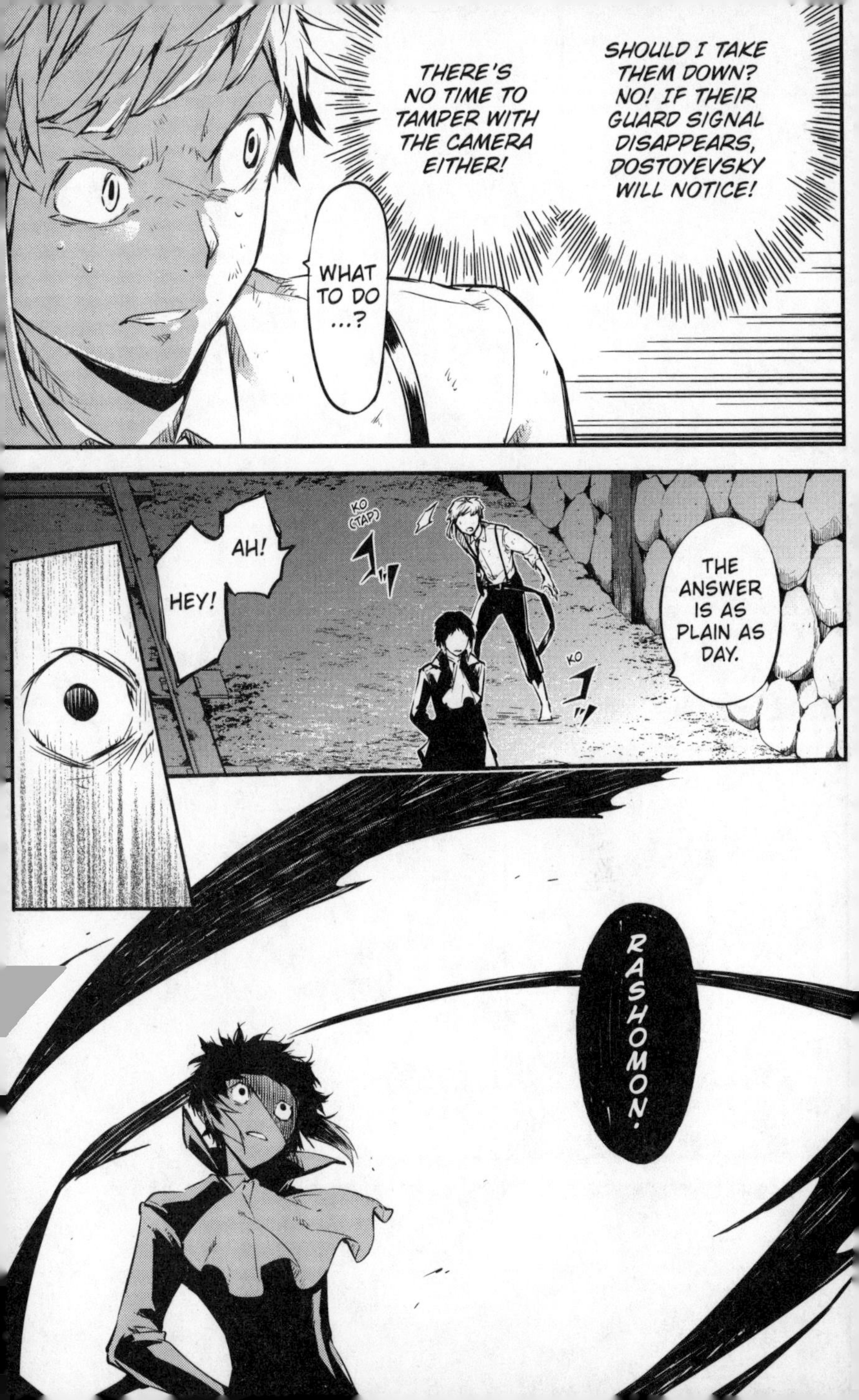
SHOULD I TAKE THEM DOWN? NO! IF THEIR GUARD SIGNAL DISAPPEARS, DOSTOYEVSKY WILL NOTICE!
THERE'S NO TIME TO TAMPER WITH THE CAMERA EITHER!
WHAT TO DO ...?
THE ANSWER IS AS PLAIN AS DAY.
KO
KO (TAP)
AH!
HEY!
RASHOMON!

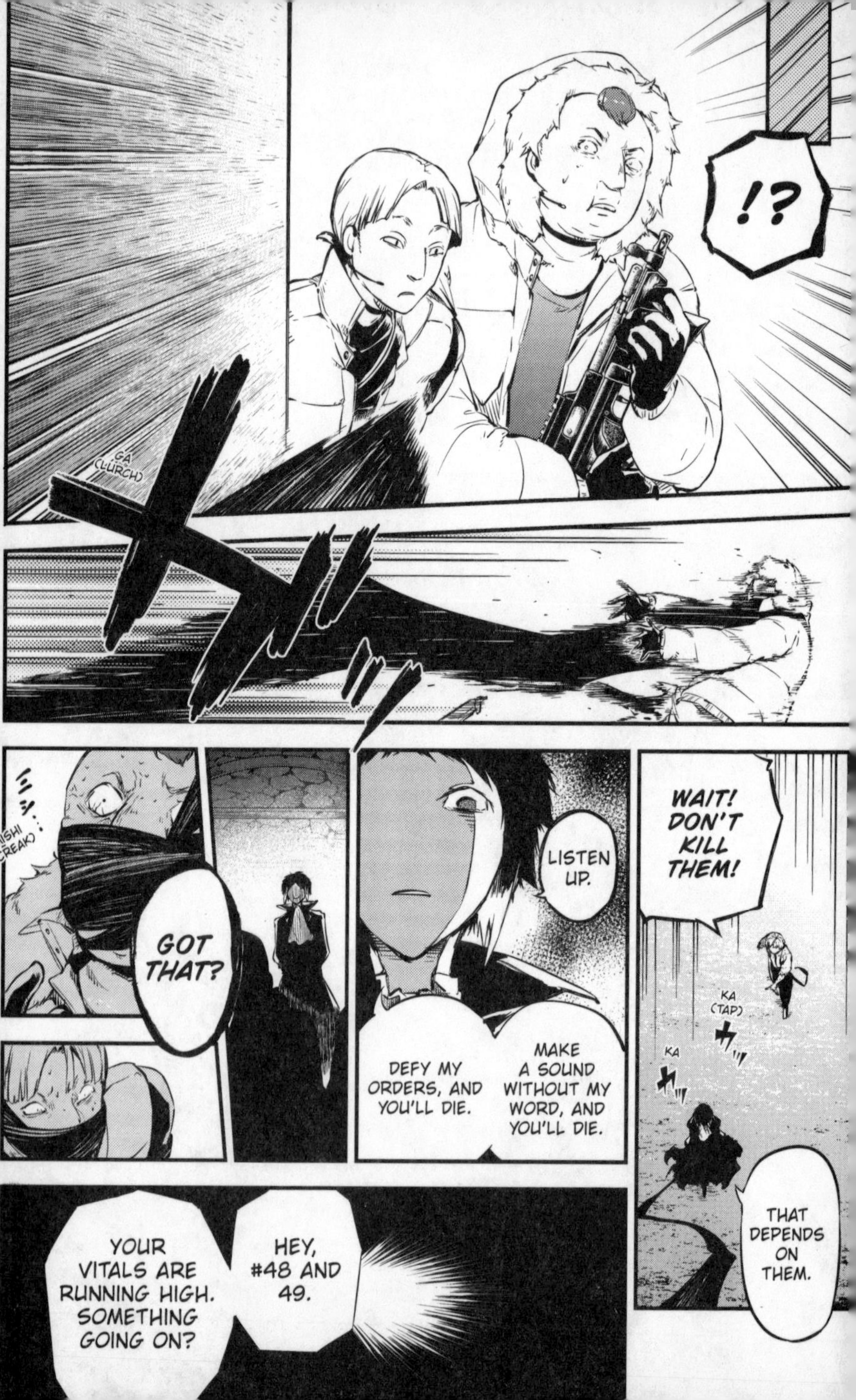
!?
GA (LURCH)
WAIT! DON'T KILL THEM!
KA (TAP)
KA
THAT DEPENDS ON THEM.
LISTEN UP.
MAKE A SOUND WITHOUT MY WORD, AND YOU'LL DIE.
DEFY MY ORDERS, AND YOU'LL DIE.
MISHI (CREAK)
GOT THAT?
HEY, #48 AND 49.
YOUR VITALS ARE RUNNING HIGH. SOMETHING GOING ON?

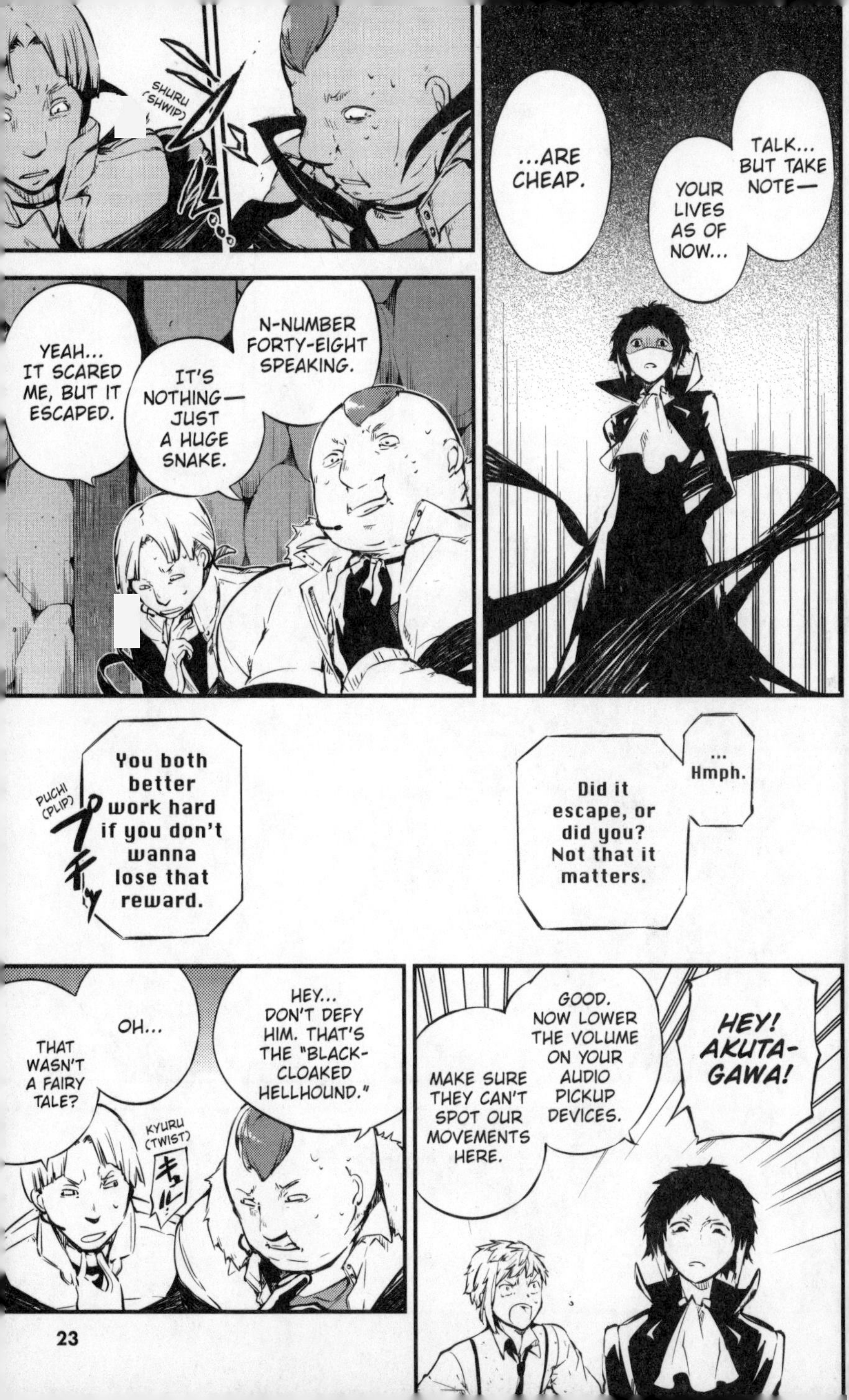
TALK... BUT TAKE NOTE—
YOUR LIVES AS OF NOW...
...ARE CHEAP.
SHURU (SHWIP)
N-NUMBER FORTY-EIGHT SPEAKING.
IT'S NOTHING— JUST A HUGE SNAKE.
YEAH... IT SCARED ME, BUT IT ESCAPED.
... Hmph.
Did it escape, or did you? Not that it matters.
You both better work hard if you don't wanna lose that reward.
PUCHI (PLIP)
HEY! AKUTA-GAWA!
GOOD. NOW LOWER THE VOLUME ON YOUR AUDIO PICKUP DEVICES.
MAKE SURE THEY CAN'T SPOT OUR MOVEMENTS HERE.
HEY... DON'T DEFY HIM. THAT'S THE "BLACK-CLOAKED HELLHOUND."
OH...
KYURU (TWIST)
THAT WASN'T A FAIRY TALE?

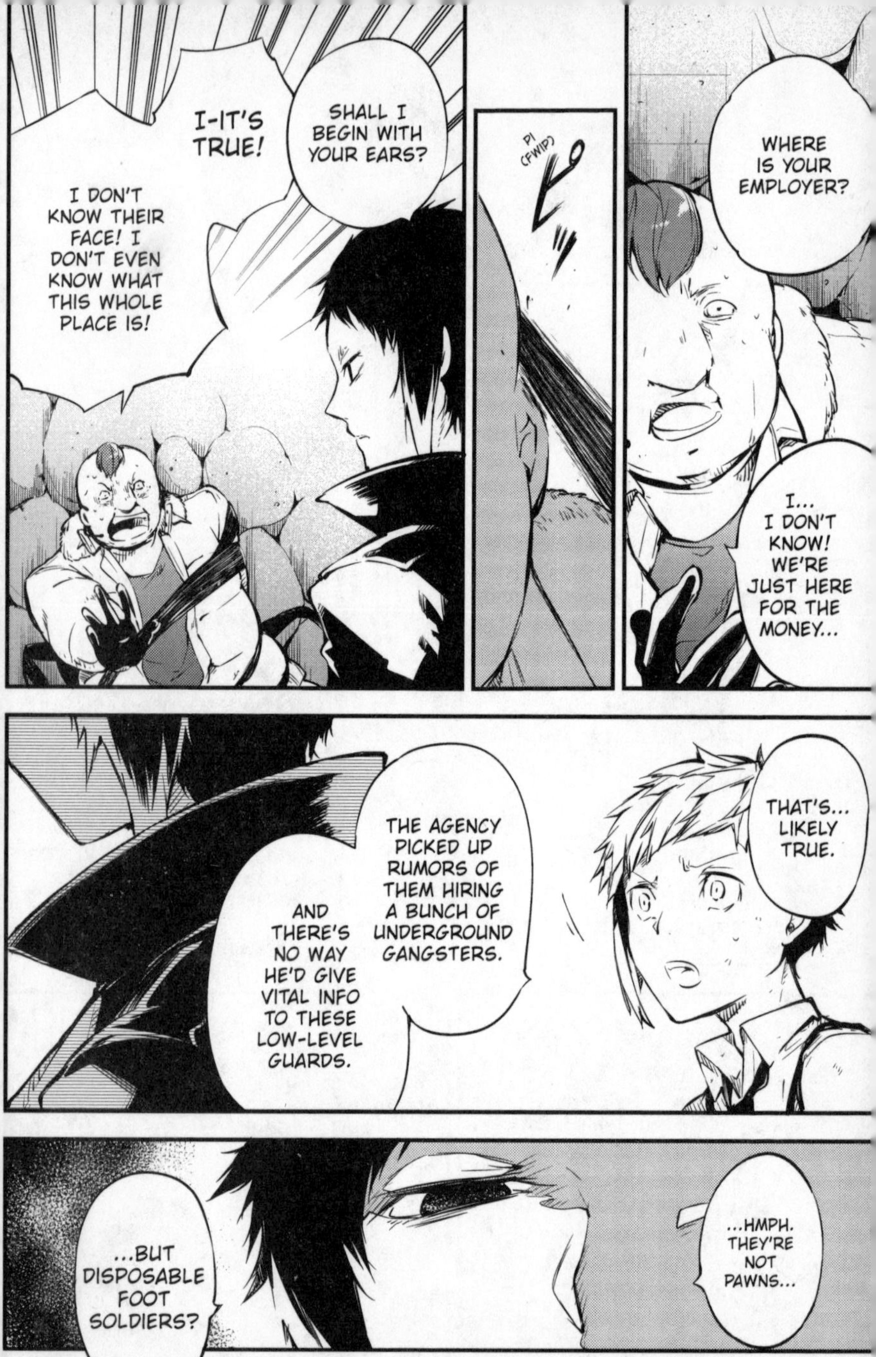
WHERE IS YOUR EMPLOYER?
I... I DON'T KNOW! WE'RE JUST HERE FOR THE MONEY...
PI (FWIP)
SHALL I BEGIN WITH YOUR EARS?
I-IT'S TRUE!
I DON'T KNOW THEIR FACE! I DON'T EVEN KNOW WHAT THIS WHOLE PLACE IS!
THAT'S... LIKELY TRUE.
THE AGENCY PICKED UP RUMORS OF THEM HIRING A BUNCH OF UNDERGROUND GANGSTERS.
AND THERE'S NO WAY HE'D GIVE VITAL INFO TO THESE LOW-LEVEL GUARDS.
...HMPH. THEY'RE NOT PAWNS...
...BUT DISPOSABLE FOOT SOLDIERS?

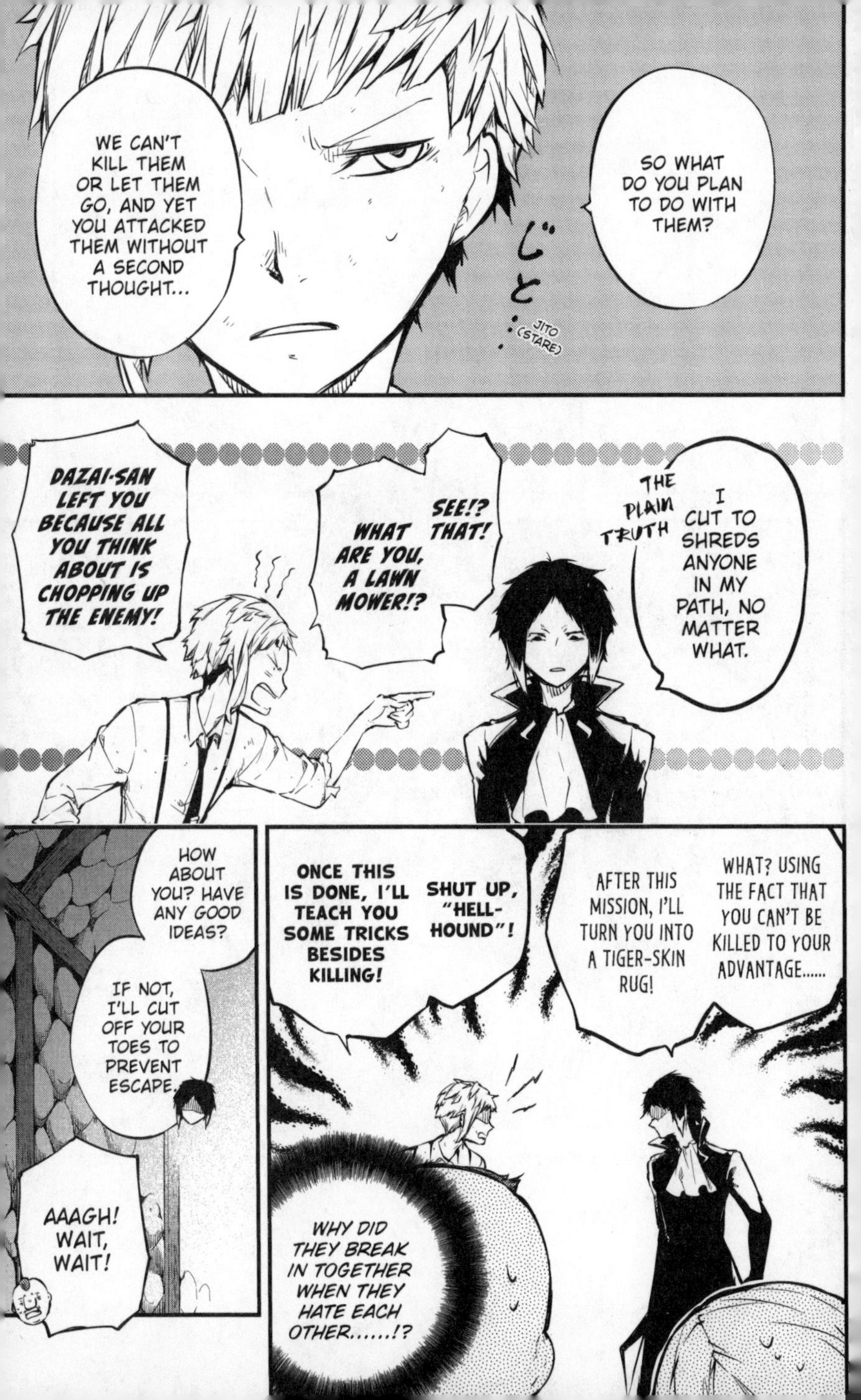
SO WHAT DO YOU PLAN TO DO WITH THEM?
じと…
JITO (STARE)
WE CAN'T KILL THEM OR LET THEM GO, AND YET YOU ATTACKED THEM WITHOUT A SECOND THOUGHT...
THE PLAIN TRUTH
I CUT TO SHREDS ANYONE IN MY PATH, NO MATTER WHAT.
SEE!? THAT!
WHAT ARE YOU, A LAWN MOWER!?
DAZAI-SAN LEFT YOU BECAUSE ALL YOU THINK ABOUT IS CHOPPING UP THE ENEMY!
WHAT? USING THE FACT THAT YOU CAN'T BE KILLED TO YOUR ADVANTAGE......
AFTER THIS MISSION, I'LL TURN YOU INTO A TIGER-SKIN RUG!
SHUT UP, "HELL-HOUND"!
ONCE THIS IS DONE, I'LL TEACH YOU SOME TRICKS BESIDES KILLING!
WHY DID THEY BREAK IN TOGETHER WHEN THEY HATE EACH OTHER......!?
HOW ABOUT YOU? HAVE ANY GOOD IDEAS?
IF NOT, I'LL CUT OFF YOUR TOES TO PREVENT ESCAPE.
AAAGH! WAIT, WAIT!

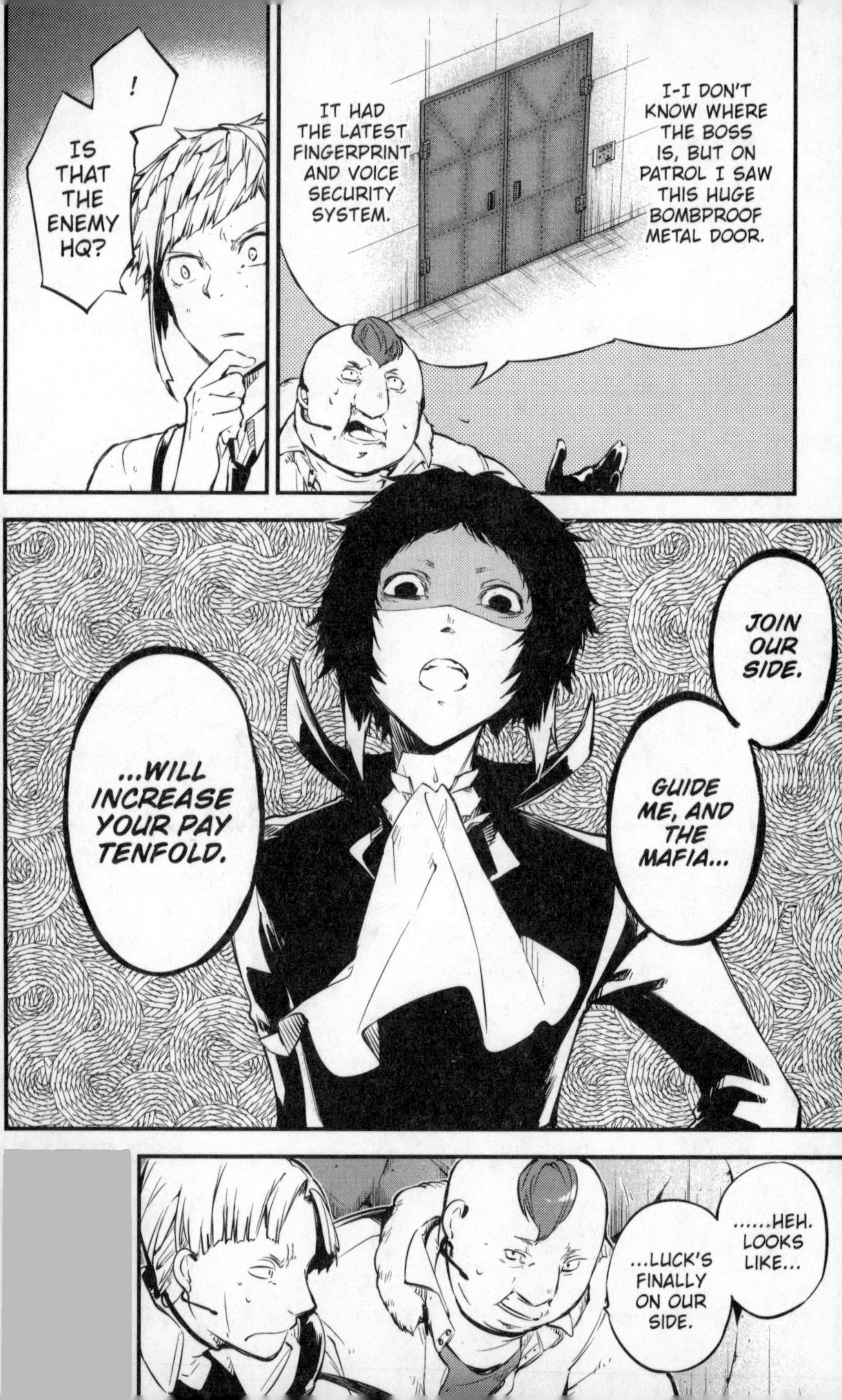
I-I DON'T KNOW WHERE THE BOSS IS, BUT ON PATROL I SAW THIS HUGE BOMBPROOF METAL DOOR.
IT HAD THE LATEST FINGERPRINT AND VOICE SECURITY SYSTEM.
!
IS THAT THE ENEMY HQ?
JOIN OUR SIDE.
GUIDE ME, AND THE MAFIA...
...WILL INCREASE YOUR PAY TENFOLD.
......HEH. LOOKS LIKE...
...LUCK'S FINALLY ON OUR SIDE.

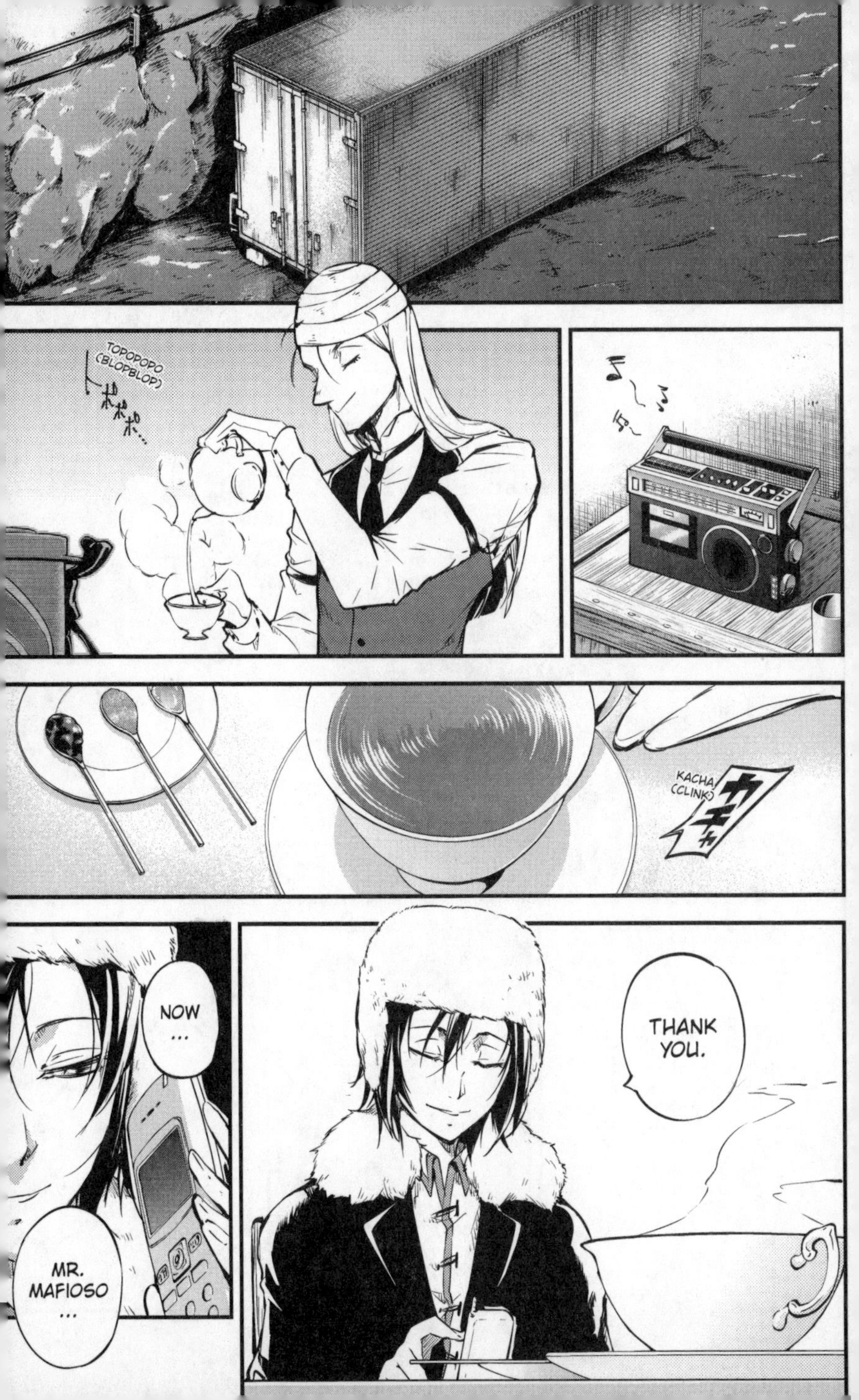
TOPOPOPO (BLOPBLOP)
トポポポ…
KACHA (CLINK)
カチャ
THANK YOU.
NOW ...
MR. MAFIOSO ...

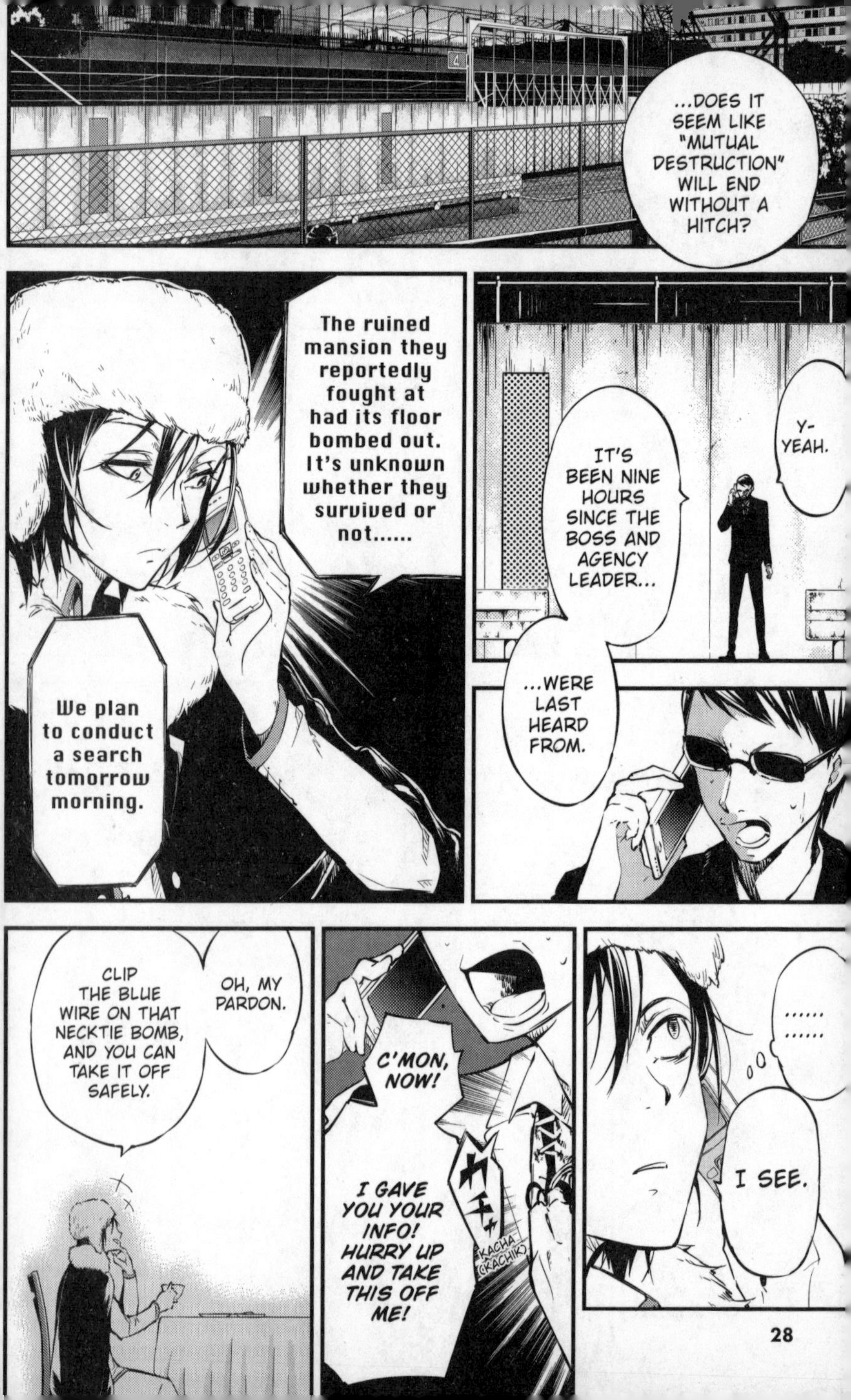
...DOES IT SEEM LIKE "MUTUAL DESTRUCTION" WILL END WITHOUT A HITCH?
Y-YEAH.
IT'S BEEN NINE HOURS SINCE THE BOSS AND AGENCY LEADER...
...WERE LAST HEARD FROM.
The ruined mansion they reportedly fought at had its floor bombed out. It's unknown whether they survived or not......
We plan to conduct a search tomorrow morning.
....
I SEE.
C'MON, NOW!
KACHA (KACHIK)
I GAVE YOU YOUR INFO! HURRY UP AND TAKE THIS OFF ME!
OH, MY PARDON.
CLIP THE BLUE WIRE ON THAT NECKTIE BOMB, AND YOU CAN TAKE IT OFF SAFELY.

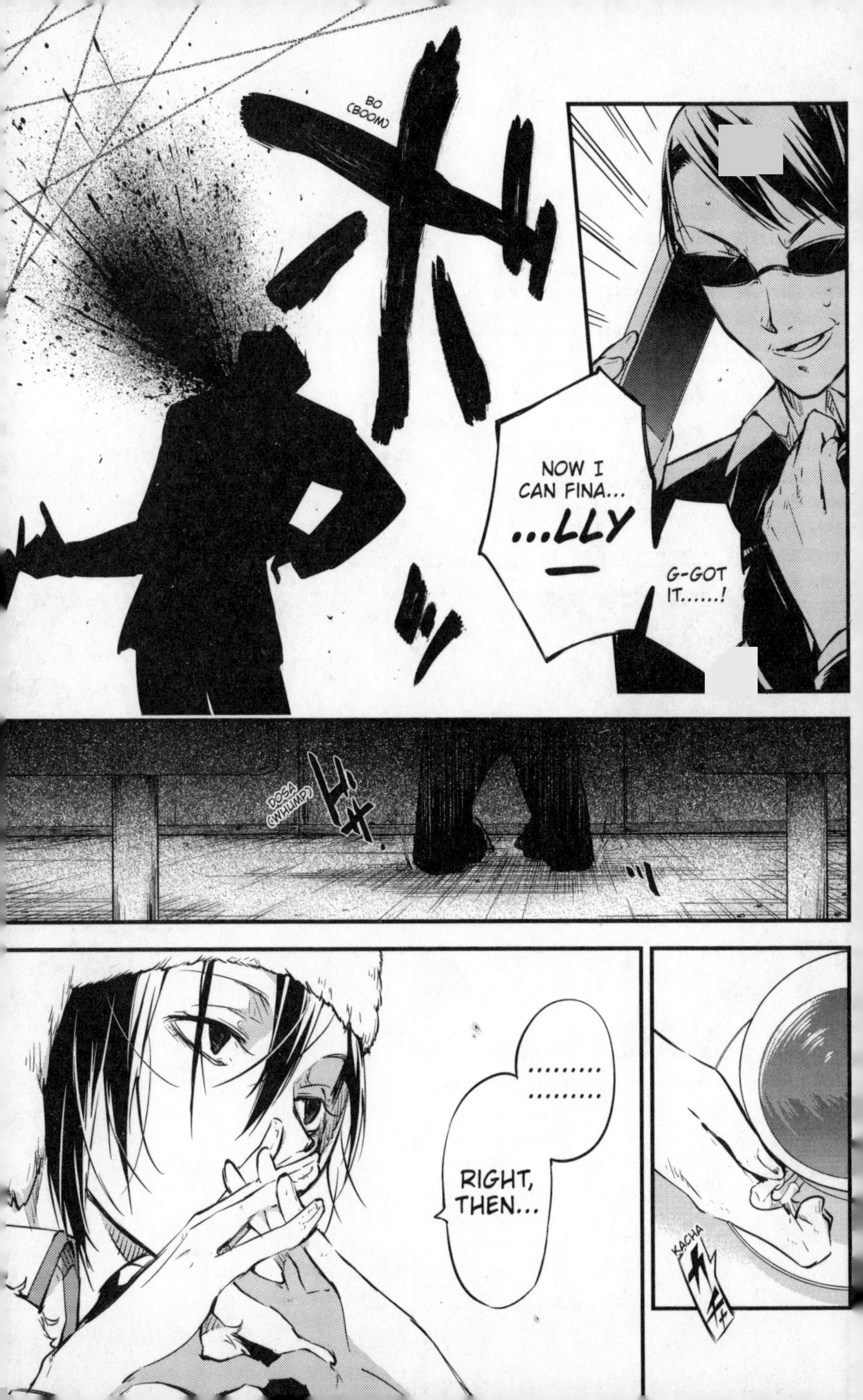

NOW I CAN FINA... ...LLY —
G-GOT IT......!
BO (BOOM)
DOSA (WHUMP)
KACHA
....
RIGHT, THEN...

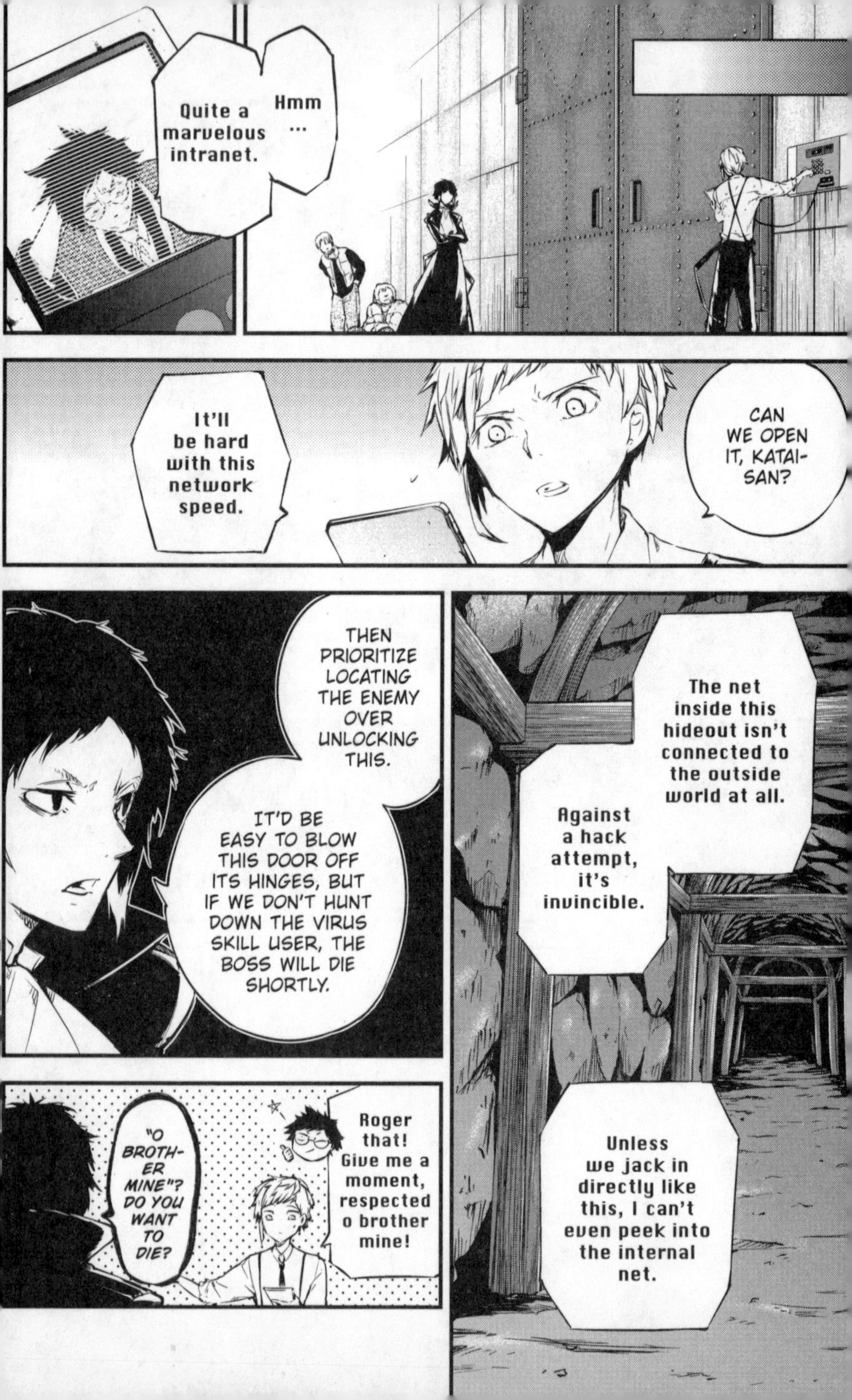
Hmm...
Quite a marvelous intranet.
CAN WE OPEN IT, KATAI-SAN?
It'll be hard with this network speed.
The net inside this hideout isn't connected to the outside world at all.
Against a hack attempt, it's invincible.
Unless we jack in directly like this, I can't even peek into the internal net.
THEN PRIORITIZE LOCATING THE ENEMY OVER UNLOCKING THIS.
IT'D BE EASY TO BLOW THIS DOOR OFF ITS HINGES, BUT IF WE DON'T HUNT DOWN THE VIRUS SKILL USER, THE BOSS WILL DIE SHORTLY.
Roger that! Give me a moment, respected o brother mine!
"O BROTHER-ER MINE"? DO YOU WANT TO DIE?

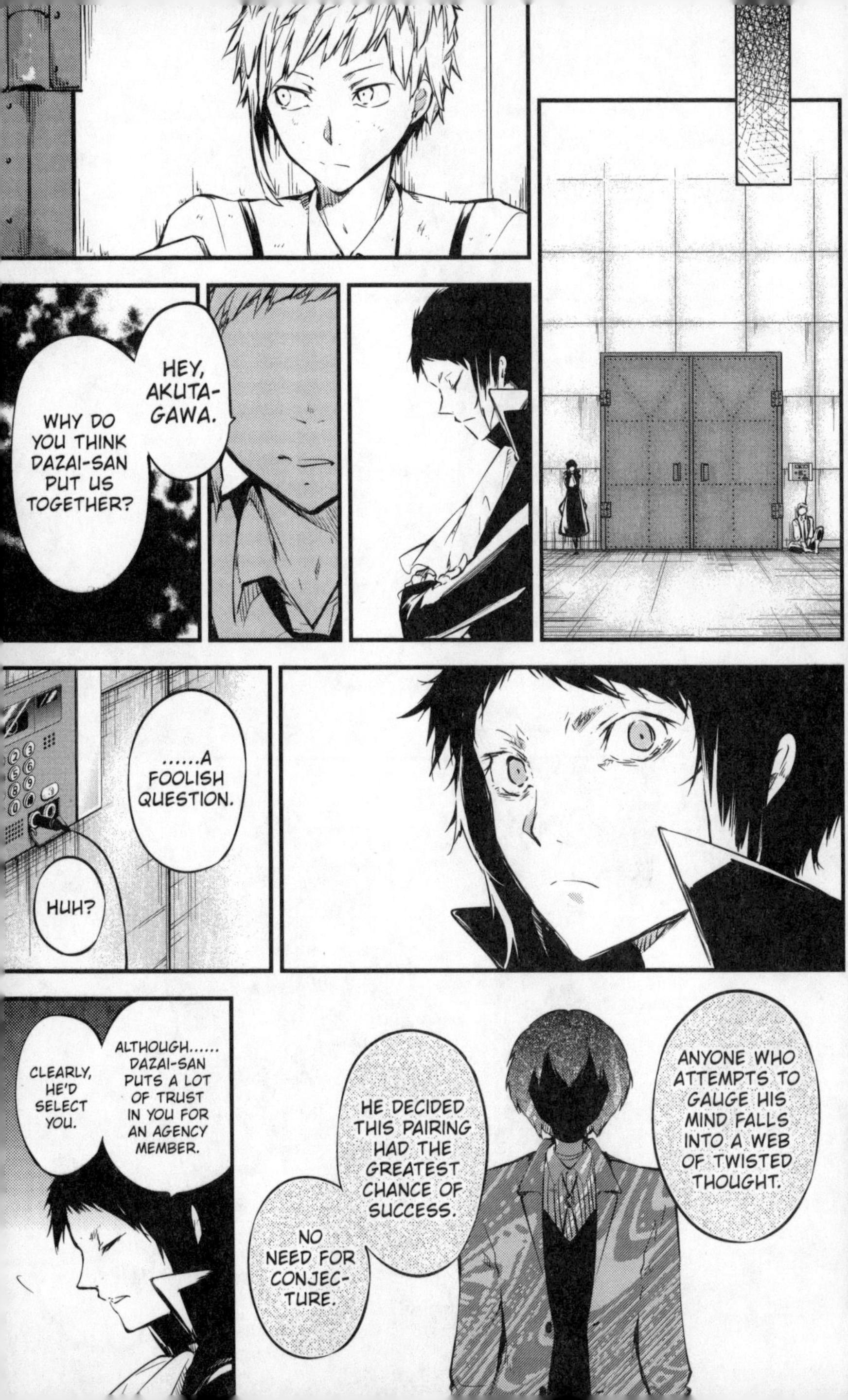
HEY, AKUTA-GAWA.
WHY DO YOU THINK DAZAI-SAN PUT US TOGETHER?
......A FOOLISH QUESTION.
HUH?
ANYONE WHO ATTEMPTS TO GAUGE HIS MIND FALLS INTO A WEB OF TWISTED THOUGHT.
HE DECIDED THIS PAIRING HAD THE GREATEST CHANCE OF SUCCESS.
NO NEED FOR CONJEC-TURE.
ALTHOUGH...... DAZAI-SAN PUTS A LOT OF TRUST IN YOU FOR AN AGENCY MEMBER.
CLEARLY, HE'D SELECT YOU.

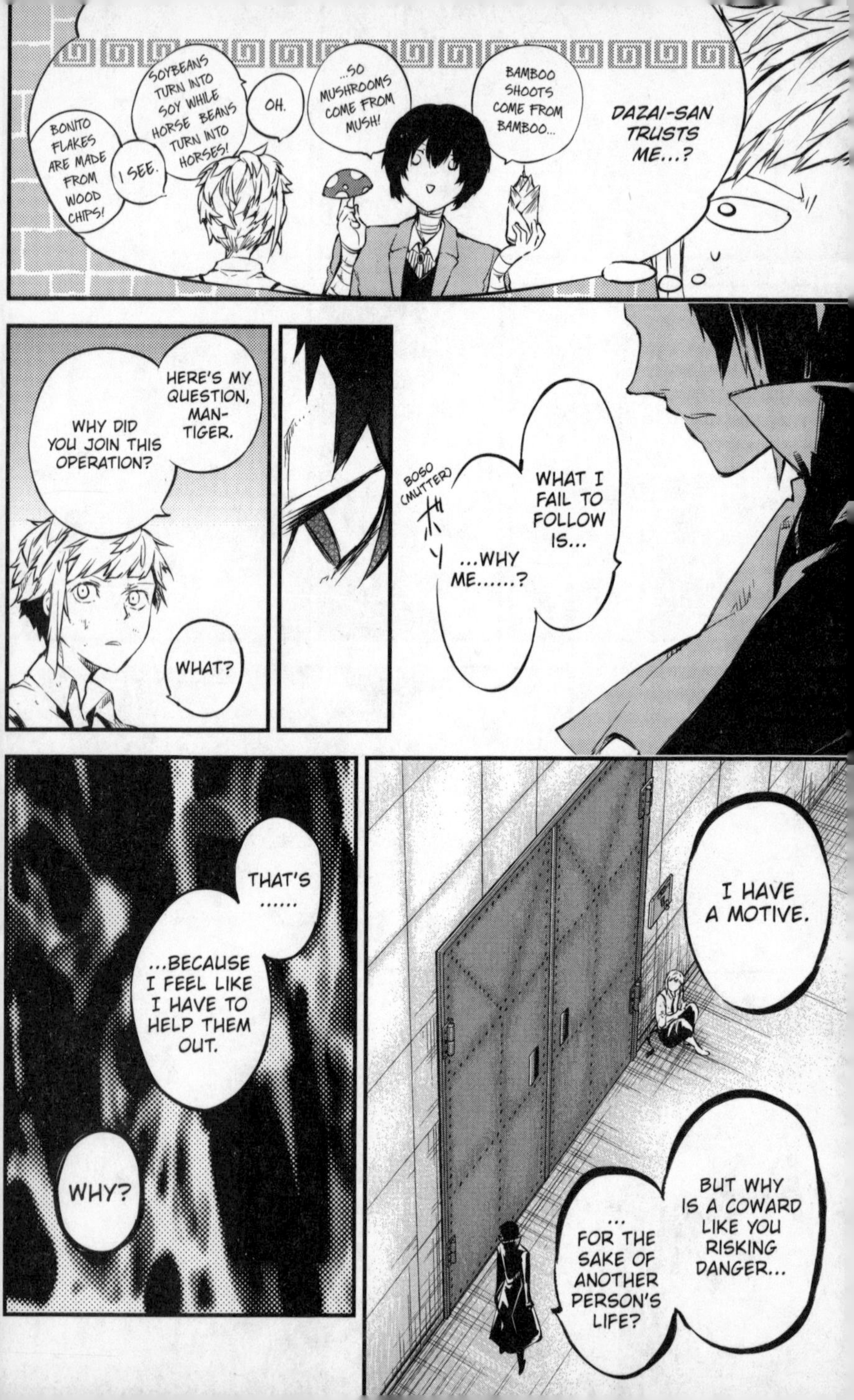
DAZAI-SAN TRUSTS ME...?
BAMBOO SHOOTS COME FROM BAMBOO...
...SO MUSHROOMS COME FROM MUSH!
OH.
SOYBEANS TURN INTO SOY WHILE HORSE BEANS TURN INTO HORSES!
I SEE.
BONITO FLAKES ARE MADE FROM WOOD CHIPS!
WHAT I FAIL TO FOLLOW IS...
...WHY ME......?
ボソ
BOSO (MUTTER)
HERE'S MY QUESTION, MAN-TIGER.
WHY DID YOU JOIN THIS OPERATION?
WHAT?
I HAVE A MOTIVE.
BUT WHY IS A COWARD LIKE YOU RISKING DANGER...
...FOR THE SAKE OF ANOTHER PERSON'S LIFE?
THAT'S......
...BECAUSE I FEEL LIKE I HAVE TO HELP THEM OUT.
WHY?

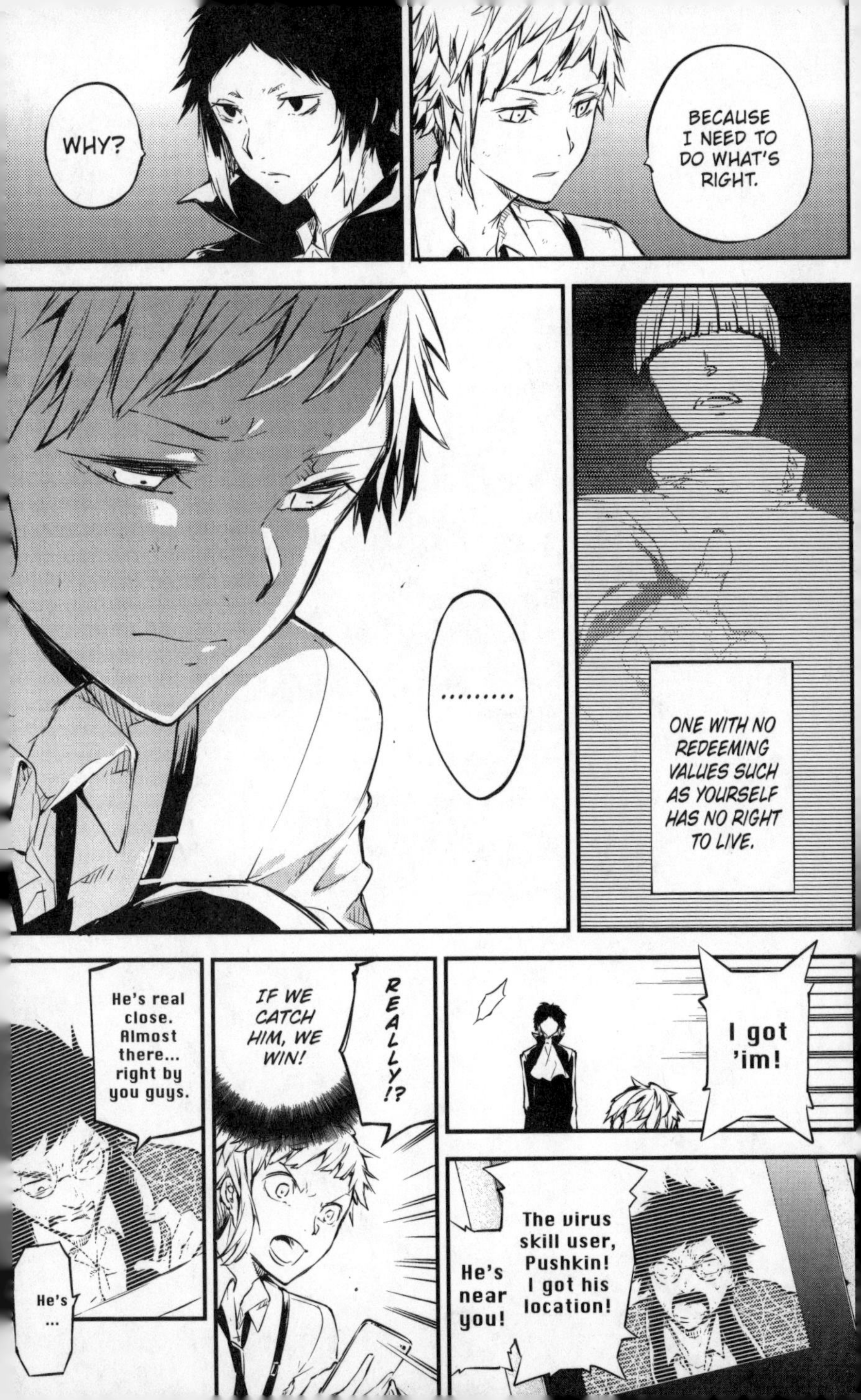
BECAUSE I NEED TO DO WHAT'S RIGHT.
WHY?
ONE WITH NO REDEEMING VALUES SUCH AS YOURSELF HAS NO RIGHT TO LIVE.
....
I got 'im!
The virus skill user, Pushkin! I got his location!
He's near you!
REALLY!?
IF WE CATCH HIM, WE WIN!
He's real close. Almost there... right by you guys.
He's ...

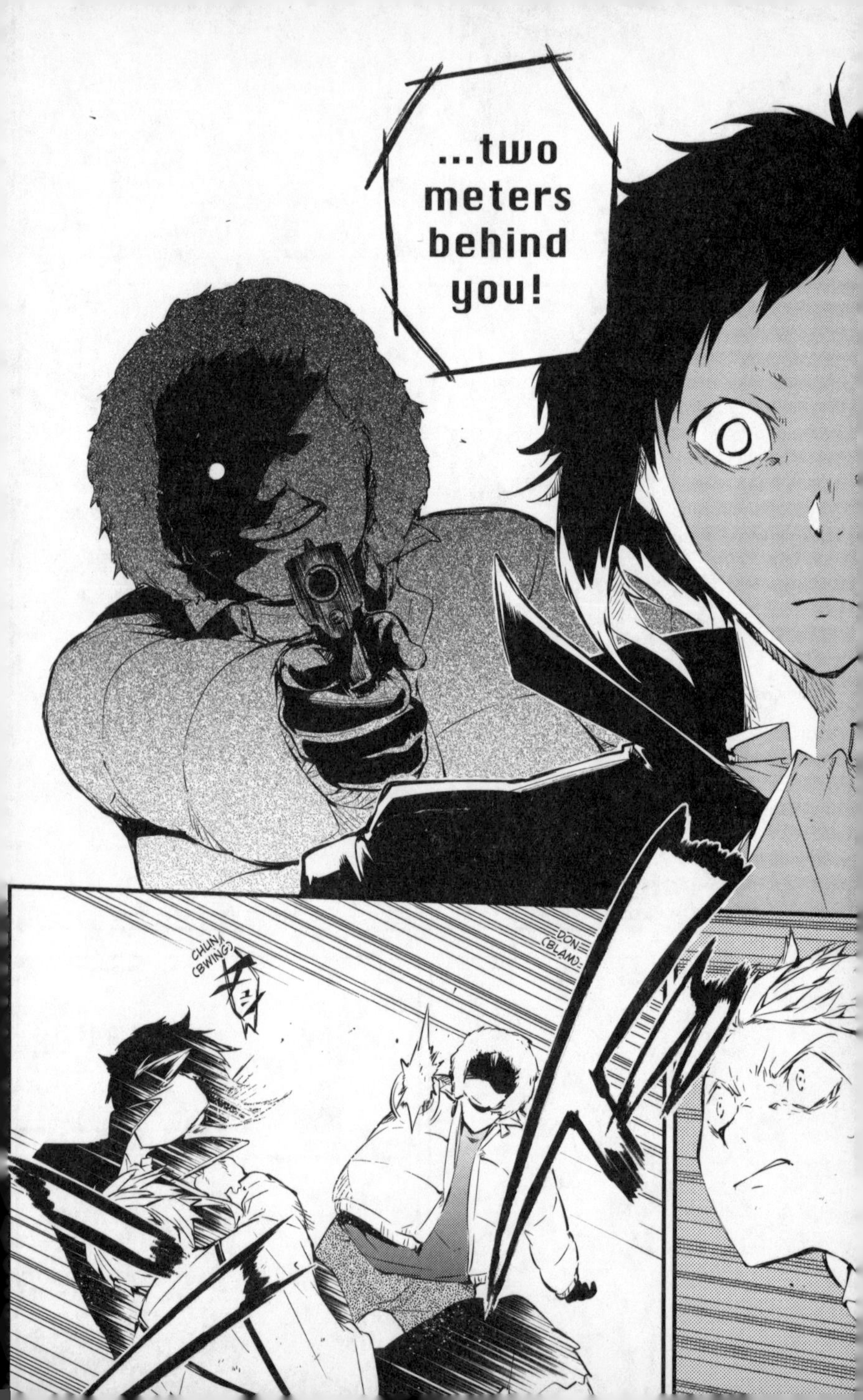
...two meters behind you!
DON (BLAM)
CHUN (BWING)

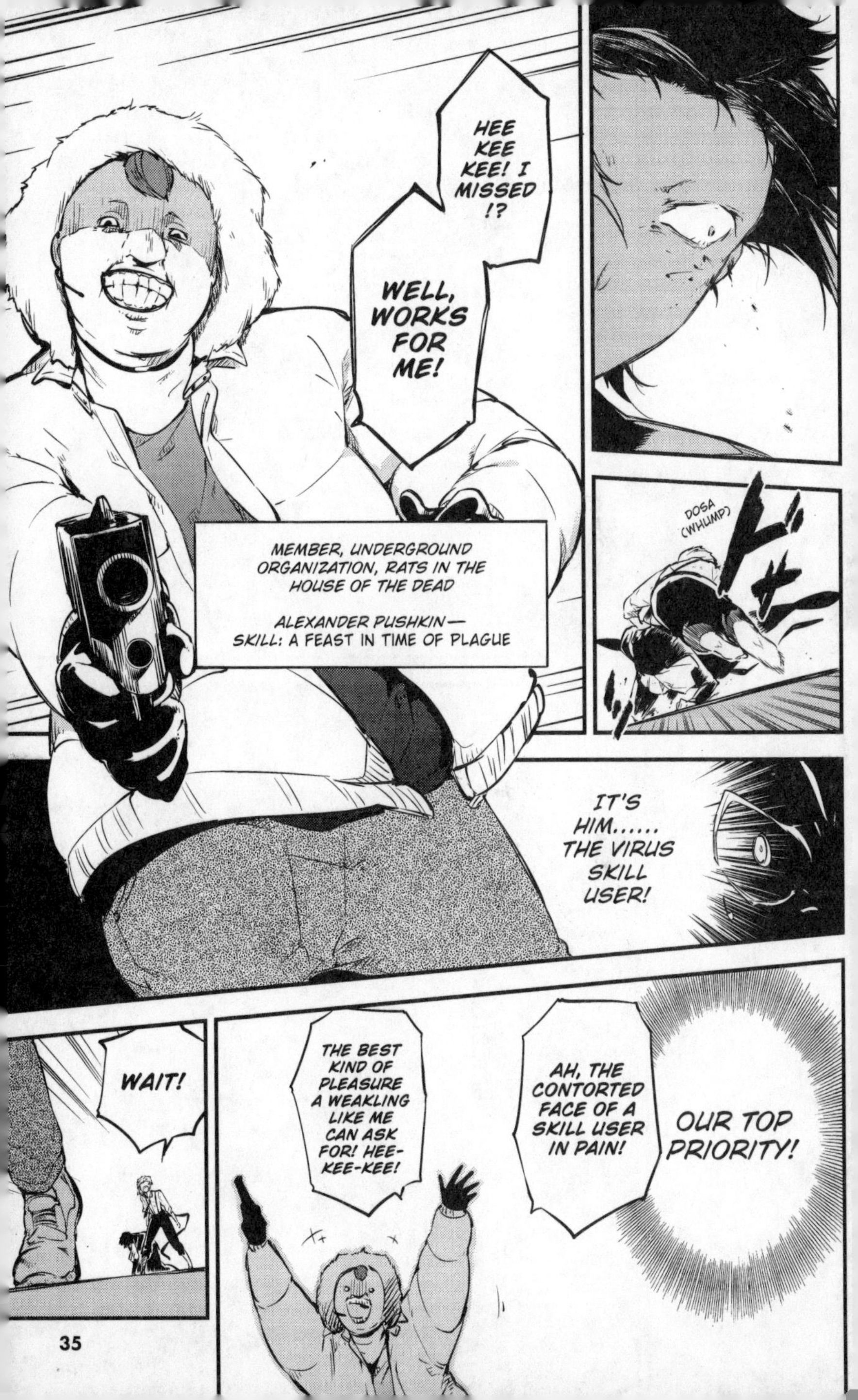
DOSA (WHUMP)
IT'S HIM...... THE VIRUS SKILL USER!
HEE KEE KEE! I MISSED !?
WELL, WORKS FOR ME!
MEMBER, UNDERGROUND ORGANIZATION, RATS IN THE HOUSE OF THE DEAD
ALEXANDER PUSHKIN— SKILL: A FEAST IN TIME OF PLAGUE
OUR TOP PRIORITY!
AH, THE CONTORTED FACE OF A SKILL USER IN PAIN!
THE BEST KIND OF PLEASURE A WEAKLING LIKE ME CAN ASK FOR! HEE-KEE-KEE!
WAIT!

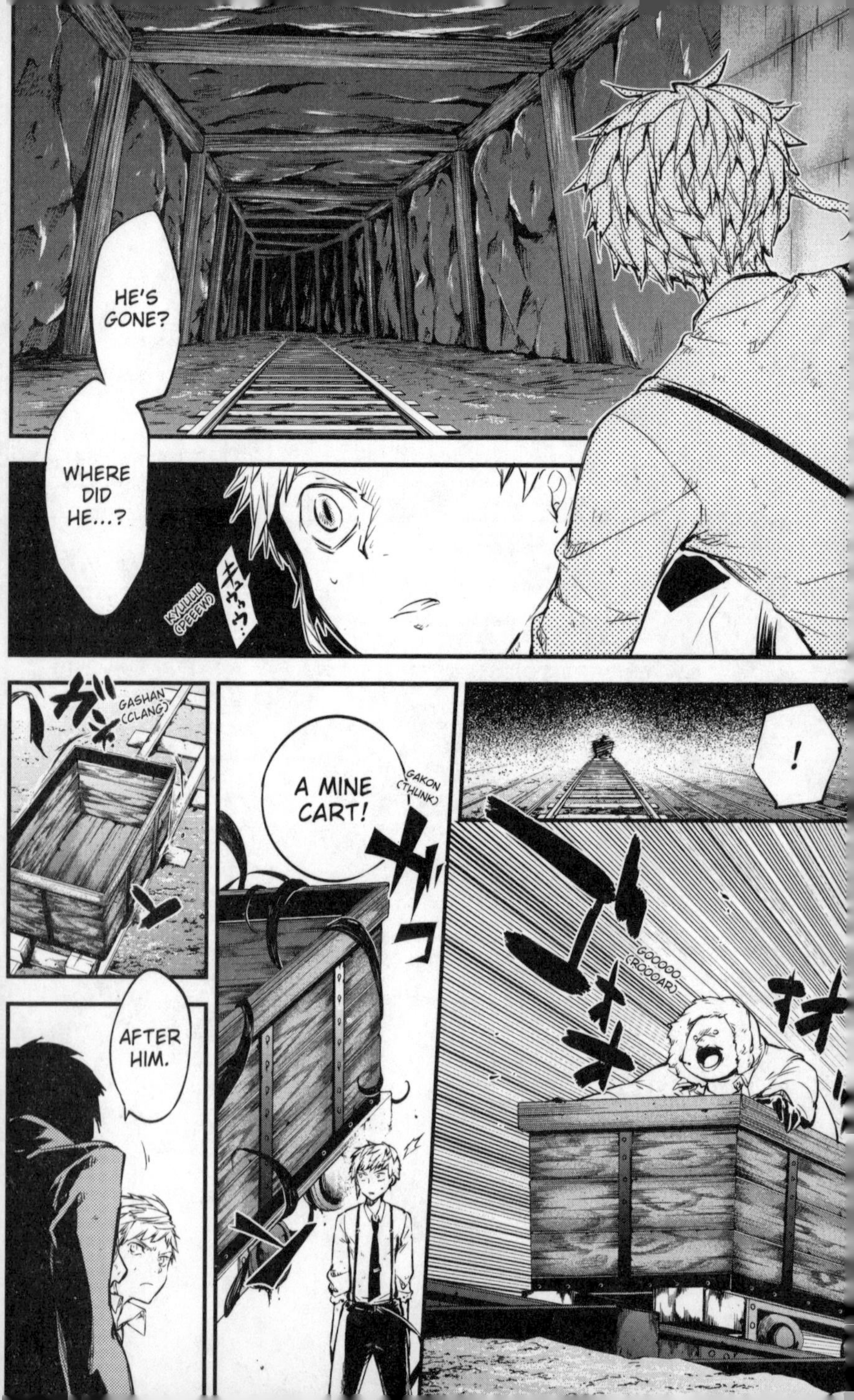
HE'S GONE?
WHERE DID HE...?
KYUUUU (PEEEW)
!
GOOOOO (ROOOAR)
A MINE CART!
GAKON (THUNK)
GASHAN (CLANG)
AFTER HIM.

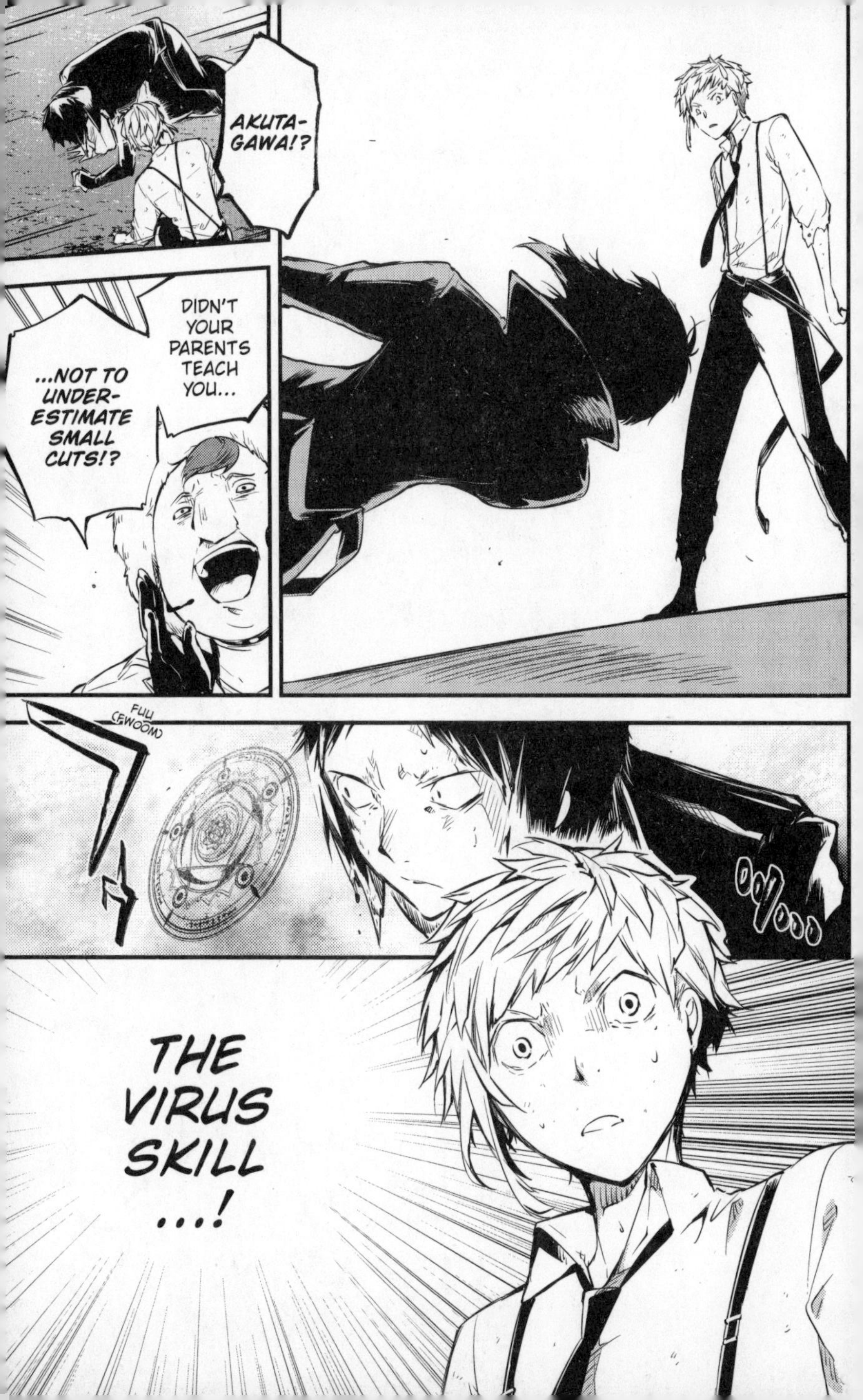
AKUTA-GAWA!?
DIDN'T YOUR PARENTS TEACH YOU...
...NOT TO UNDER-ESTIMATE SMALL CUTS!?
FUU (FWOOM)
THE VIRUS SKILL ...!

BUNGO
STRAY DOGS

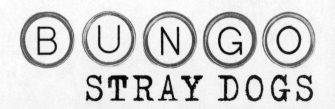

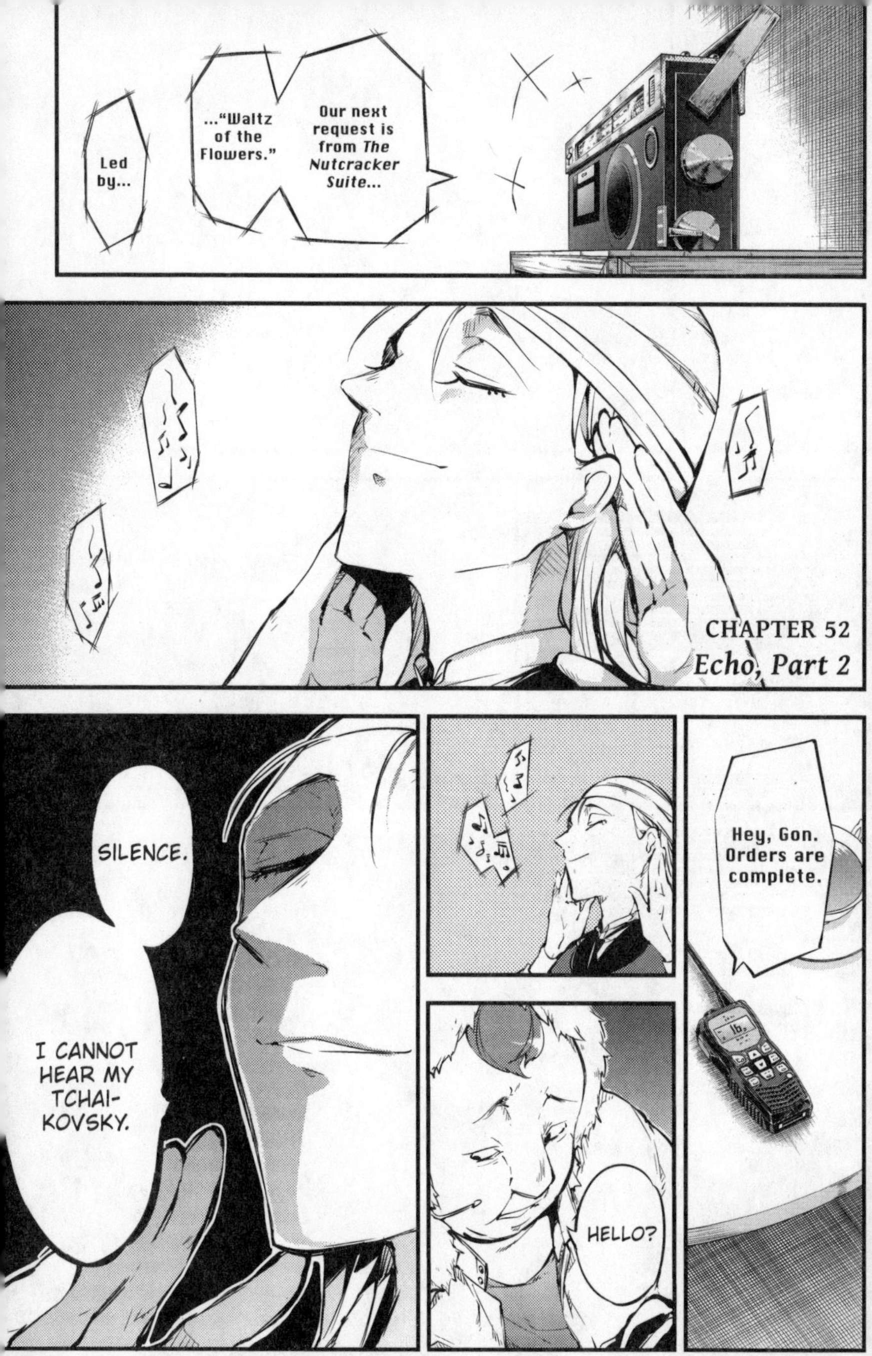
Our next request is from *The Nutcracker Suite*...
..."Waltz of the Flowers."
Led by...
CHAPTER 52
Echo, Part 2
Hey, Gon. Orders are complete.
HELLO?
SILENCE.
I CANNOT HEAR MY TCHAIKOVSKY.

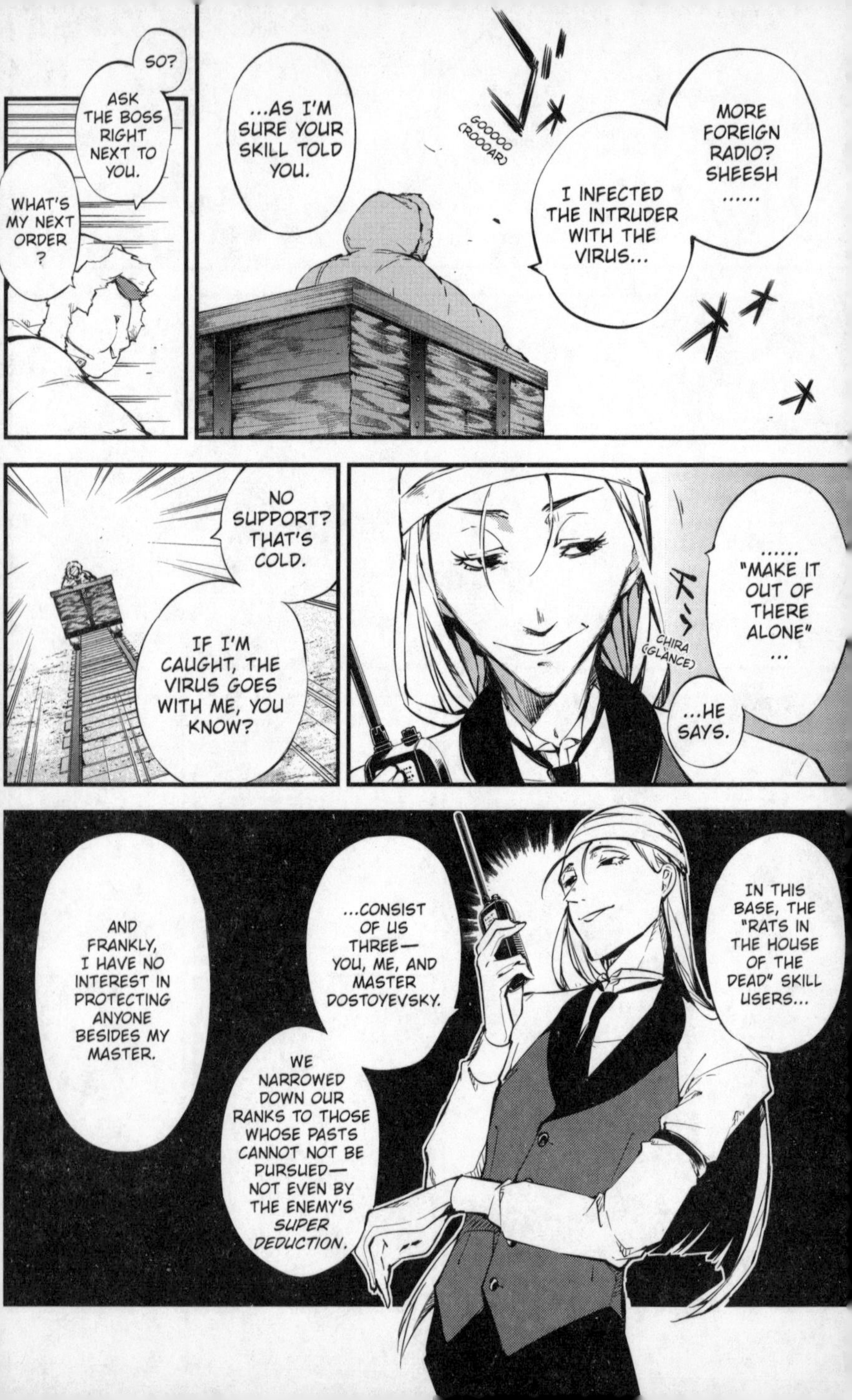
MORE FOREIGN RADIO? SHEESH......
GOOOOO (ROOOAR)
I INFECTED THE INTRUDER WITH THE VIRUS...
...AS I'M SURE YOUR SKILL TOLD YOU.
SO?
ASK THE BOSS RIGHT NEXT TO YOU.
WHAT'S MY NEXT ORDER?
......“MAKE IT OUT OF THERE ALONE”...
CHIRA (GLANCE)
...HE SAYS.
NO SUPPORT? THAT'S COLD.
IF I'M CAUGHT, THE VIRUS GOES WITH ME, YOU KNOW?
IN THIS BASE, THE “RATS IN THE HOUSE OF THE DEAD” SKILL USERS...
...CONSIST OF US THREE—YOU, ME, AND MASTER DOSTOYEVSKY.
WE NARROWED DOWN OUR RANKS TO THOSE WHOSE PASTS CANNOT NOT BE PURSUED—NOT EVEN BY THE ENEMY'S *SUPER DEDUCTION*.
AND FRANKLY, I HAVE NO INTEREST IN PROTECTING ANYONE BESIDES MY MASTER.

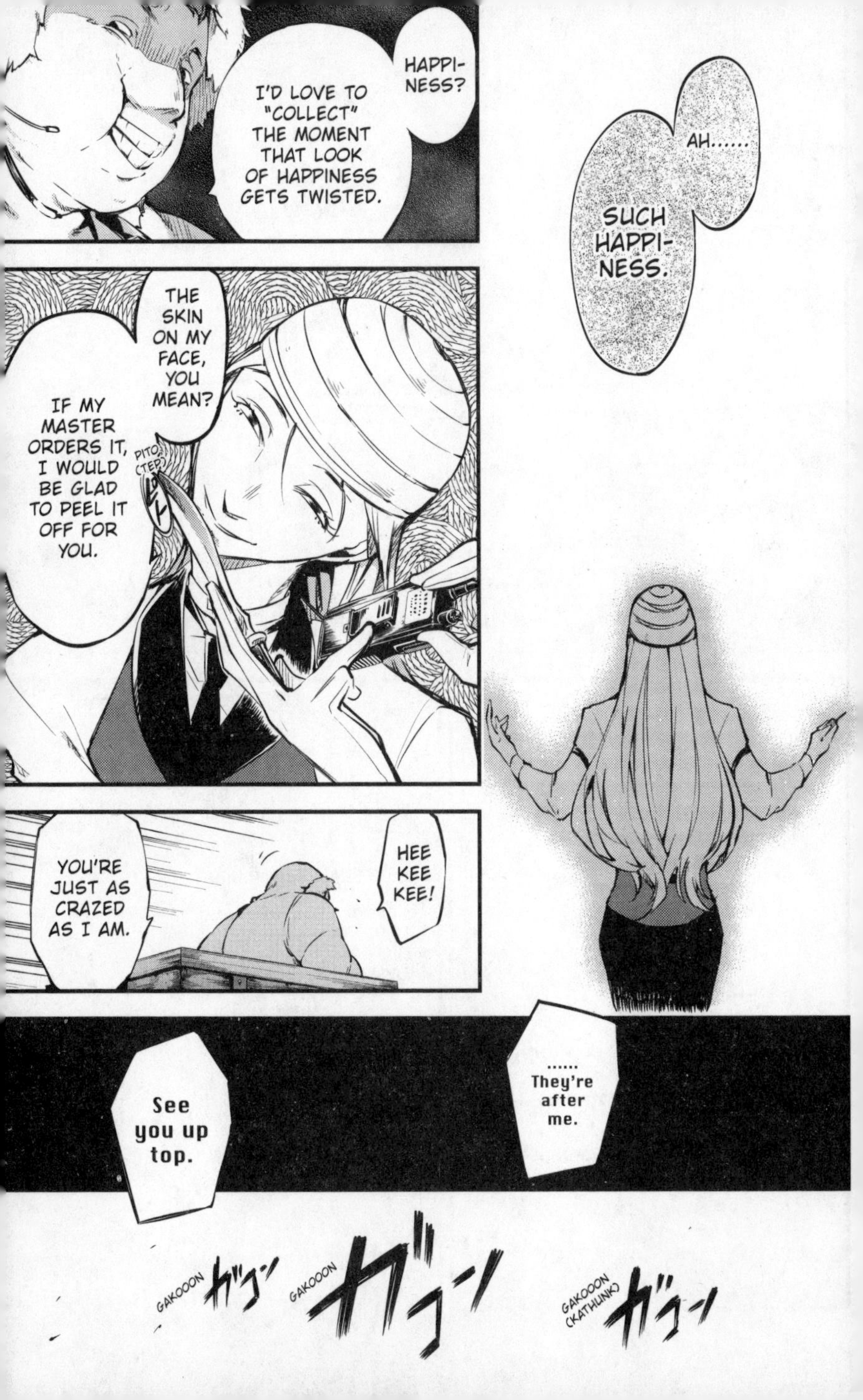
AH...... SUCH HAPPINESS.
HAPPINESS?
I'D LOVE TO "COLLECT" THE MOMENT THAT LOOK OF HAPPINESS GETS TWISTED.
THE SKIN ON MY FACE, YOU MEAN?
PITO (TEP)
IF MY MASTER ORDERS IT, I WOULD BE GLAD TO PEEL IT OFF FOR YOU.
HEE KEE KEE!
YOU'RE JUST AS CRAZED AS I AM.
...... They're after me.
See you up top.
GAKOOON (KATHUNK)
GAKOOON
GAKOOON

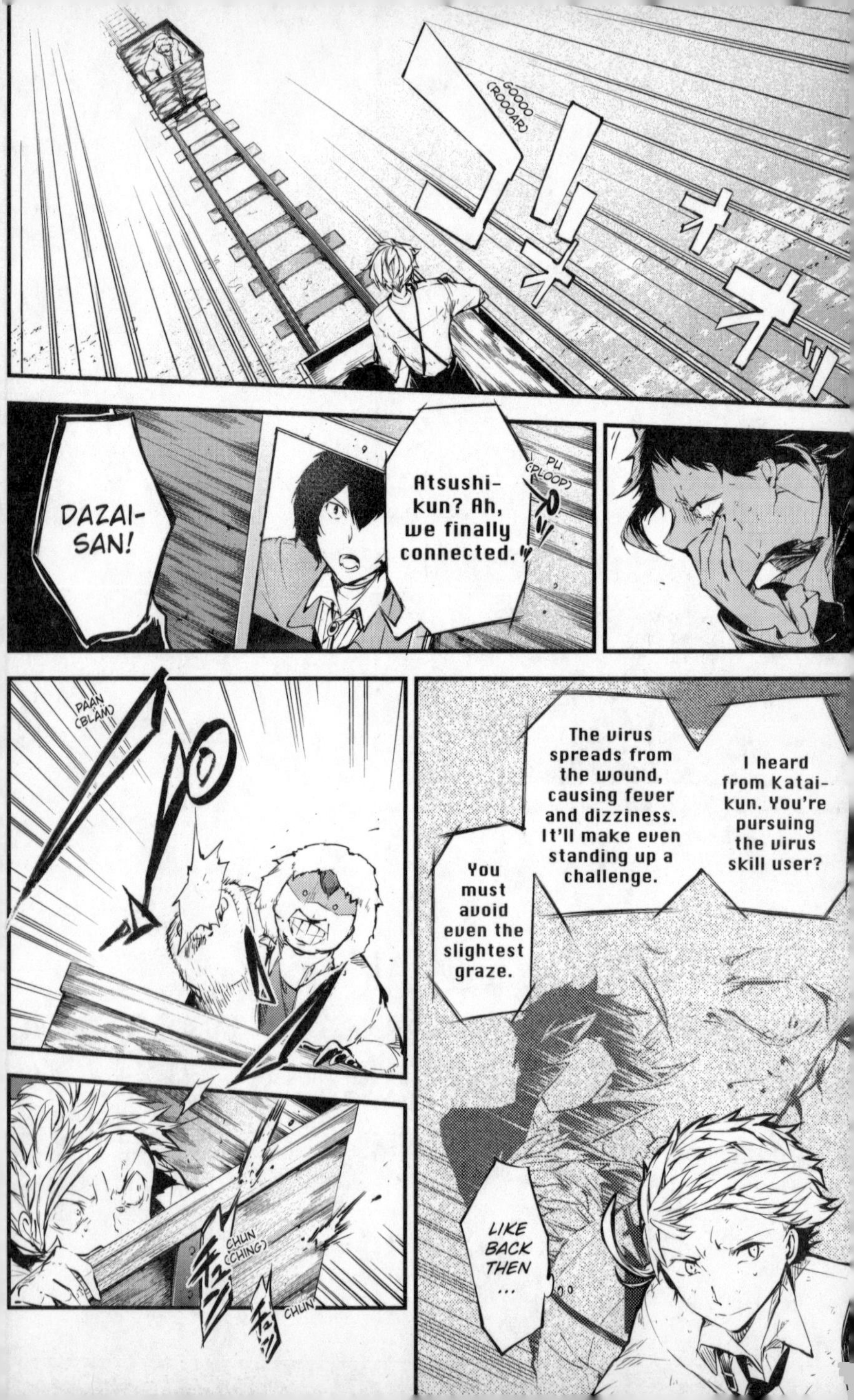
GOOOO (ROOOAR)
PU (PLOOP)
Atsushi-kun? Ah, we finally connected.
DAZAI-SAN!
I heard from Katai-kun. You're pursuing the virus skill user?
The virus spreads from the wound, causing fever and dizziness. It'll make even standing up a challenge.
You must avoid even the slightest graze.
LIKE BACK THEN ...
PAAN (BLAM)
CHUN (CHING)
CHUN

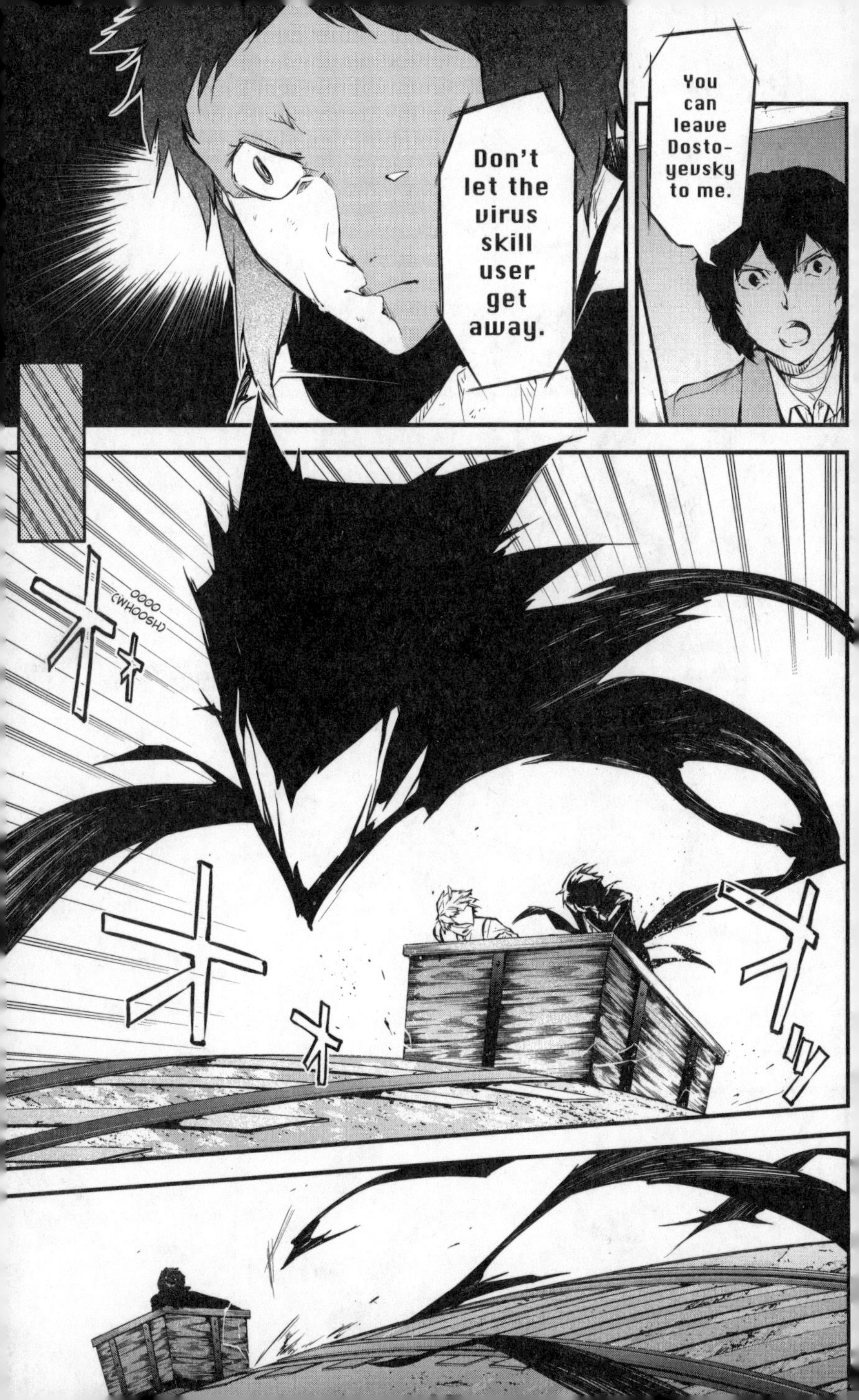
You can leave Dostoyevsky to me.
Don't let the virus skill user get away.
(WHOOSH)

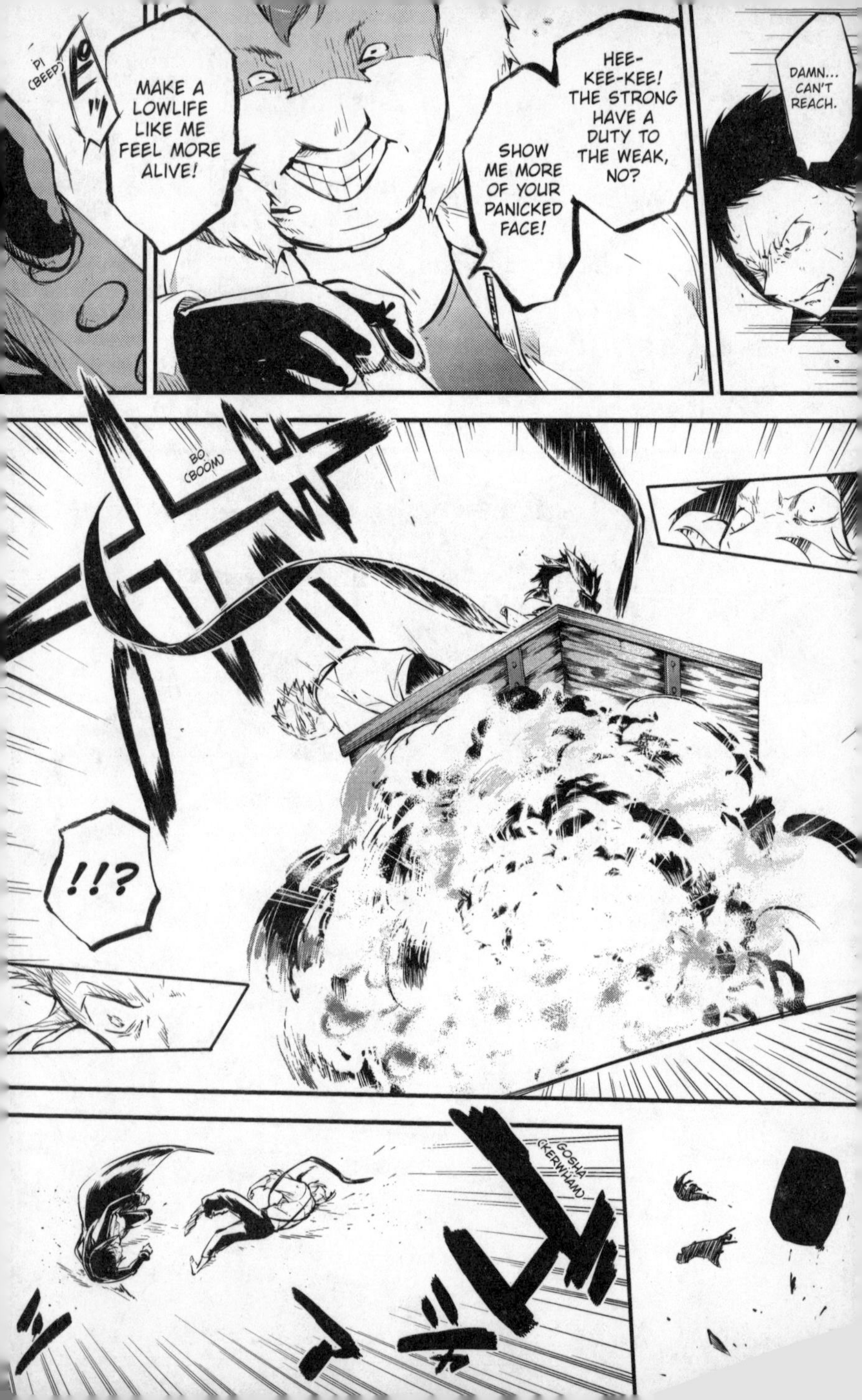
DAMN... CAN'T REACH.
HEE-KEE-KEE! THE STRONG HAVE A DUTY TO THE WEAK, NO?
SHOW ME MORE OF YOUR PANICKED FACE!
MAKE A LOWLIFE LIKE ME FEEL MORE ALIVE!
PI (BEEP)
BO (BOOM)
!!?
GOSHA (KERWHAM)

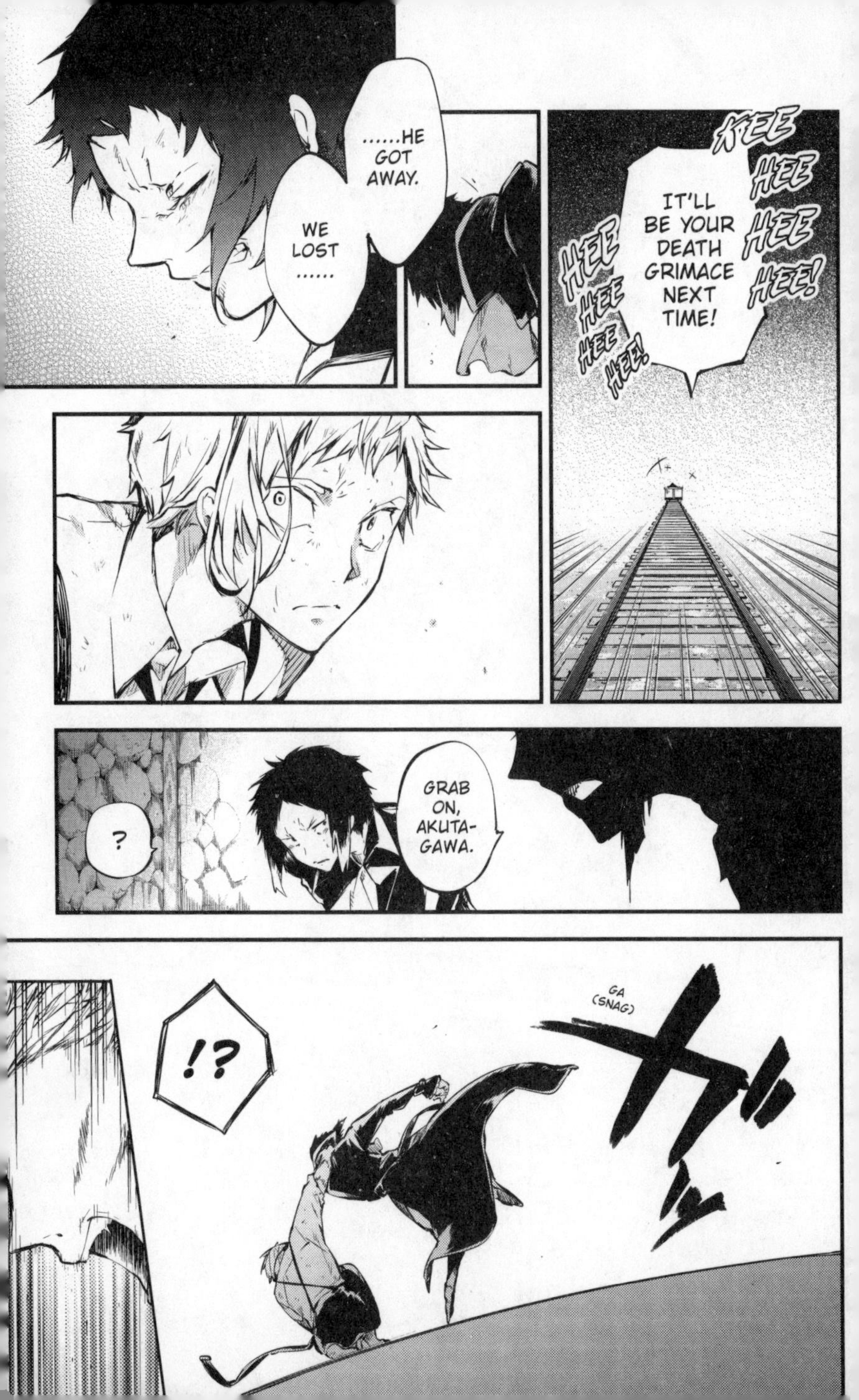
KEE HEE HEE HEE!
IT'LL BE YOUR DEATH GRIMACE NEXT TIME!
HEE HEE HEE HEE!
......HE GOT AWAY.
WE LOST ......
GRAB ON, AKUTAGAWA.
?
GA (SNAG)
!?

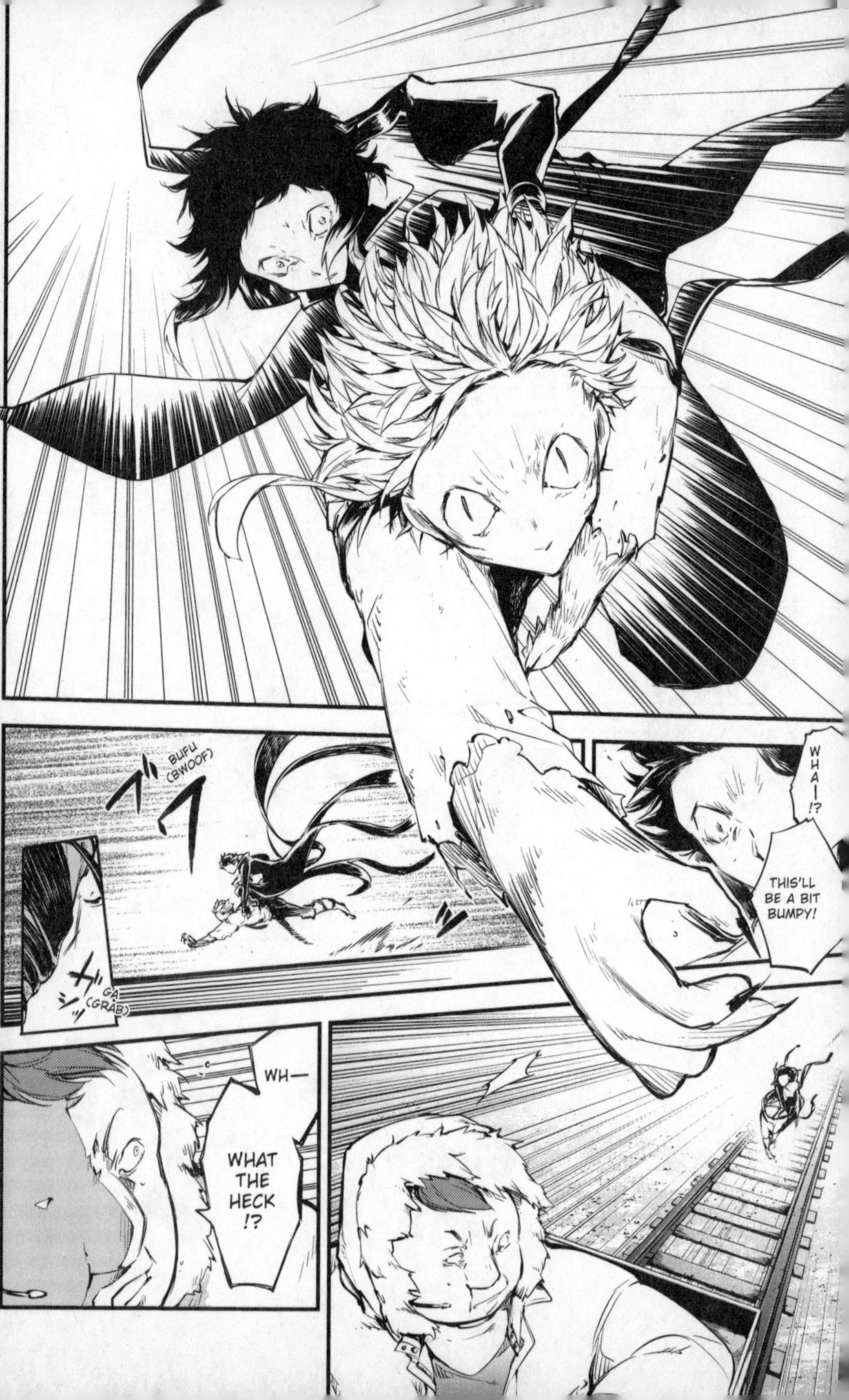
WHA—!?
THIS'LL BE A BIT BUMPY!
BUFU (BWOOF)
GA (GRAB)
WH—
WHAT THE HECK !?

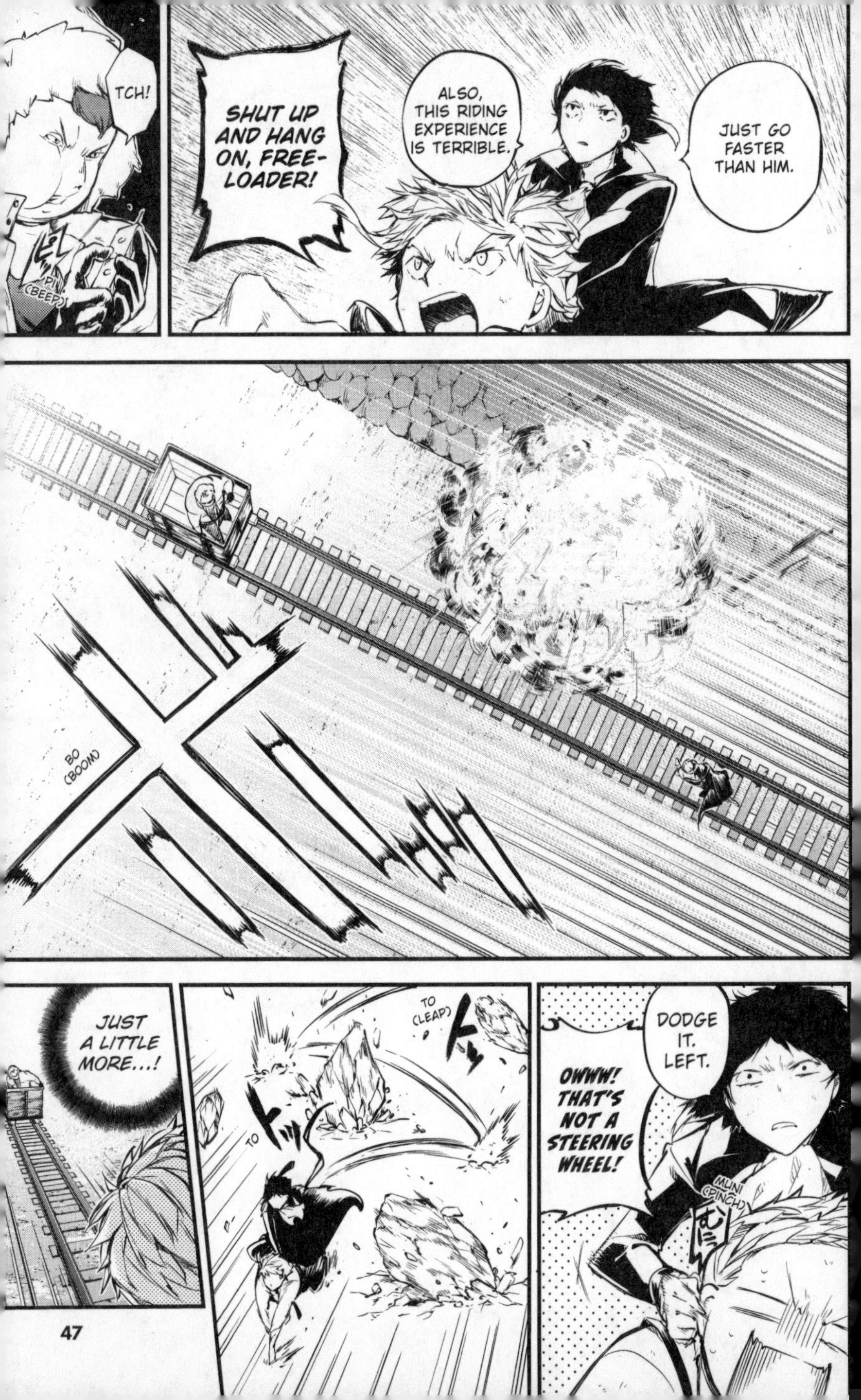
JUST GO FASTER THAN HIM.
ALSO, THIS RIDING EXPERIENCE IS TERRIBLE.
SHUT UP AND HANG ON, FREE-LOADER!
TCH!
PI (BEEP)
BO (BOOM)
DODGE IT. LEFT.
OWWW! THAT'S NOT A STEERING WHEEL!
MUNI (PINCH)
TO (LEAP)
TO
JUST A LITTLE MORE...!

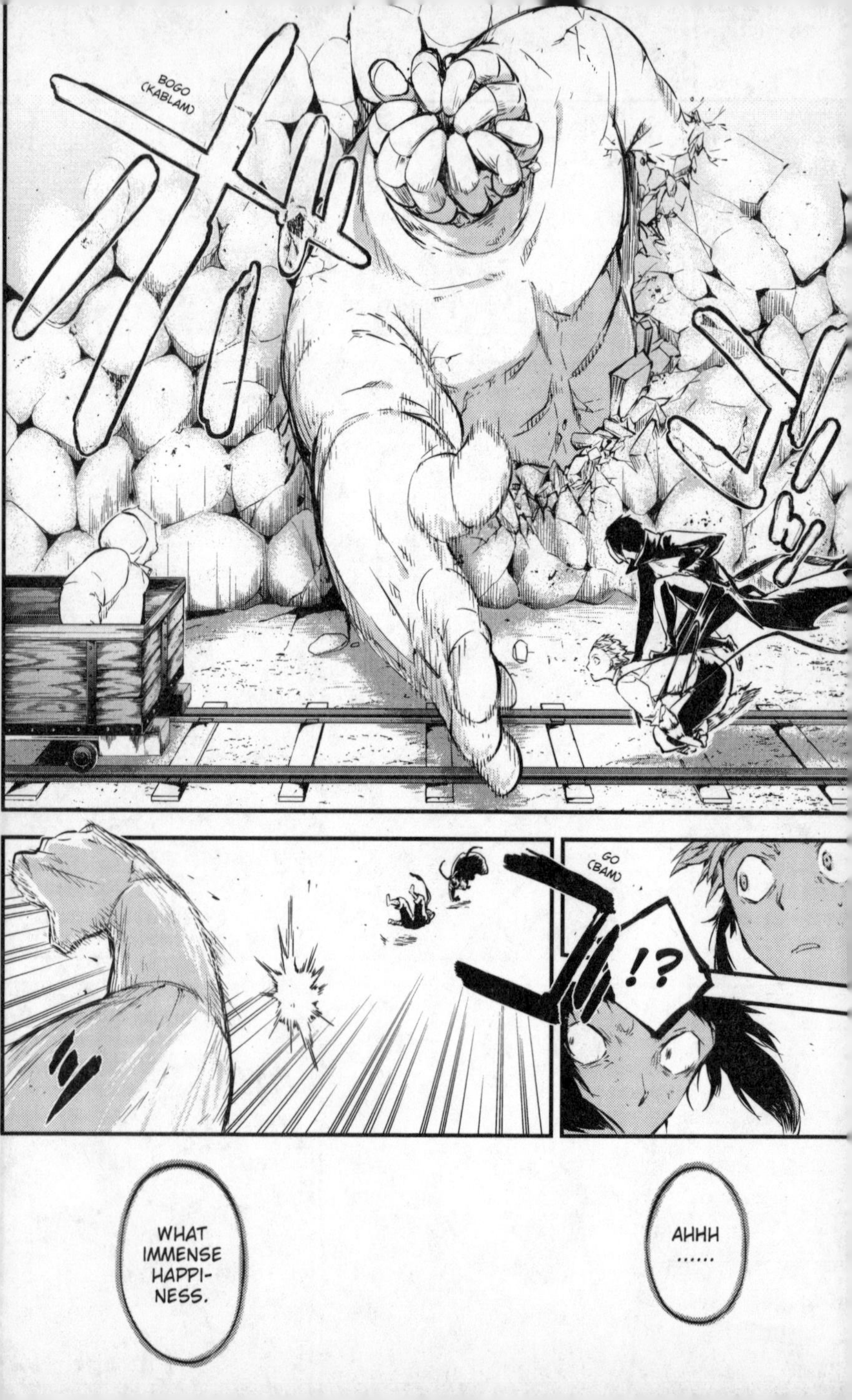
BOGO (KABLAM)
GO (BAM)
!?
AHHH ......
WHAT IMMENSE HAPPI-NESS.

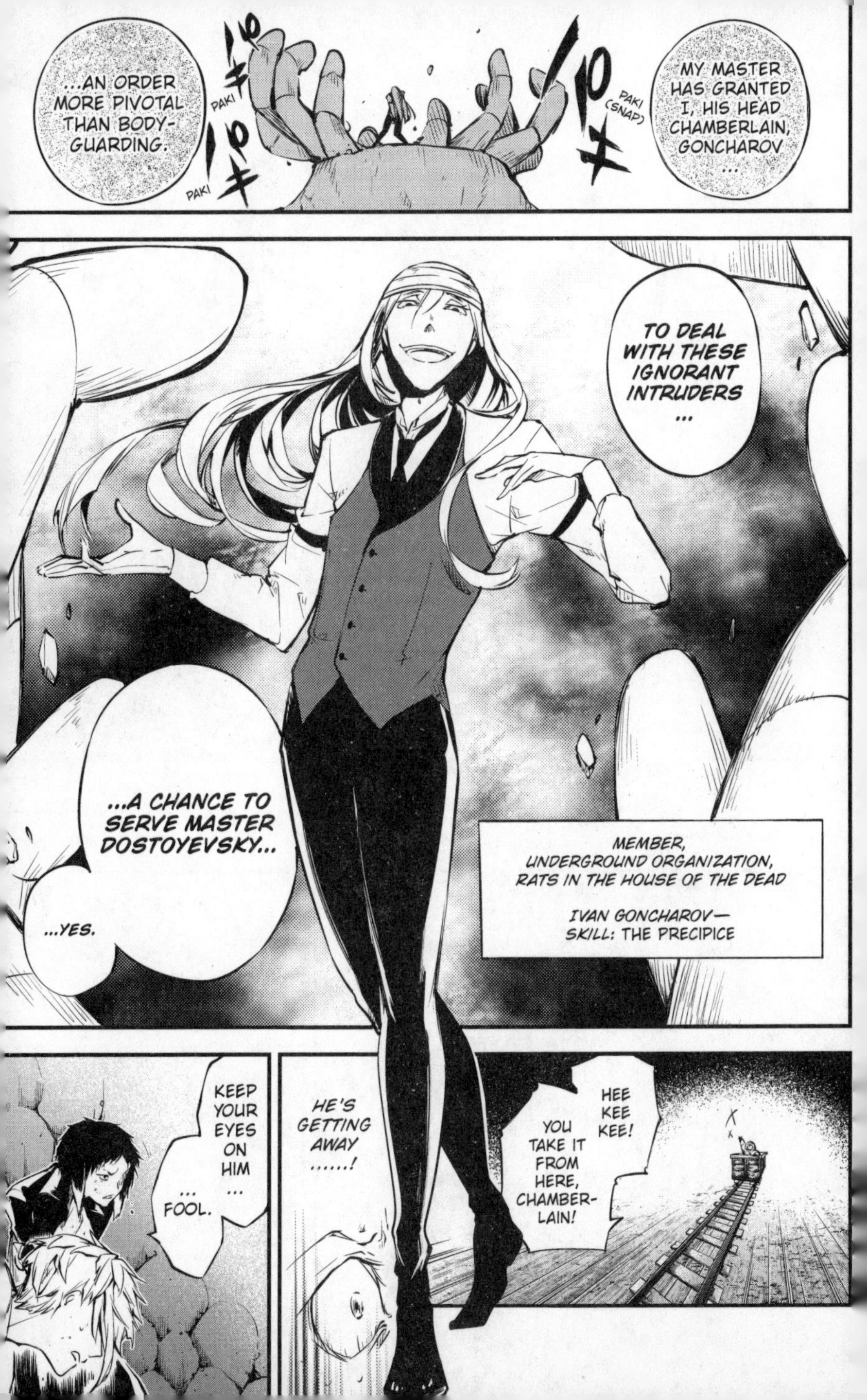
MY MASTER HAS GRANTED I, HIS HEAD CHAMBERLAIN, GONCHAROV ...
PAKI (SNAP)
PAKI
PAKI
...AN ORDER MORE PIVOTAL THAN BODY-GUARDING.
TO DEAL WITH THESE IGNORANT INTRUDERS ...
MEMBER, UNDERGROUND ORGANIZATION, RATS IN THE HOUSE OF THE DEAD
IVAN GONCHAROV— SKILL: THE PRECIPICE
...A CHANCE TO SERVE MASTER DOSTOYEVSKY...
...YES.
HEE KEE KEE!
YOU TAKE IT FROM HERE, CHAMBERLAIN!
HE'S GETTING AWAY ......!
KEEP YOUR EYES ON HIM ... FOOL.

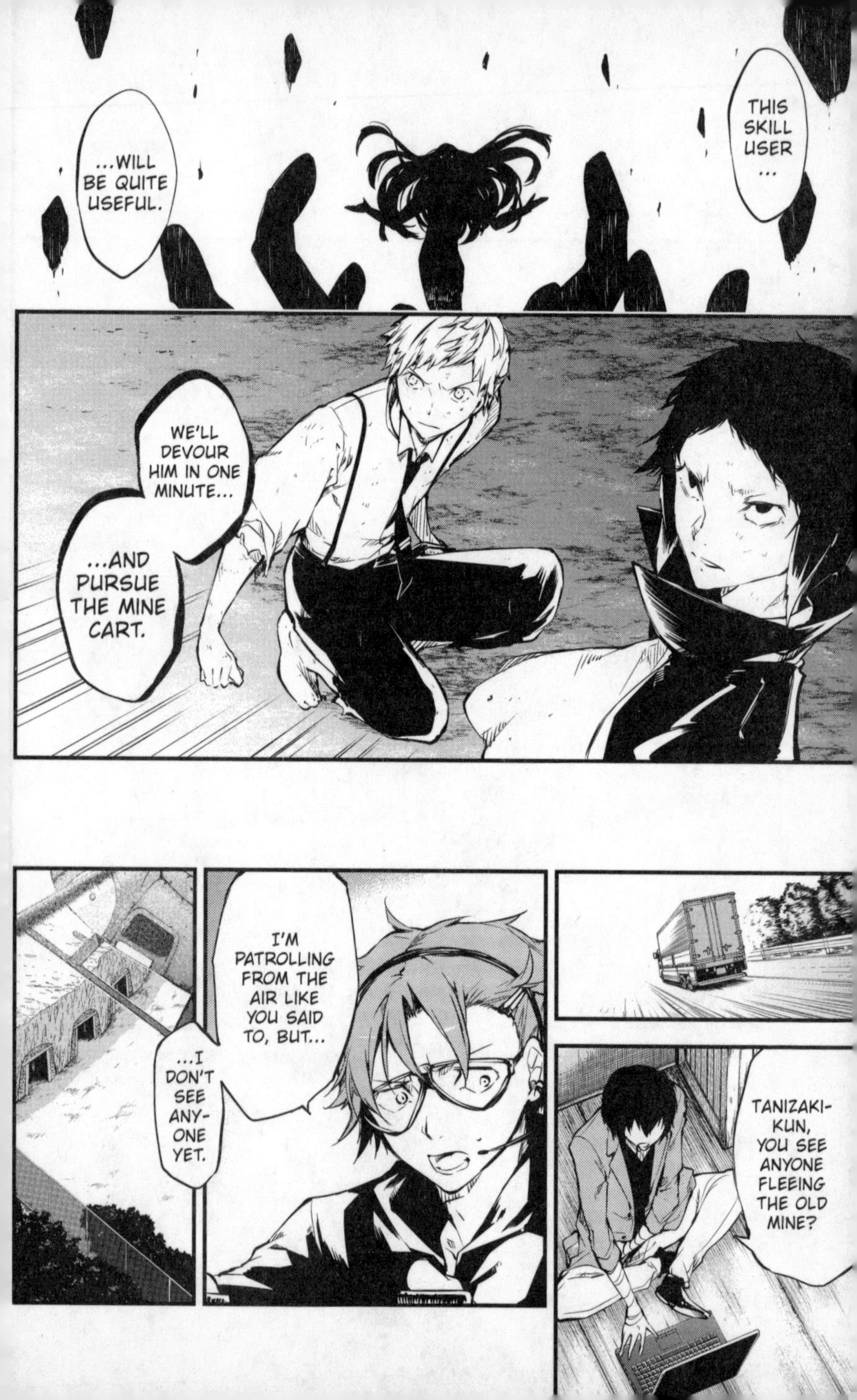
THIS SKILL USER...
...WILL BE QUITE USEFUL.
WE'LL DEVOUR HIM IN ONE MINUTE...
...AND PURSUE THE MINE CART.
TANIZAKI-KUN, YOU SEE ANYONE FLEEING THE OLD MINE?
I'M PATROLLING FROM THE AIR LIKE YOU SAID TO, BUT...
...I DON'T SEE ANY-ONE YET.

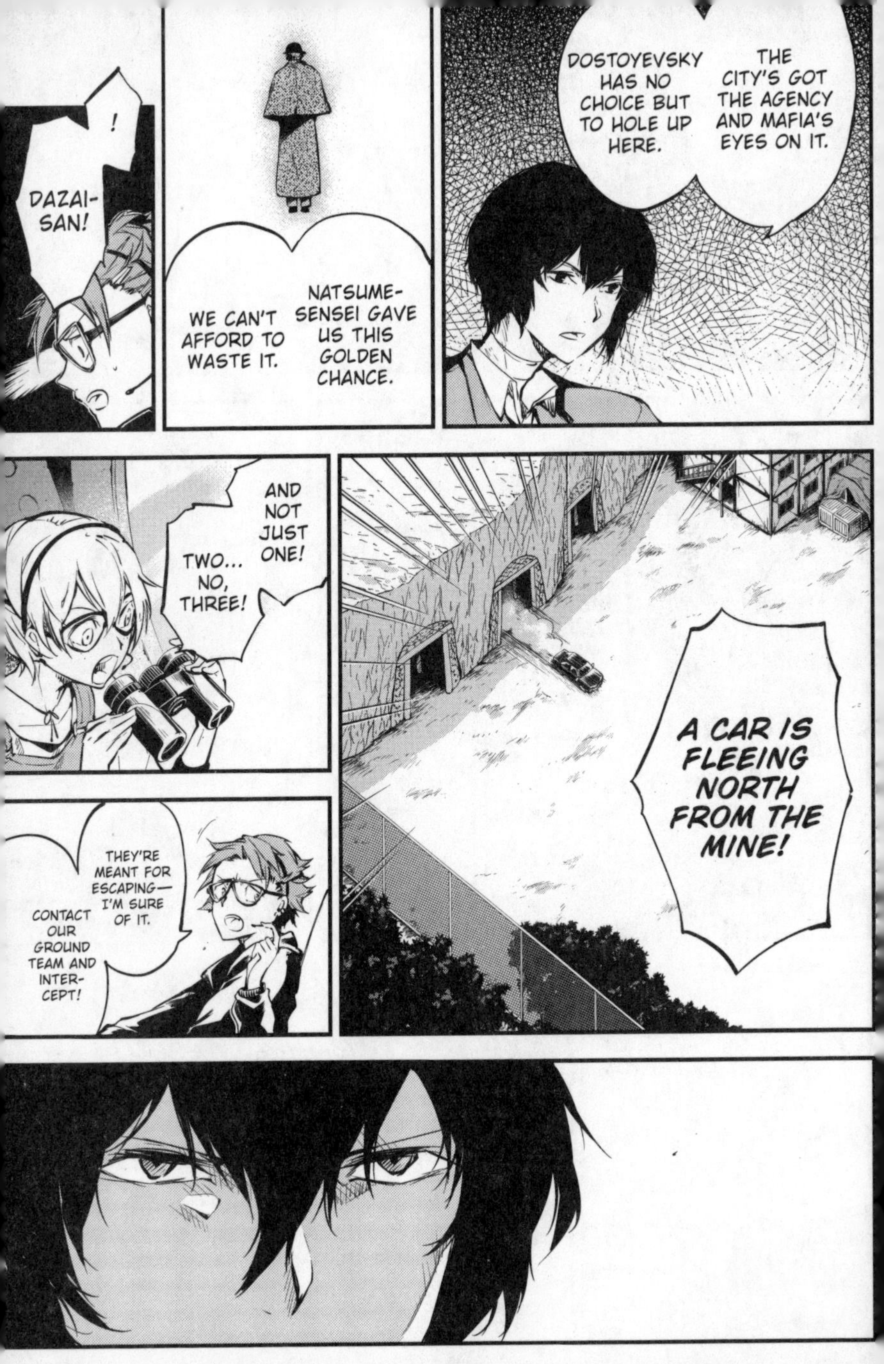
THE CITY'S GOT THE AGENCY AND MAFIA'S EYES ON IT.
DOSTOYEVSKY HAS NO CHOICE BUT TO HOLE UP HERE.
NATSUME-SENSEI GAVE US THIS GOLDEN CHANCE.
WE CAN'T AFFORD TO WASTE IT.
!
DAZAI-SAN!
A CAR IS FLEEING NORTH FROM THE MINE!
AND NOT JUST ONE!
TWO... NO, THREE!
THEY'RE MEANT FOR ESCAPING—I'M SURE OF IT.
CONTACT OUR GROUND TEAM AND INTER-CEPT!

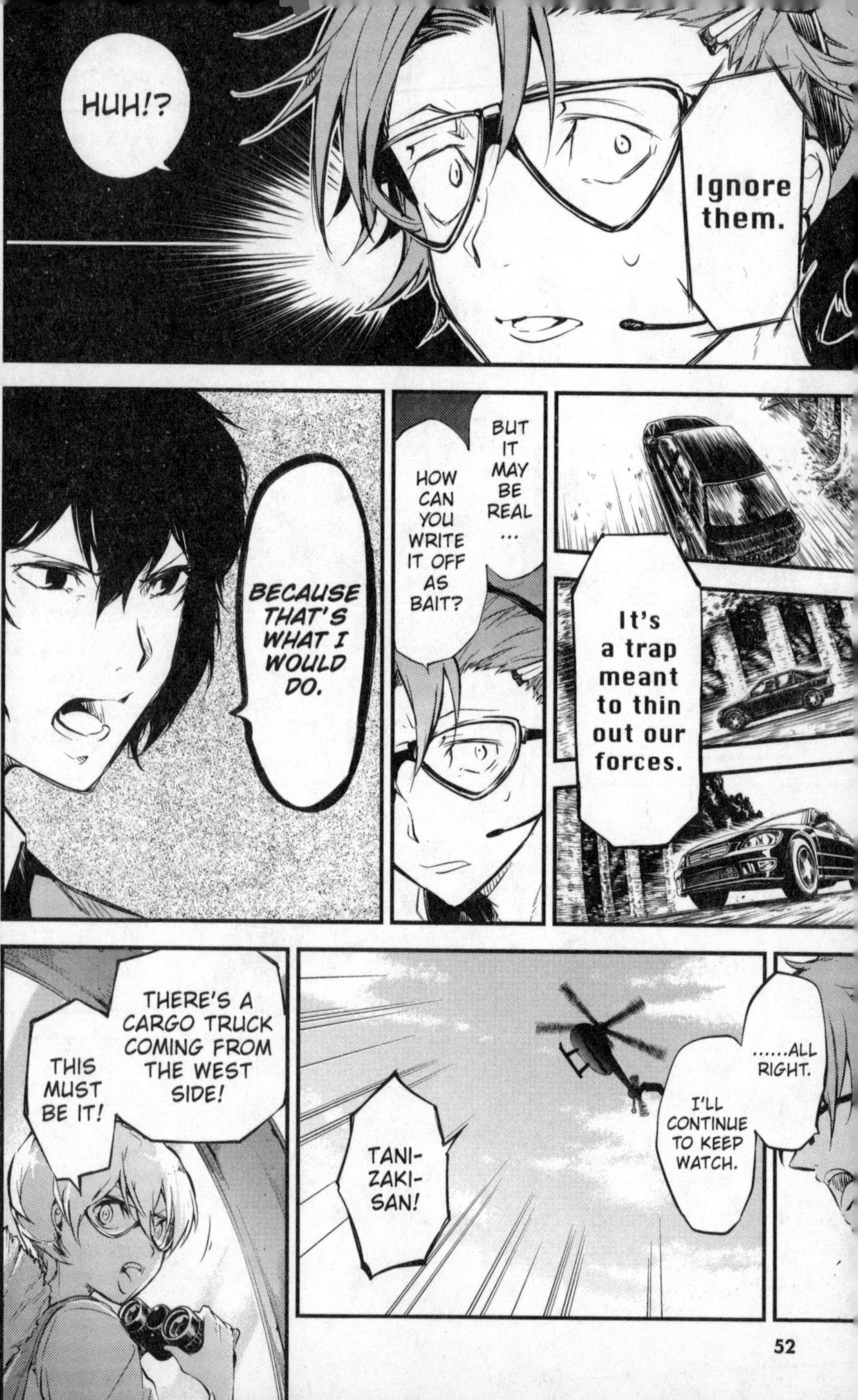
Ignore them.
HUH!?
It's a trap meant to thin out our forces.
BUT IT MAY BE REAL...
HOW CAN YOU WRITE IT OFF AS BAIT?
BECAUSE THAT'S WHAT I WOULD DO.
......ALL RIGHT.
I'LL CONTINUE TO KEEP WATCH.
TANI-ZAKI-SAN!
THERE'S A CARGO TRUCK COMING FROM THE WEST SIDE!
THIS MUST BE IT!

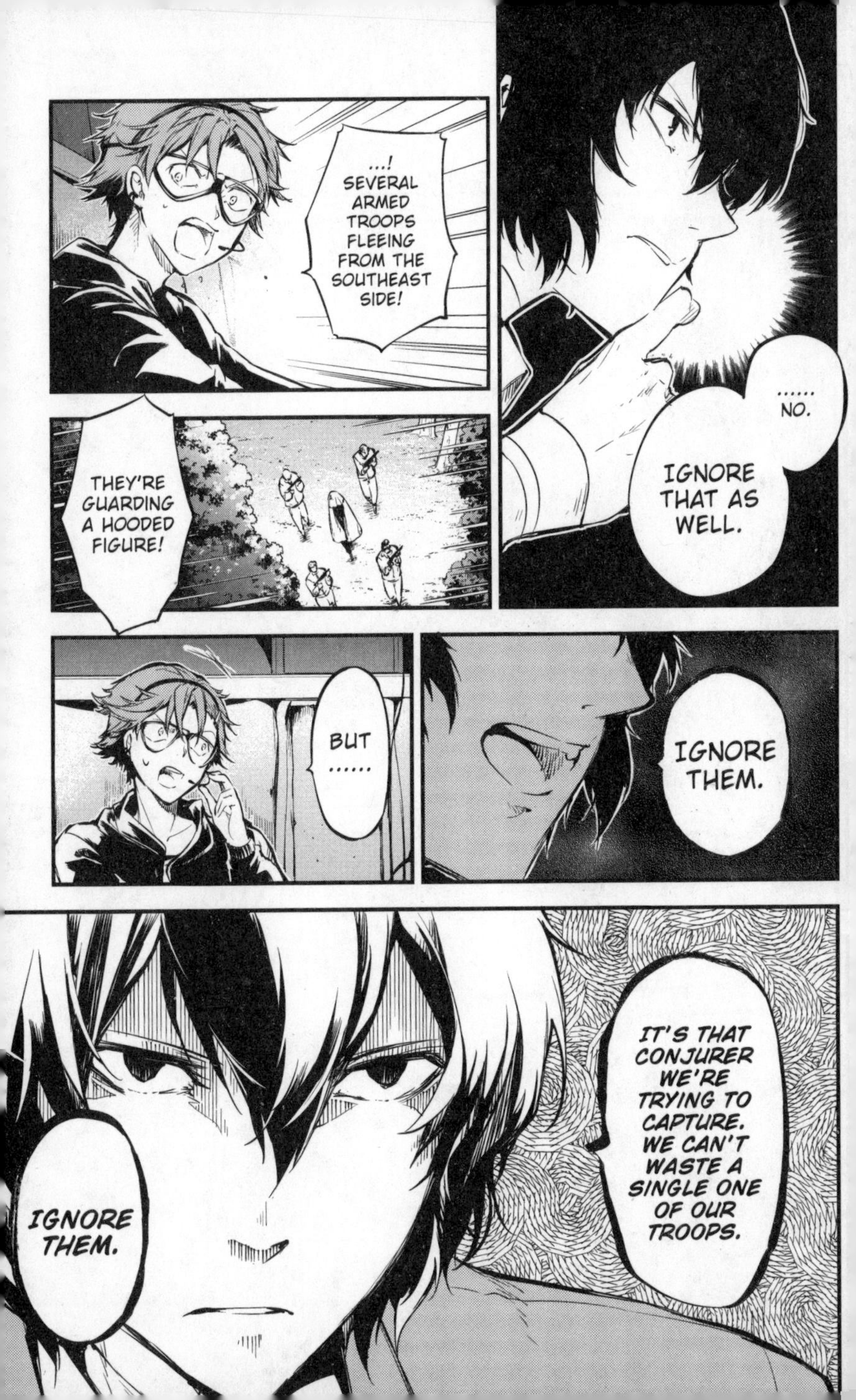
......
NO.
IGNORE THAT AS WELL.
...! SEVERAL ARMED TROOPS FLEEING FROM THE SOUTHEAST SIDE!
THEY'RE GUARDING A HOODED FIGURE!
IGNORE THEM.
BUT ......
IT'S THAT CONJURER WE'RE TRYING TO CAPTURE. WE CAN'T WASTE A SINGLE ONE OF OUR TROOPS.
IGNORE THEM.

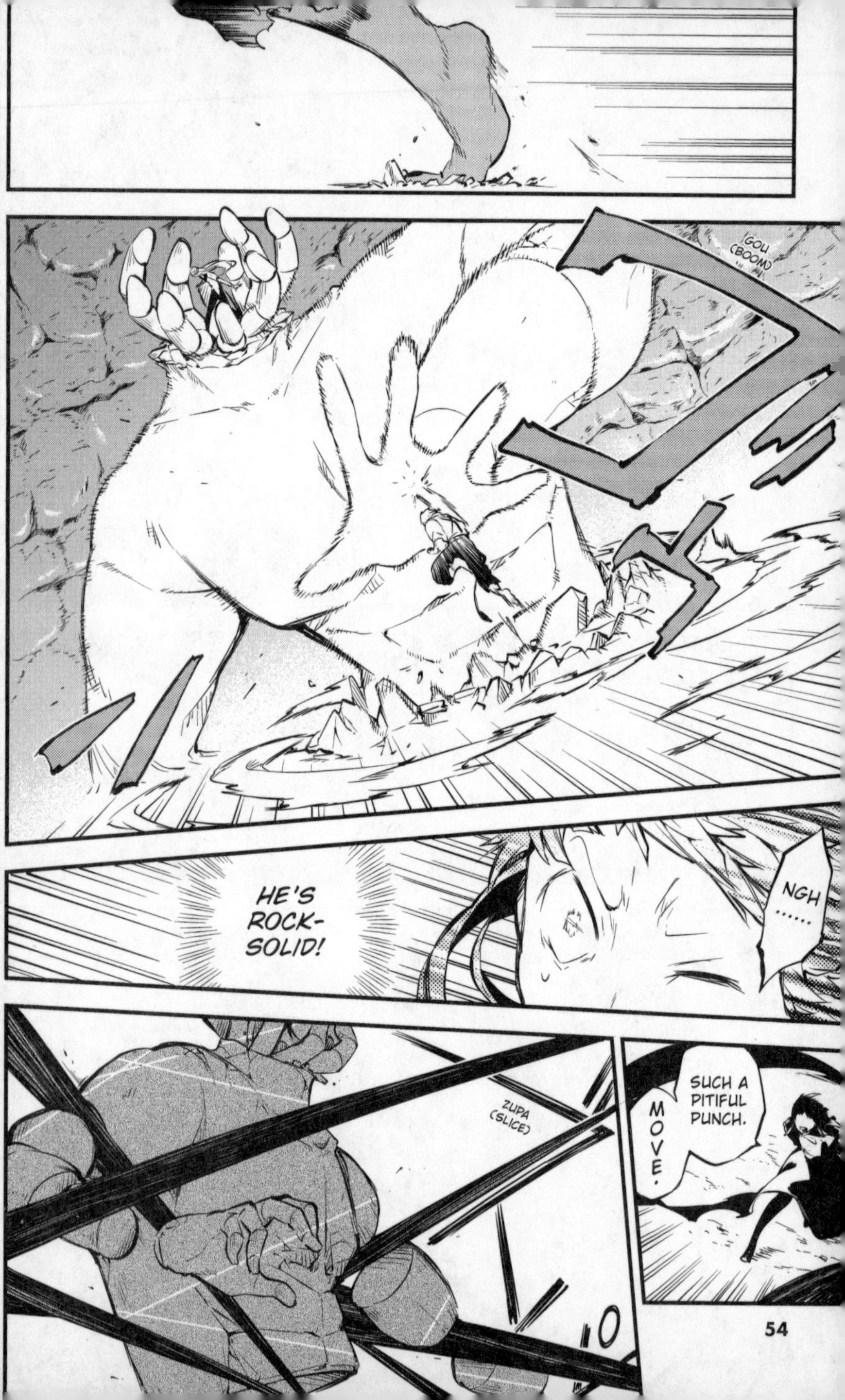
GOU (BOOM)
NGH ......
HE'S ROCK-SOLID!
MOVE.
SUCH A PITIFUL PUNCH.
ZUPA (SLICE)

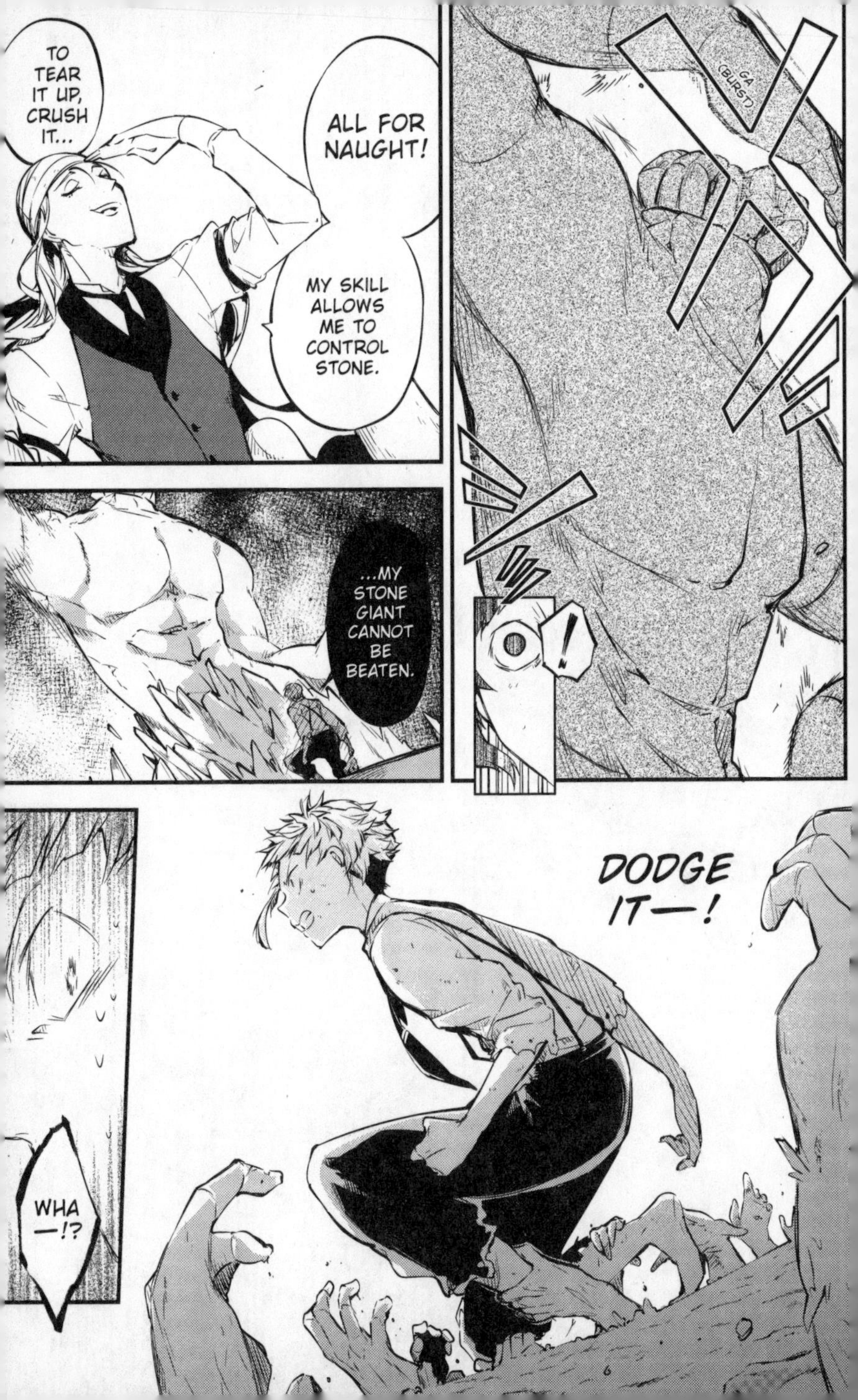
GA (BURST)
!
TO TEAR IT UP, CRUSH IT...
ALL FOR NAUGHT!
MY SKILL ALLOWS ME TO CONTROL STONE.
...MY STONE GIANT CANNOT BE BEATEN.
DODGE IT—!
WHA—!?

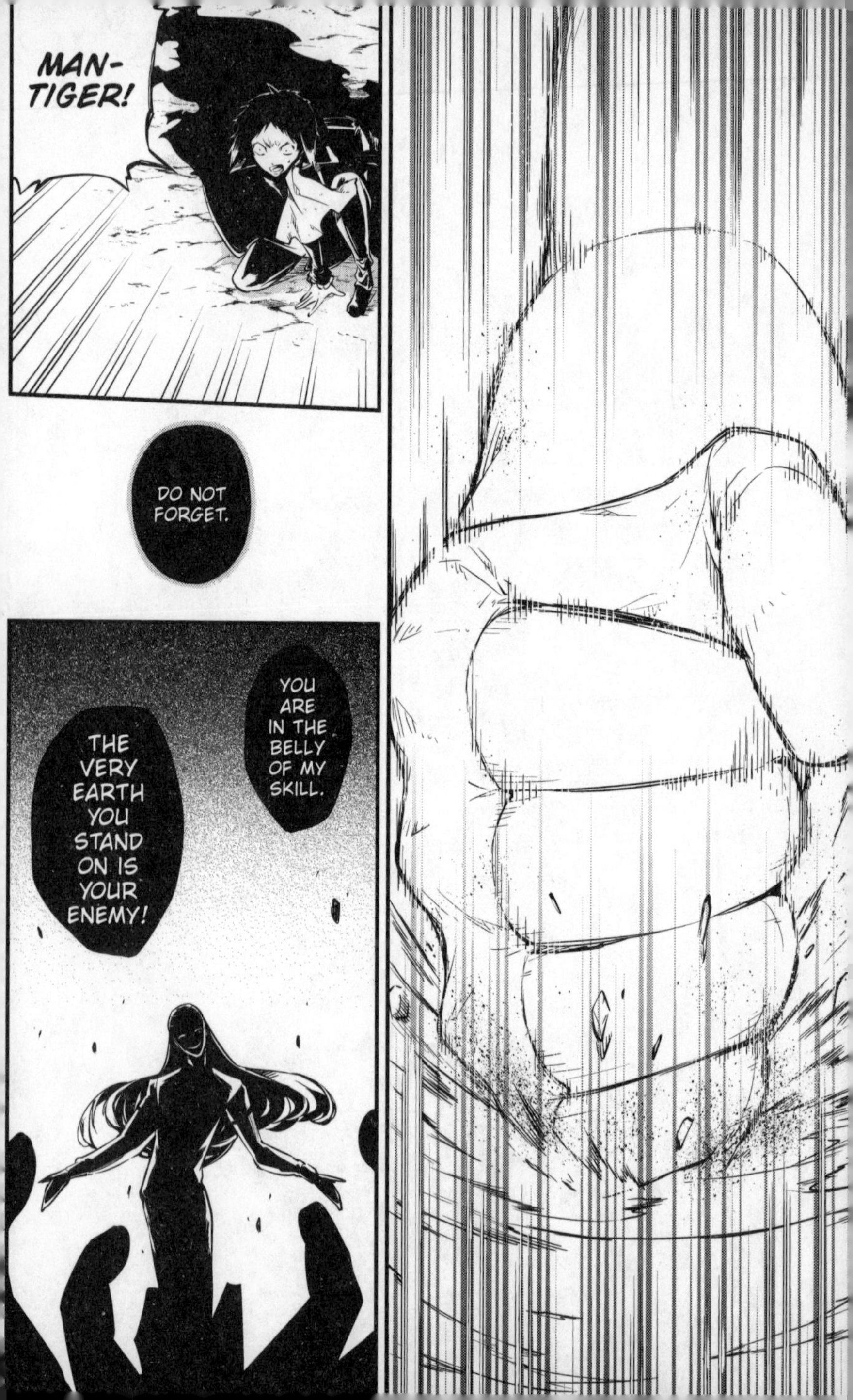
MAN-TIGER!
DO NOT FORGET.
YOU ARE IN THE BELLY OF MY SKILL.
THE VERY EARTH YOU STAND ON IS YOUR ENEMY!

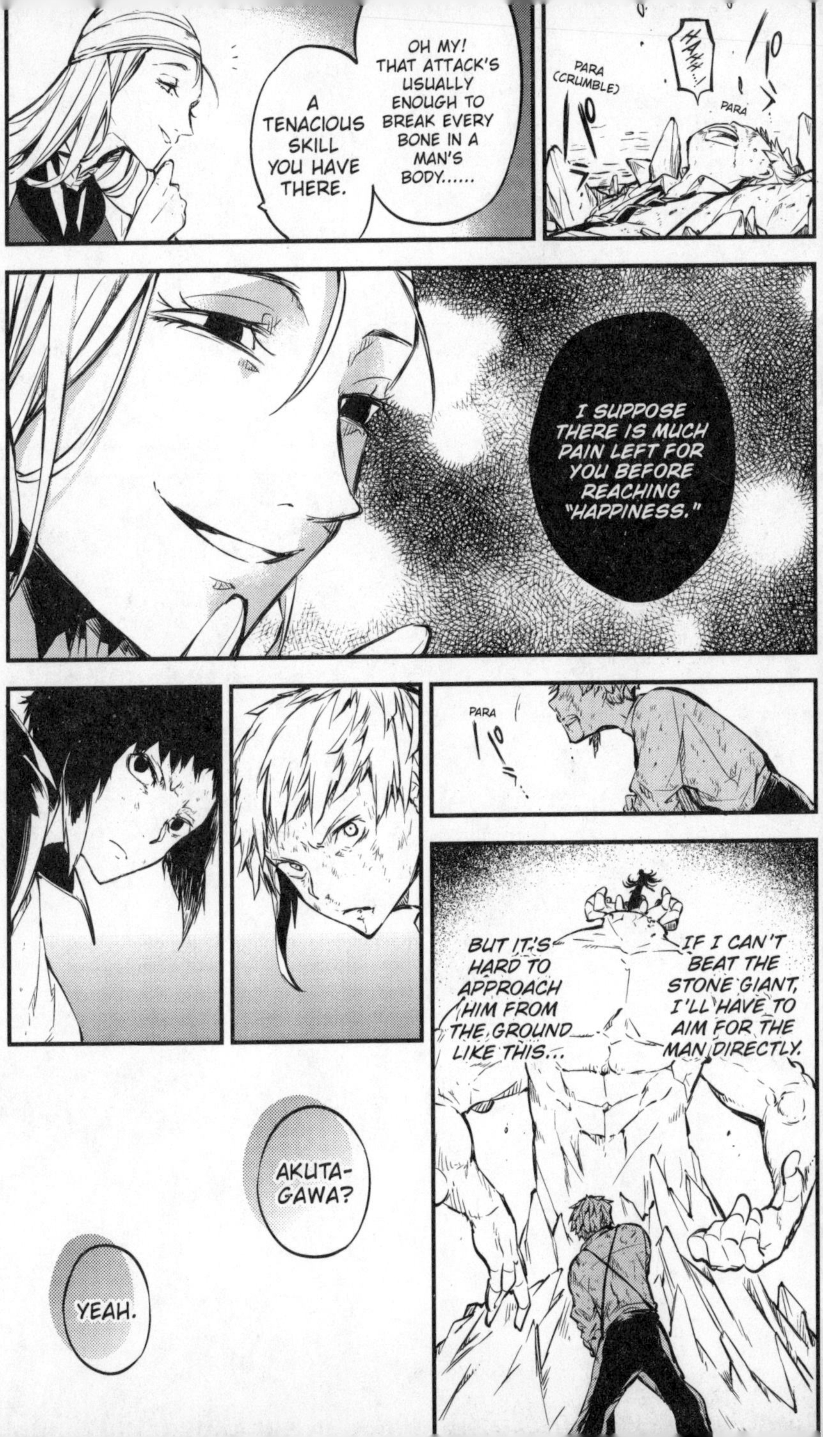
PARA (CRUMBLE)
PARA
OH MY! THAT ATTACK'S USUALLY ENOUGH TO BREAK EVERY BONE IN A MAN'S BODY......
A TENACIOUS SKILL YOU HAVE THERE.
I SUPPOSE THERE IS MUCH PAIN LEFT FOR YOU BEFORE REACHING "HAPPINESS."
PARA
IF I CAN'T BEAT THE STONE GIANT, I'LL HAVE TO AIM FOR THE MAN DIRECTLY.
BUT IT'S HARD TO APPROACH HIM FROM THE GROUND LIKE THIS...
AKUTA-GAWA?
YEAH.

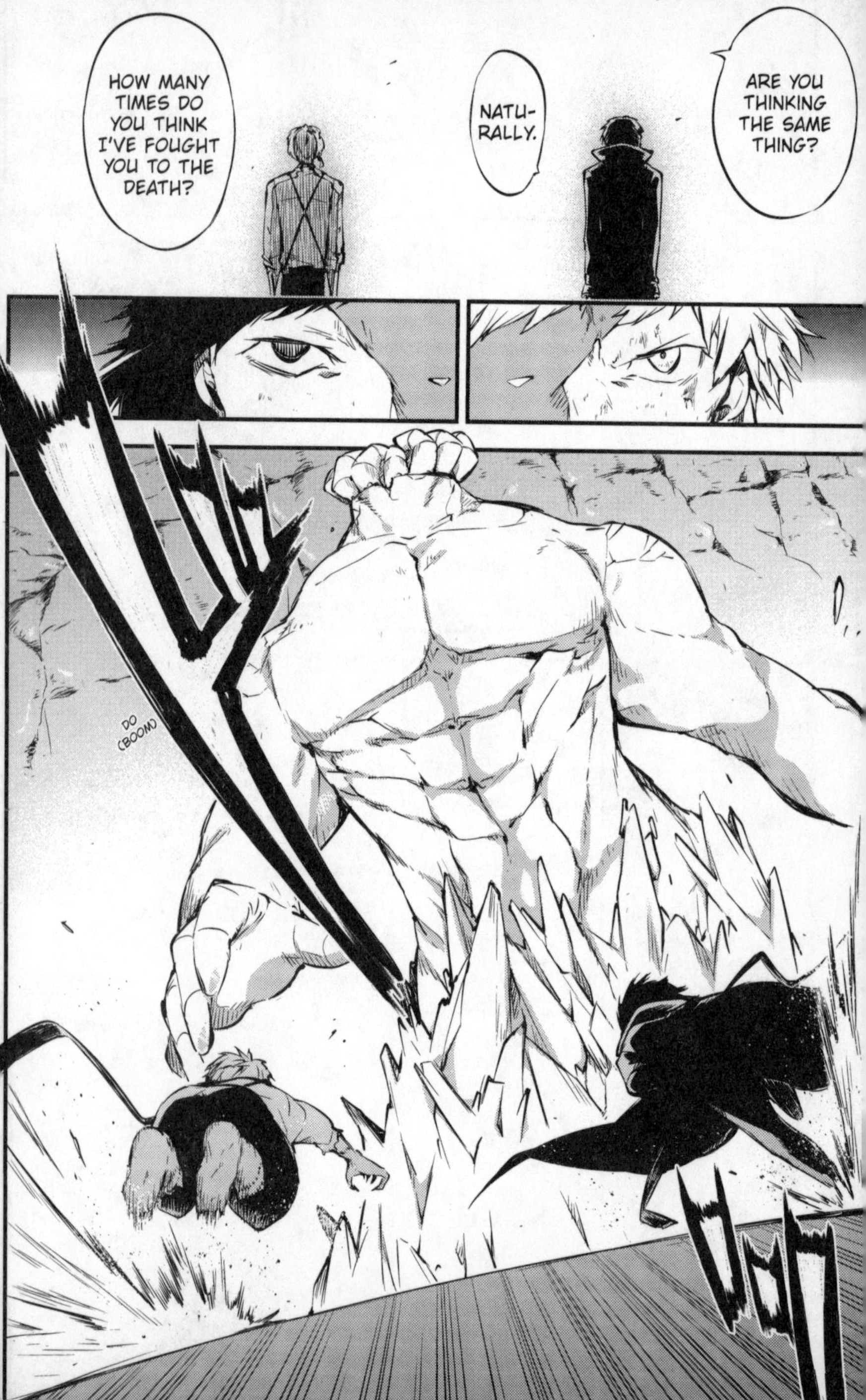
ARE YOU THINKING THE SAME THING?
NATU-RALLY.
HOW MANY TIMES DO YOU THINK I'VE FOUGHT YOU TO THE DEATH?
DO (BOOM)

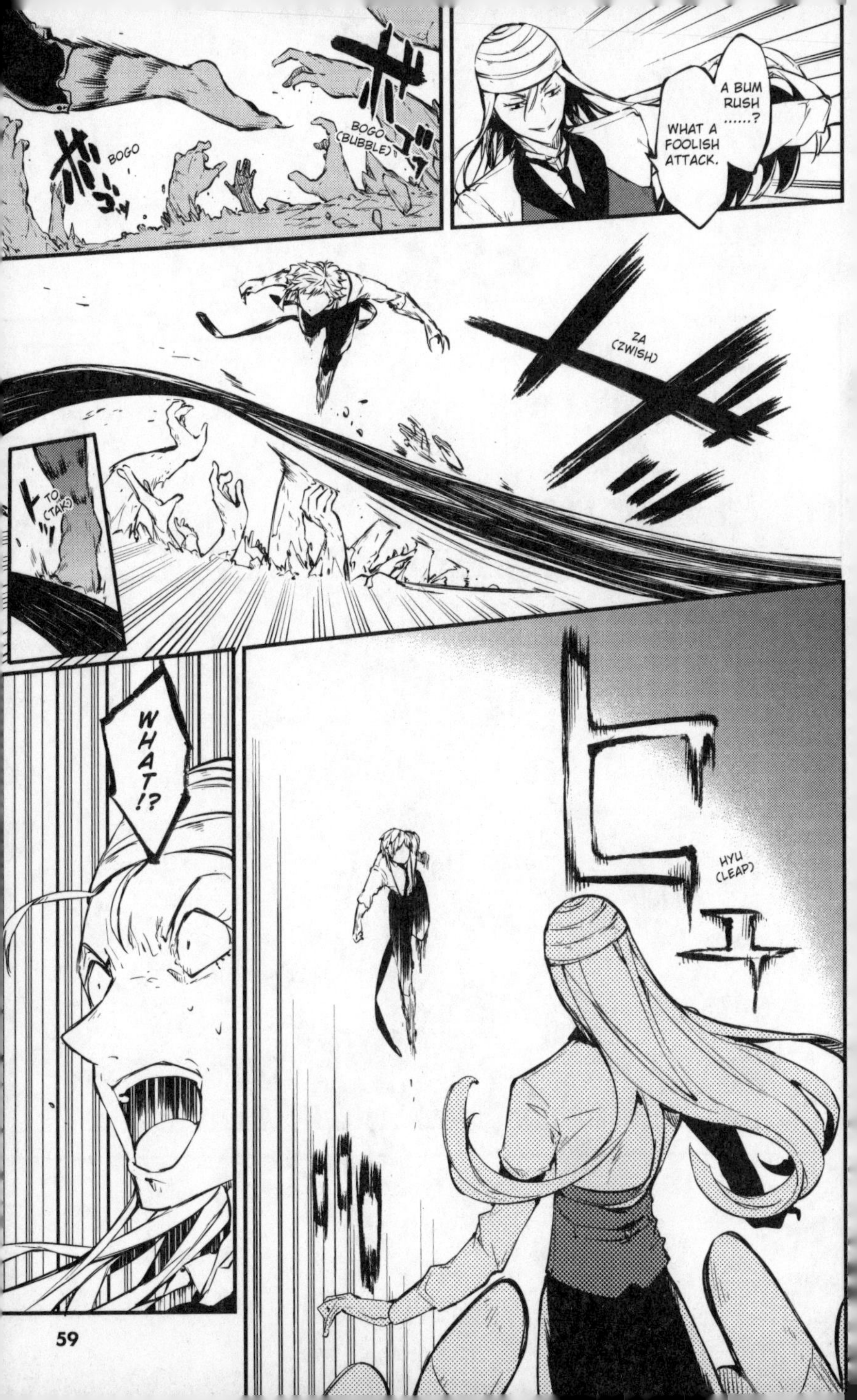
A BUM RUSH ......?
WHAT A FOOLISH ATTACK.
BOGO (BUBBLE)
BOGO
ZA (ZWISH)
TO (TAK)
HYU (LEAP)
WHAT!?

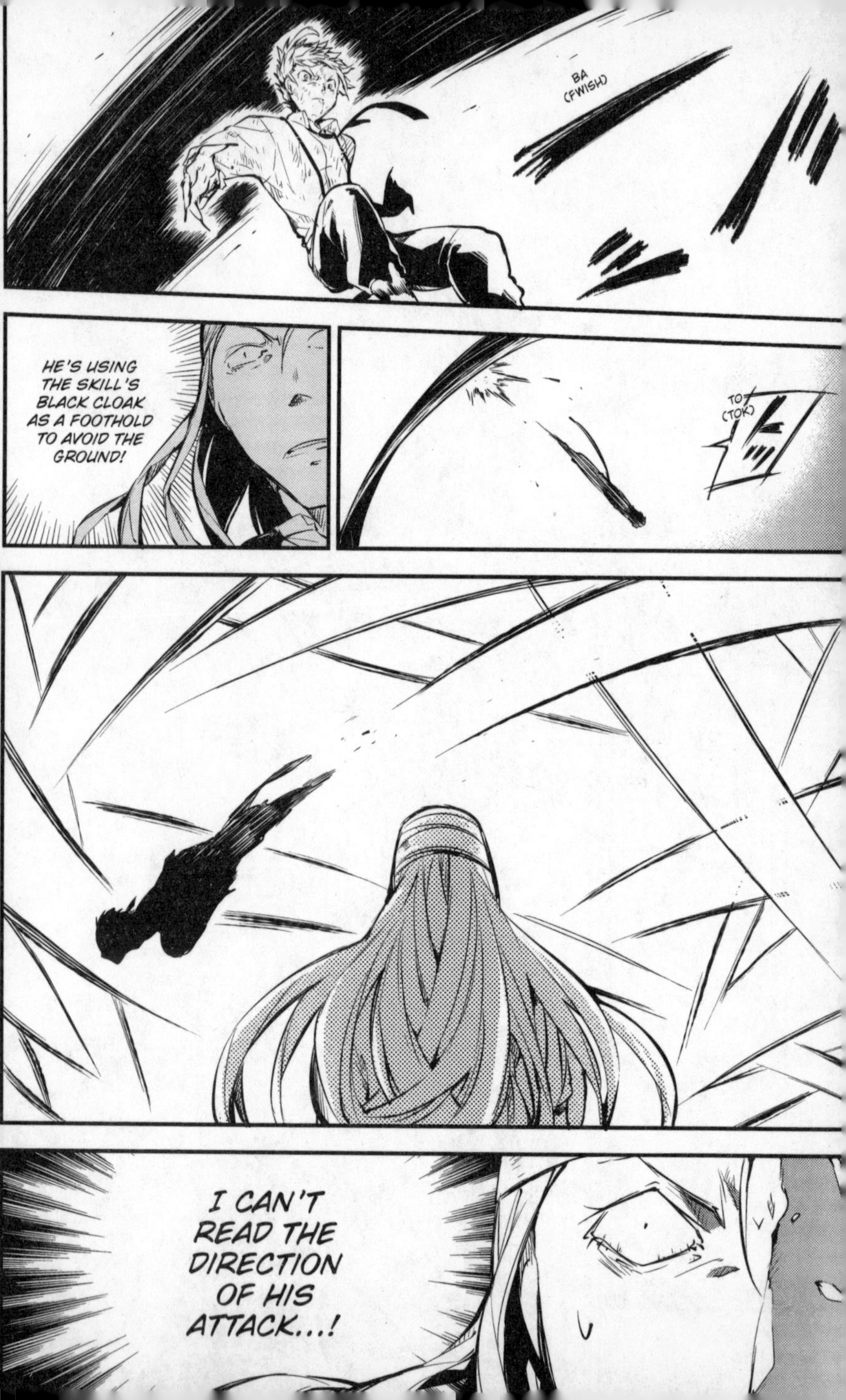
BA
(FWISH)
TO
(TOK)
HE'S USING THE SKILL'S BLACK CLOAK AS A FOOTHOLD TO AVOID THE GROUND!
I CAN'T READ THE DIRECTION OF HIS ATTACK...!

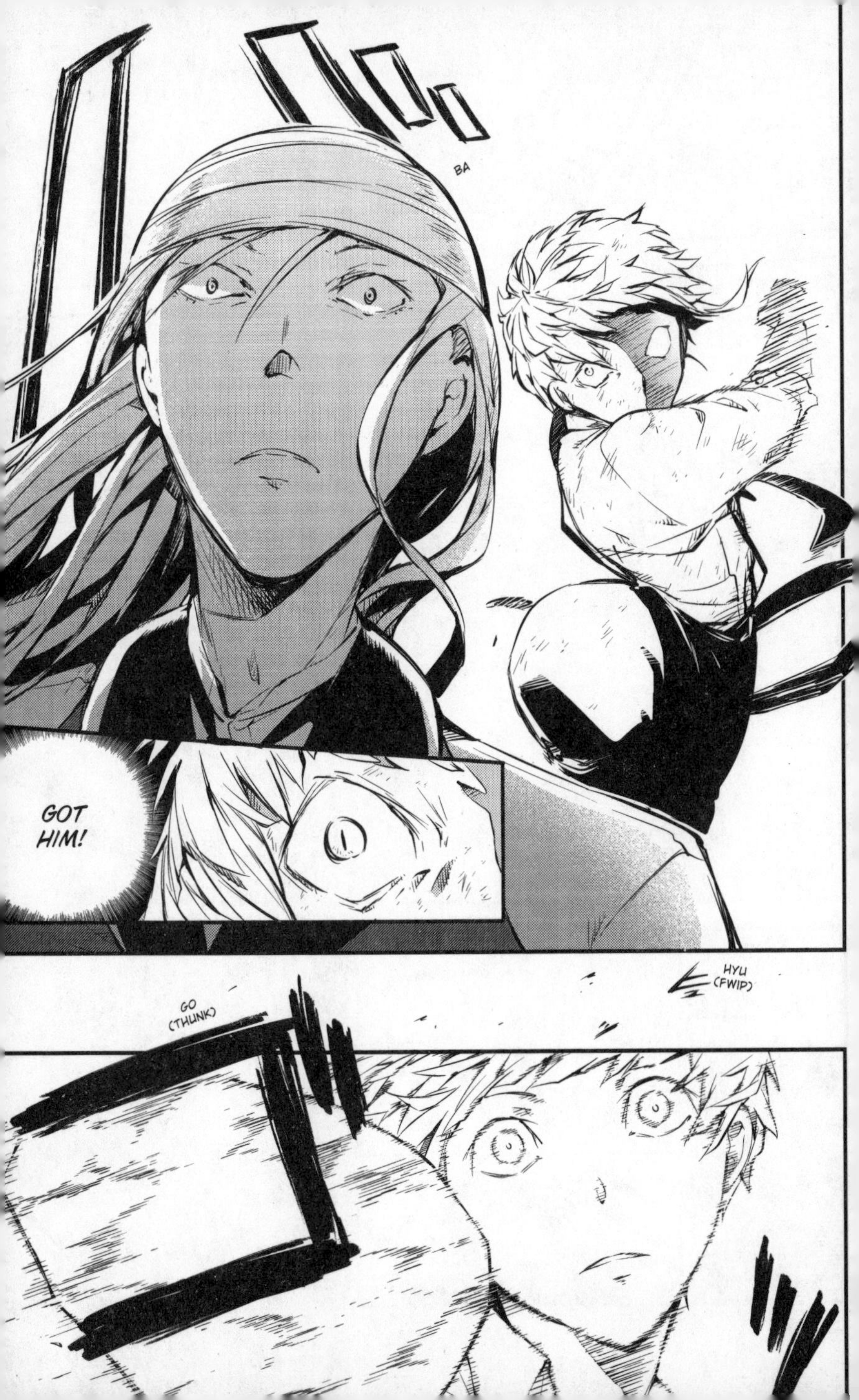
BA
GOT HIM!
HYU (FWIP)
GO (THUNK)

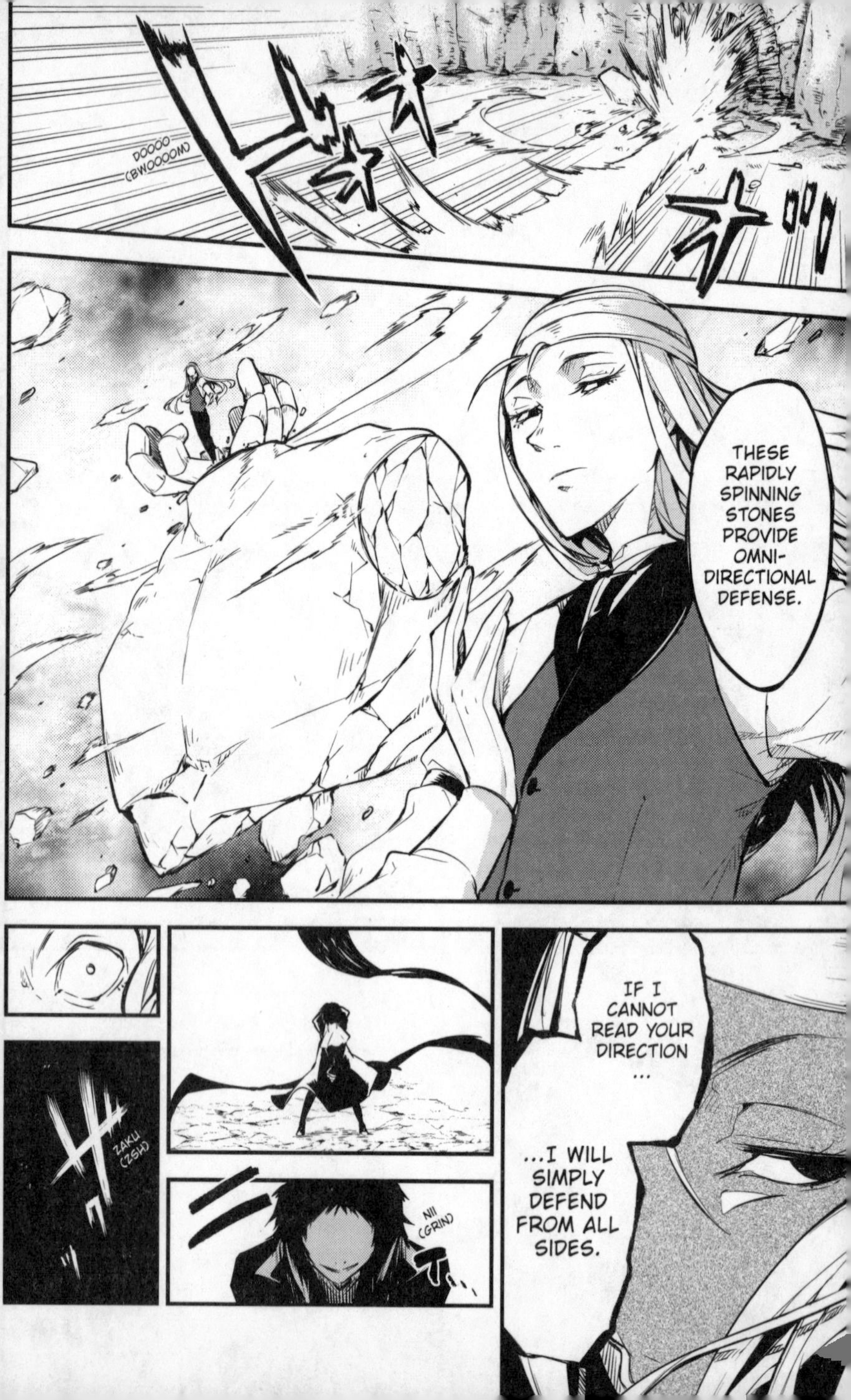
DOOOO
(BWOOOOM)
THESE RAPIDLY SPINNING STONES PROVIDE OMNI-DIRECTIONAL DEFENSE.
IF I CANNOT READ YOUR DIRECTION ...
...I WILL SIMPLY DEFEND FROM ALL SIDES.
NII
(GRIN)
ZAKU
(ZSH)

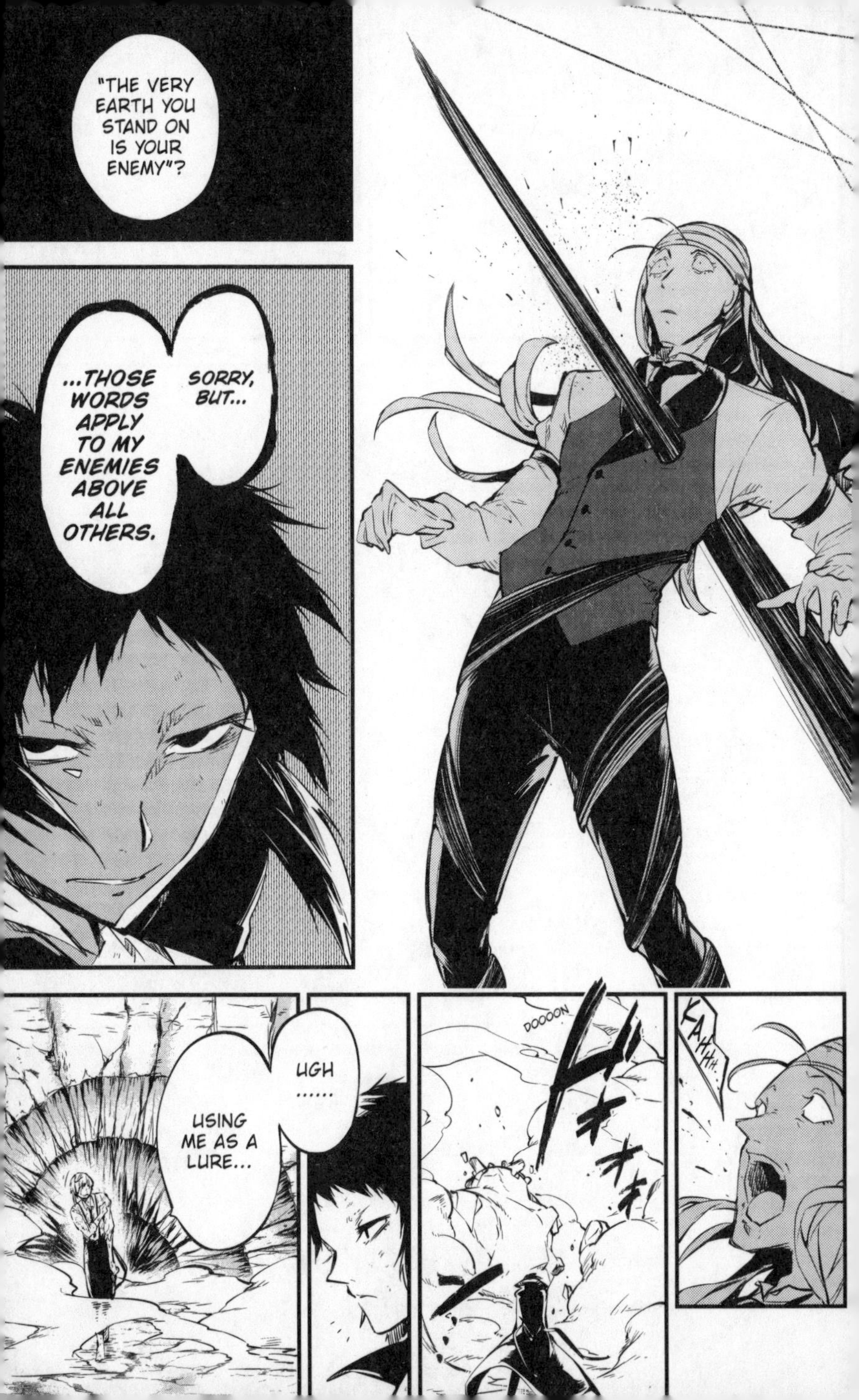
"THE VERY EARTH YOU STAND ON IS YOUR ENEMY"?
SORRY, BUT...
...THOSE WORDS APPLY TO MY ENEMIES ABOVE ALL OTHERS.
KAHHH
DOOOON
UGH ......
USING ME AS A LURE...

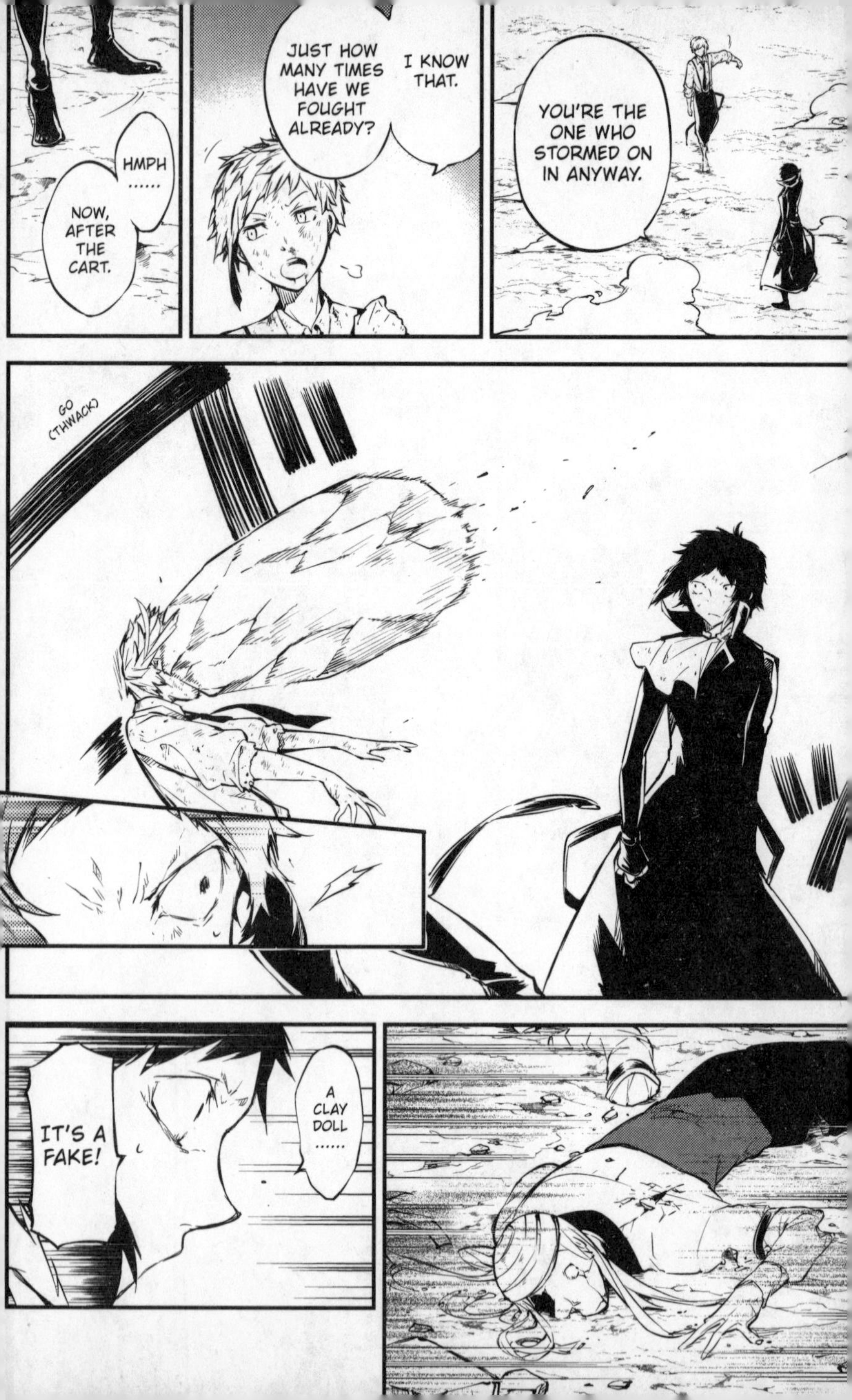
YOU'RE THE ONE WHO STORMED ON IN ANYWAY.
I KNOW THAT.
JUST HOW MANY TIMES HAVE WE FOUGHT ALREADY?
HMPH ......
NOW, AFTER THE CART.
GO (THWACK)
A CLAY DOLL ......
IT'S A FAKE!

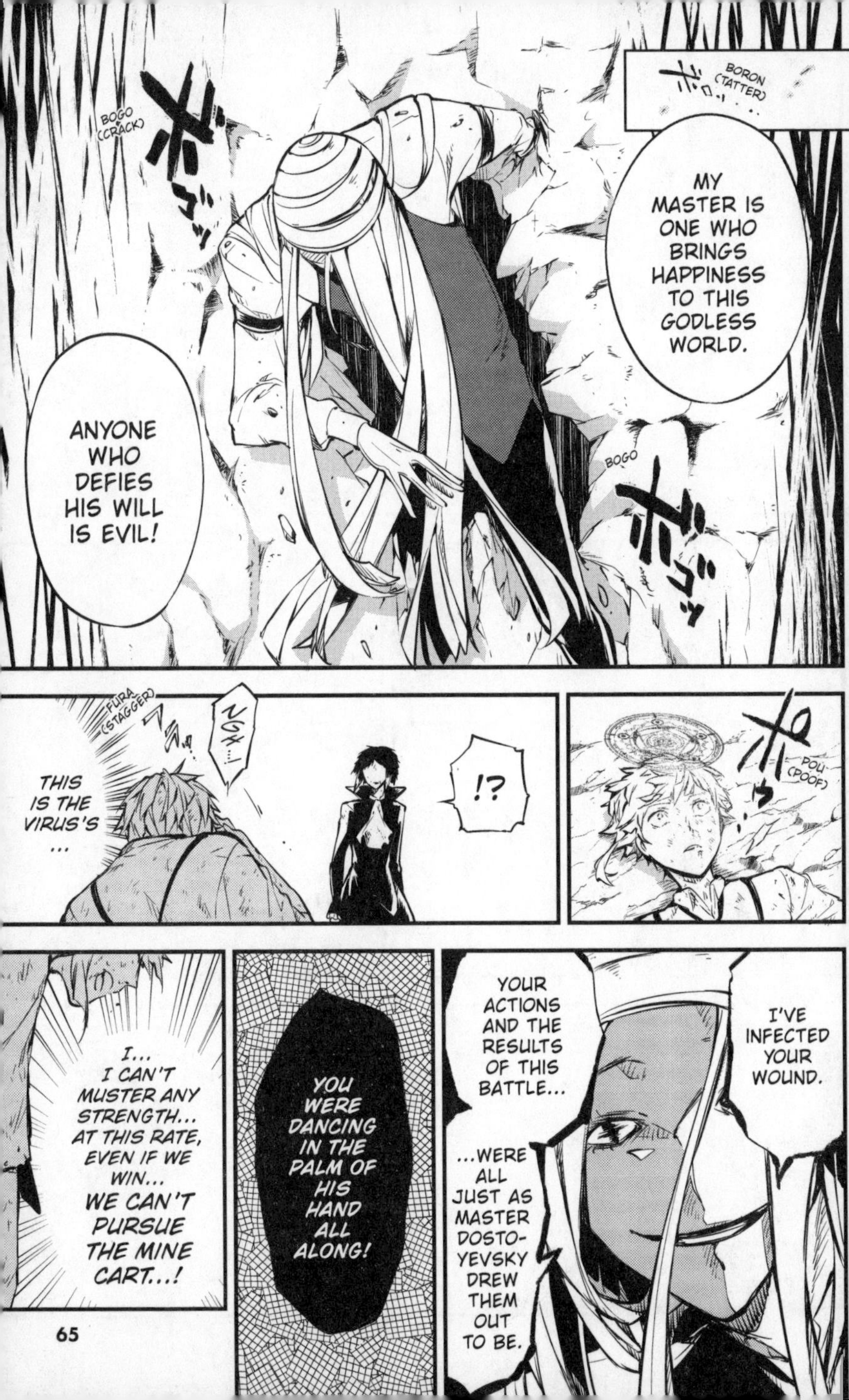
BORON (TATTER)
MY MASTER IS ONE WHO BRINGS HAPPINESS TO THIS GODLESS WORLD.
BOGO
BOGO (CRACK)
ANYONE WHO DEFIES HIS WILL IS EVIL!
POU (POOF)
!?
NGK...!
FURA (STAGGER)
THIS IS THE VIRUS'S...
I'VE INFECTED YOUR WOUND.
YOUR ACTIONS AND THE RESULTS OF THIS BATTLE...
...WERE ALL JUST AS MASTER DOSTO-YEVSKY DREW THEM OUT TO BE.
YOU WERE DANCING IN THE PALM OF HIS HAND ALL ALONG!
I... I CAN'T MUSTER ANY STRENGTH... AT THIS RATE, EVEN IF WE WIN... WE CAN'T PURSUE THE MINE CART...!

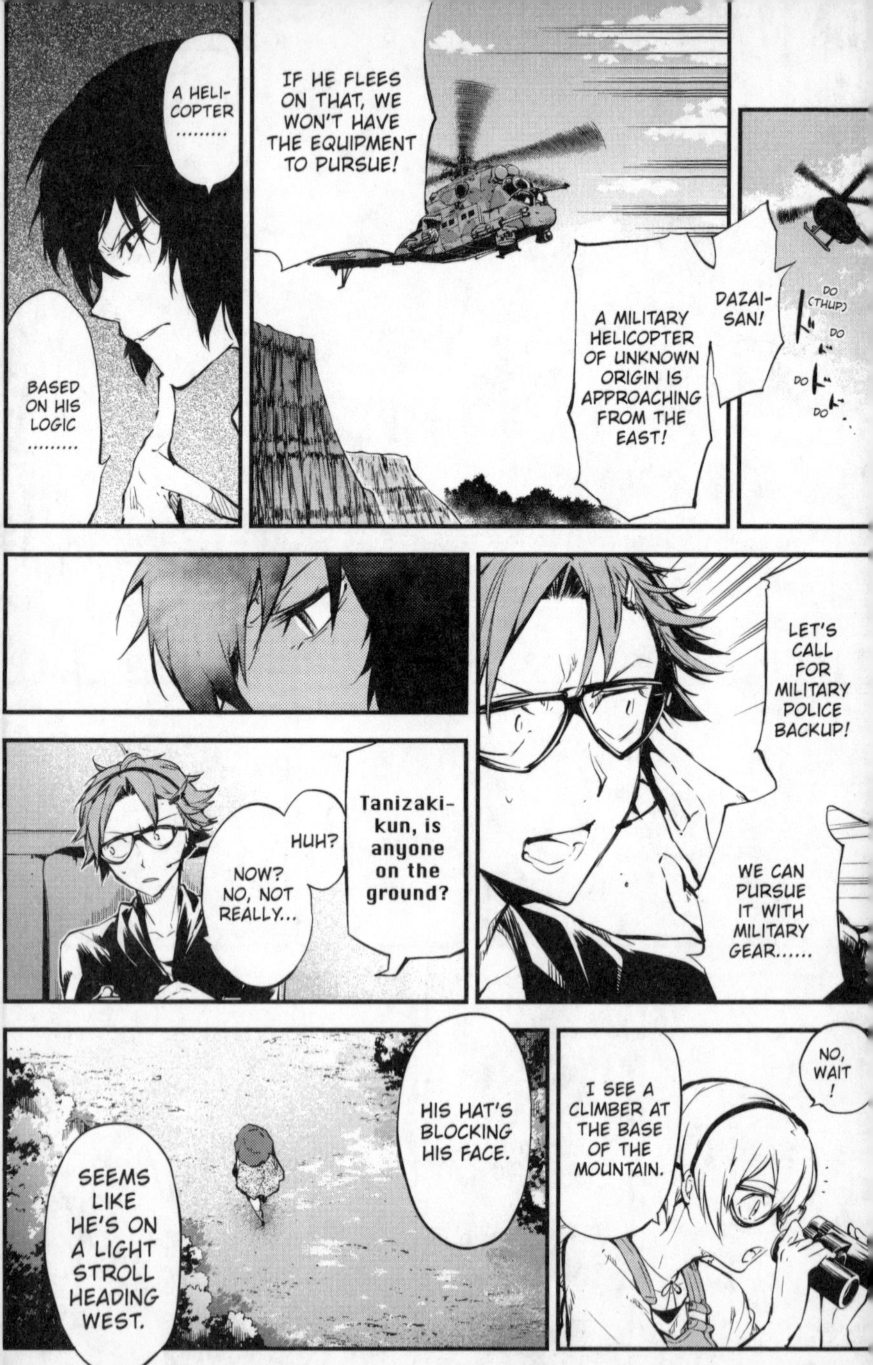
DO (THUP)
DO
DO
DO
DAZAI-SAN!
A MILITARY HELICOPTER OF UNKNOWN ORIGIN IS APPROACHING FROM THE EAST!
IF HE FLEES ON THAT, WE WON'T HAVE THE EQUIPMENT TO PURSUE!
A HELI-COPTER ....
BASED ON HIS LOGIC ....
LET'S CALL FOR MILITARY POLICE BACKUP!
WE CAN PURSUE IT WITH MILITARY GEAR......
Tanizaki-kun, is anyone on the ground?
HUH?
NOW? NO, NOT REALLY...
NO, WAIT!
I SEE A CLIMBER AT THE BASE OF THE MOUNTAIN.
HIS HAT'S BLOCKING HIS FACE.
SEEMS LIKE HE'S ON A LIGHT STROLL HEADING WEST.

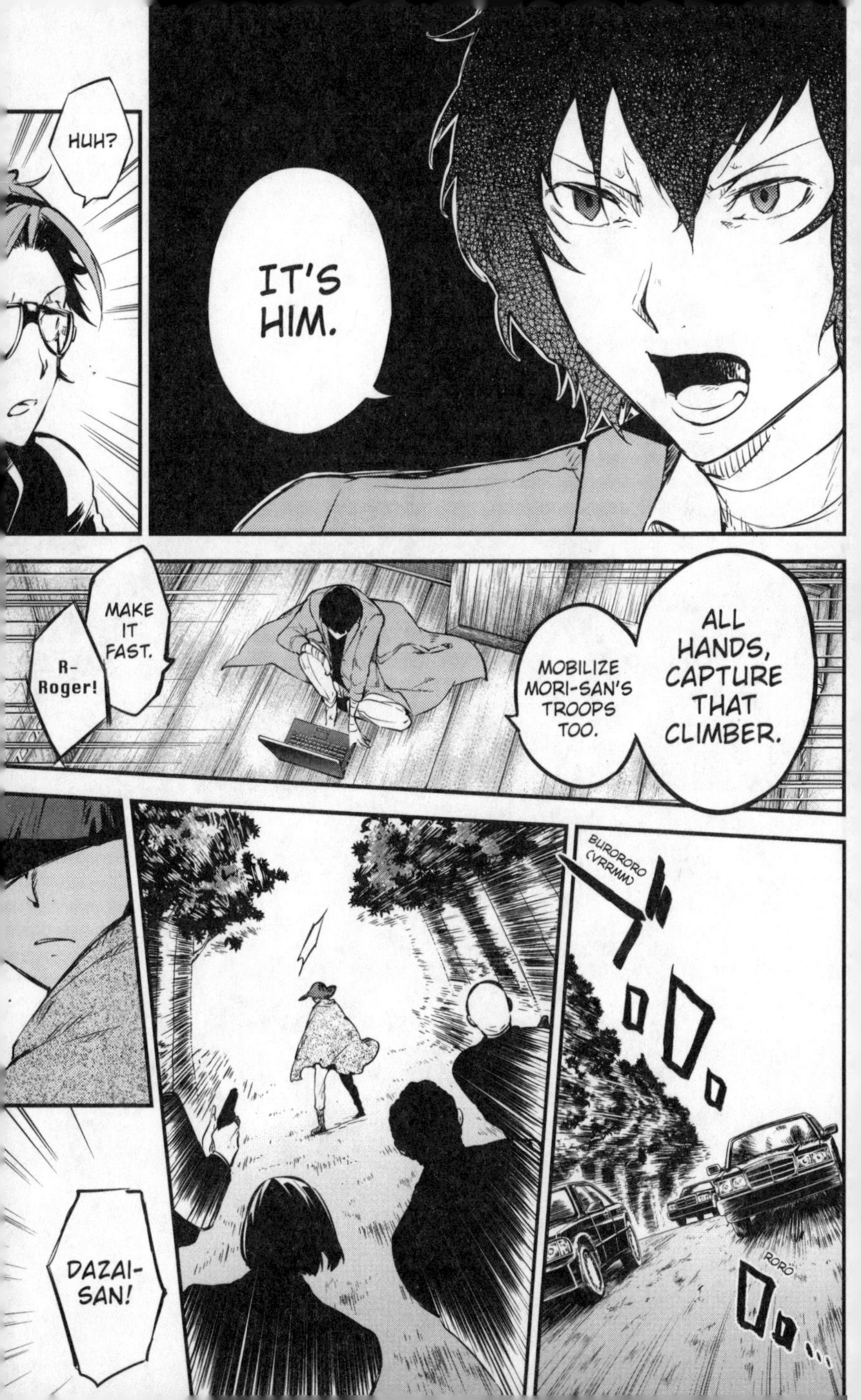
IT'S HIM.
HUH?
ALL HANDS, CAPTURE THAT CLIMBER.
MOBILIZE MORI-SAN'S TROOPS TOO.
MAKE IT FAST.
R-Roger!
BURORORO (VRRMM)
RORO
DAZAI-SAN!

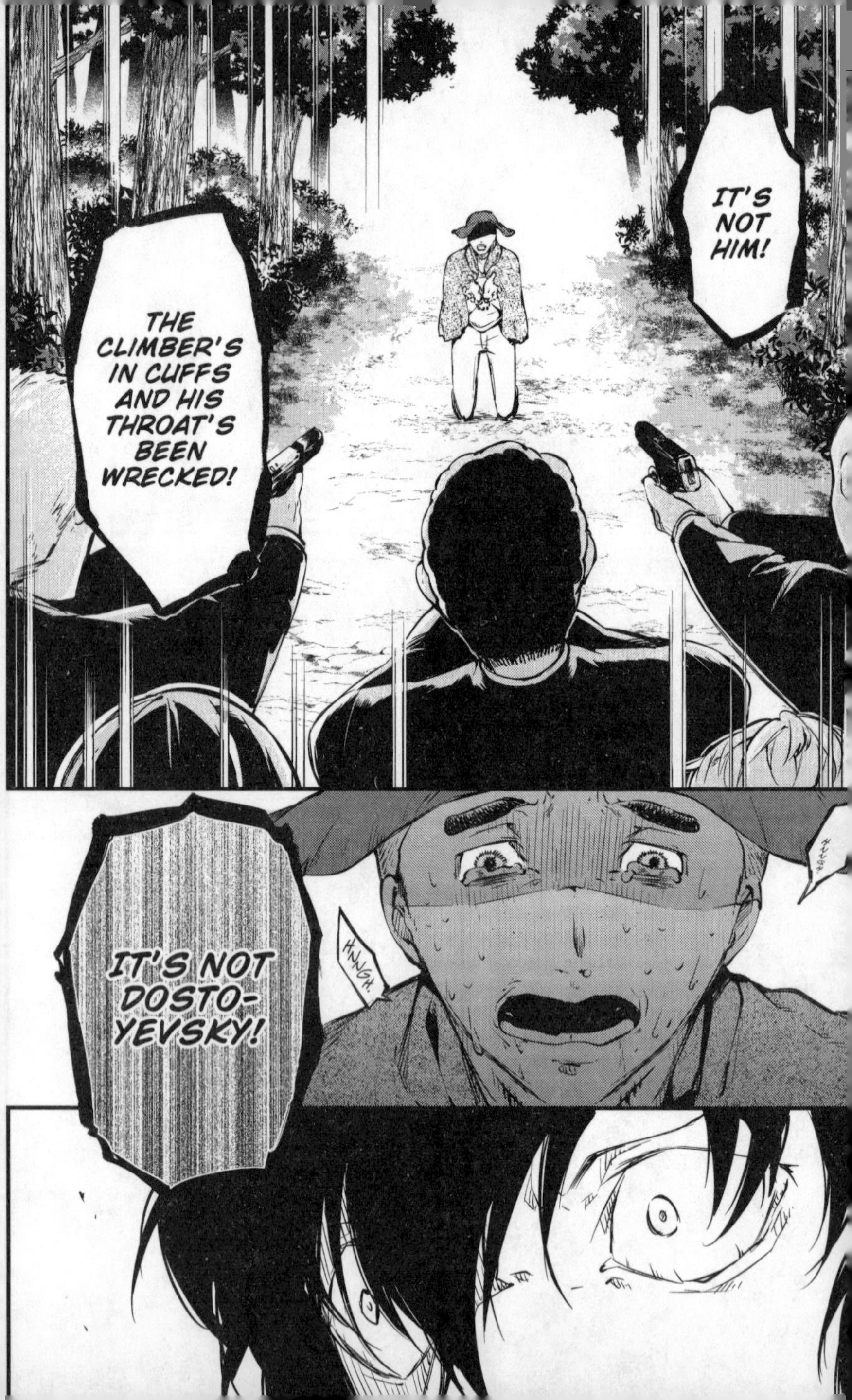
IT'S NOT HIM!
THE CLIMBER'S IN CUFFS AND HIS THROAT'S BEEN WRECKED!
HNNGH.
IT'S NOT DOSTO-YEVSKY!

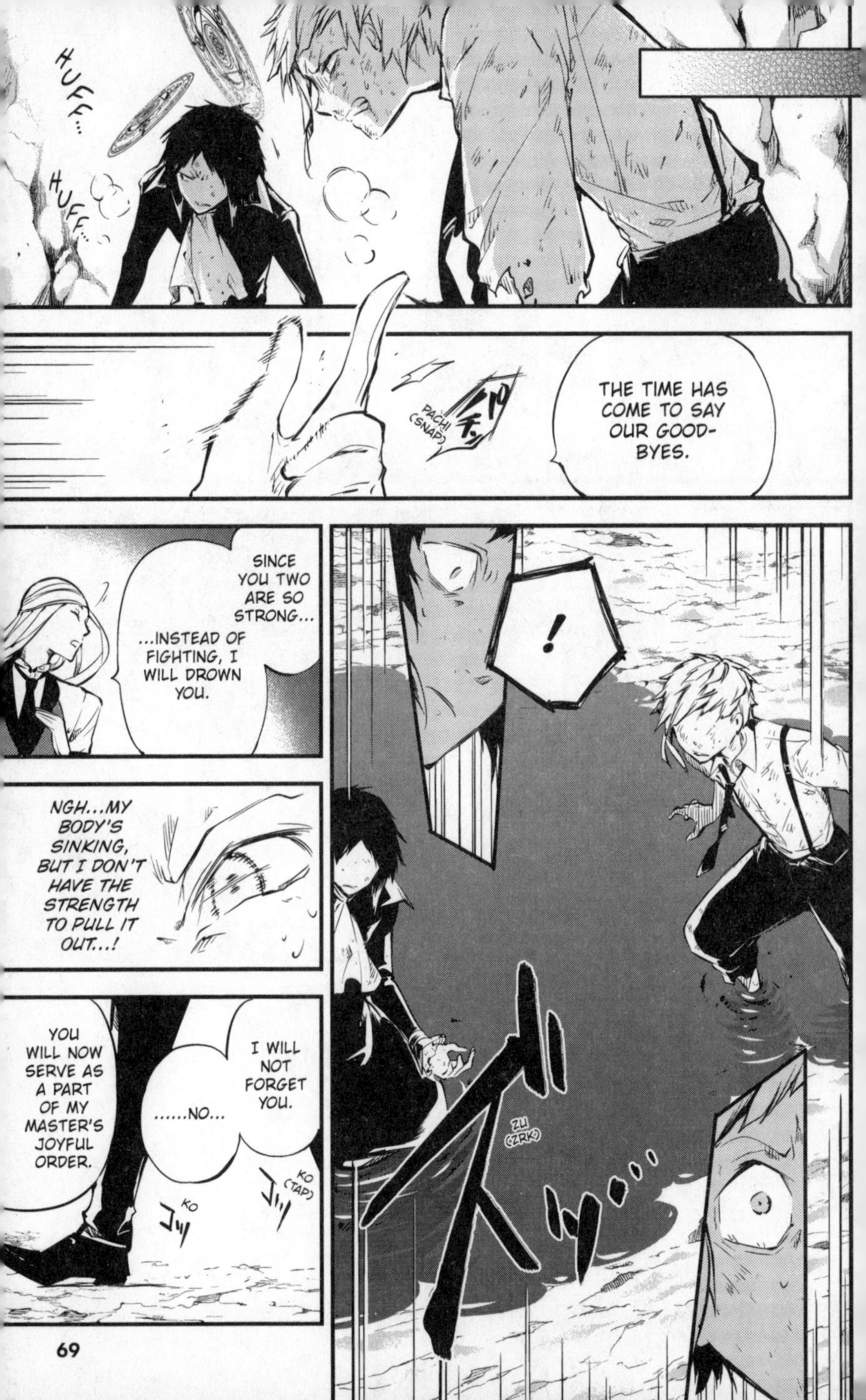
HUFF...
HUFF...
THE TIME HAS COME TO SAY OUR GOOD-BYES.
PACHI (SNAP)
!
ZU (ZRK)
SINCE YOU TWO ARE SO STRONG...
...INSTEAD OF FIGHTING, I WILL DROWN YOU.
NGH...MY BODY'S SINKING, BUT I DON'T HAVE THE STRENGTH TO PULL IT OUT...!
I WILL NOT FORGET YOU.
YOU WILL NOW SERVE AS A PART OF MY MASTER'S JOYFUL ORDER.
......NO...
KO (TAP)
KO

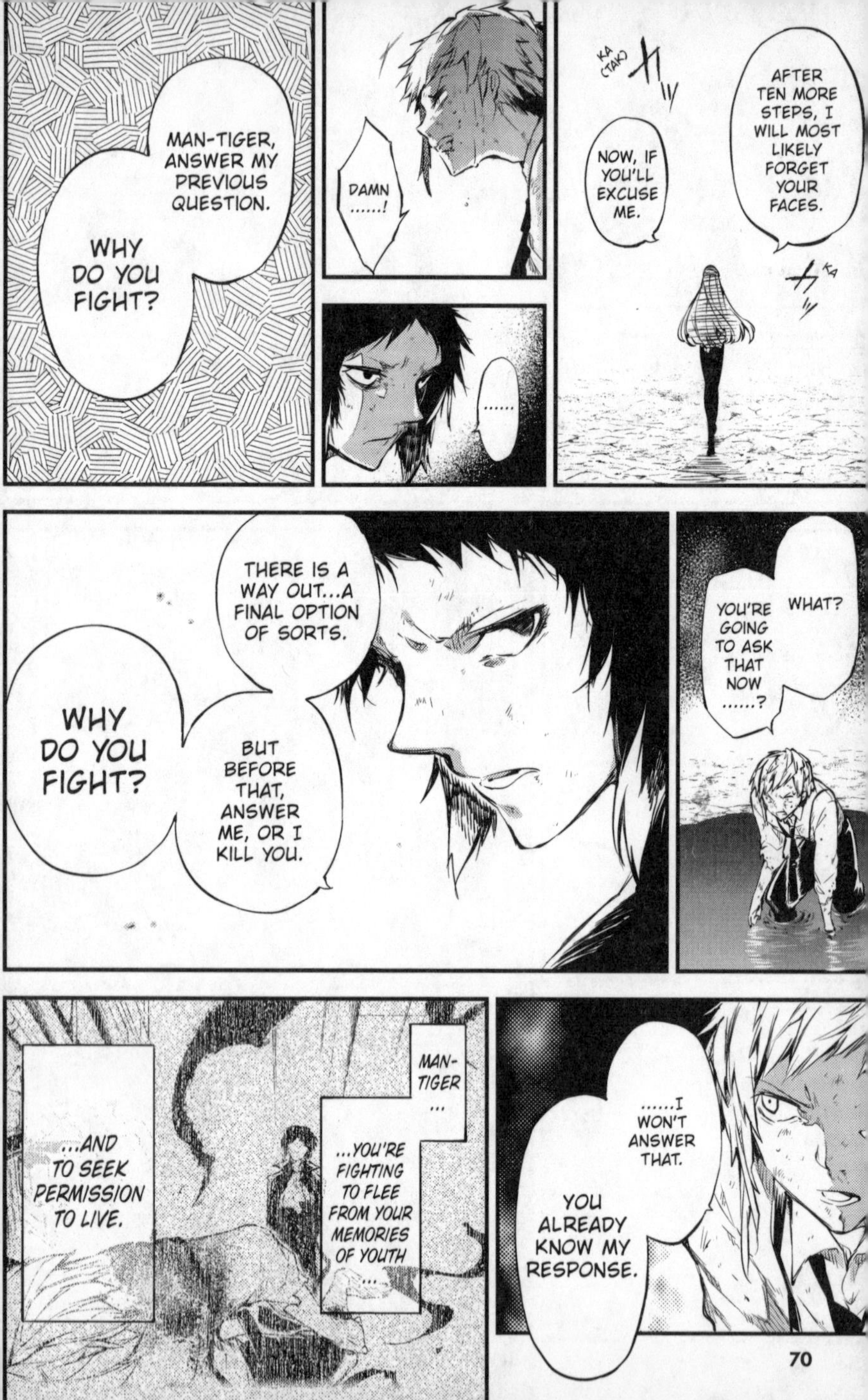
KA (TAK)
AFTER TEN MORE STEPS, I WILL MOST LIKELY FORGET YOUR FACES.
NOW, IF YOU'LL EXCUSE ME.
KA
DAMN ......!
......
MAN-TIGER, ANSWER MY PREVIOUS QUESTION.
WHY DO YOU FIGHT?
WHAT?
YOU'RE GOING TO ASK THAT NOW ......?
THERE IS A WAY OUT...A FINAL OPTION OF SORTS.
BUT BEFORE THAT, ANSWER ME, OR I KILL YOU.
WHY DO YOU FIGHT?
......I WON'T ANSWER THAT.
YOU ALREADY KNOW MY RESPONSE.
MAN-TIGER...
...YOU'RE FIGHTING TO FLEE FROM YOUR MEMORIES OF YOUTH...
...AND TO SEEK PERMISSION TO LIVE.

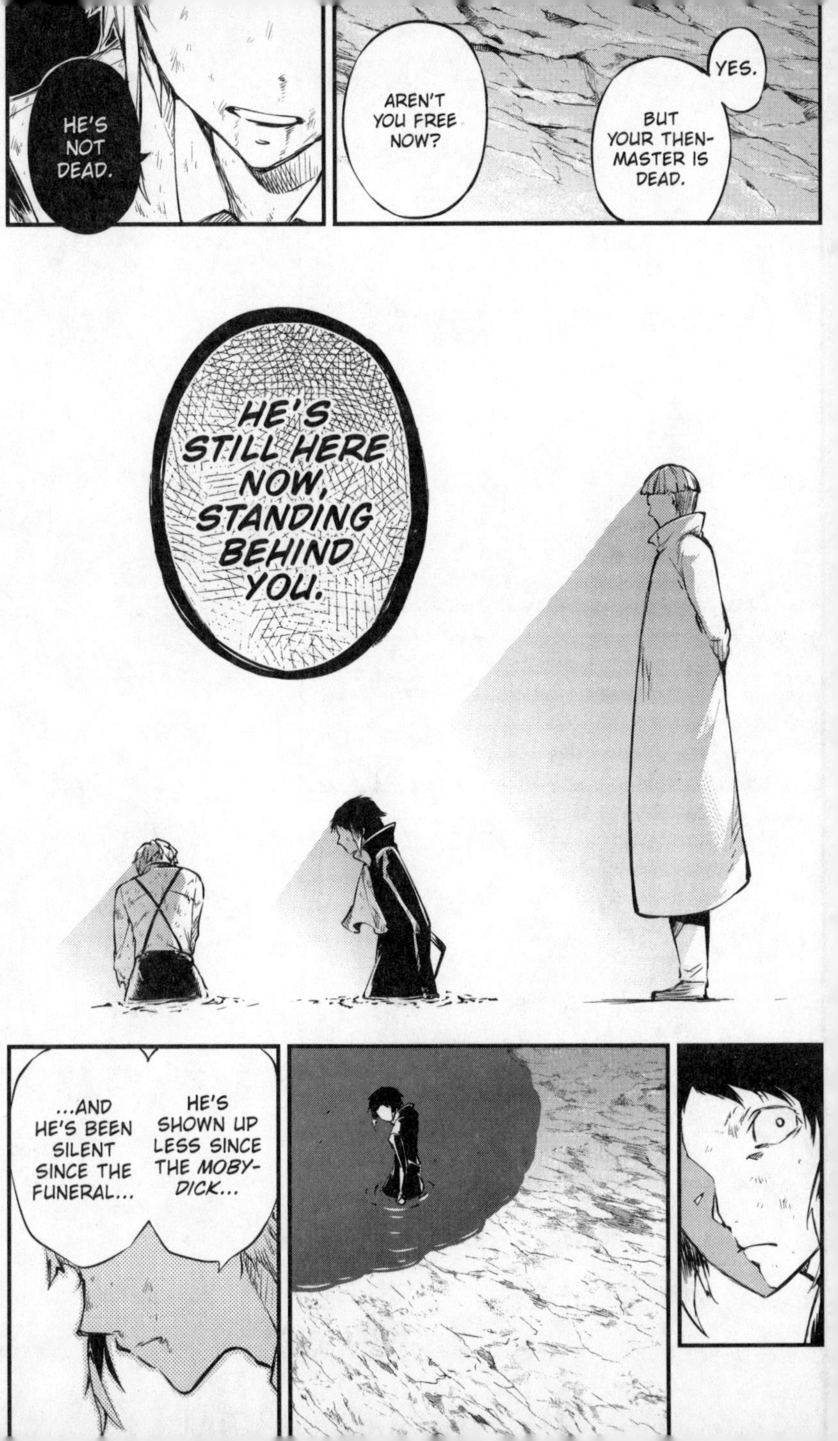

YES.
BUT YOUR THEN-MASTER IS DEAD.
AREN'T YOU FREE NOW?
HE'S NOT DEAD.
HE'S STILL HERE NOW, STANDING BEHIND YOU.
HE'S SHOWN UP LESS SINCE THE *MOBY-DICK*...
...AND HE'S BEEN SILENT SINCE THE FUNERAL...

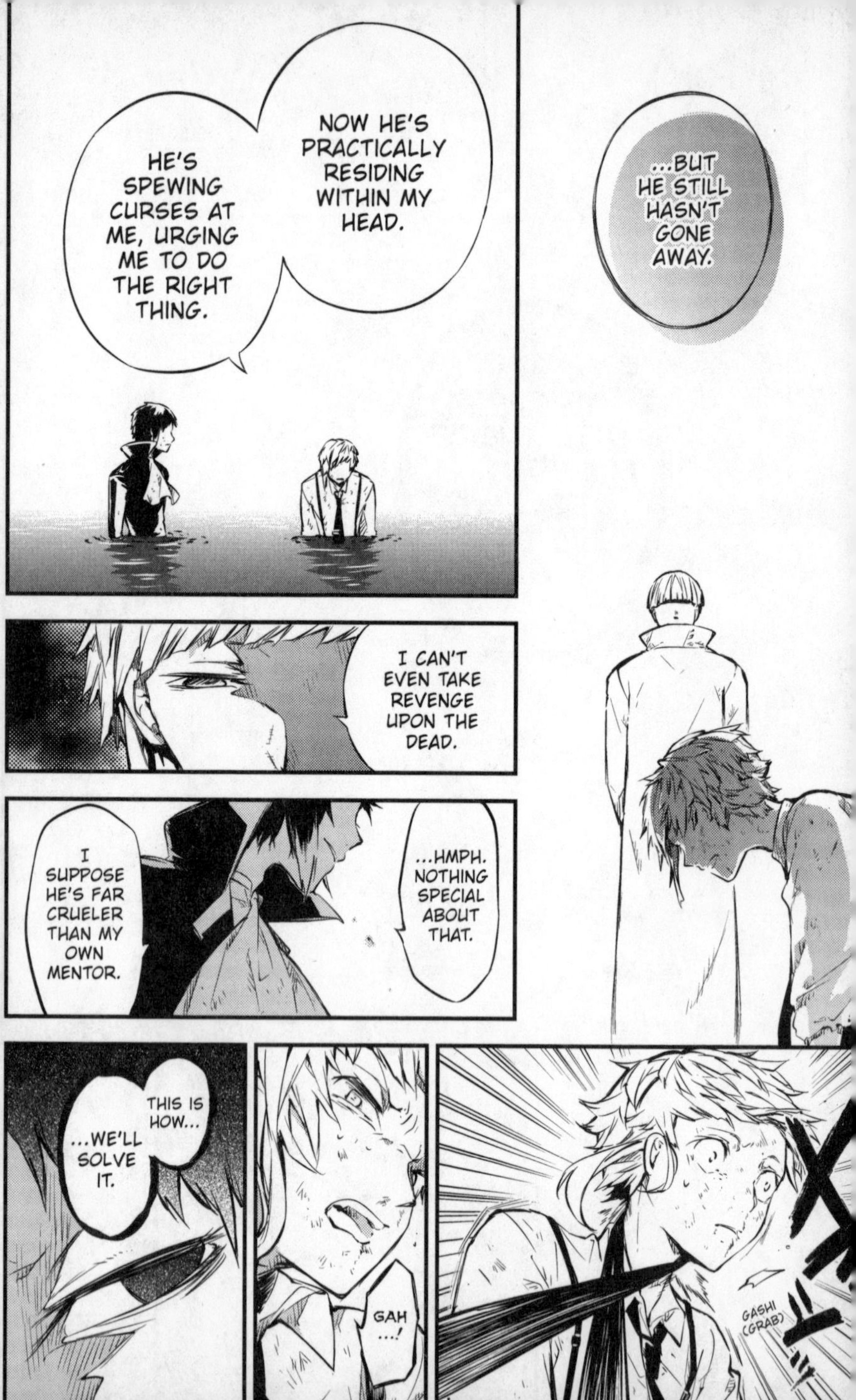
...BUT HE STILL HASN'T GONE AWAY.
NOW HE'S PRACTICALLY RESIDING WITHIN MY HEAD.
HE'S SPEWING CURSES AT ME, URGING ME TO DO THE RIGHT THING.
I CAN'T EVEN TAKE REVENGE UPON THE DEAD.
...HMPH. NOTHING SPECIAL ABOUT THAT.
I SUPPOSE HE'S FAR CRUELER THAN MY OWN MENTOR.
GASHI (GRAB)
GAH ...!
THIS IS HOW...
...WE'LL SOLVE IT.

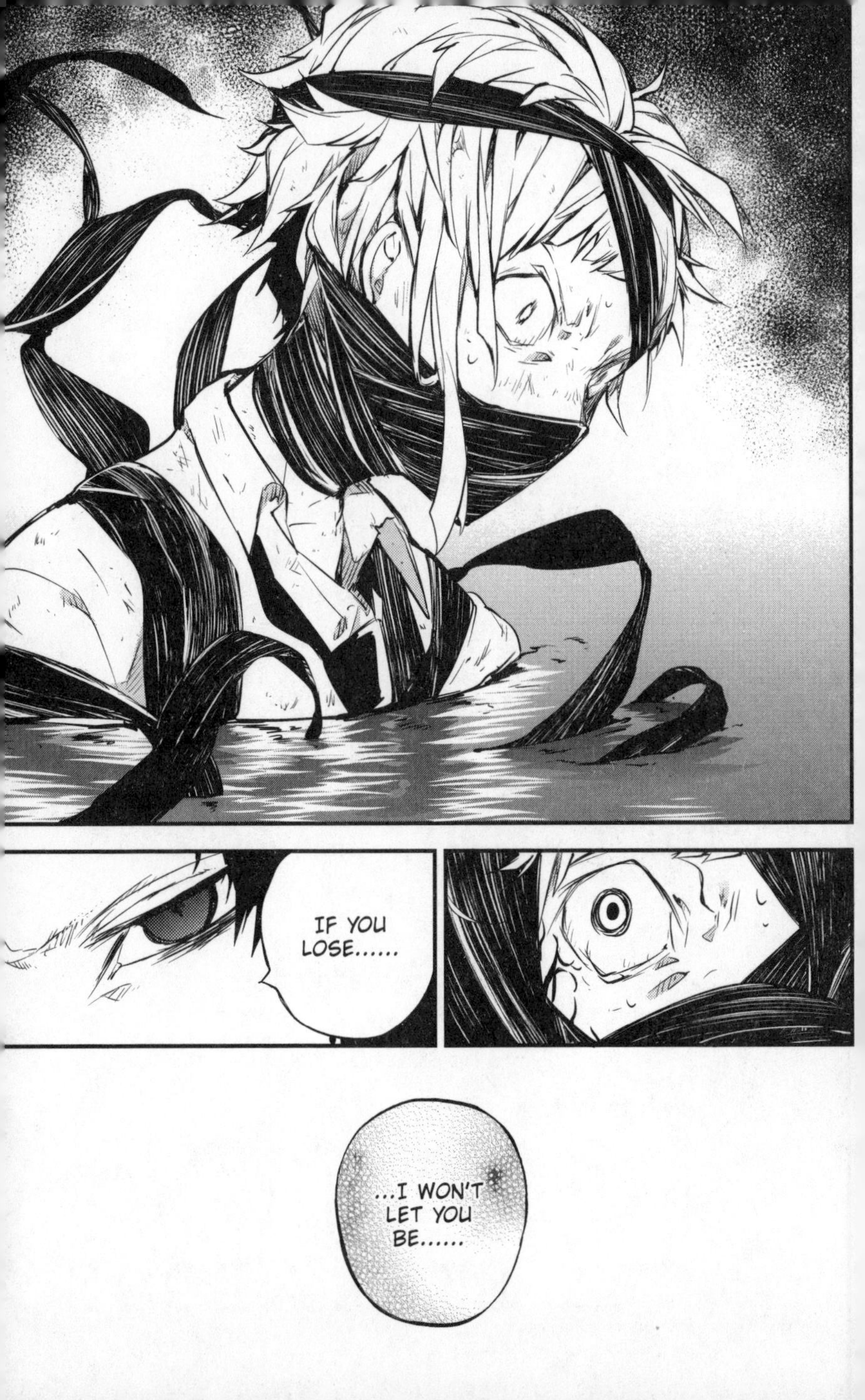
IF YOU LOSE......
...I WON'T LET YOU BE......

BUNGO
STRAY DOGS

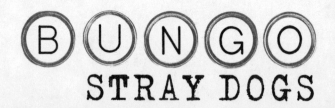

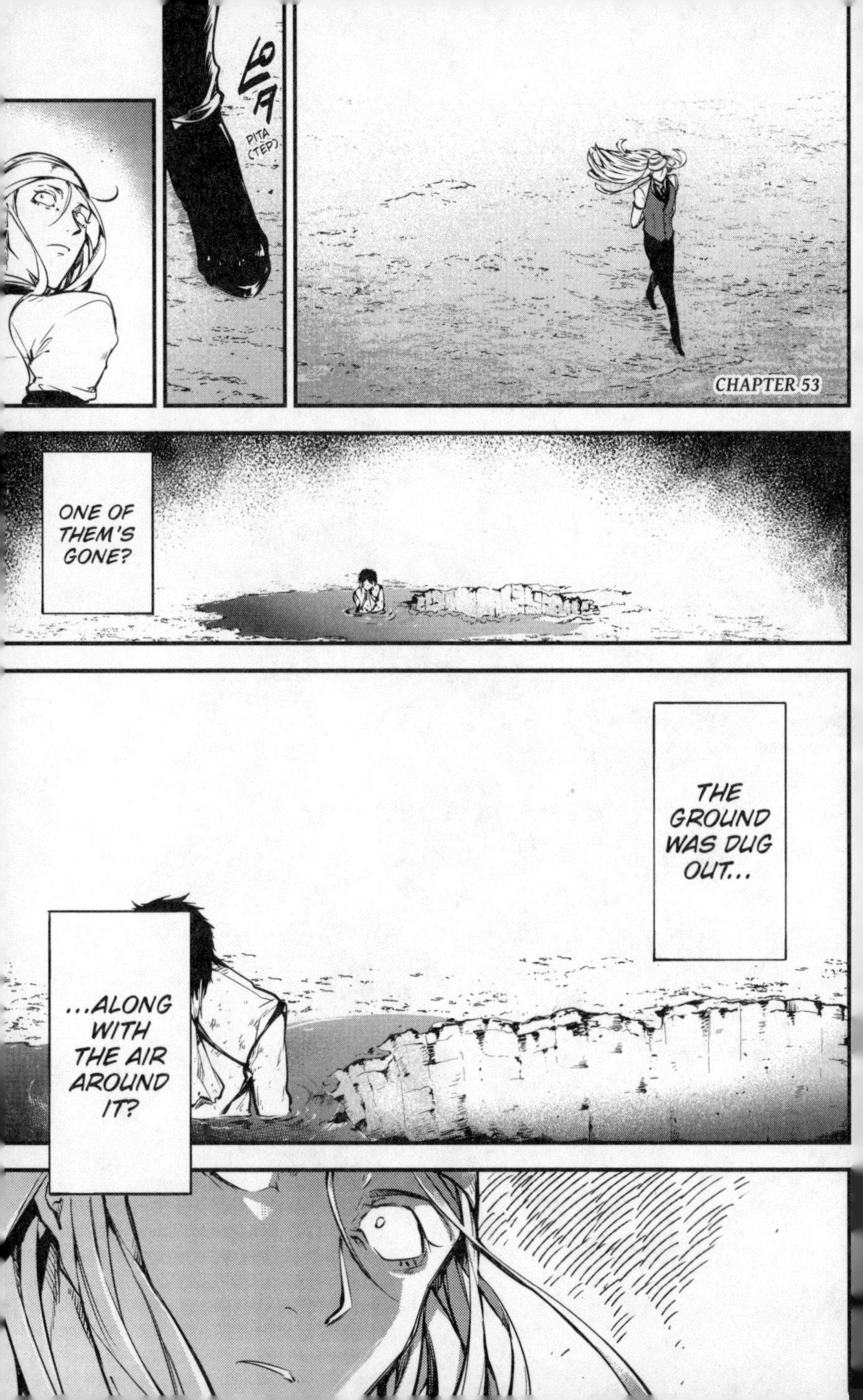
CHAPTER 53
PITA (TEP)
ONE OF THEM'S GONE?
THE GROUND WAS DUG OUT...
...ALONG WITH THE AIR AROUND IT?

CHAPTER 53
Echo, Part 3

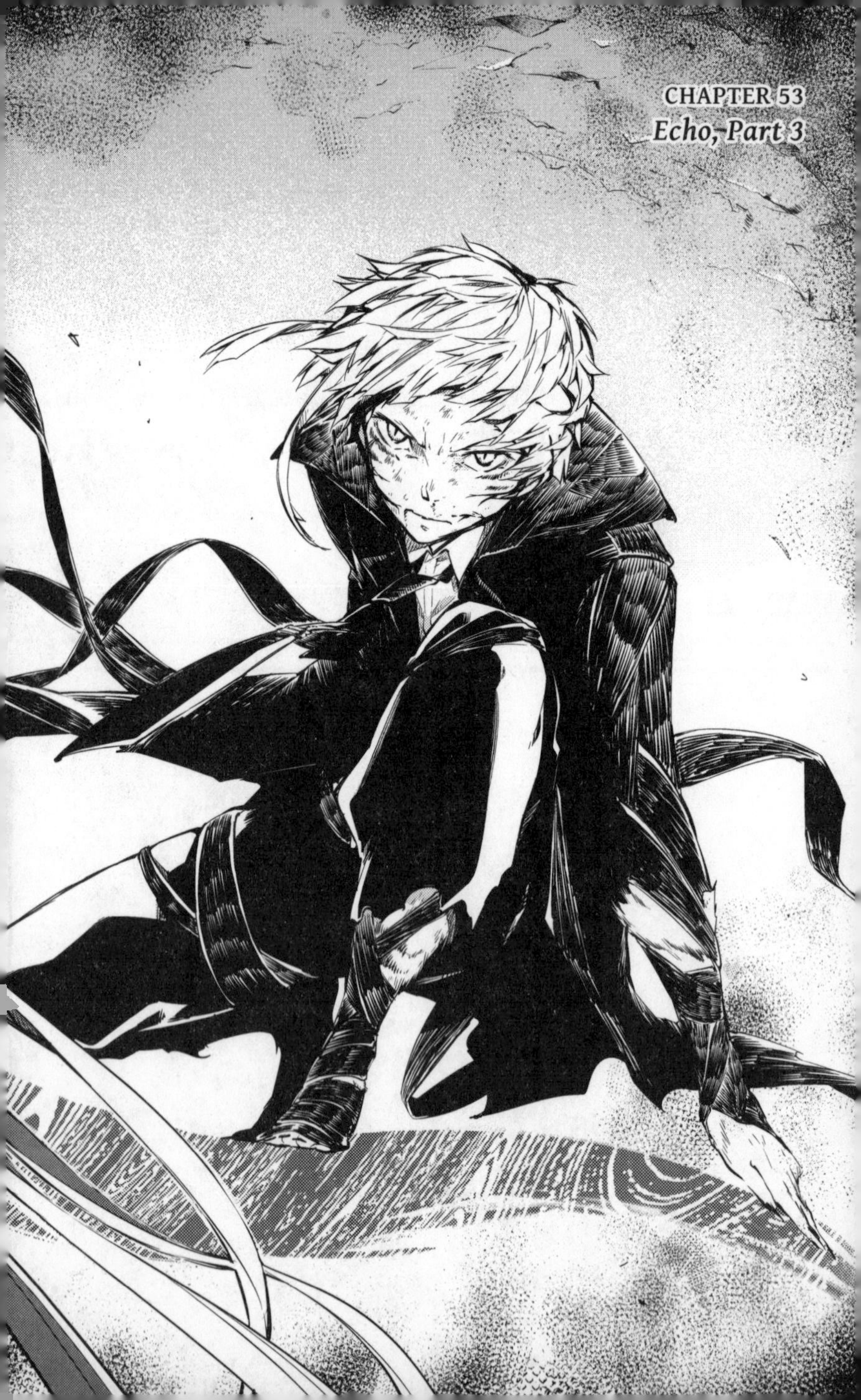

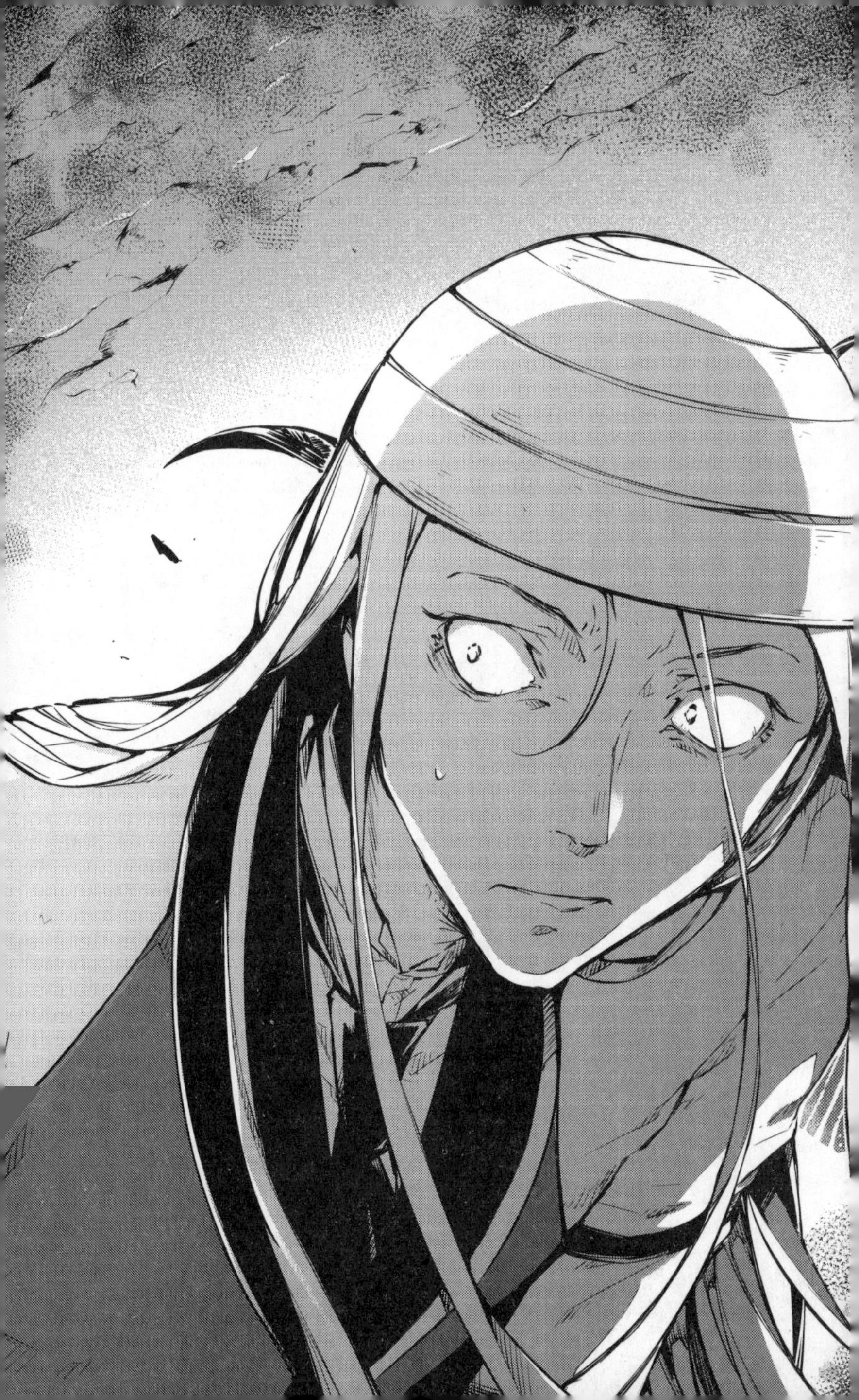

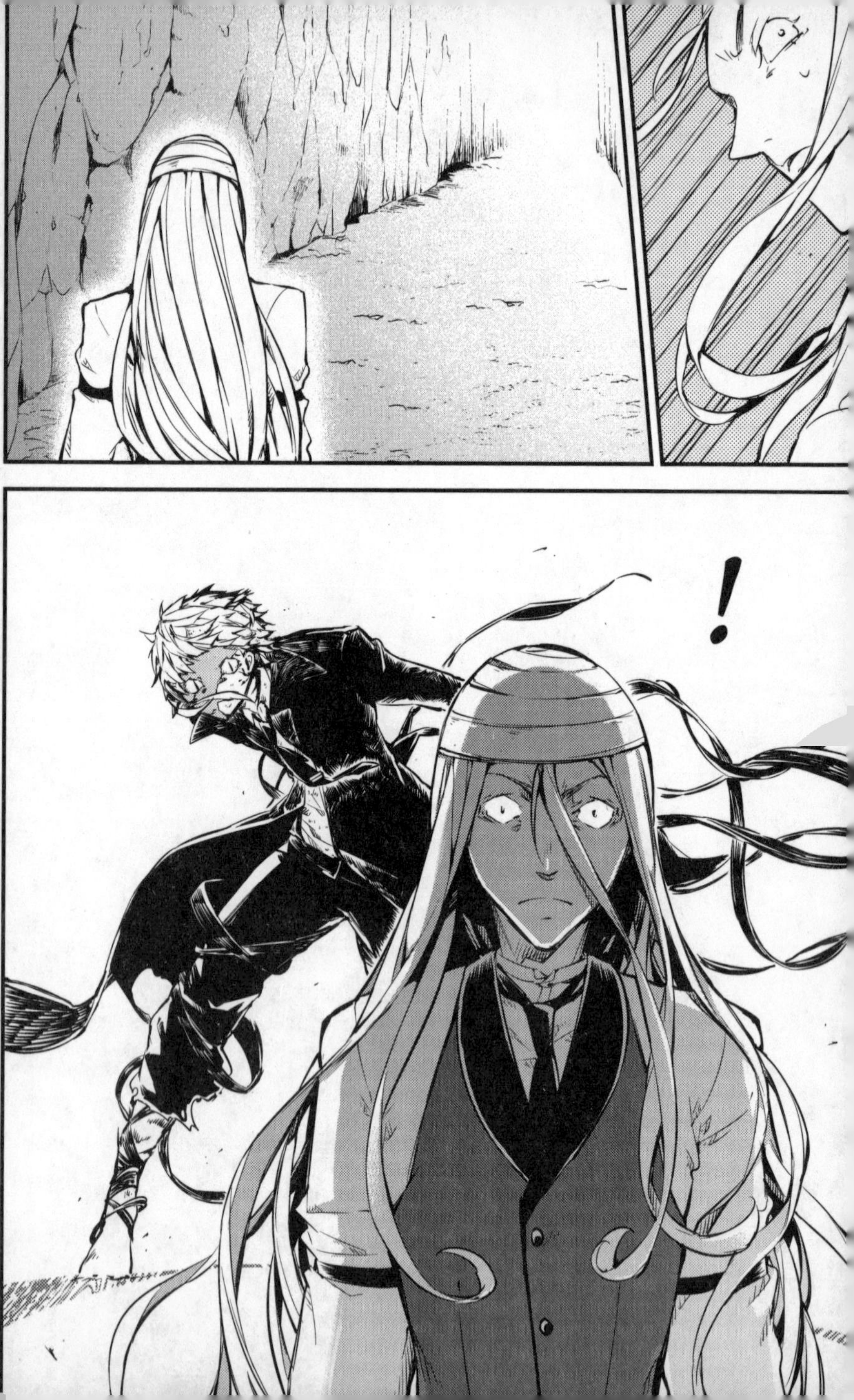
!

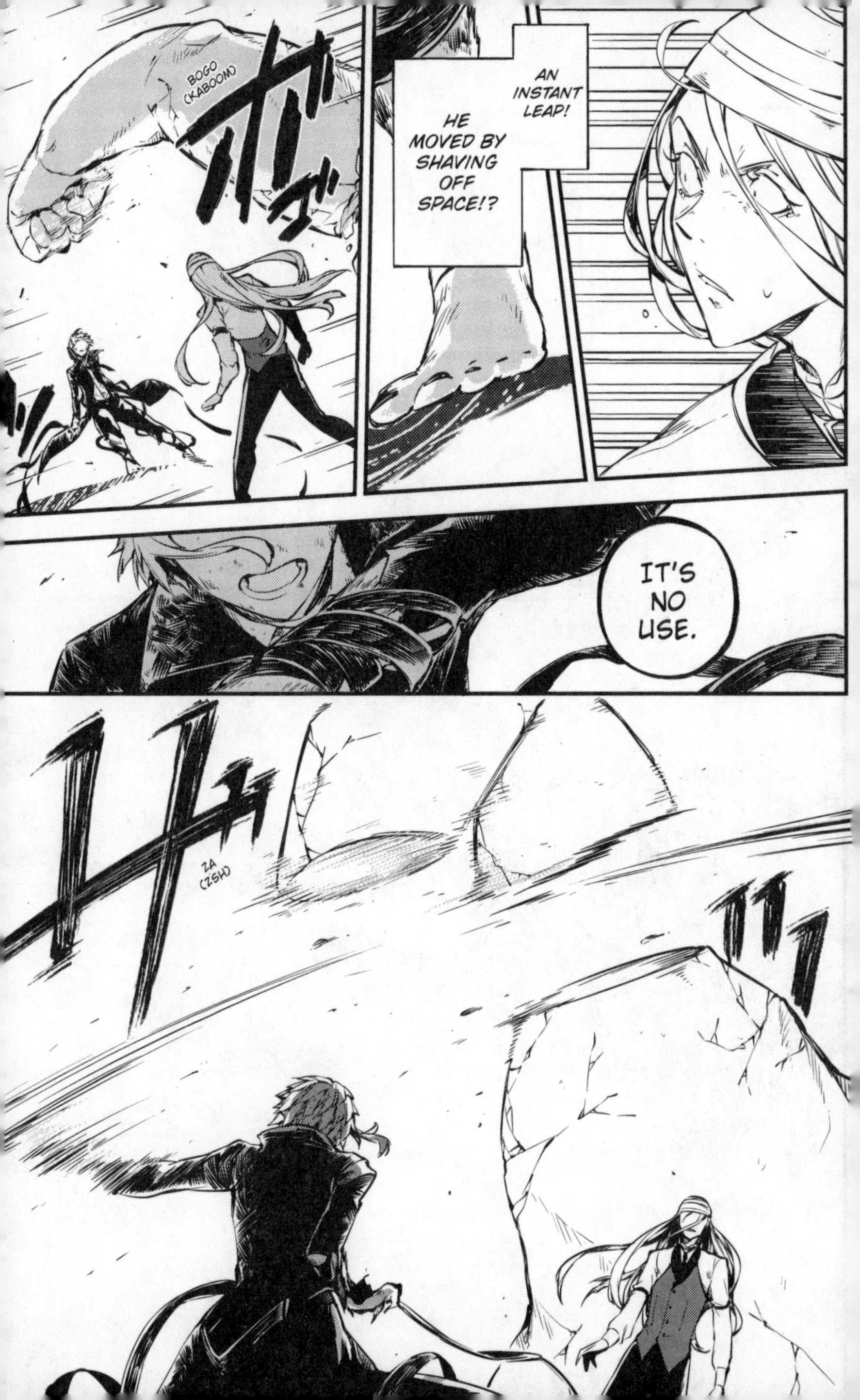
AN INSTANT LEAP!
HE MOVED BY SHAVING OFF SPACE!?
BOGO (KABOOM)
IT'S NO USE.
ZA (ZSH)

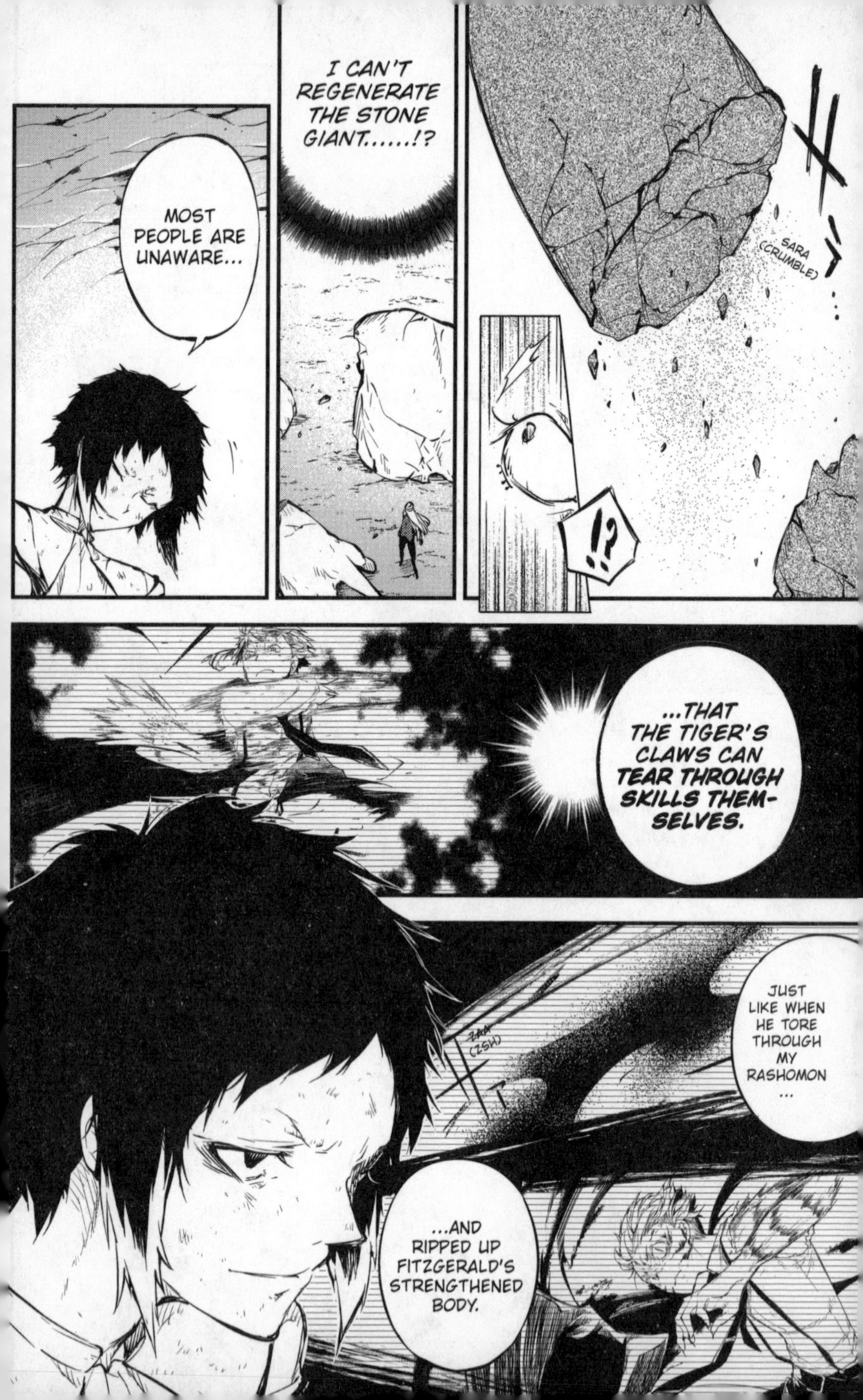
SARA (CRUMBLE)
!?
I CAN'T REGENERATE THE STONE GIANT......!?
MOST PEOPLE ARE UNAWARE...
...THAT THE TIGER'S CLAWS CAN TEAR THROUGH SKILLS THEM-SELVES.
JUST LIKE WHEN HE TORE THROUGH MY RASHOMON ...
ZAA (ZSH)
...AND RIPPED UP FITZGERALD'S STRENGTHENED BODY.

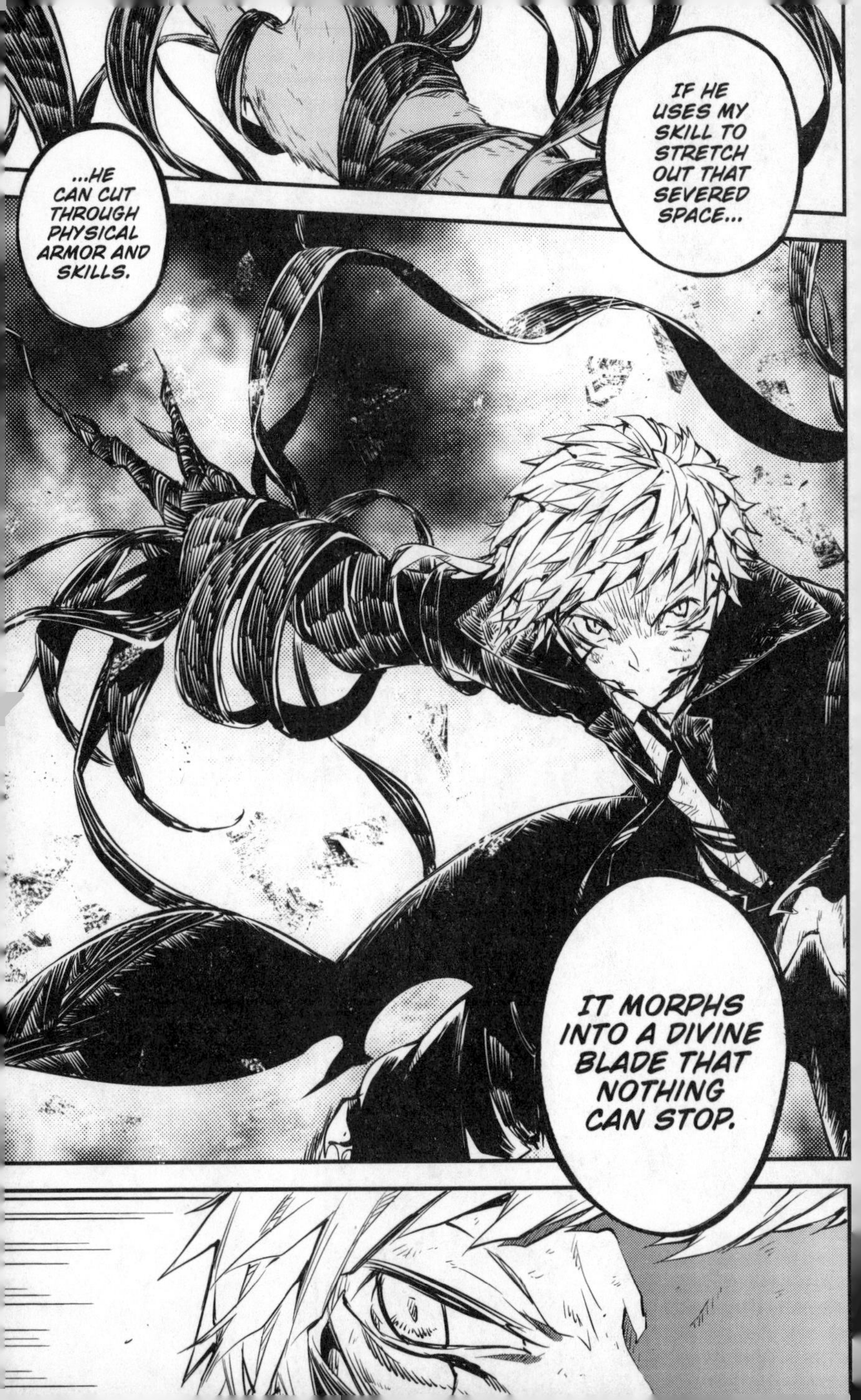
IF HE USES MY SKILL TO STRETCH OUT THAT SEVERED SPACE...
...HE CAN CUT THROUGH PHYSICAL ARMOR AND SKILLS.
IT MORPHS INTO A DIVINE BLADE THAT NOTHING CAN STOP.

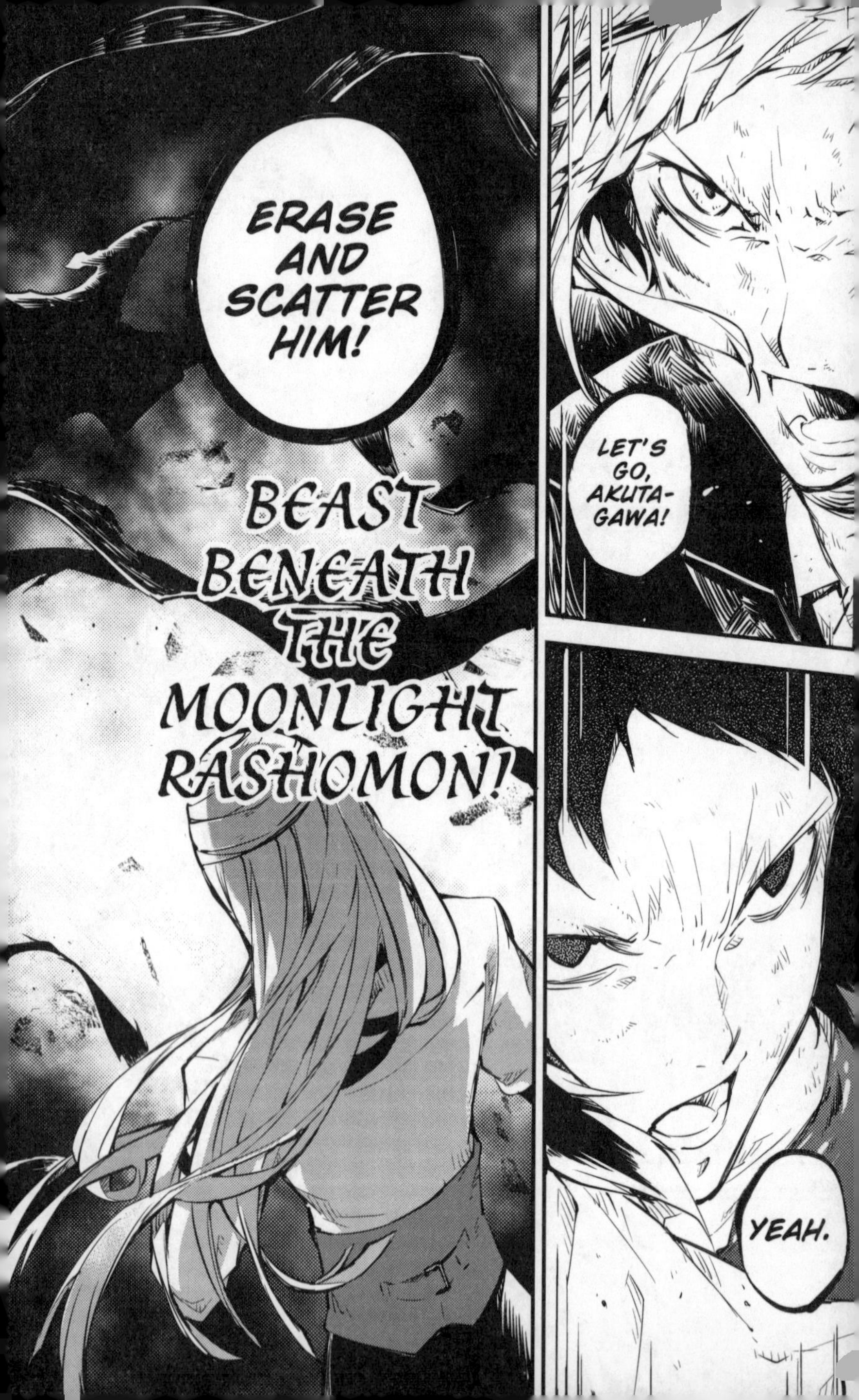
LET'S GO, AKUTAGAWA!
YEAH.
ERASE AND SCATTER HIM!
BEAST BENEATH THE MOONLIGHT
RASHOMON!

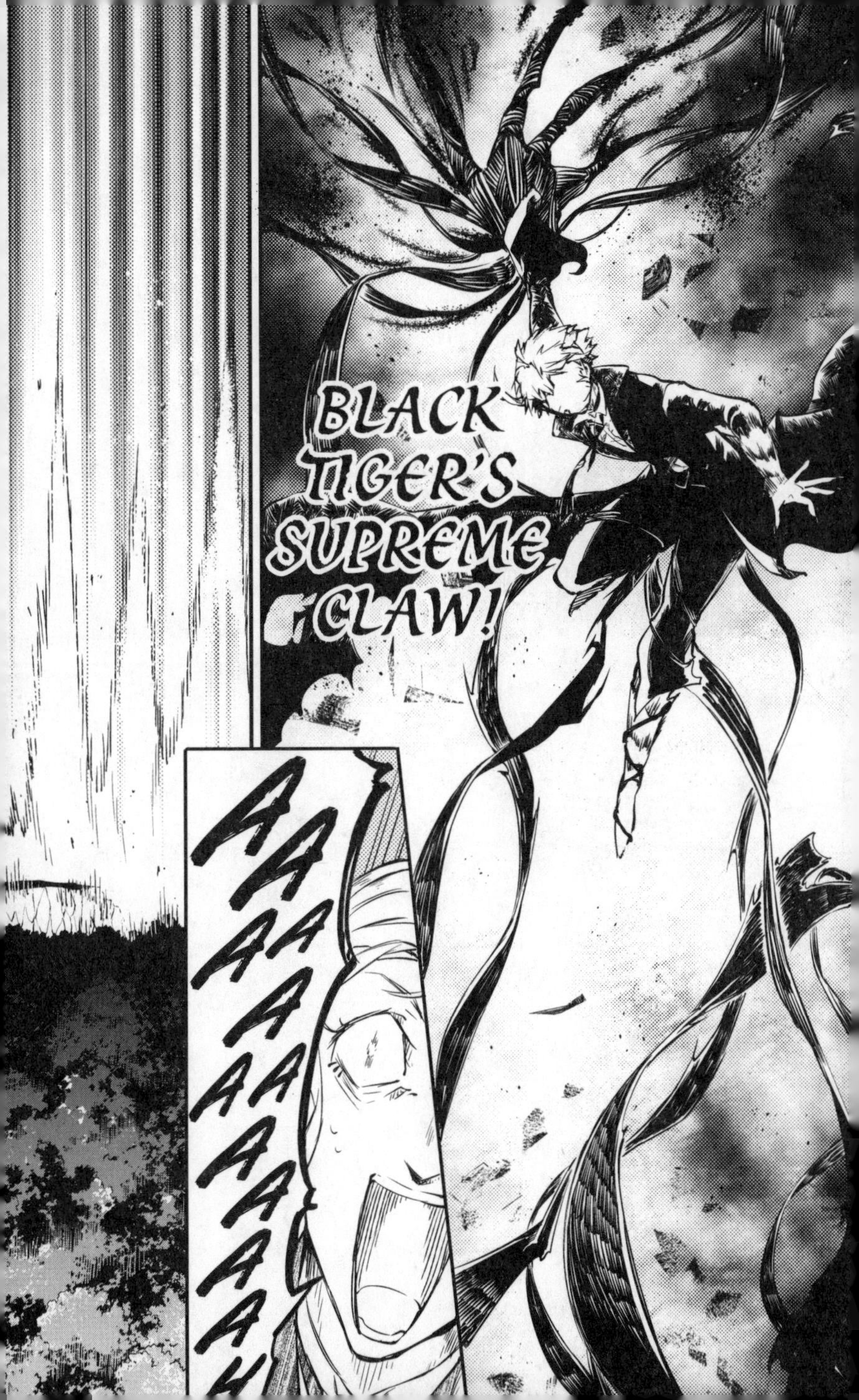
BLACK TIGER'S SUPREME CLAW!
AAAAAAAAAAAAAAAAAAAAAAAAH

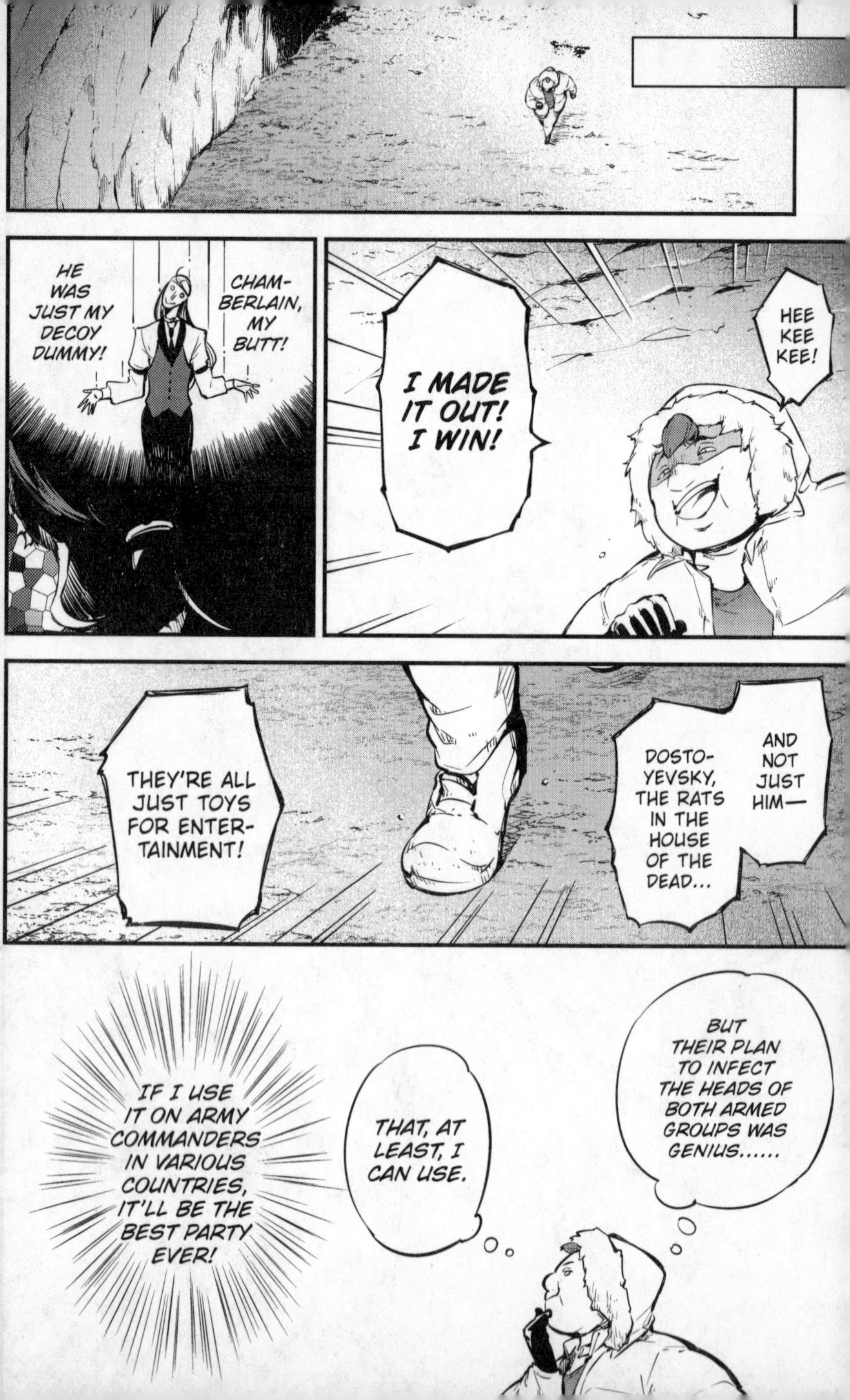
HEE KEE KEE!
I MADE IT OUT! I WIN!
CHAM-BERLAIN, MY BUTT!
HE WAS JUST MY DECOY DUMMY!
AND NOT JUST HIM—
DOSTO-YEVSKY, THE RATS IN THE HOUSE OF THE DEAD...
THEY'RE ALL JUST TOYS FOR ENTER-TAINMENT!
BUT THEIR PLAN TO INFECT THE HEADS OF BOTH ARMED GROUPS WAS GENIUS......
THAT, AT LEAST, I CAN USE.
IF I USE IT ON ARMY COMMANDERS IN VARIOUS COUNTRIES, IT'LL BE THE BEST PARTY EVER!

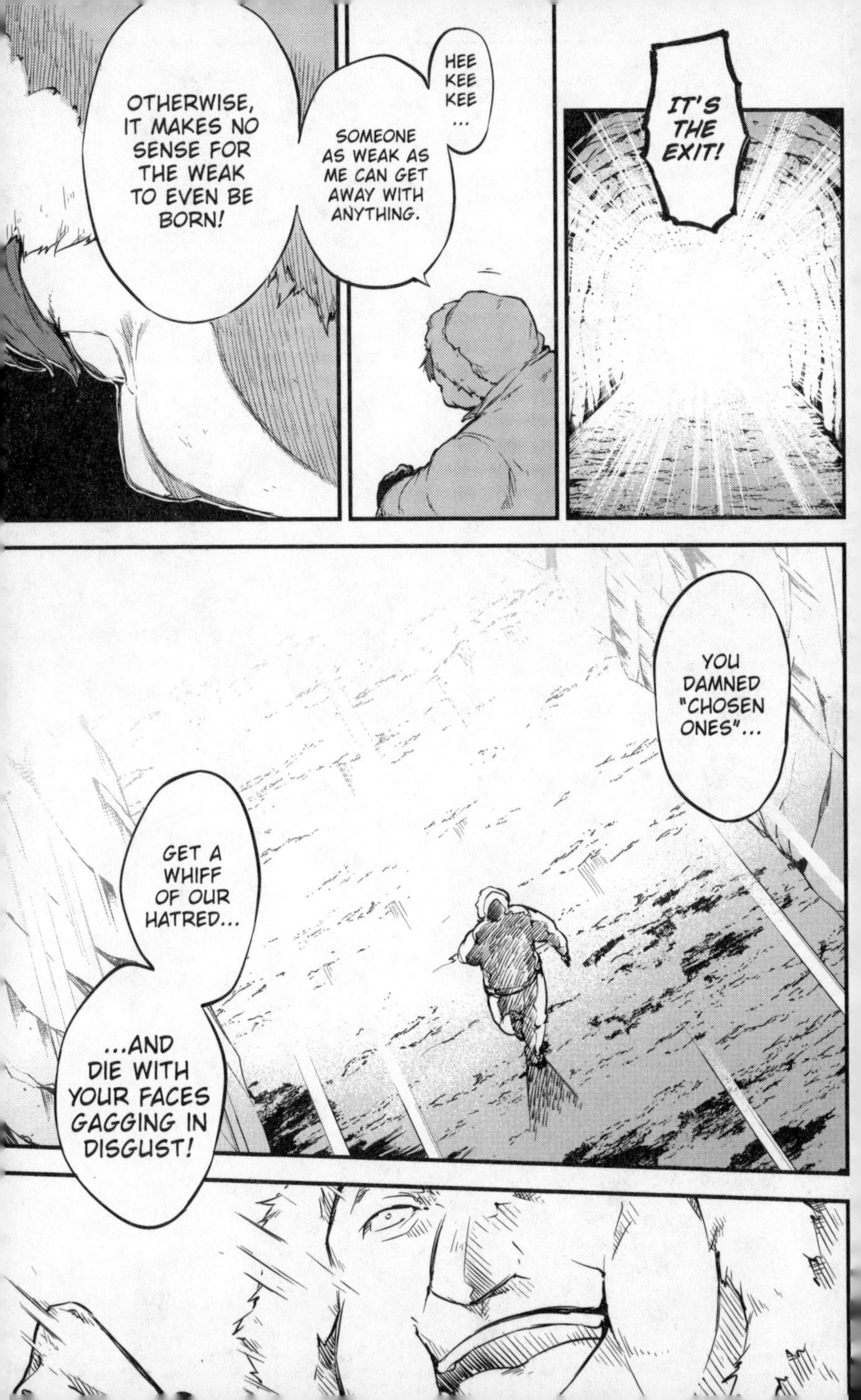
IT'S THE EXIT!
HEE KEE KEE...
SOMEONE AS WEAK AS ME CAN GET AWAY WITH ANYTHING.
OTHERWISE, IT MAKES NO SENSE FOR THE WEAK TO EVEN BE BORN!
YOU DAMNED "CHOSEN ONES"...
GET A WHIFF OF OUR HATRED...
...AND DIE WITH YOUR FACES GAGGING IN DISGUST!

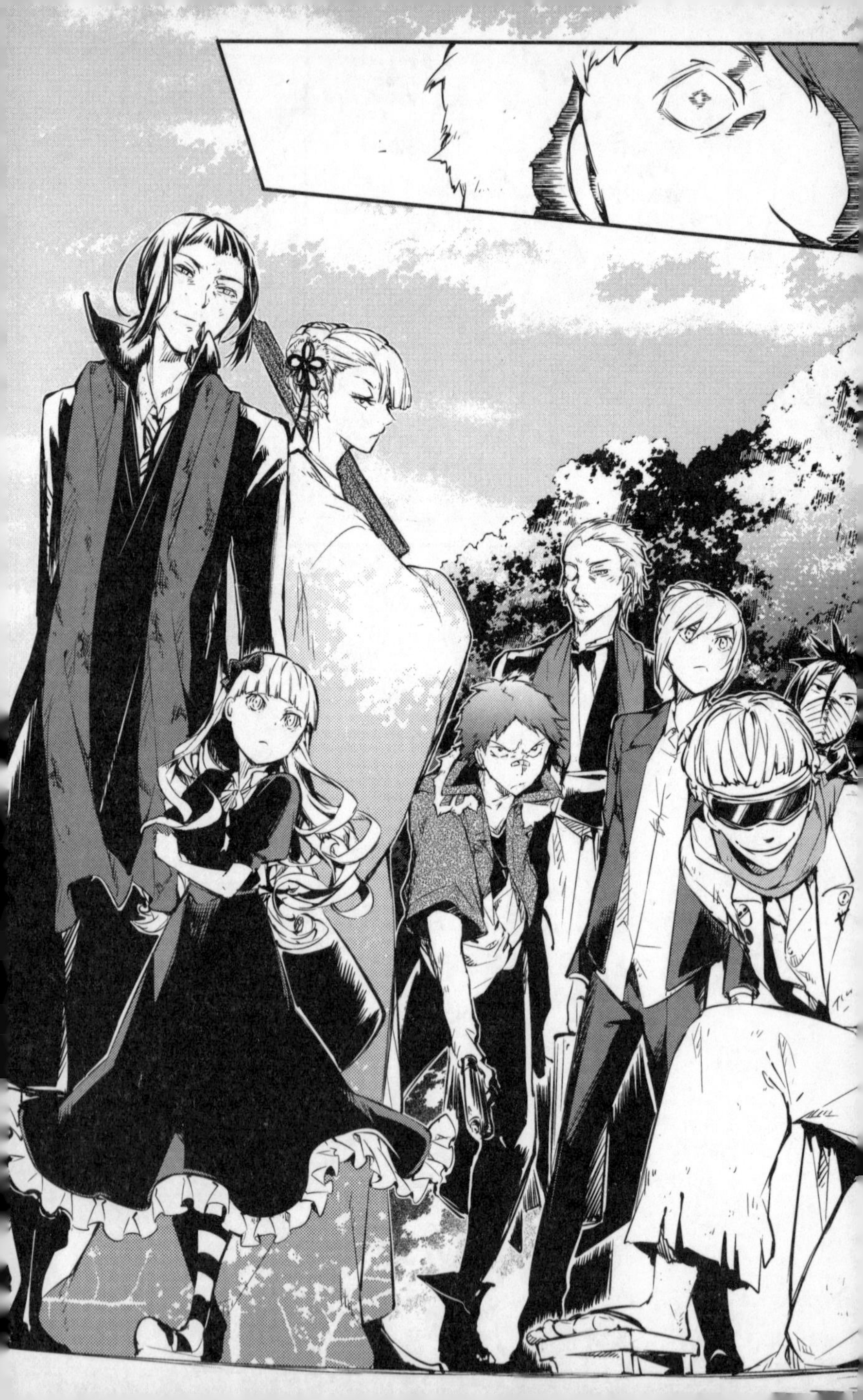

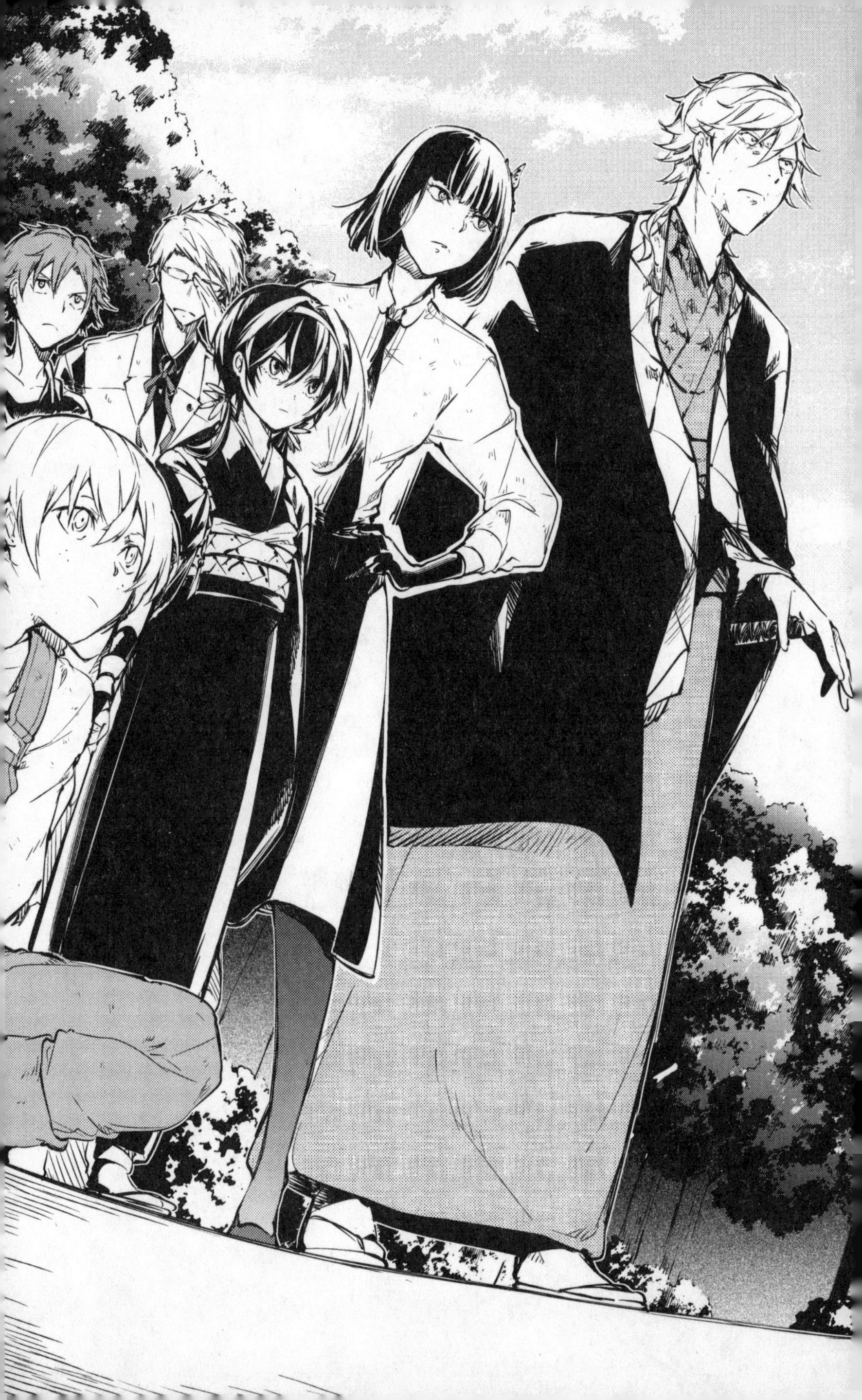

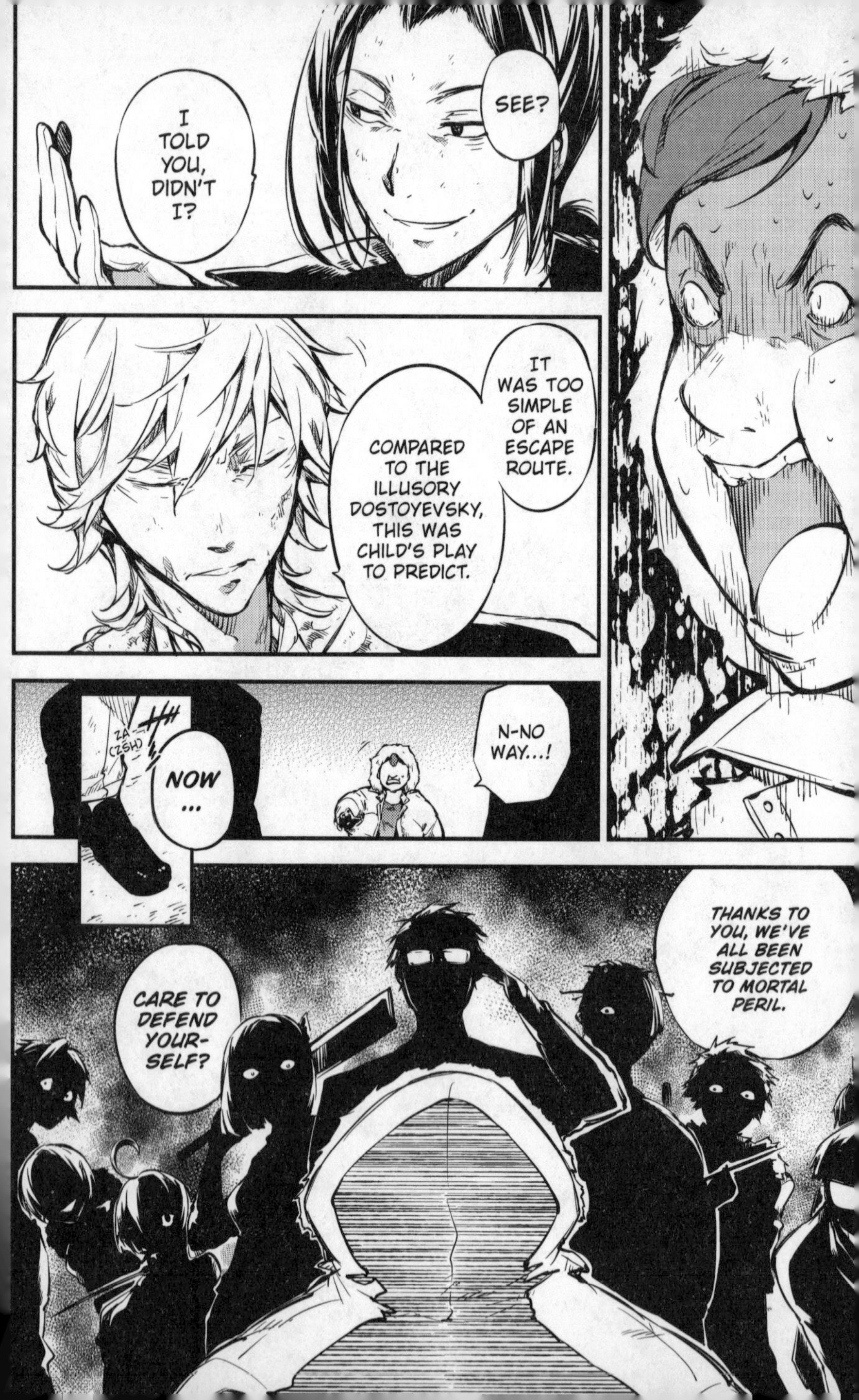
SEE?
I TOLD YOU, DIDN'T I?
IT WAS TOO SIMPLE OF AN ESCAPE ROUTE.
COMPARED TO THE ILLUSORY DOSTOYEVSKY, THIS WAS CHILD'S PLAY TO PREDICT.
N-NO WAY...!
ZA (ZSH)
NOW...
THANKS TO YOU, WE'VE ALL BEEN SUBJECTED TO MORTAL PERIL.
CARE TO DEFEND YOURSELF?

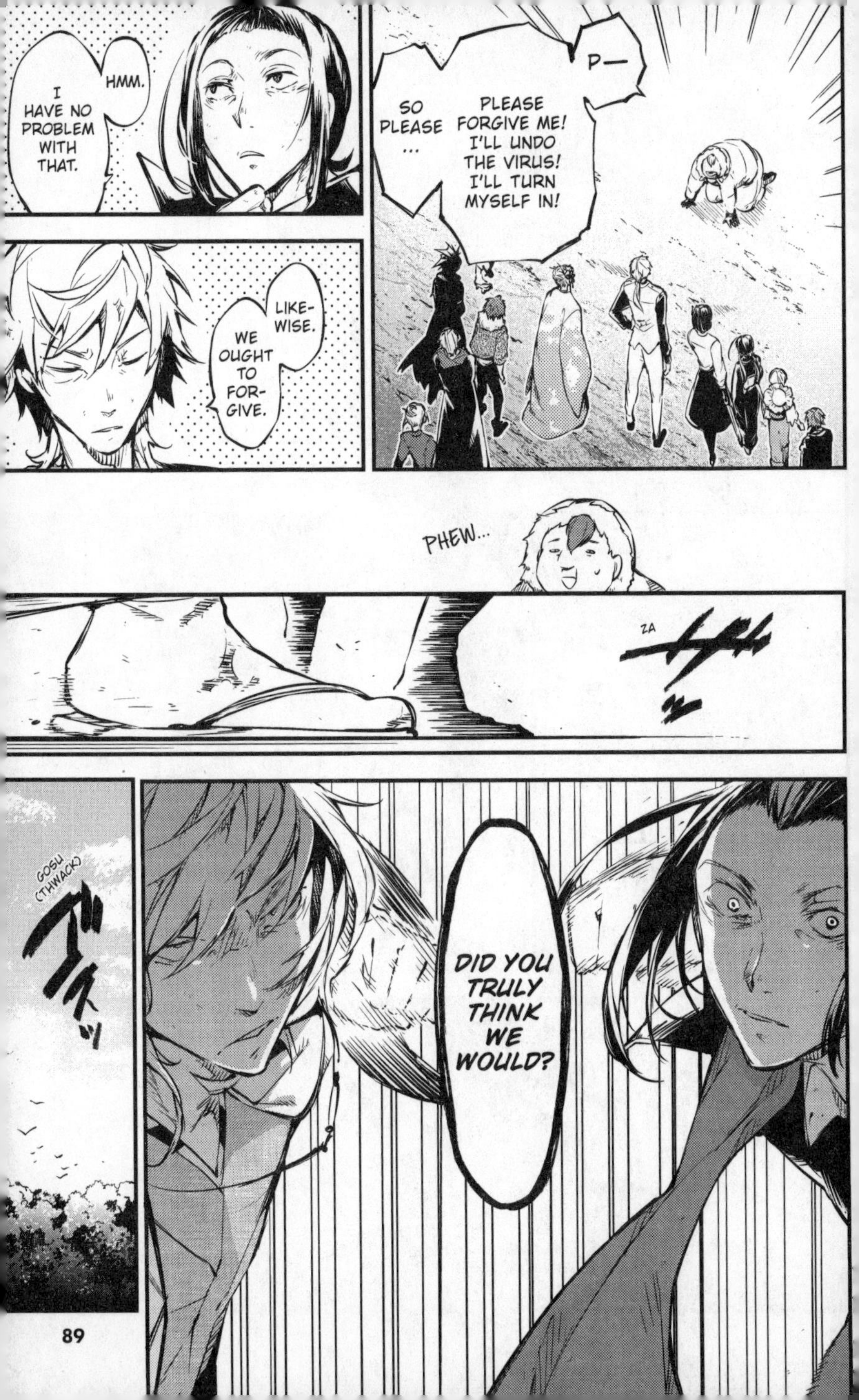
P—
PLEASE FORGIVE ME! I'LL UNDO THE VIRUS! I'LL TURN MYSELF IN!
SO PLEASE ...
HMM.
I HAVE NO PROBLEM WITH THAT.
LIKE-WISE.
WE OUGHT TO FOR-GIVE.
PHEW...
ZA
DID YOU TRULY THINK WE WOULD?
GOSU (THWACK)

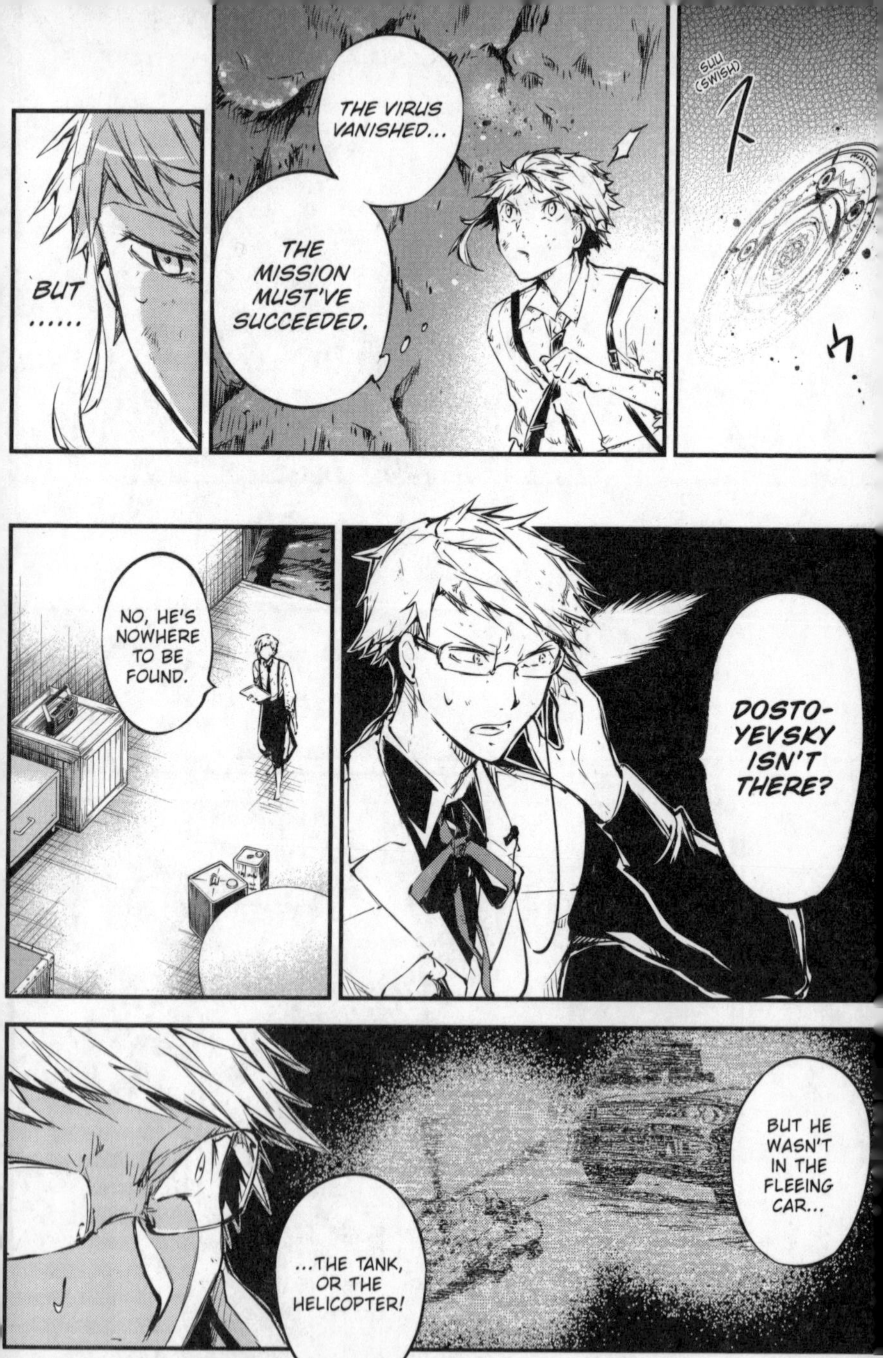
SUU
(SWISH)
THE VIRUS VANISHED...
THE MISSION MUST'VE SUCCEEDED.
BUT ......
DOSTO-YEVSKY ISN'T THERE?
NO, HE'S NOWHERE TO BE FOUND.
BUT HE WASN'T IN THE FLEEING CAR...
...THE TANK, OR THE HELICOPTER!

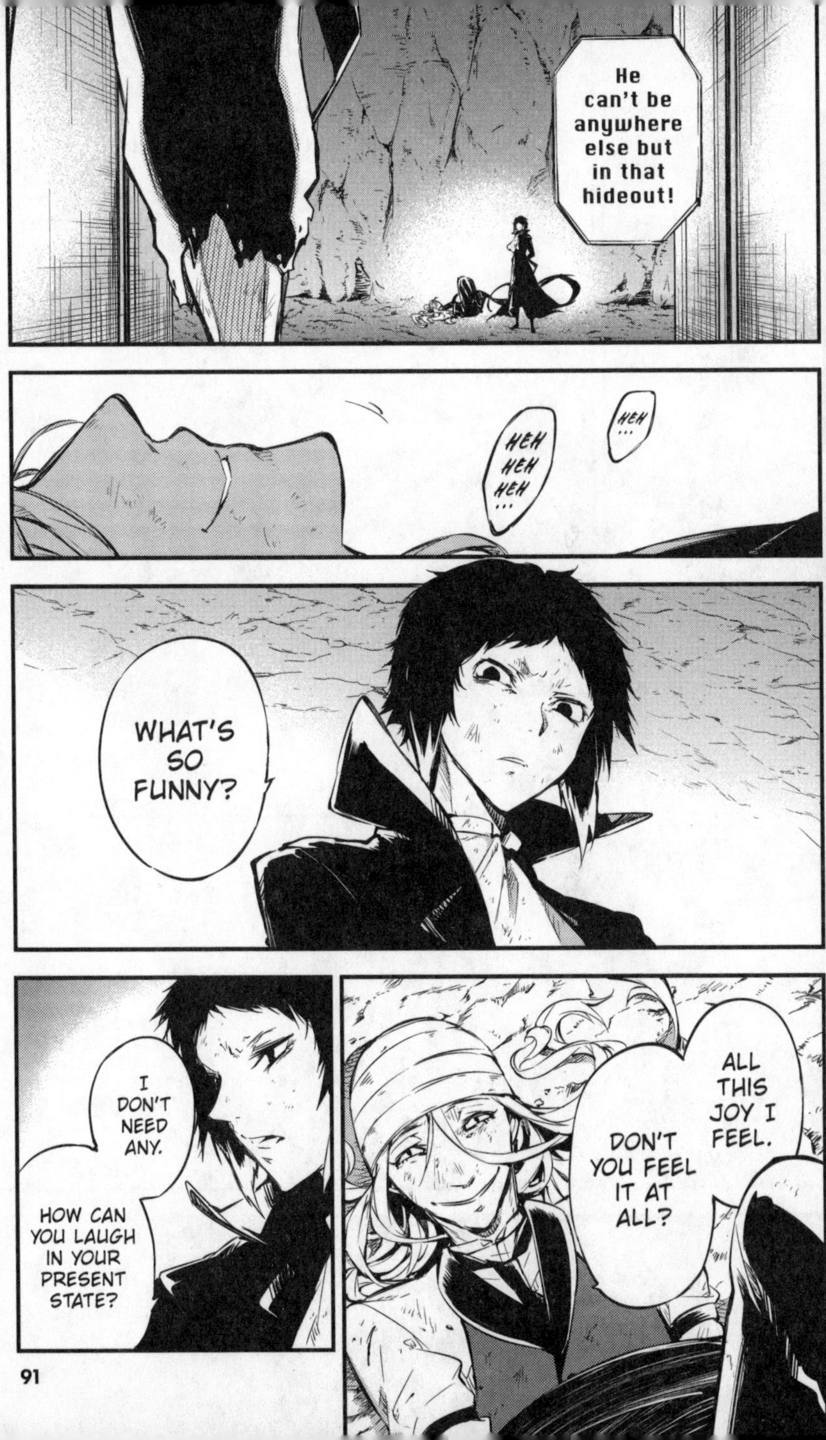
He can't be anywhere else but in that hideout!
HEH...
HEH HEH HEH...
WHAT'S SO FUNNY?
ALL THIS JOY I FEEL.
DON'T YOU FEEL IT AT ALL?
I DON'T NEED ANY.
HOW CAN YOU LAUGH IN YOUR PRESENT STATE?

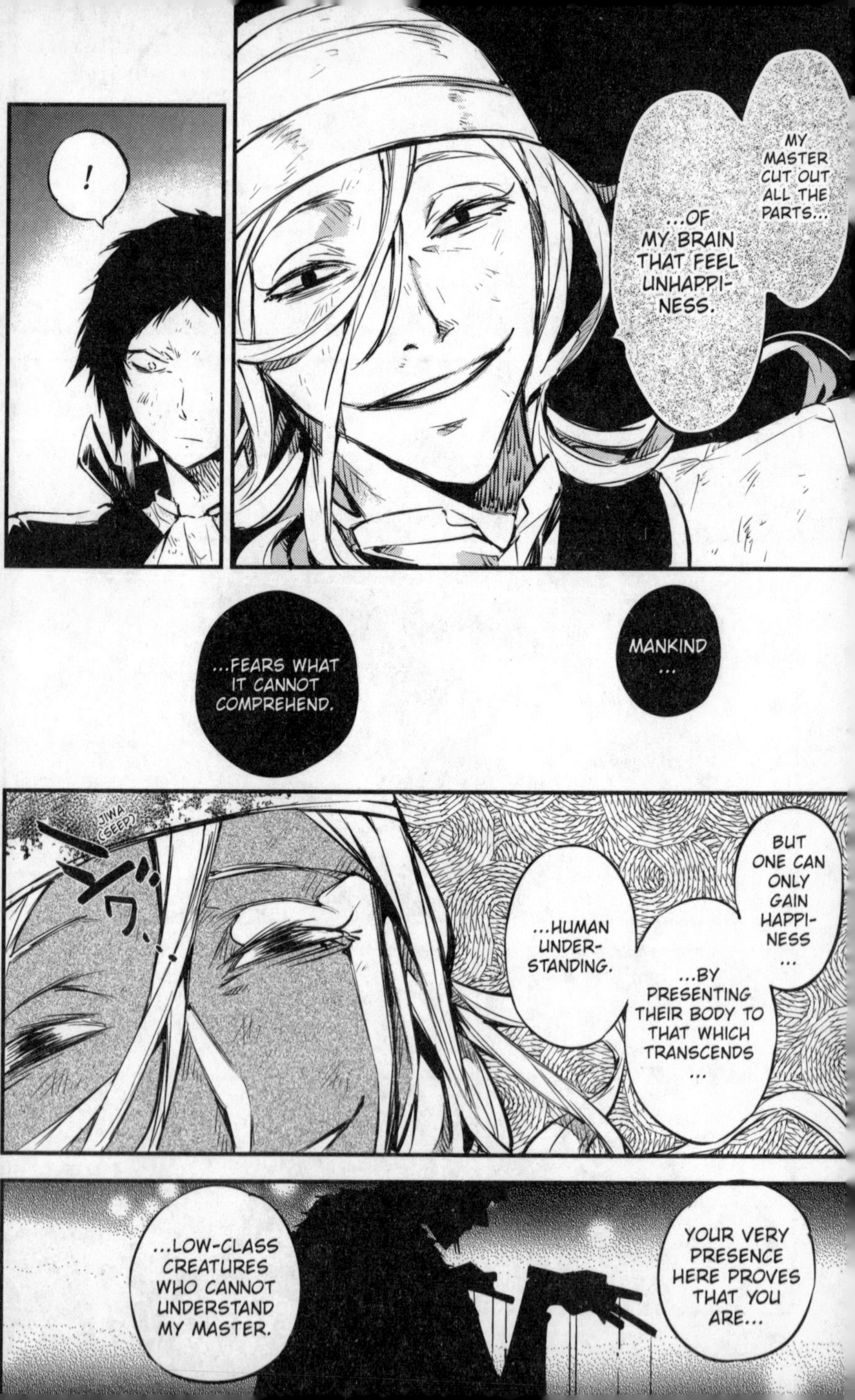
MY MASTER CUT OUT ALL THE PARTS...
...OF MY BRAIN THAT FEEL UNHAPPINESS.
!
MANKIND...
...FEARS WHAT IT CANNOT COMPREHEND.
BUT ONE CAN ONLY GAIN HAPPINESS...
...BY PRESENTING THEIR BODY TO THAT WHICH TRANSCENDS...
...HUMAN UNDERSTANDING.
JIWA (SEEP)
YOUR VERY PRESENCE HERE PROVES THAT YOU ARE...
...LOW-CLASS CREATURES WHO CANNOT UNDERSTAND MY MASTER.

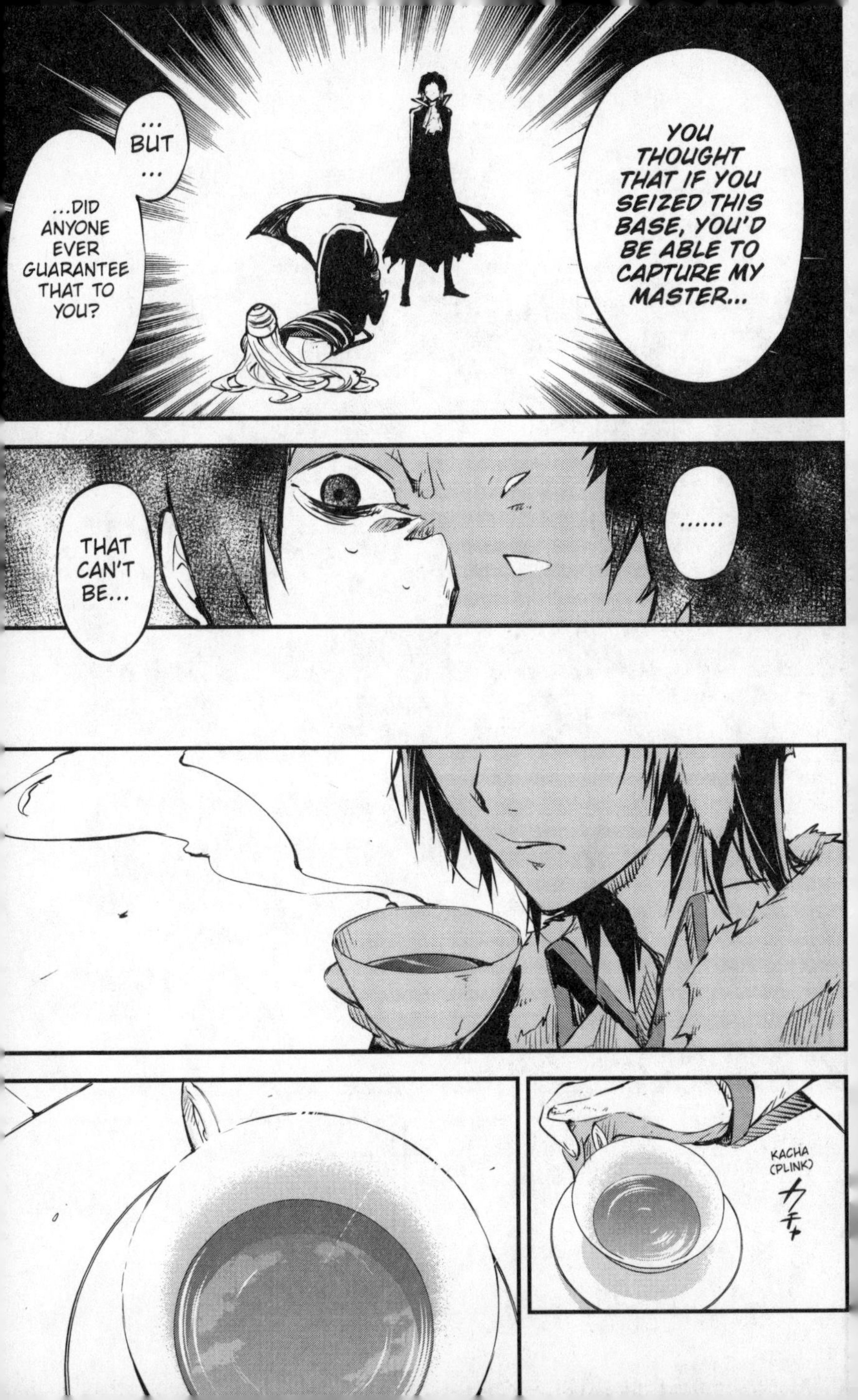
YOU THOUGHT THAT IF YOU SEIZED THIS BASE, YOU'D BE ABLE TO CAPTURE MY MASTER...
... BUT ...
...DID ANYONE EVER GUARANTEE THAT TO YOU?
......
THAT CAN'T BE...
KACHA (PLINK)

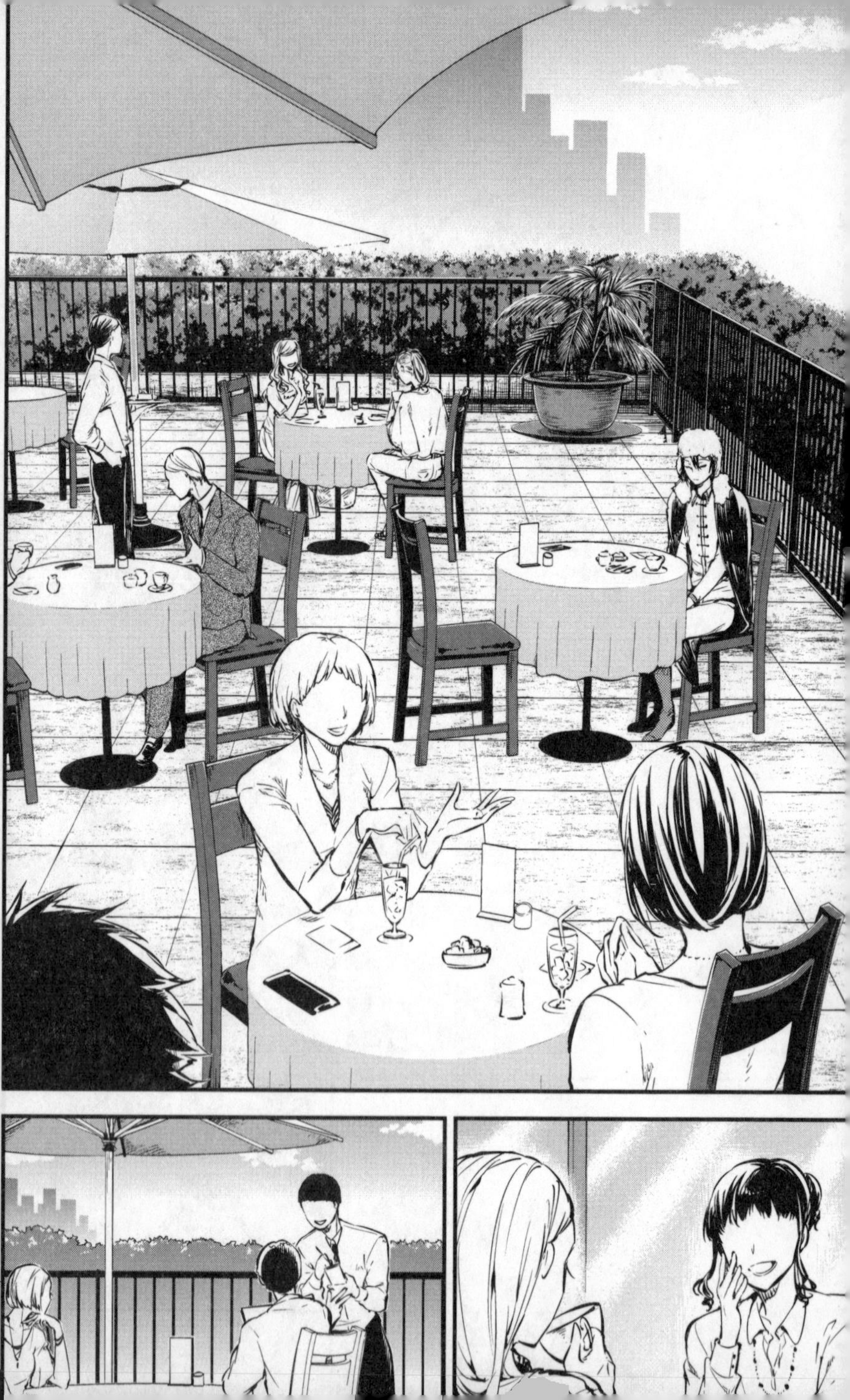

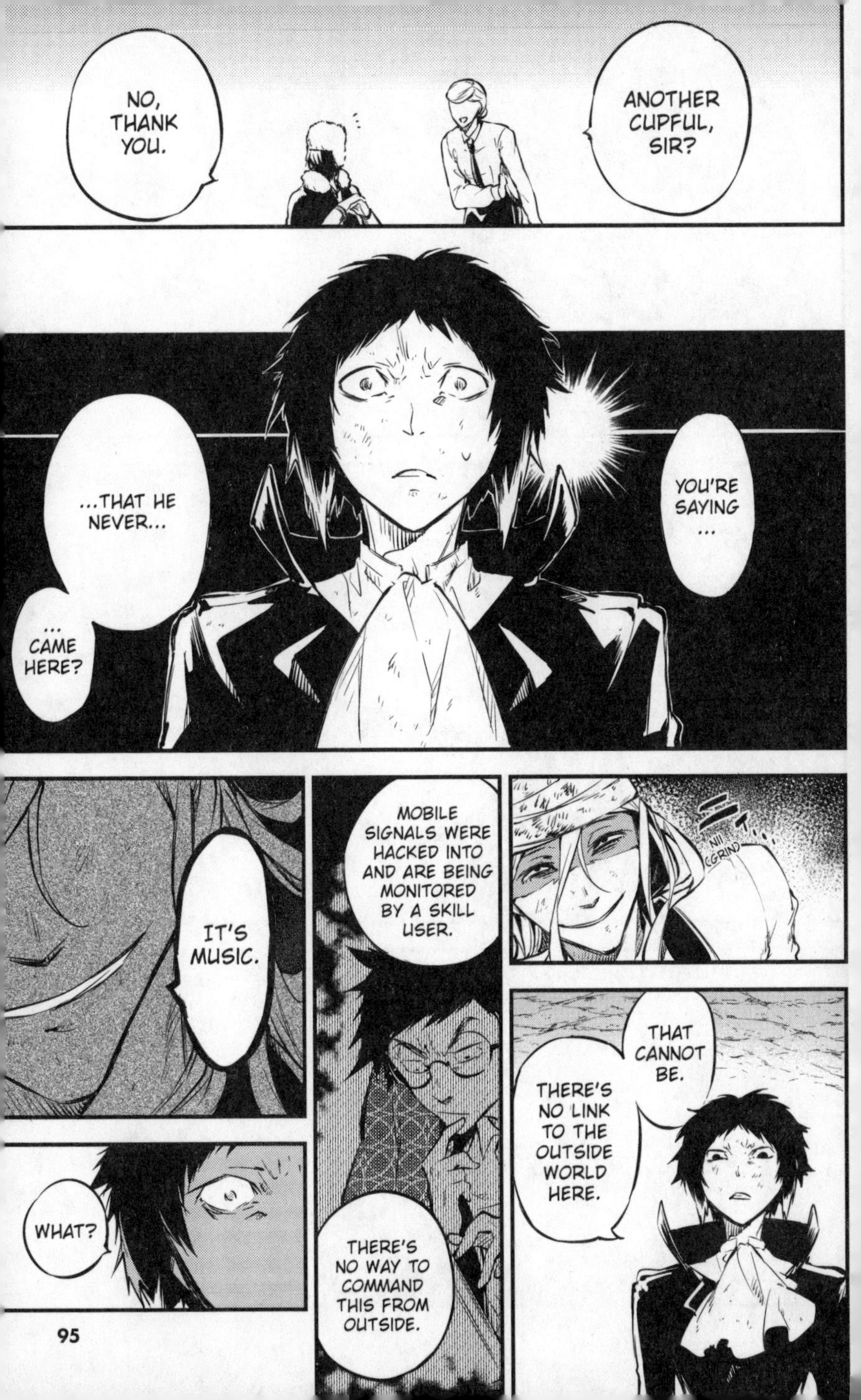
ANOTHER CUPFUL, SIR?
NO, THANK YOU.
YOU'RE SAYING...
...THAT HE NEVER...
...CAME HERE?
NII (GRIN)
THAT CANNOT BE.
THERE'S NO LINK TO THE OUTSIDE WORLD HERE.
MOBILE SIGNALS WERE HACKED INTO AND ARE BEING MONITORED BY A SKILL USER.
THERE'S NO WAY TO COMMAND THIS FROM OUTSIDE.
IT'S MUSIC.
WHAT?

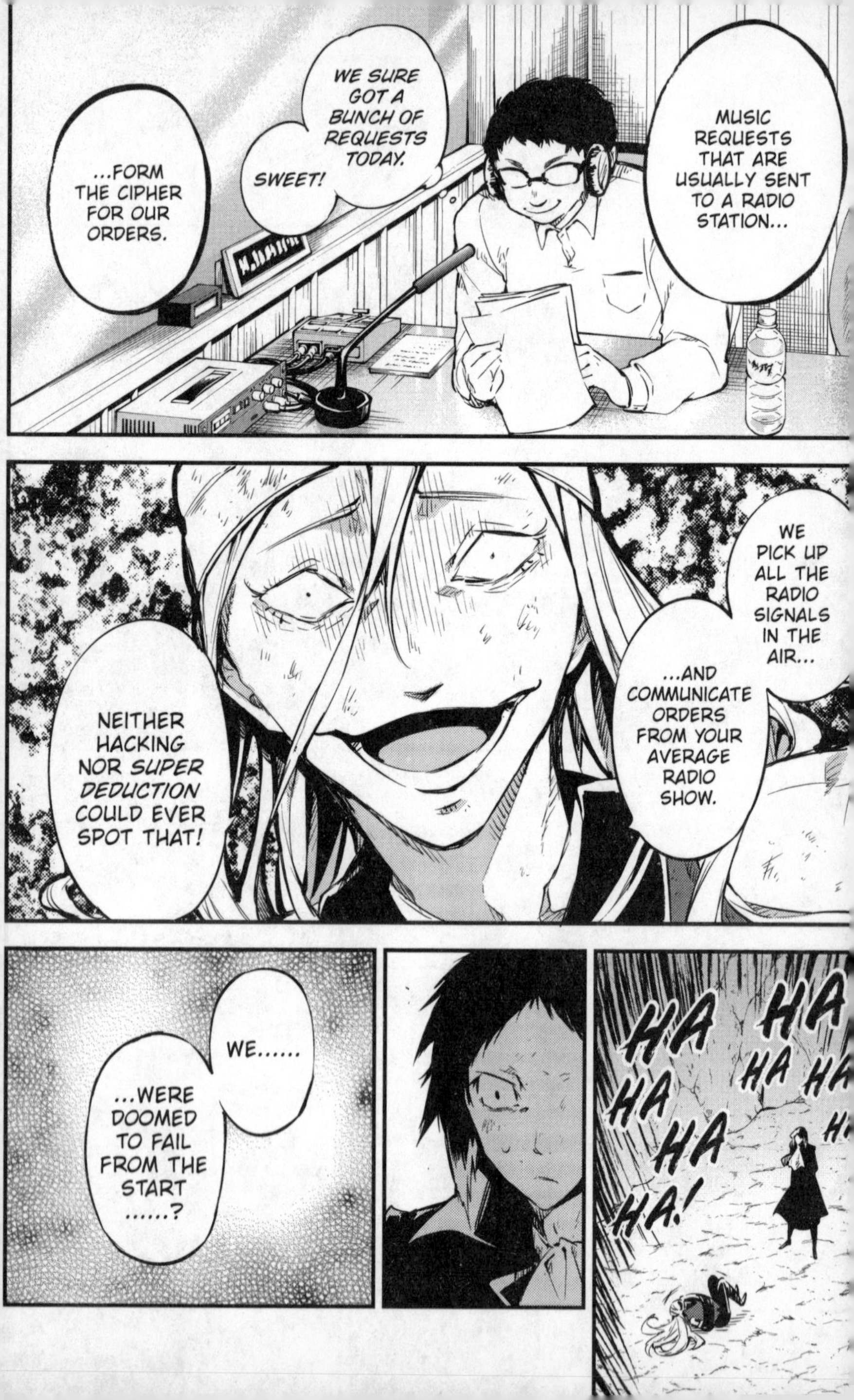
MUSIC REQUESTS THAT ARE USUALLY SENT TO A RADIO STATION...
WE SURE GOT A BUNCH OF REQUESTS TODAY.
SWEET!
...FORM THE CIPHER FOR OUR ORDERS.
WE PICK UP ALL THE RADIO SIGNALS IN THE AIR...
...AND COMMUNICATE ORDERS FROM YOUR AVERAGE RADIO SHOW.
NEITHER HACKING NOR *SUPER DEDUCTION* COULD EVER SPOT THAT!
HA HA HA HA HA HA HA HA HA!
WE......
...WERE DOOMED TO FAIL FROM THE START ......?

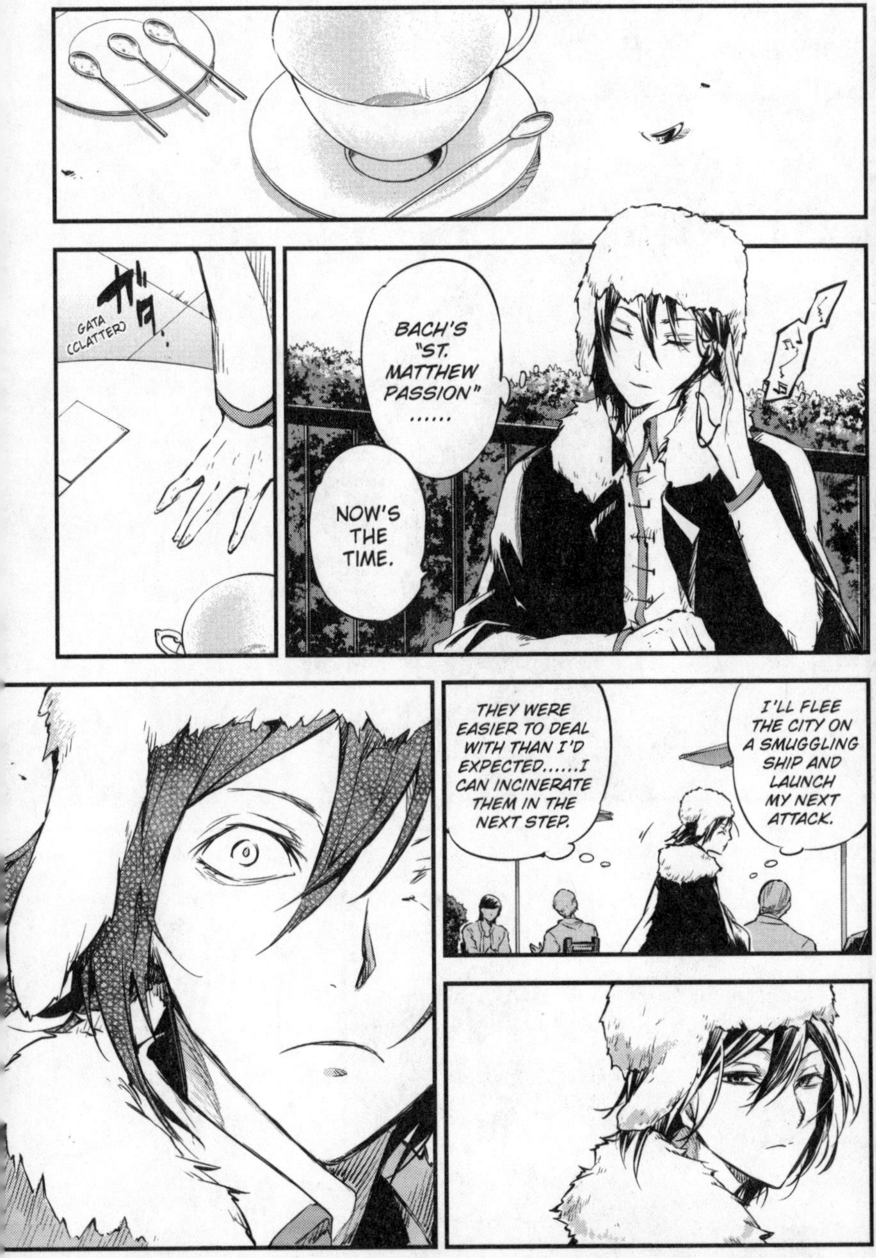
BACH'S "ST. MATTHEW PASSION" ......
NOW'S THE TIME.
GATA (CLATTER)
I'LL FLEE THE CITY ON A SMUGGLING SHIP AND LAUNCH MY NEXT ATTACK.
THEY WERE EASIER TO DEAL WITH THAN I'D EXPECTED......I CAN INCINERATE THEM IN THE NEXT STEP.

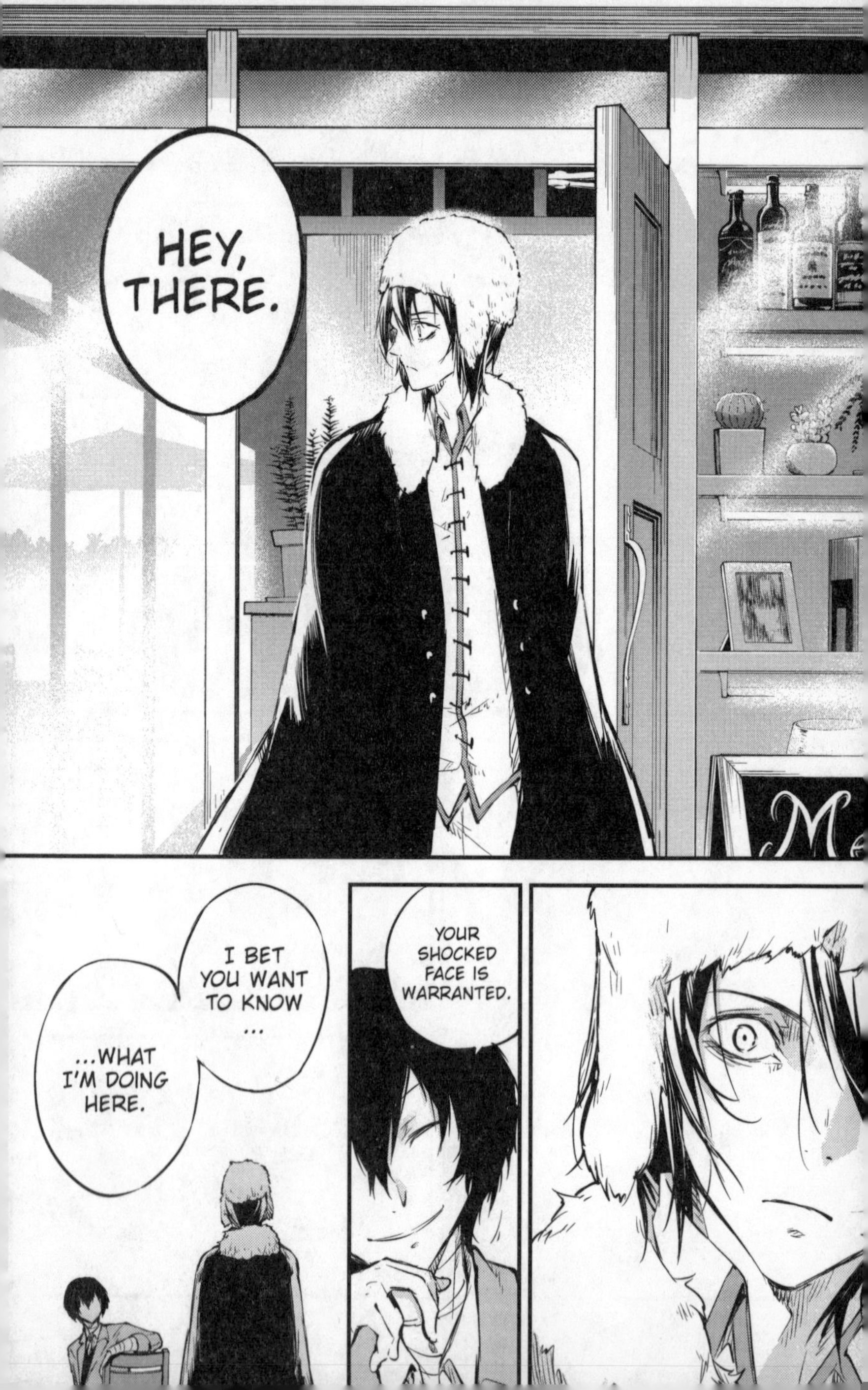
HEY, THERE.
YOUR SHOCKED FACE IS WARRANTED.
I BET YOU WANT TO KNOW ...
...WHAT I'M DOING HERE.

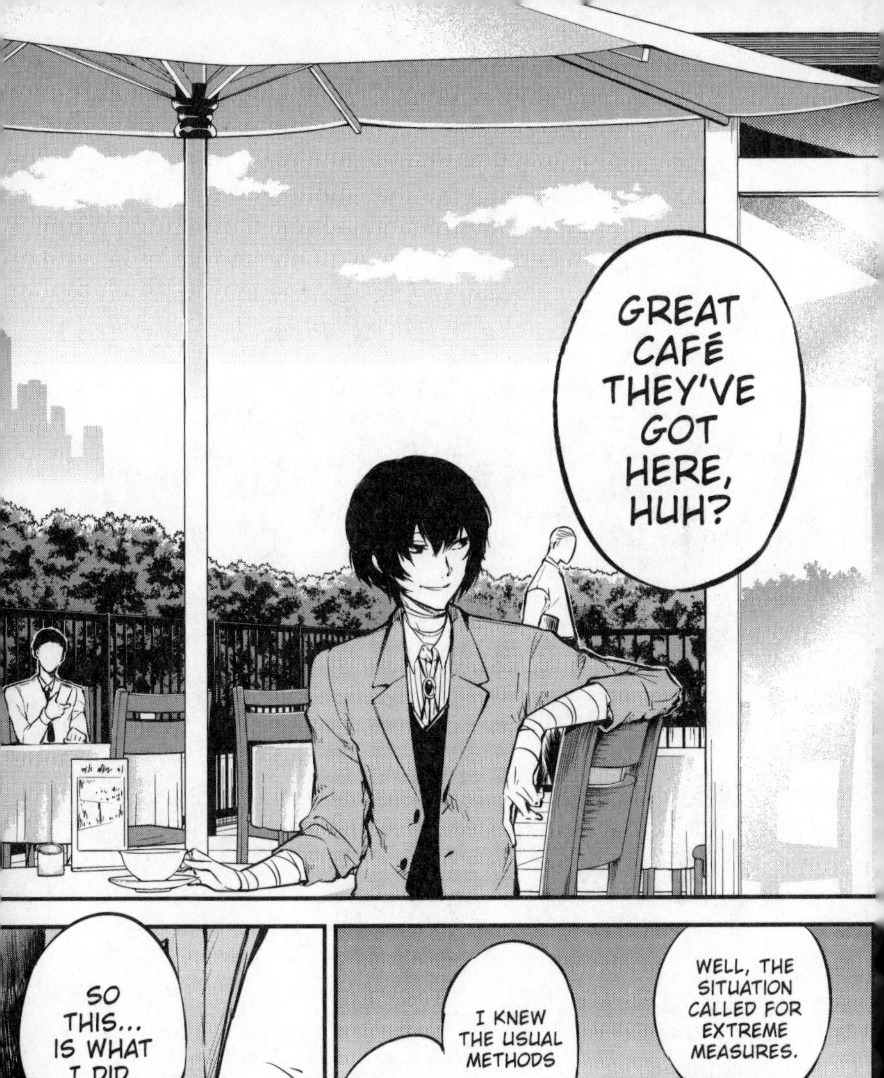
GREAT CAFÉ THEY'VE GOT HERE, HUH?
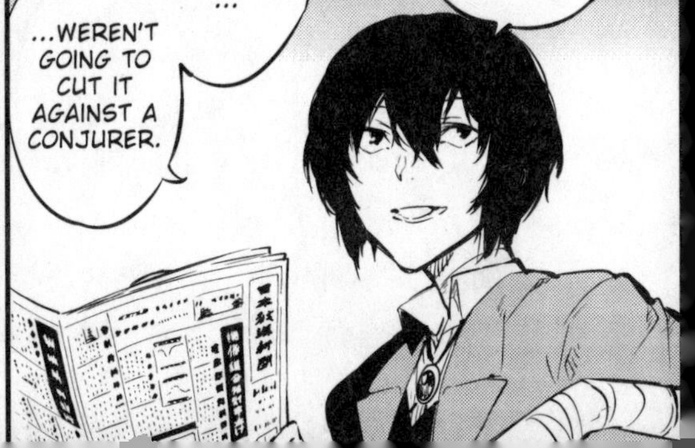
WELL, THE SITUATION CALLED FOR EXTREME MEASURES.
I KNEW THE USUAL METHODS ...
...WEREN'T GOING TO CUT IT AGAINST A CONJURER.
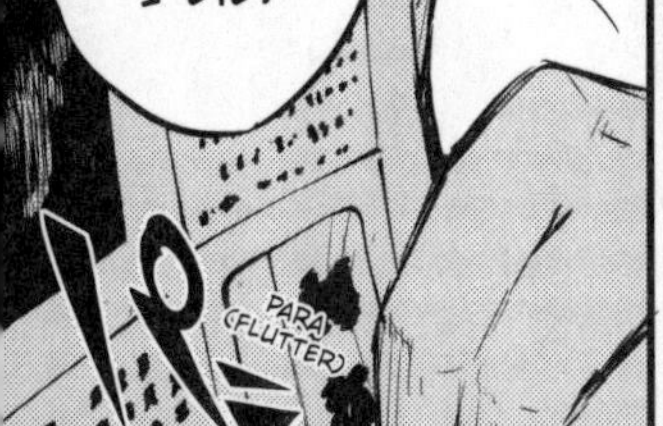
SO THIS... IS WHAT I DID.
PARA (FLUTTER)

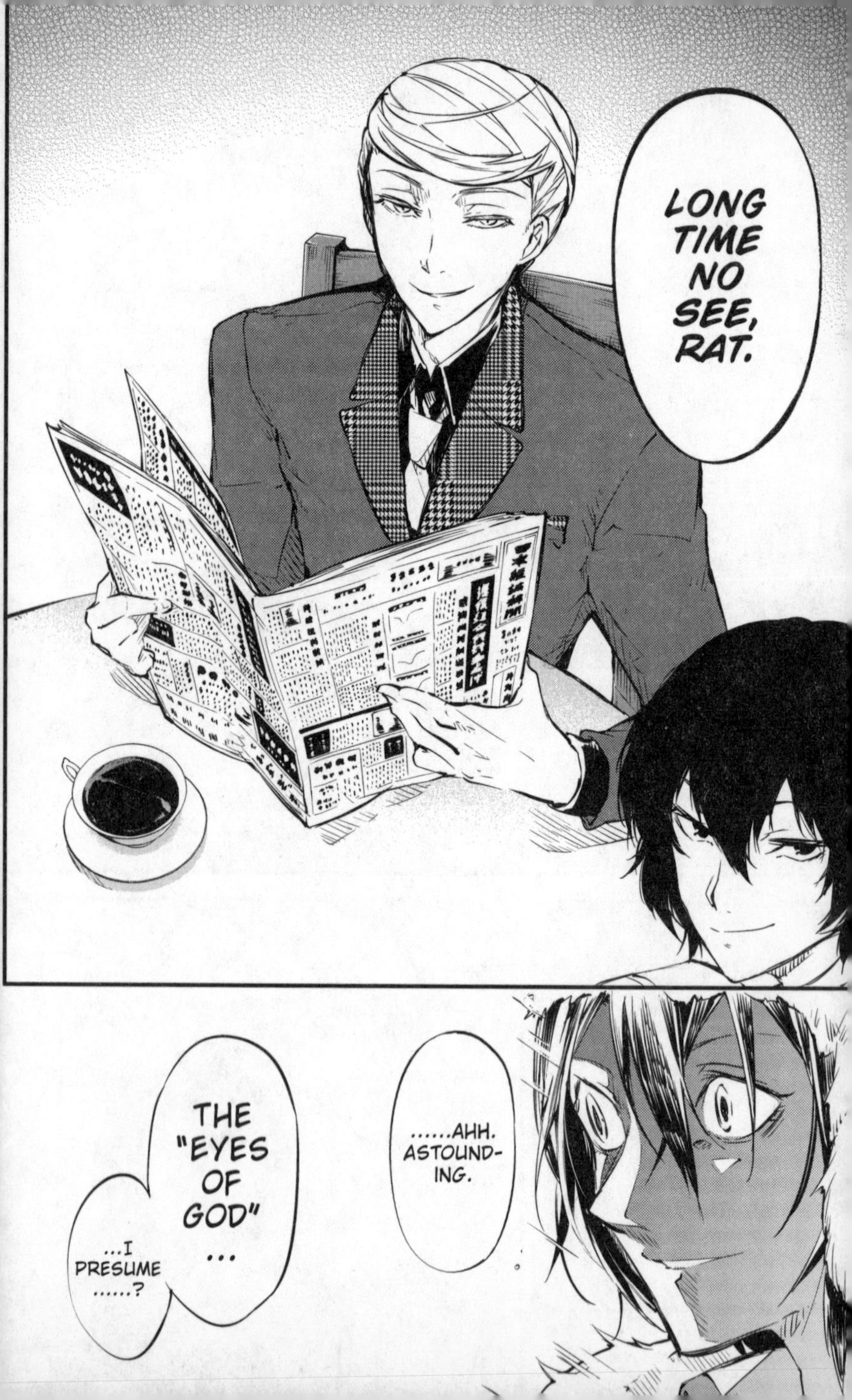
LONG TIME NO SEE, RAT.
......AHH. ASTOUND-ING.
THE "EYES OF GOD" ...
...I PRESUME ......?

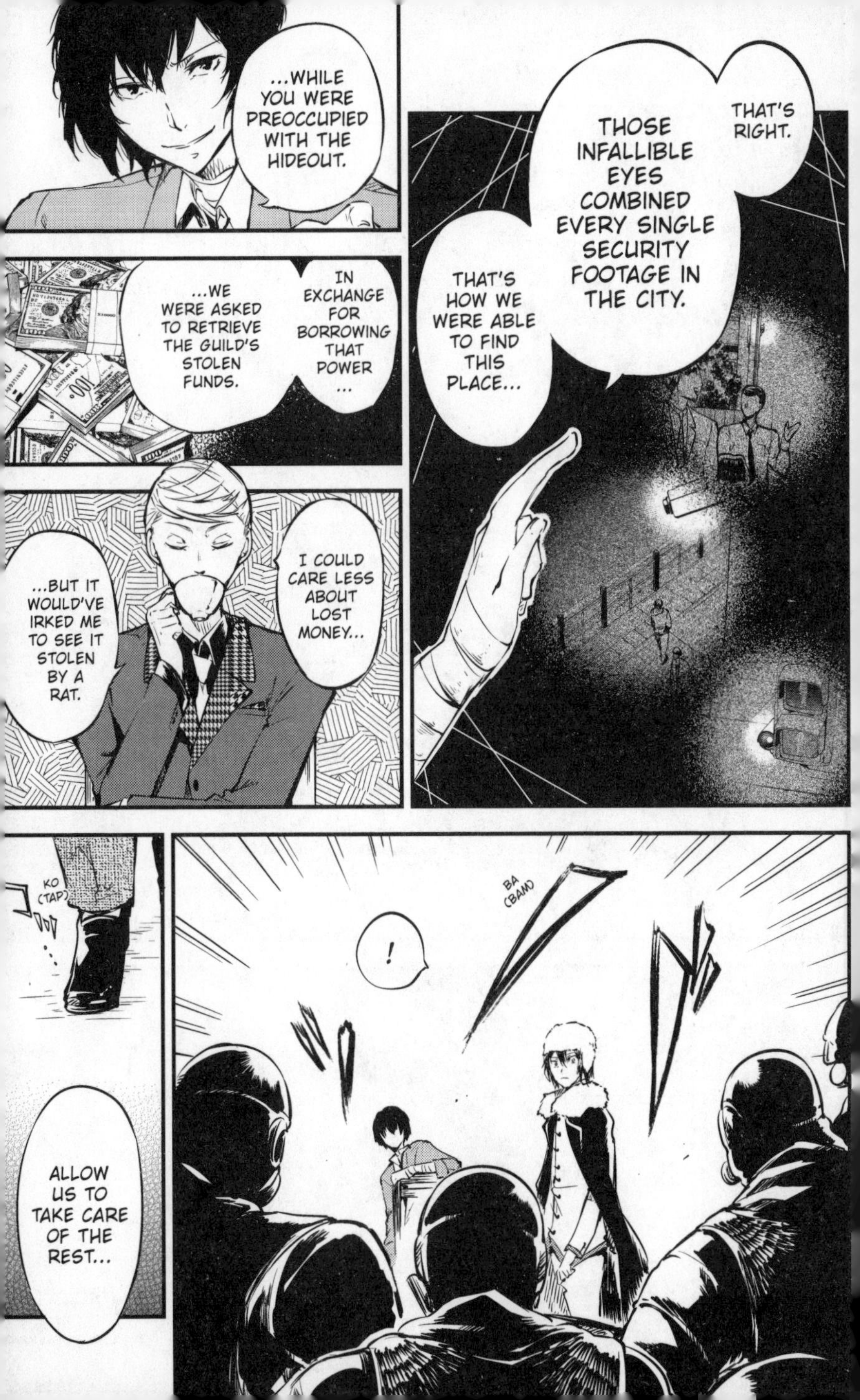
THAT'S RIGHT.
THOSE INFALLIBLE EYES COMBINED EVERY SINGLE SECURITY FOOTAGE IN THE CITY.
THAT'S HOW WE WERE ABLE TO FIND THIS PLACE...
...WHILE YOU WERE PREOCCUPIED WITH THE HIDEOUT.
IN EXCHANGE FOR BORROWING THAT POWER...
...WE WERE ASKED TO RETRIEVE THE GUILD'S STOLEN FUNDS.
I COULD CARE LESS ABOUT LOST MONEY...
...BUT IT WOULD'VE IRKED ME TO SEE IT STOLEN BY A RAT.
BA (BAM)
!
KO (TAP)
ALLOW US TO TAKE CARE OF THE REST...

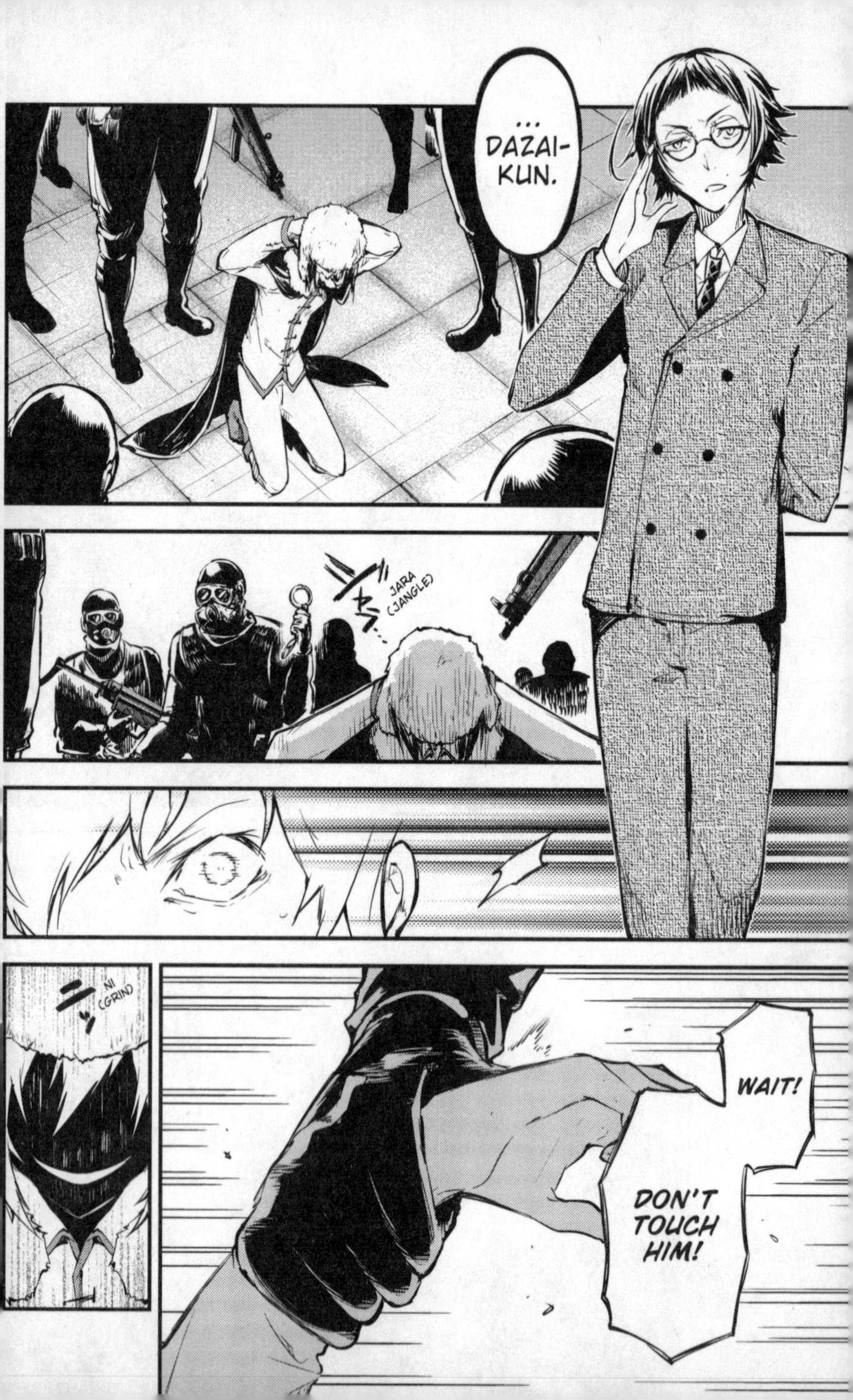
... DAZAI-KUN.
JARA (JANGLE)
WAIT!
DON'T TOUCH HIM!
NI (GRIN)

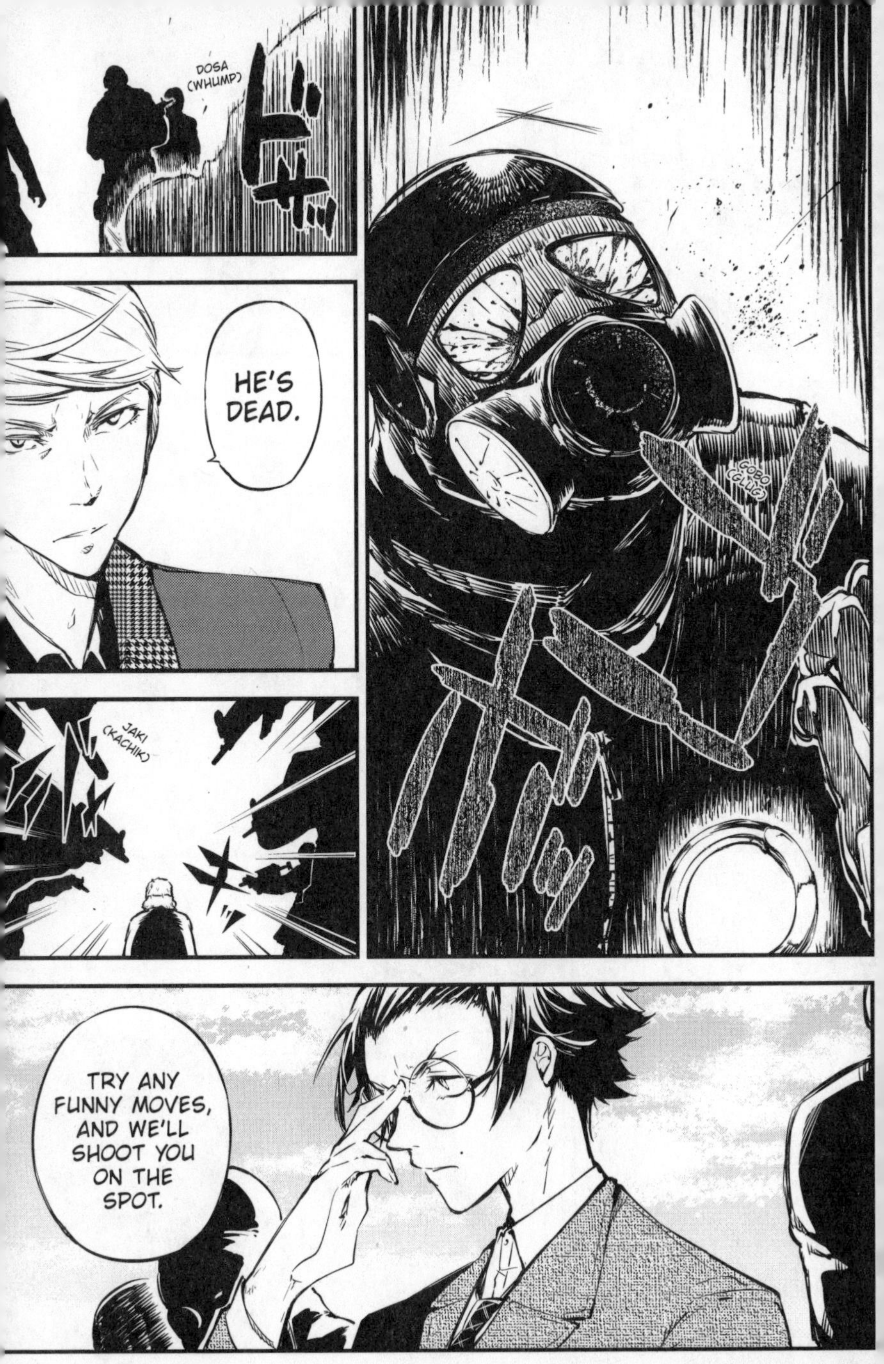
GOBO (GLUG)
DOSA (WHUMP)
HE'S DEAD.
JAKI (KACHIK)
TRY ANY FUNNY MOVES, AND WE'LL SHOOT YOU ON THE SPOT.

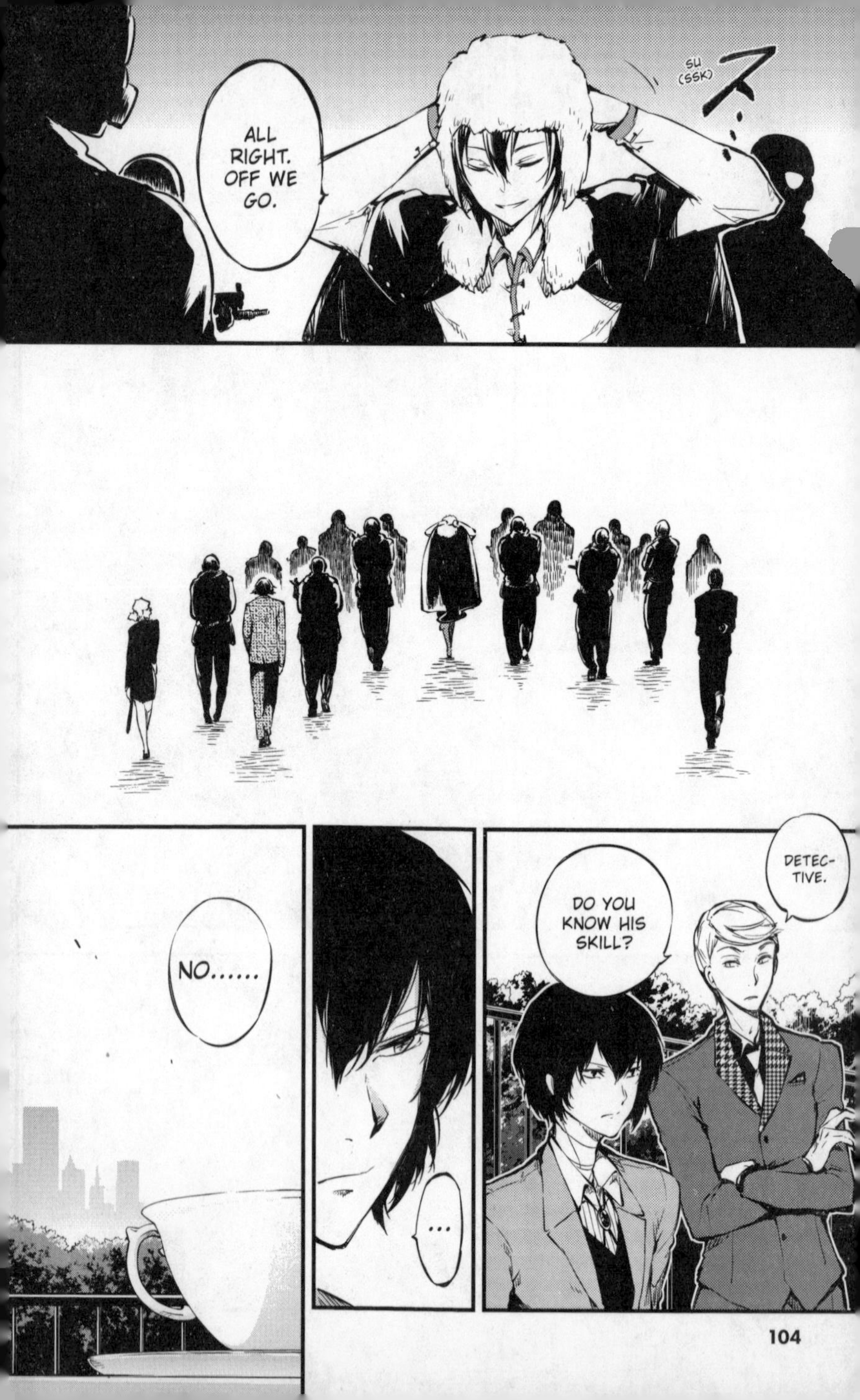
SU (SSK)
ALL RIGHT. OFF WE GO.
DETEC-TIVE.
DO YOU KNOW HIS SKILL?
...
NO......

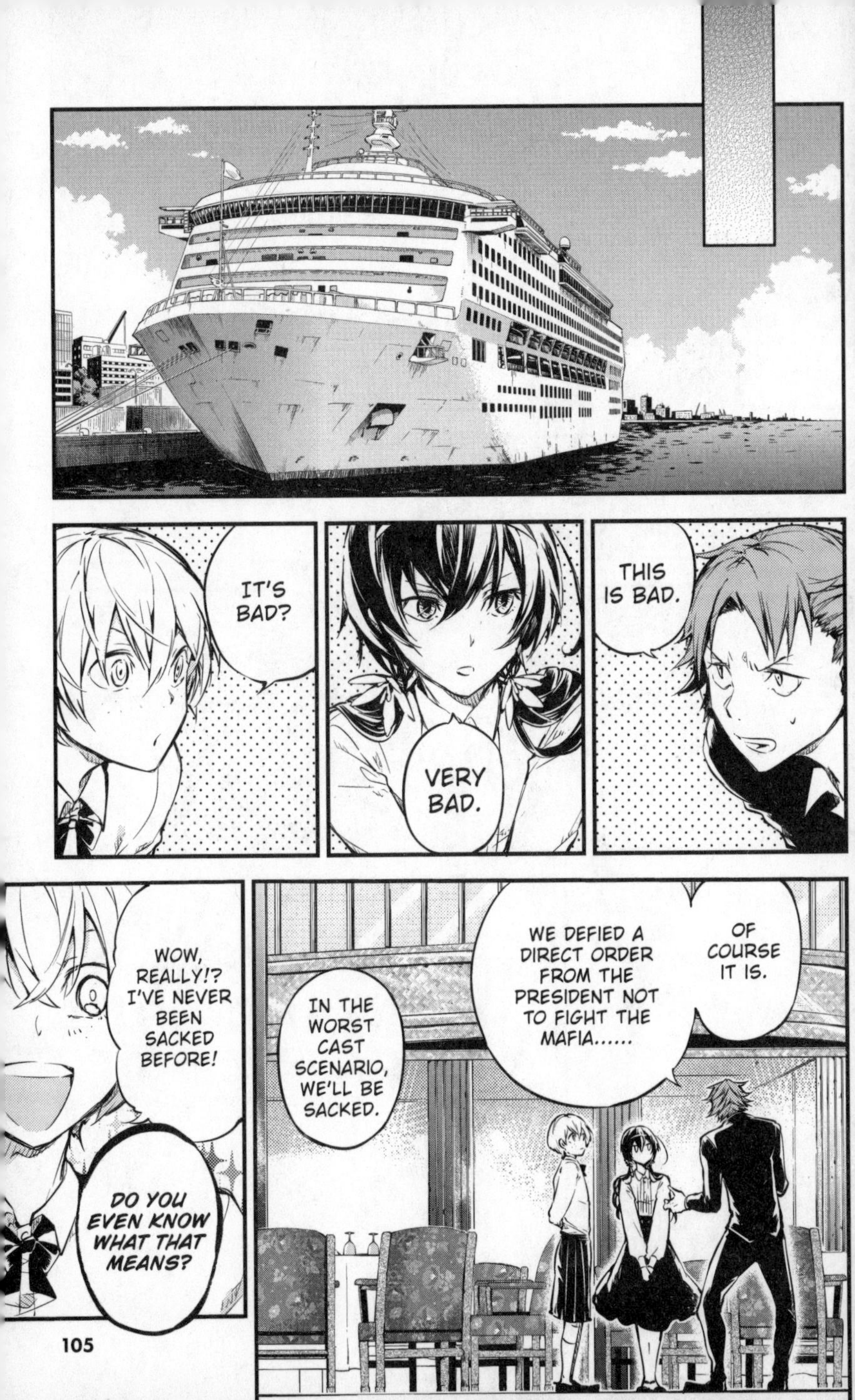
THIS IS BAD.
VERY BAD.
IT'S BAD?
OF COURSE IT IS.
WE DEFIED A DIRECT ORDER FROM THE PRESIDENT NOT TO FIGHT THE MAFIA......
IN THE WORST CAST SCENARIO, WE'LL BE SACKED.
WOW, REALLY!? I'VE NEVER BEEN SACKED BEFORE!
DO YOU EVEN KNOW WHAT THAT MEANS?

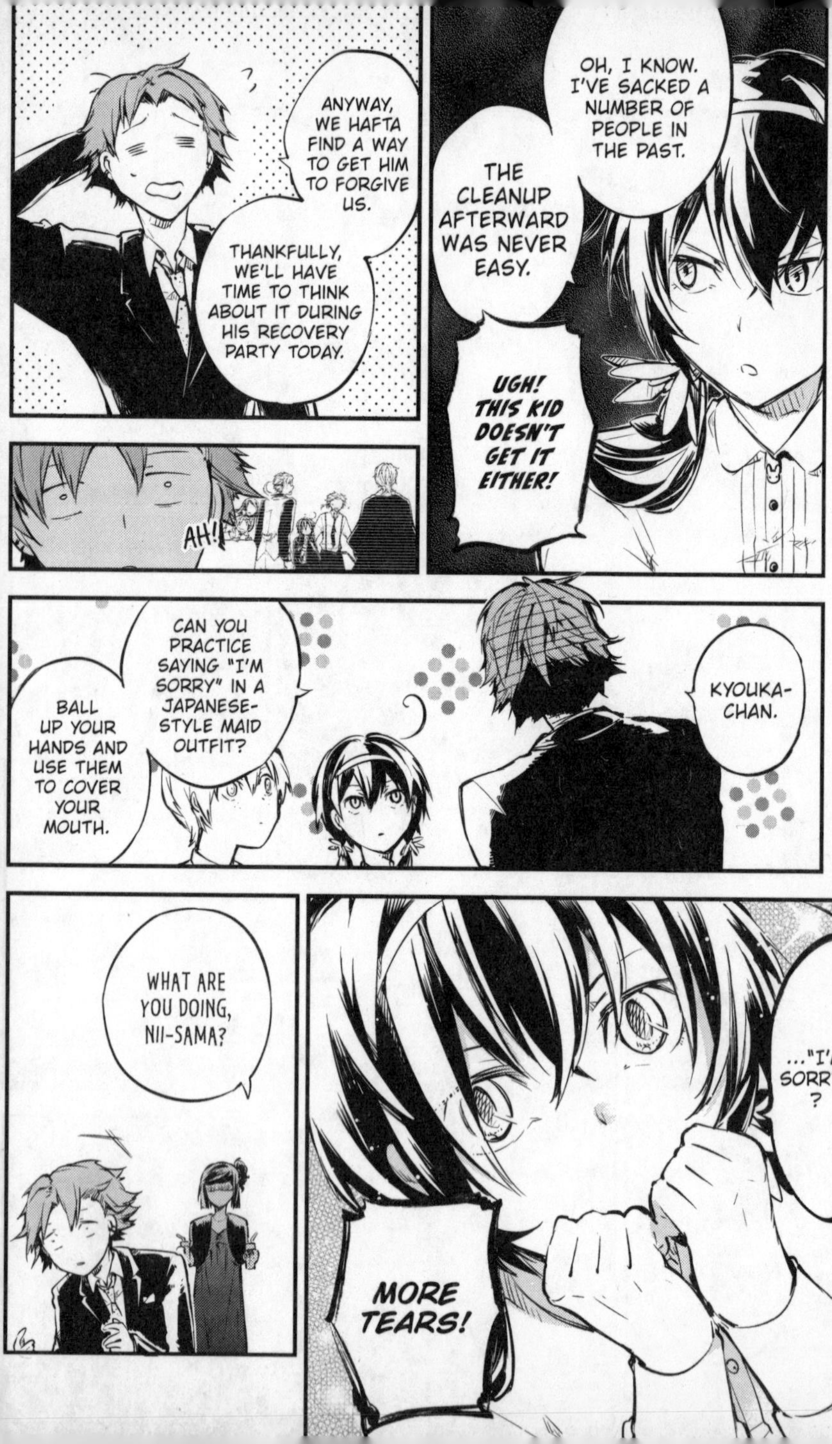
OH, I KNOW. I'VE SACKED A NUMBER OF PEOPLE IN THE PAST.
THE CLEANUP AFTERWARD WAS NEVER EASY.
UGH! THIS KID DOESN'T GET IT EITHER!
ANYWAY, WE HAFTA FIND A WAY TO GET HIM TO FORGIVE US.
THANKFULLY, WE'LL HAVE TIME TO THINK ABOUT IT DURING HIS RECOVERY PARTY TODAY.
AH!
KYOUKA-CHAN.
CAN YOU PRACTICE SAYING "I'M SORRY" IN A JAPANESE-STYLE MAID OUTFIT?
BALL UP YOUR HANDS AND USE THEM TO COVER YOUR MOUTH.
..."I'M SORRY"?
MORE TEARS!
WHAT ARE YOU DOING, NII-SAMA?

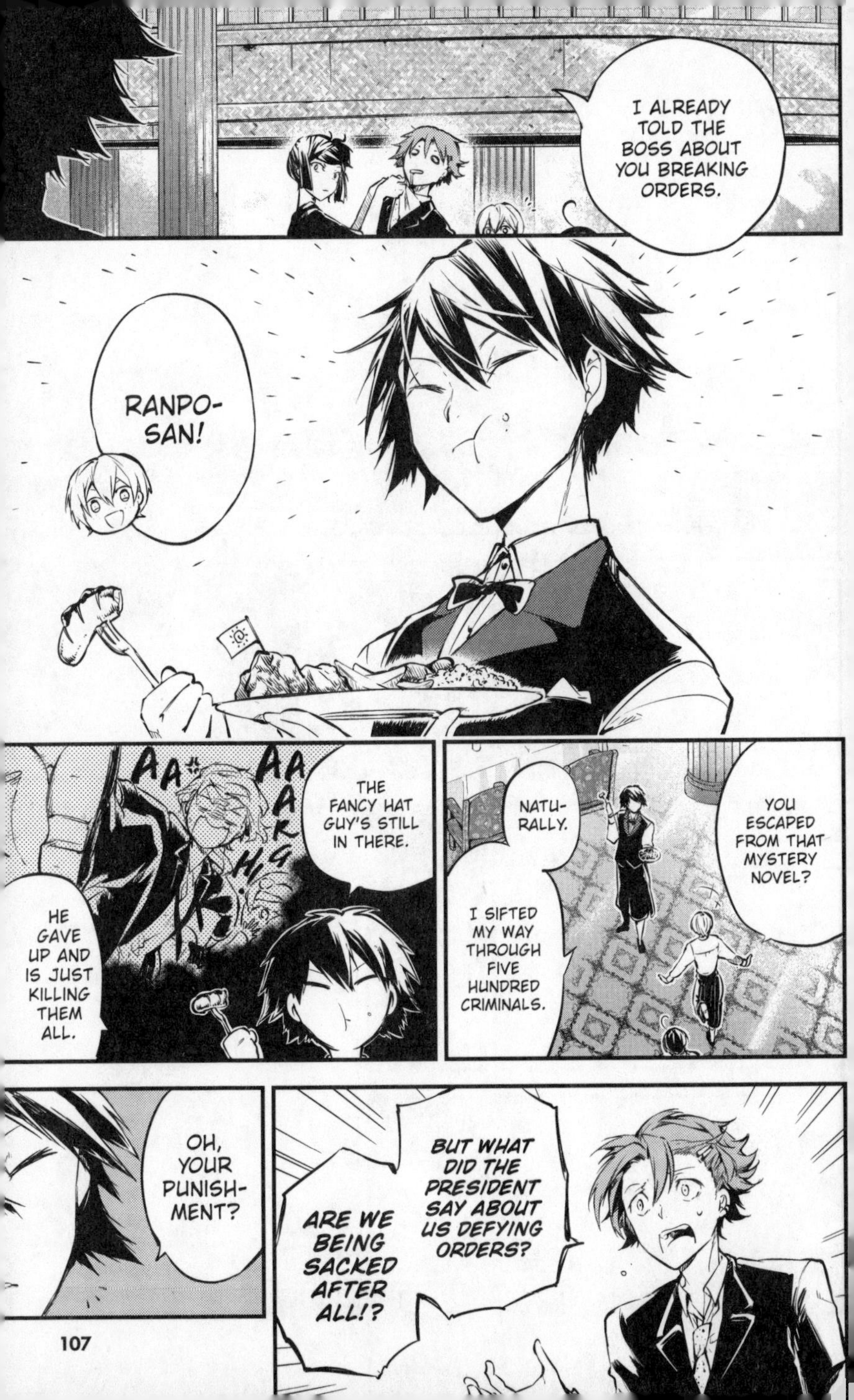
I ALREADY TOLD THE BOSS ABOUT YOU BREAKING ORDERS.
RANPO-SAN!
YOU ESCAPED FROM THAT MYSTERY NOVEL?
NATU-RALLY.
I SIFTED MY WAY THROUGH FIVE HUNDRED CRIMINALS.
THE FANCY HAT GUY'S STILL IN THERE.
AAAAAKGH!
HE GAVE UP AND IS JUST KILLING THEM ALL.
BUT WHAT DID THE PRESIDENT SAY ABOUT US DEFYING ORDERS?
ARE WE BEING SACKED AFTER ALL!?
OH, YOUR PUNISH-MENT?

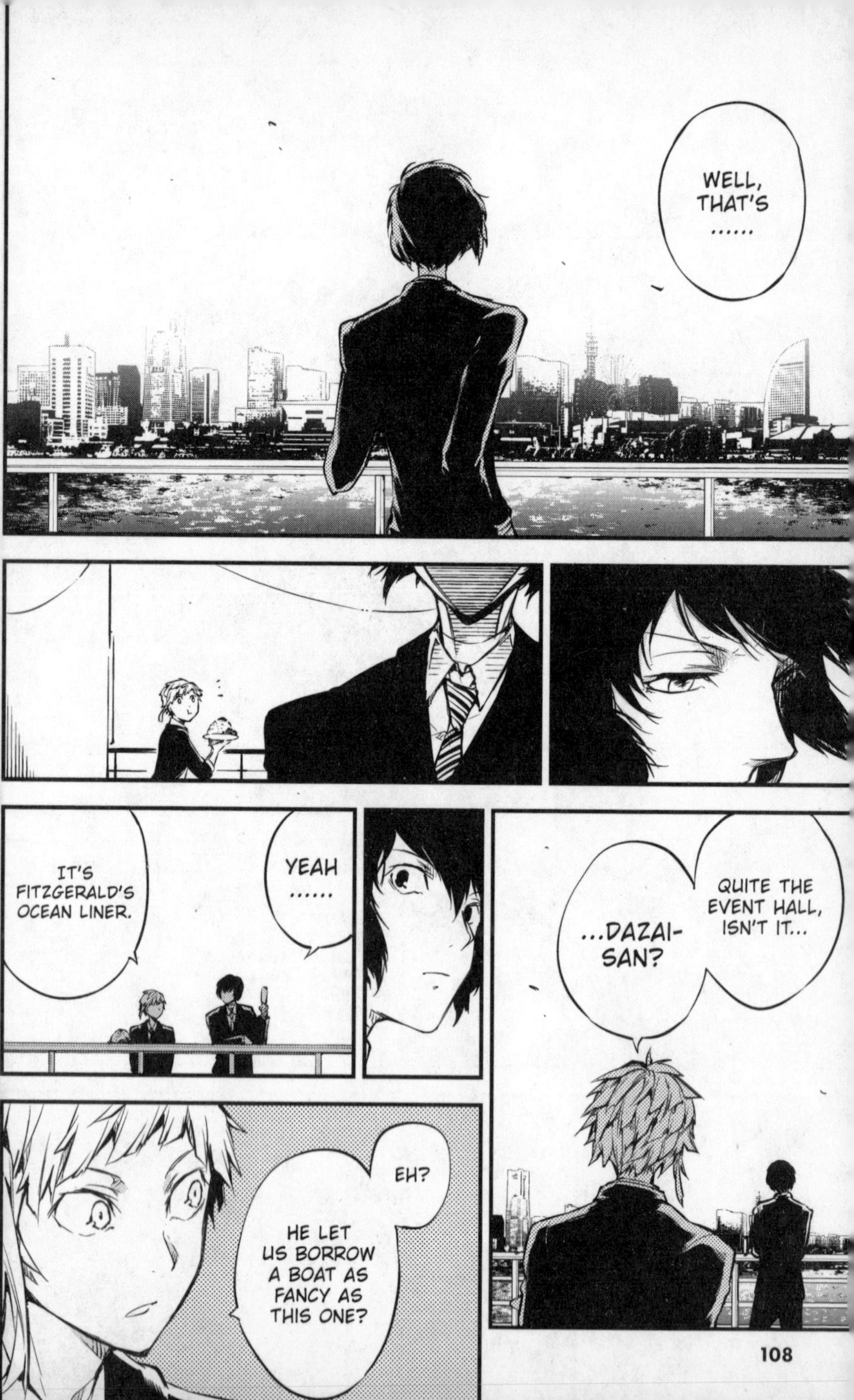
WELL, THAT'S ......
QUITE THE EVENT HALL, ISN'T IT...
...DAZAI-SAN?
YEAH ......
IT'S FITZGERALD'S OCEAN LINER.
EH?
HE LET US BORROW A BOAT AS FANCY AS THIS ONE?

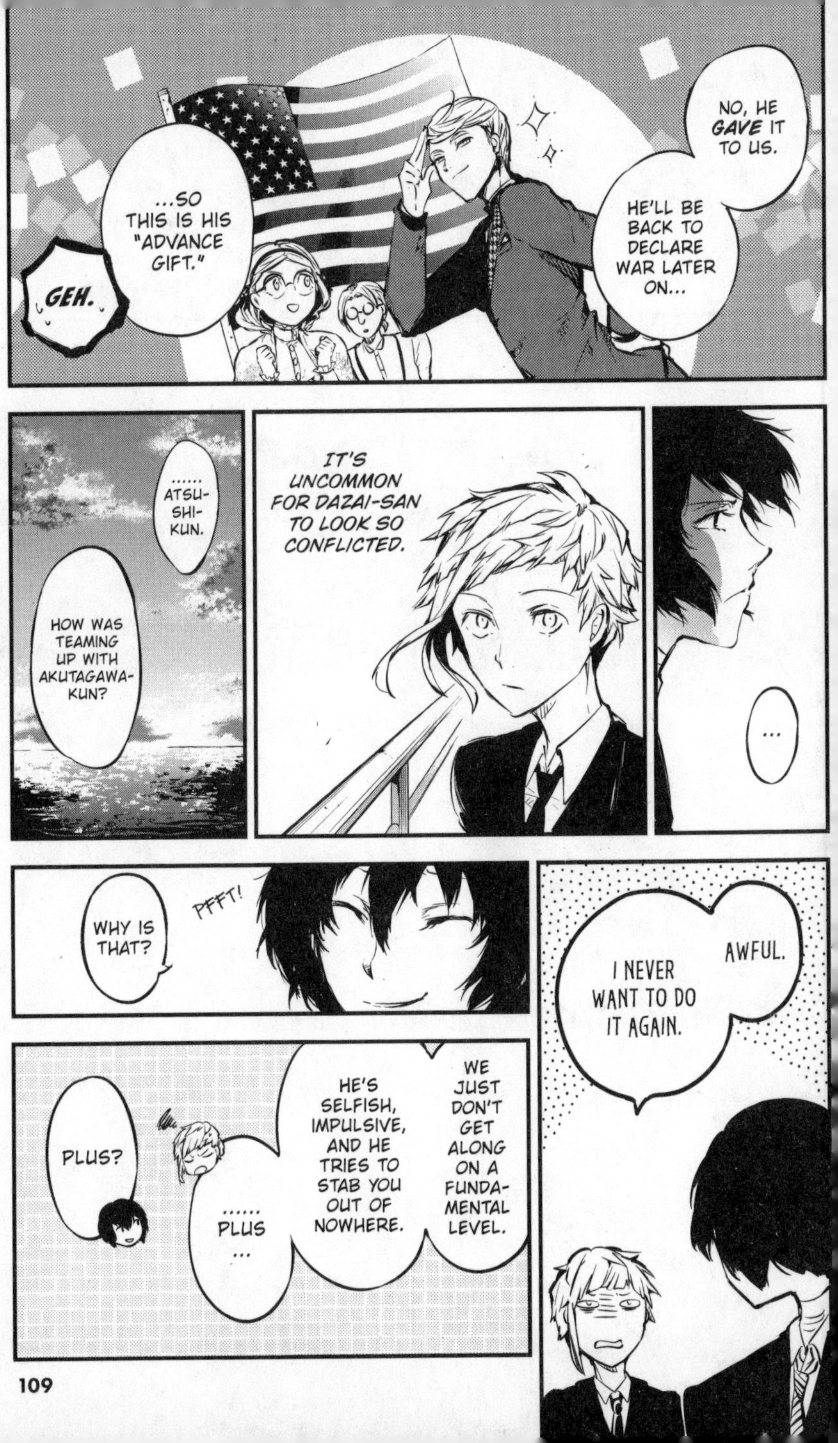
NO, HE *GAVE* IT TO US.
HE'LL BE BACK TO DECLARE WAR LATER ON...
...SO THIS IS HIS "ADVANCE GIFT."
GEH.
...
IT'S UNCOMMON FOR DAZAI-SAN TO LOOK SO CONFLICTED.
......ATSUSHI-KUN.
HOW WAS TEAMING UP WITH AKUTAGAWA-KUN?
AWFUL.
I NEVER WANT TO DO IT AGAIN.
PFFT!
WHY IS THAT?
WE JUST DON'T GET ALONG ON A FUNDAMENTAL LEVEL.
HE'S SELFISH, IMPULSIVE, AND HE TRIES TO STAB YOU OUT OF NOWHERE.
......PLUS...
PLUS?

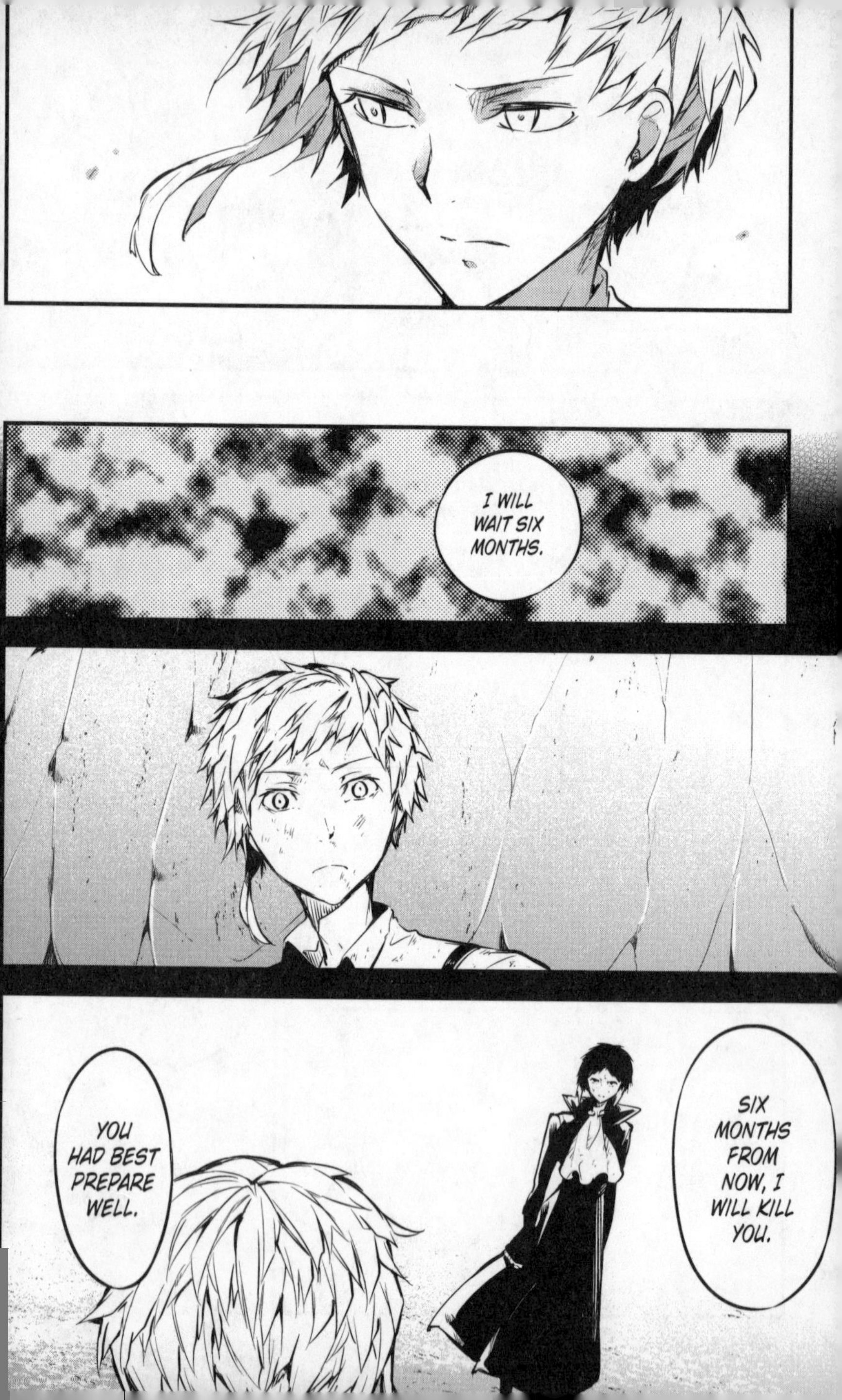
I WILL WAIT SIX MONTHS.
SIX MONTHS FROM NOW, I WILL KILL YOU.
YOU HAD BEST PREPARE WELL.

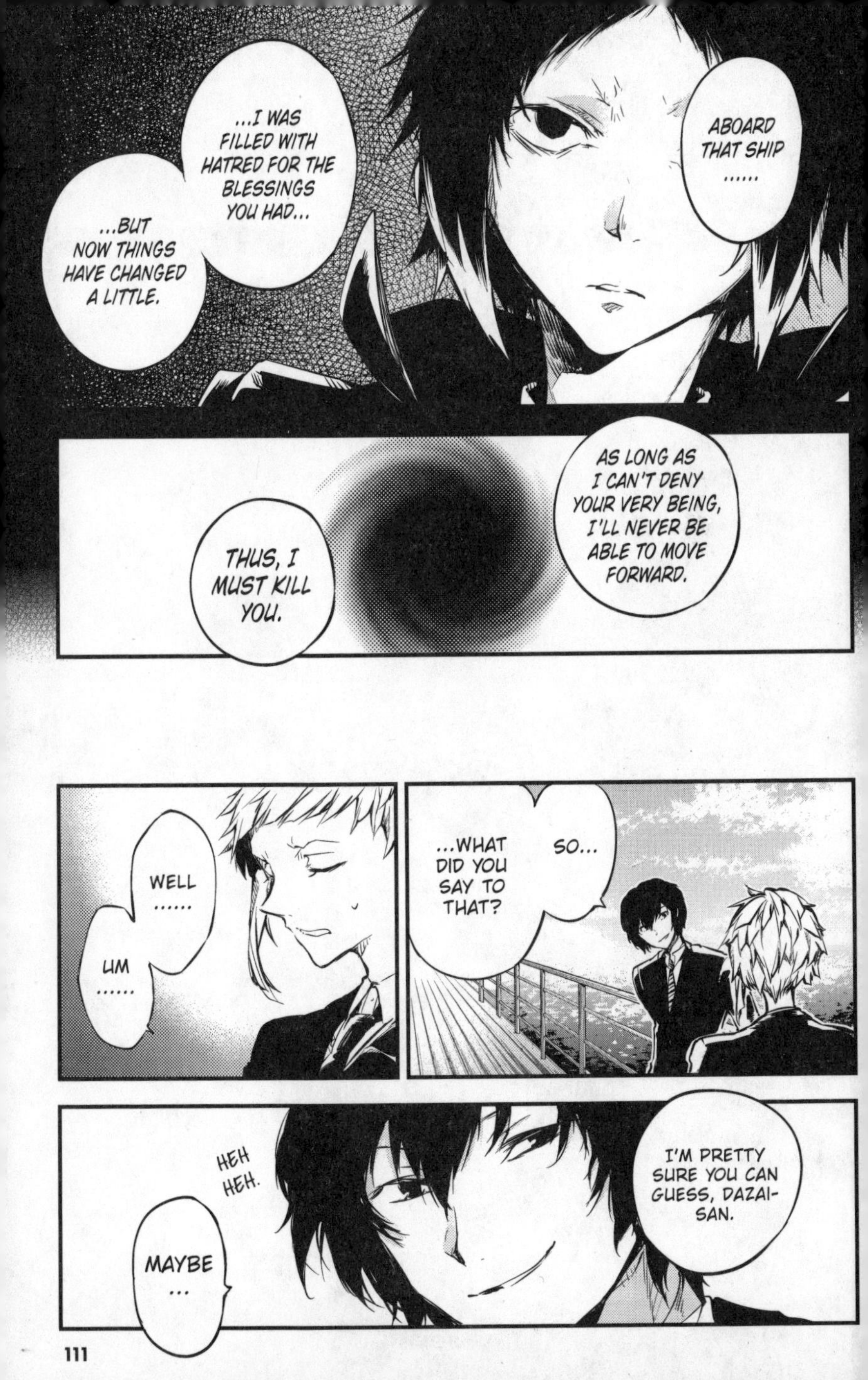
ABOARD THAT SHIP ......
...I WAS FILLED WITH HATRED FOR THE BLESSINGS YOU HAD...
...BUT NOW THINGS HAVE CHANGED A LITTLE.
AS LONG AS I CAN'T DENY YOUR VERY BEING, I'LL NEVER BE ABLE TO MOVE FORWARD.
THUS, I MUST KILL YOU.
SO...
...WHAT DID YOU SAY TO THAT?
WELL ......
UM ......
I'M PRETTY SURE YOU CAN GUESS, DAZAI-SAN.
HEH HEH.
MAYBE ...

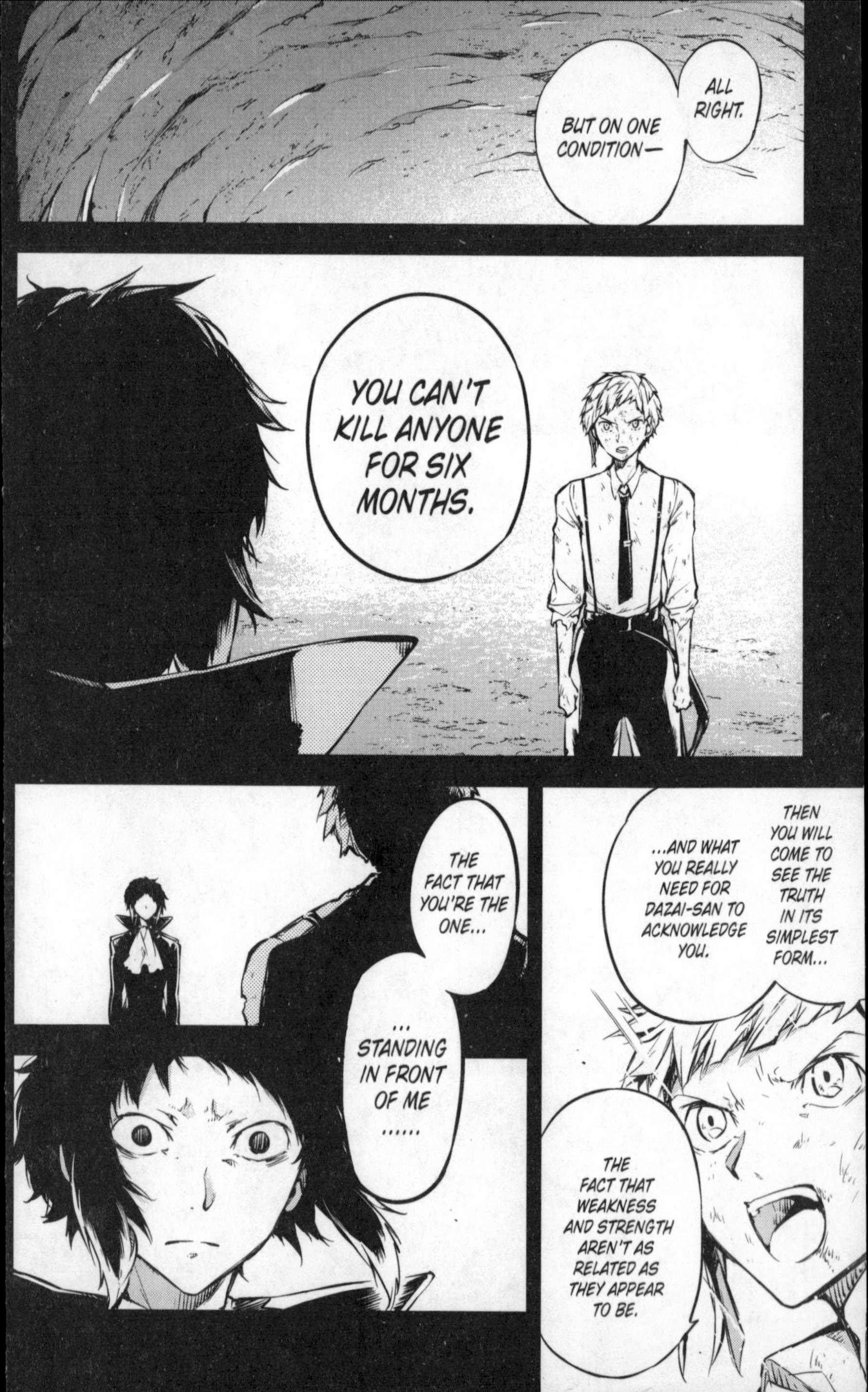
ALL RIGHT.
BUT ON ONE CONDITION—
YOU CAN'T KILL ANYONE FOR SIX MONTHS.
THEN YOU WILL COME TO SEE THE TRUTH IN ITS SIMPLEST FORM...
...AND WHAT YOU REALLY NEED FOR DAZAI-SAN TO ACKNOWLEDGE YOU.
THE FACT THAT WEAKNESS AND STRENGTH AREN'T AS RELATED AS THEY APPEAR TO BE.
THE FACT THAT YOU'RE THE ONE...
... STANDING IN FRONT OF ME ......

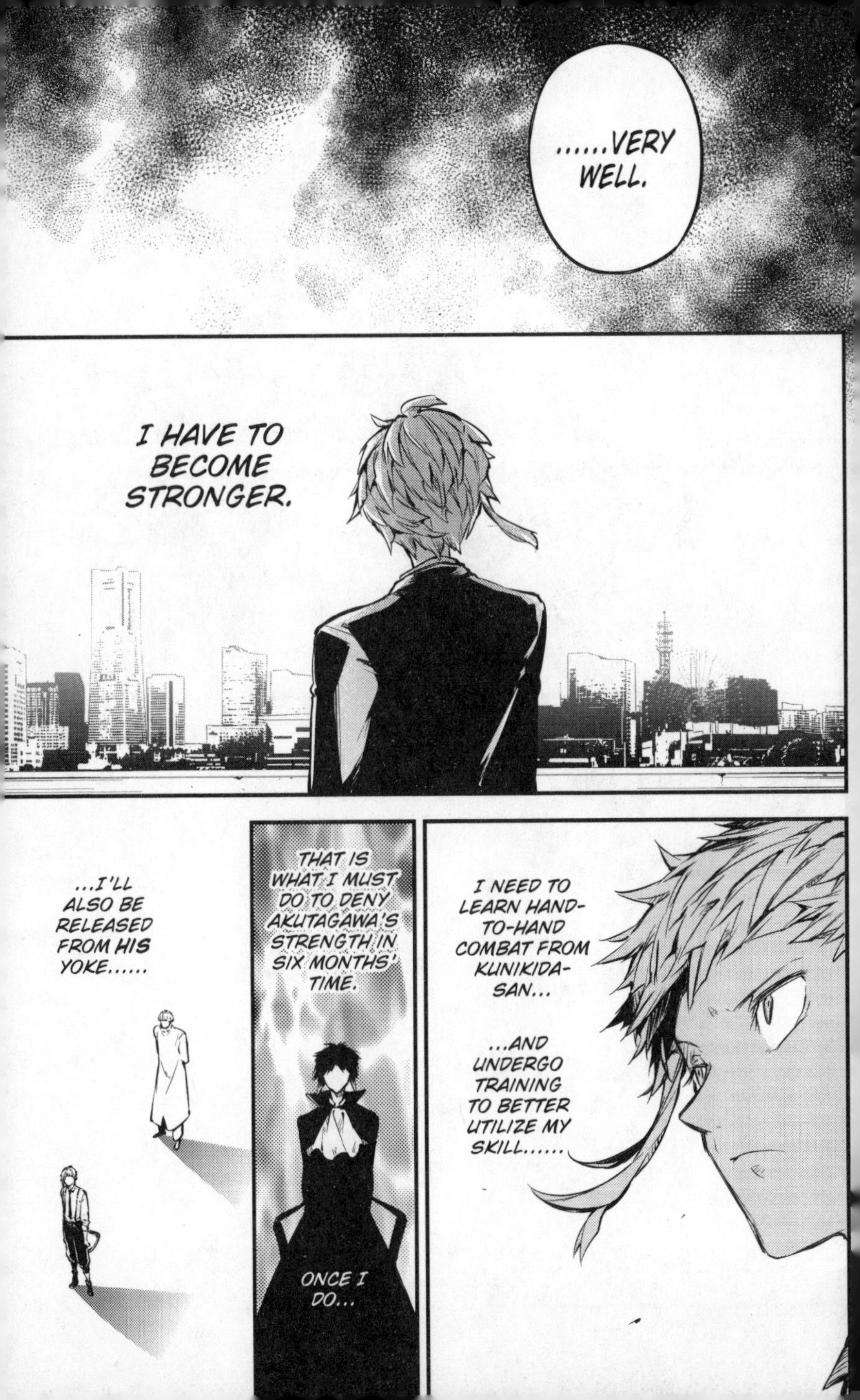
......VERY WELL.
I HAVE TO BECOME STRONGER.
I NEED TO LEARN HAND-TO-HAND COMBAT FROM KUNIKIDA-SAN...
...AND UNDERGO TRAINING TO BETTER UTILIZE MY SKILL......
THAT IS WHAT I MUST DO TO DENY AKUTAGAWA'S STRENGTH IN SIX MONTHS' TIME.
ONCE I DO...
...I'LL ALSO BE RELEASED FROM HIS YOKE......

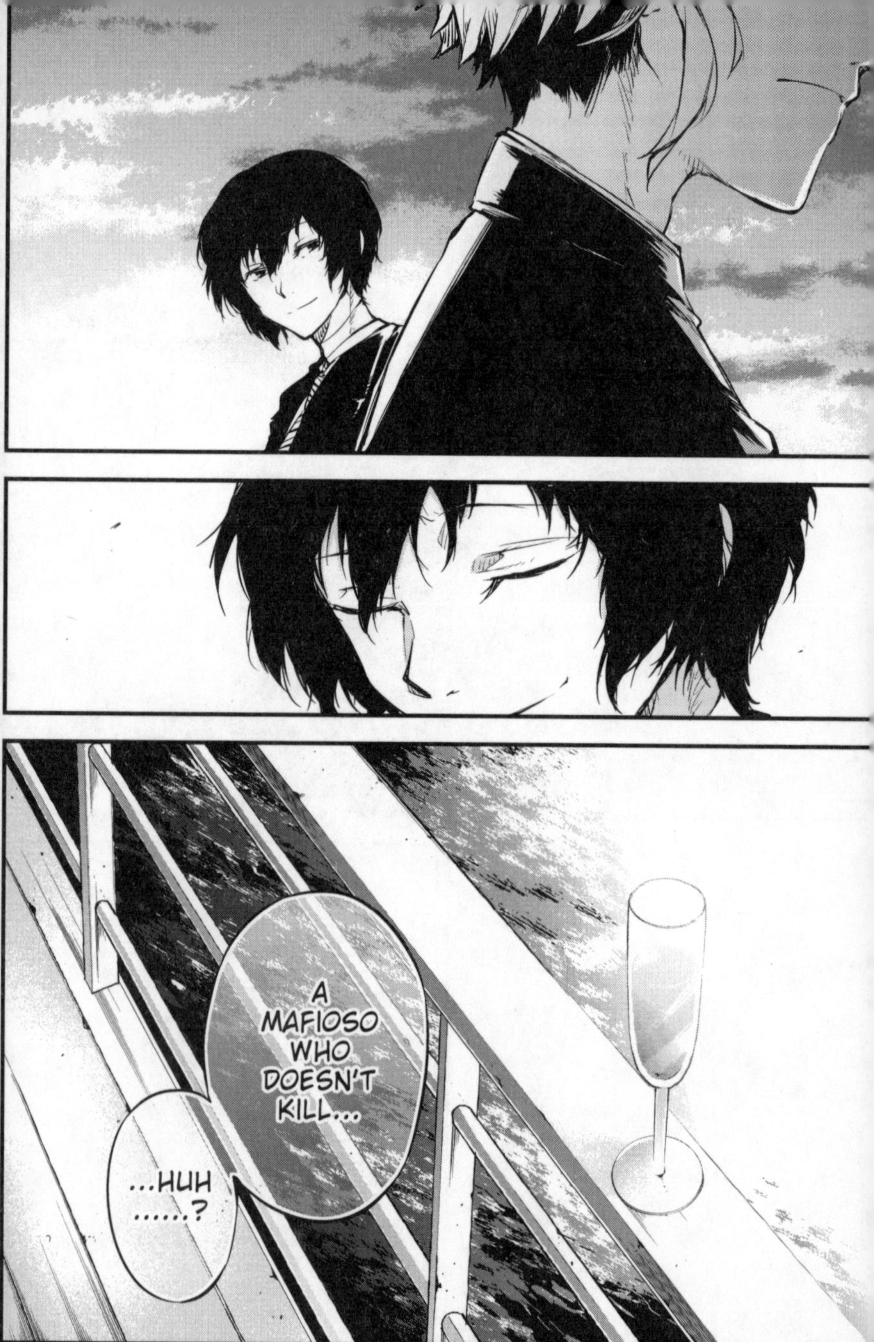
A MAFIOSO WHO DOESN'T KILL...
...HUH ......?

LOUISA MAY ALCOTT

SKILL: Little Women
When thinking alone in a room, time passes at 1/8000th the normal speed for her.

AGE: *18*

BIRTH DATE: *November 29*

HEIGHT: *165cm*

WEIGHT: *50kg*

BLOOD TYPE: *O*

LIKES: *The country, nature, printed type, books*

DISLIKES: *Cities, discrimination, being in public*

BUNGO STRAY DOGS

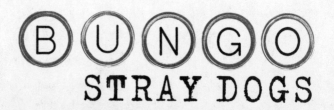

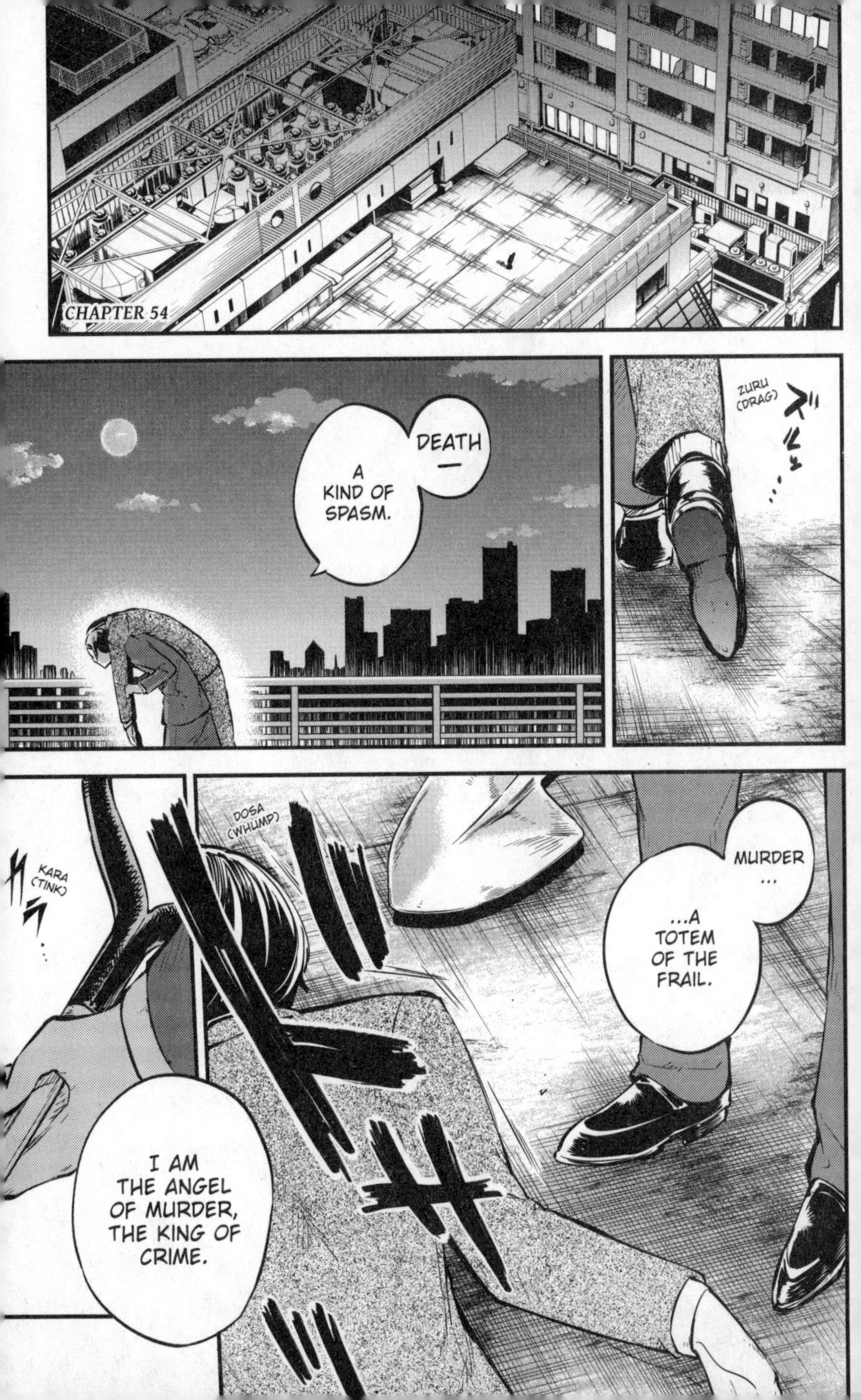
CHAPTER 54
ZURU (DRAG)
DEATH — A KIND OF SPASM.
MURDER ... ...A TOTEM OF THE FRAIL.
DOSA (WHUMP)
KARA (TINK)
I AM THE ANGEL OF MURDER, THE KING OF CRIME.

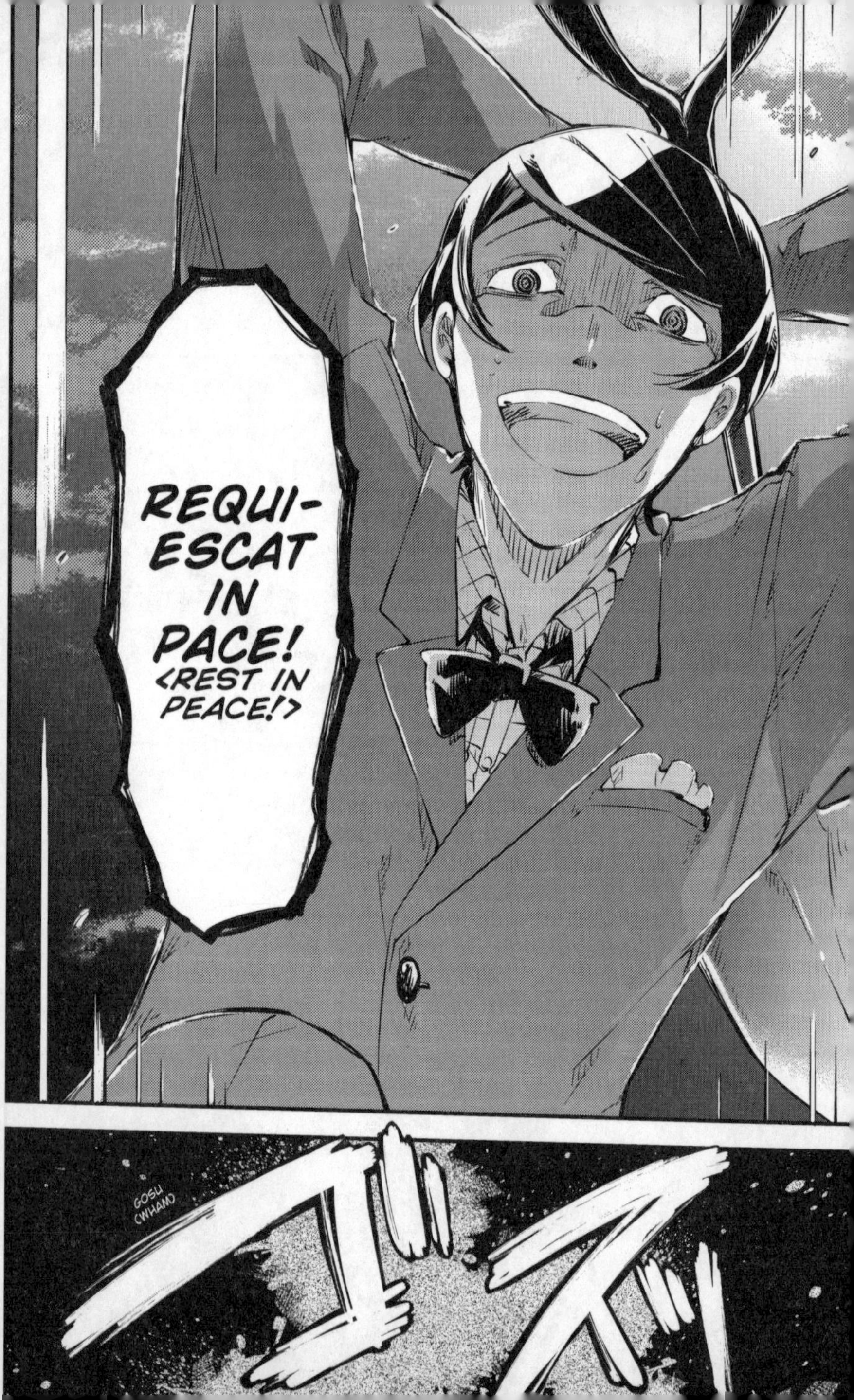
REQUIESCAT IN PACE! <REST IN PEACE!>
GOSU (WHAM)

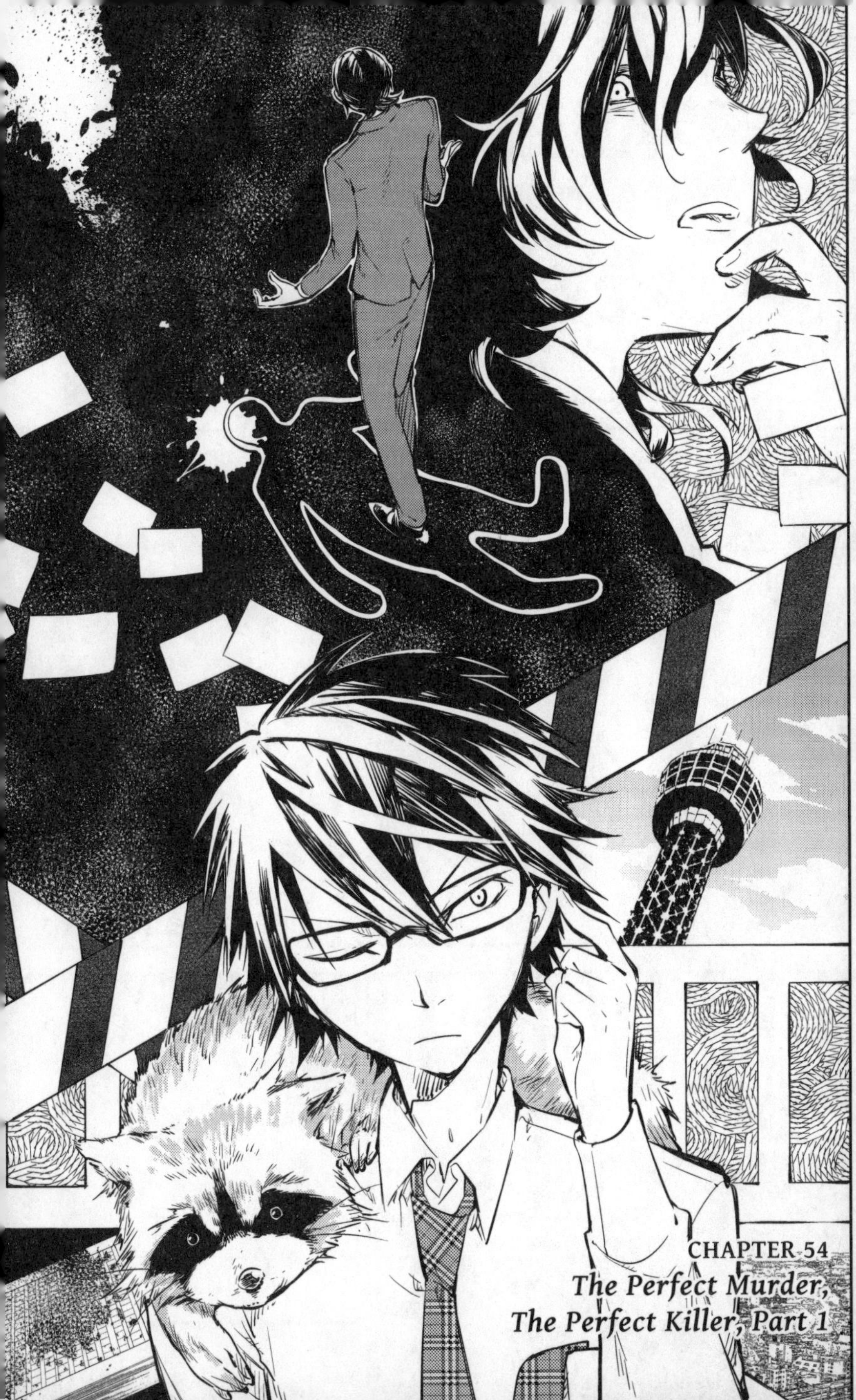
CHAPTER 54
The Perfect Murder,
The Perfect Killer, Part 1

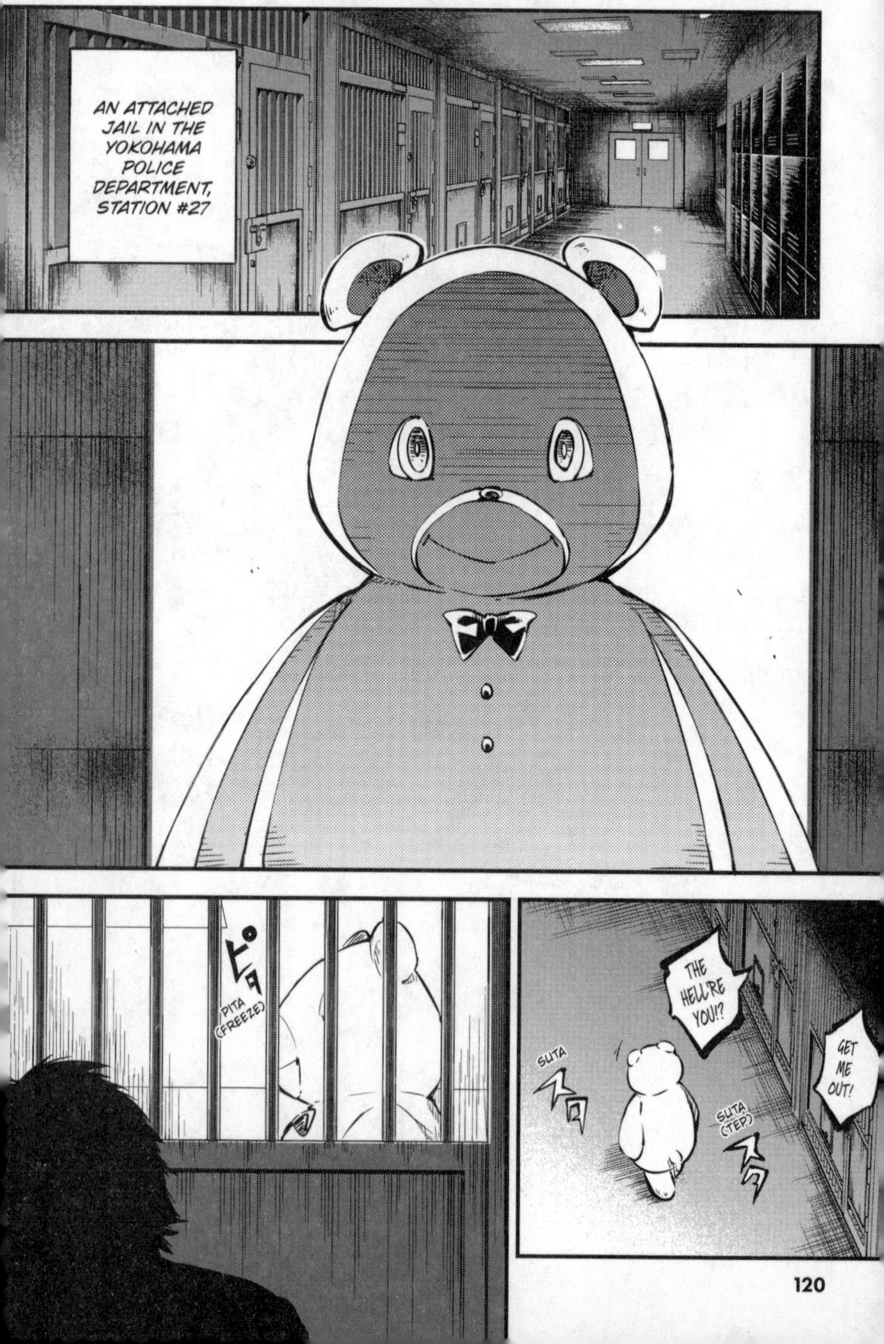
AN ATTACHED JAIL IN THE YOKOHAMA POLICE DEPARTMENT, STATION #27
THE HELL'RE YOU!?
GET ME OUT!
SUTA (TEP)
SUTA
PITA (FREEZE)

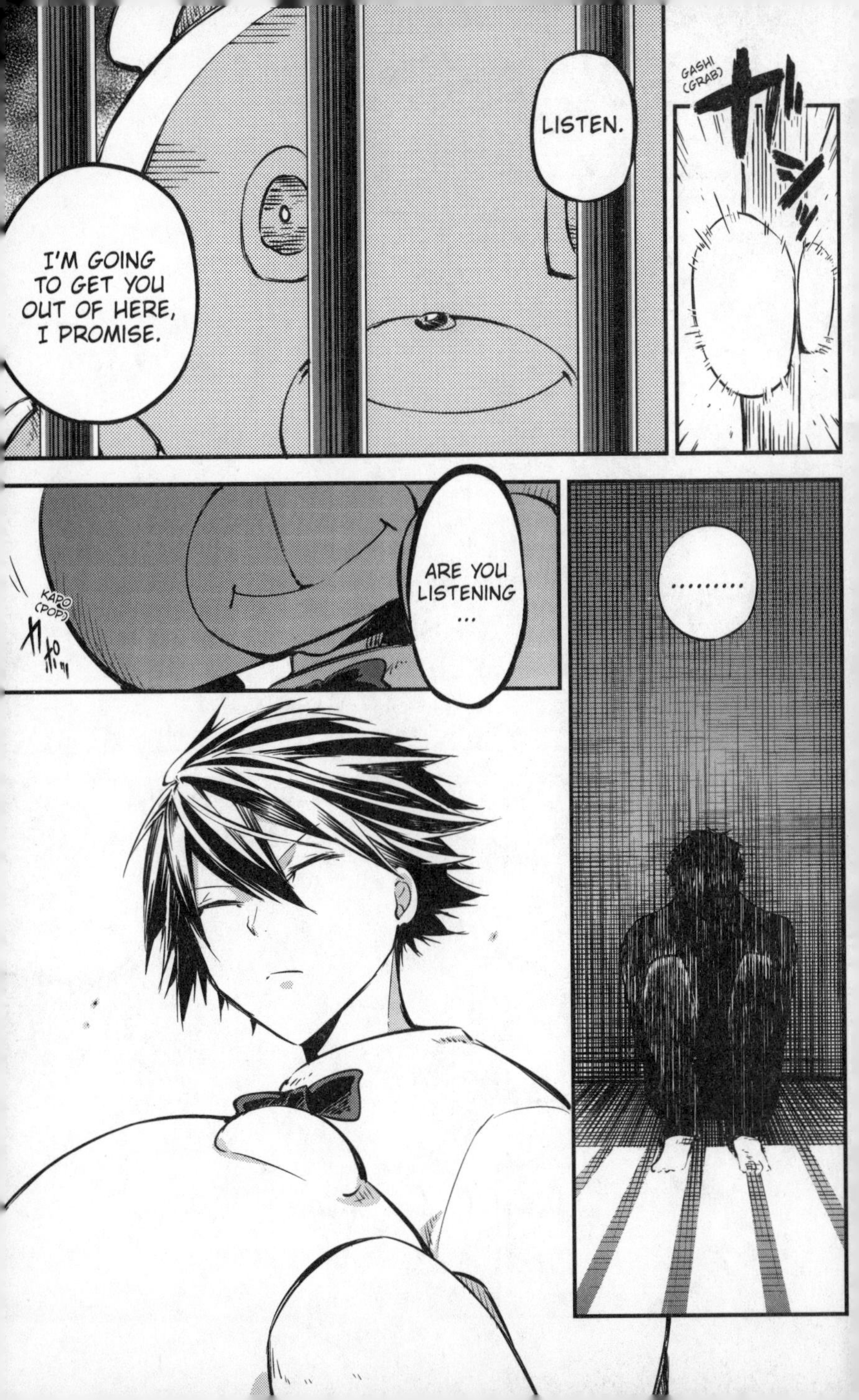
GASHI (GRAB)
LISTEN.
I'M GOING TO GET YOU OUT OF HERE, I PROMISE.
....
ARE YOU LISTENING ...
KAPO (POP)

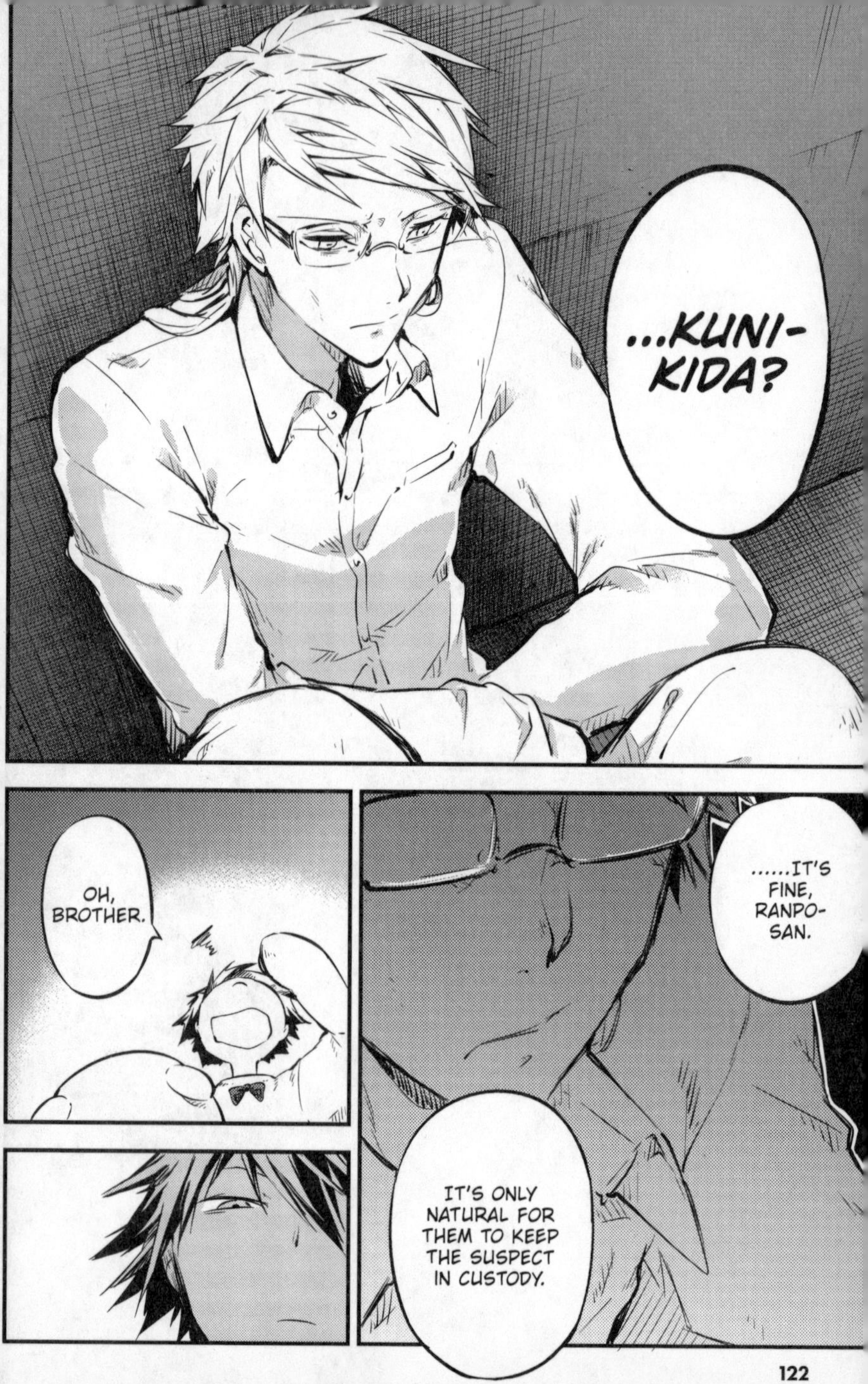
...KUNI-KIDA?
......IT'S FINE, RANPO-SAN.
IT'S ONLY NATURAL FOR THEM TO KEEP THE SUSPECT IN CUSTODY.
OH, BROTHER.

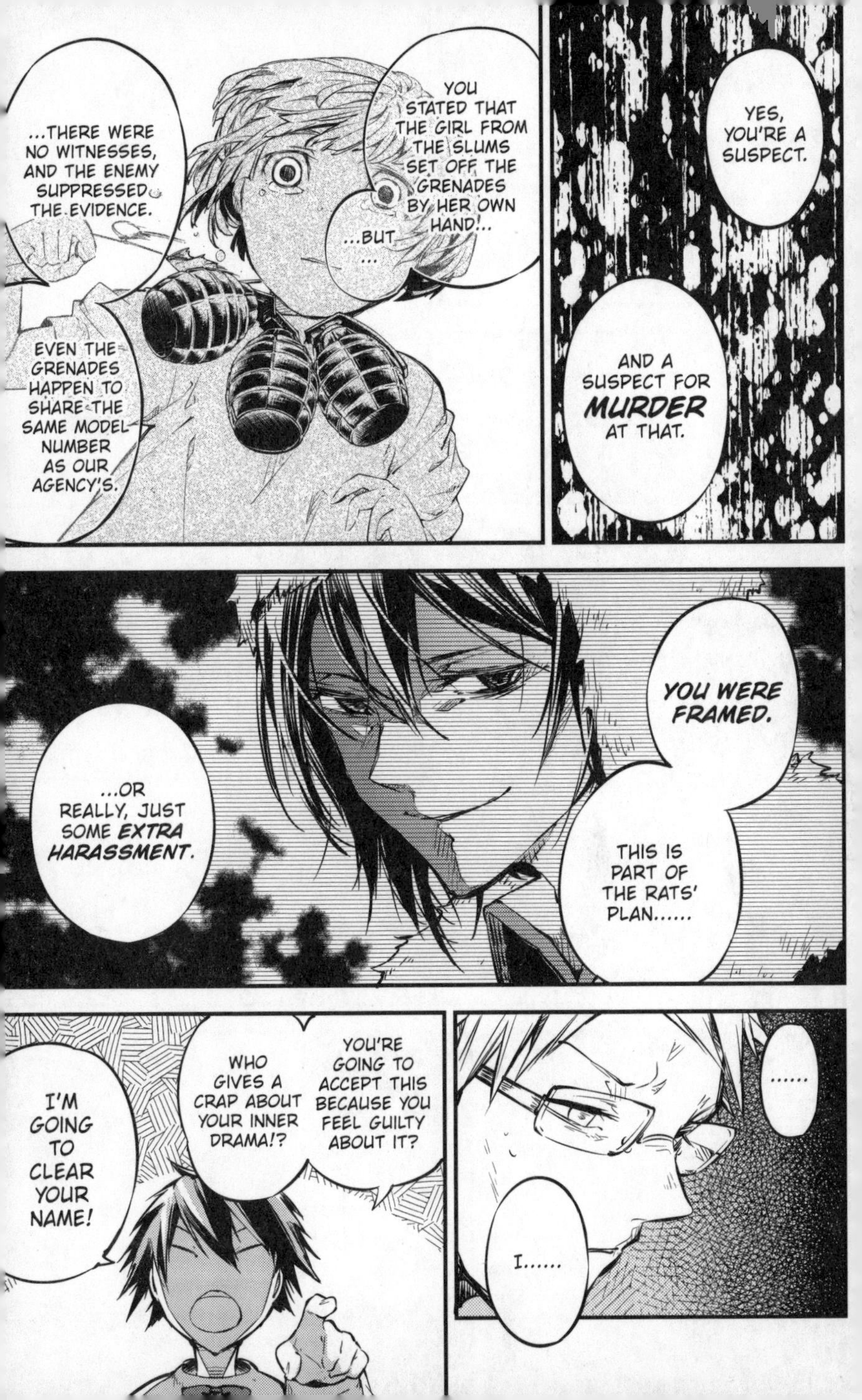
YES, YOU'RE A SUSPECT.
AND A SUSPECT FOR **MURDER** AT THAT.
YOU STATED THAT THE GIRL FROM THE SLUMS SET OFF THE GRENADES BY HER OWN HAND!...
...BUT ...
...THERE WERE NO WITNESSES, AND THE ENEMY SUPPRESSED THE EVIDENCE.
EVEN THE GRENADES HAPPEN TO SHARE THE SAME MODEL NUMBER AS OUR AGENCY'S.
YOU WERE FRAMED.
THIS IS PART OF THE RATS' PLAN......
...OR REALLY, JUST SOME ***EXTRA HARASSMENT***.
......
I......
YOU'RE GOING TO ACCEPT THIS BECAUSE YOU FEEL GUILTY ABOUT IT?
WHO GIVES A CRAP ABOUT YOUR INNER DRAMA!?
I'M GOING TO CLEAR YOUR NAME!

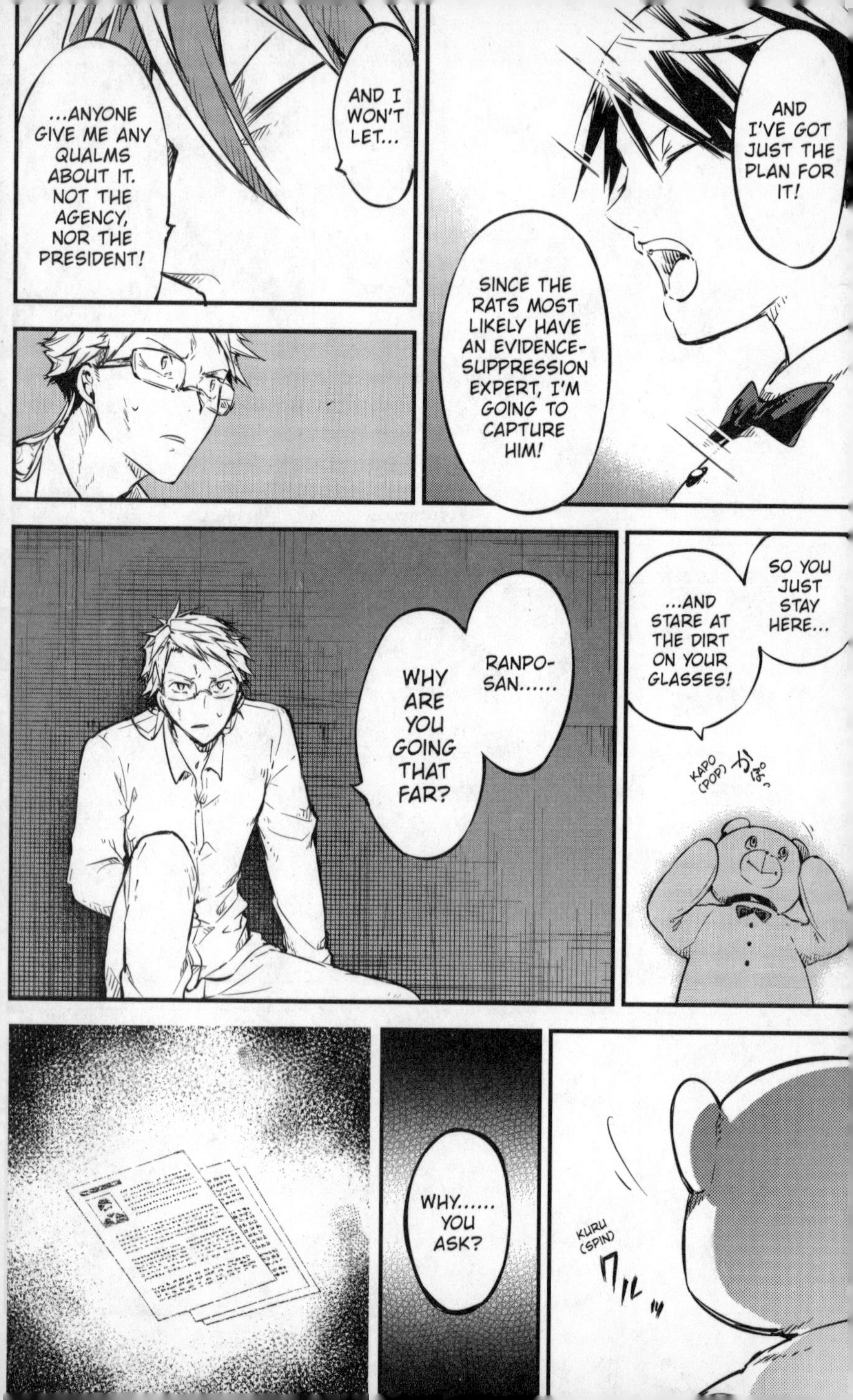
AND I'VE GOT JUST THE PLAN FOR IT!
SINCE THE RATS MOST LIKELY HAVE AN EVIDENCE-SUPPRESSION EXPERT, I'M GOING TO CAPTURE HIM!
AND I WON'T LET...
...ANYONE GIVE ME ANY QUALMS ABOUT IT. NOT THE AGENCY, NOR THE PRESIDENT!
SO YOU JUST STAY HERE...
...AND STARE AT THE DIRT ON YOUR GLASSES!
KAPO (POP)
かぽっ
RANPO-SAN......
WHY ARE YOU GOING THAT FAR?
KURU (SPIN)
クル
WHY...... YOU ASK?

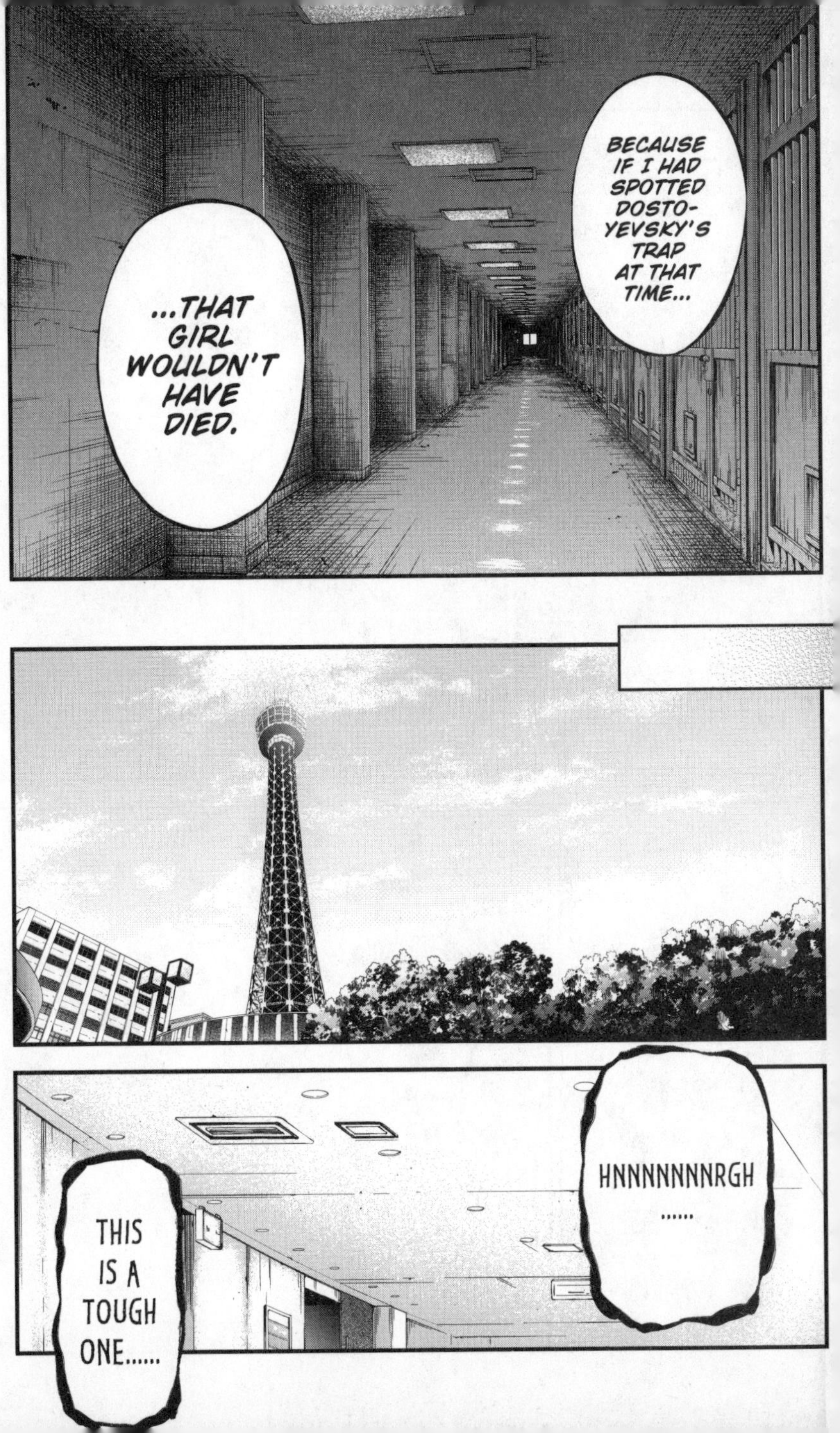
BECAUSE IF I HAD SPOTTED DOSTO-YEVSKY'S TRAP AT THAT TIME...
...THAT GIRL WOULDN'T HAVE DIED.
HNNNNNNNRGH ......
THIS IS A TOUGH ONE......

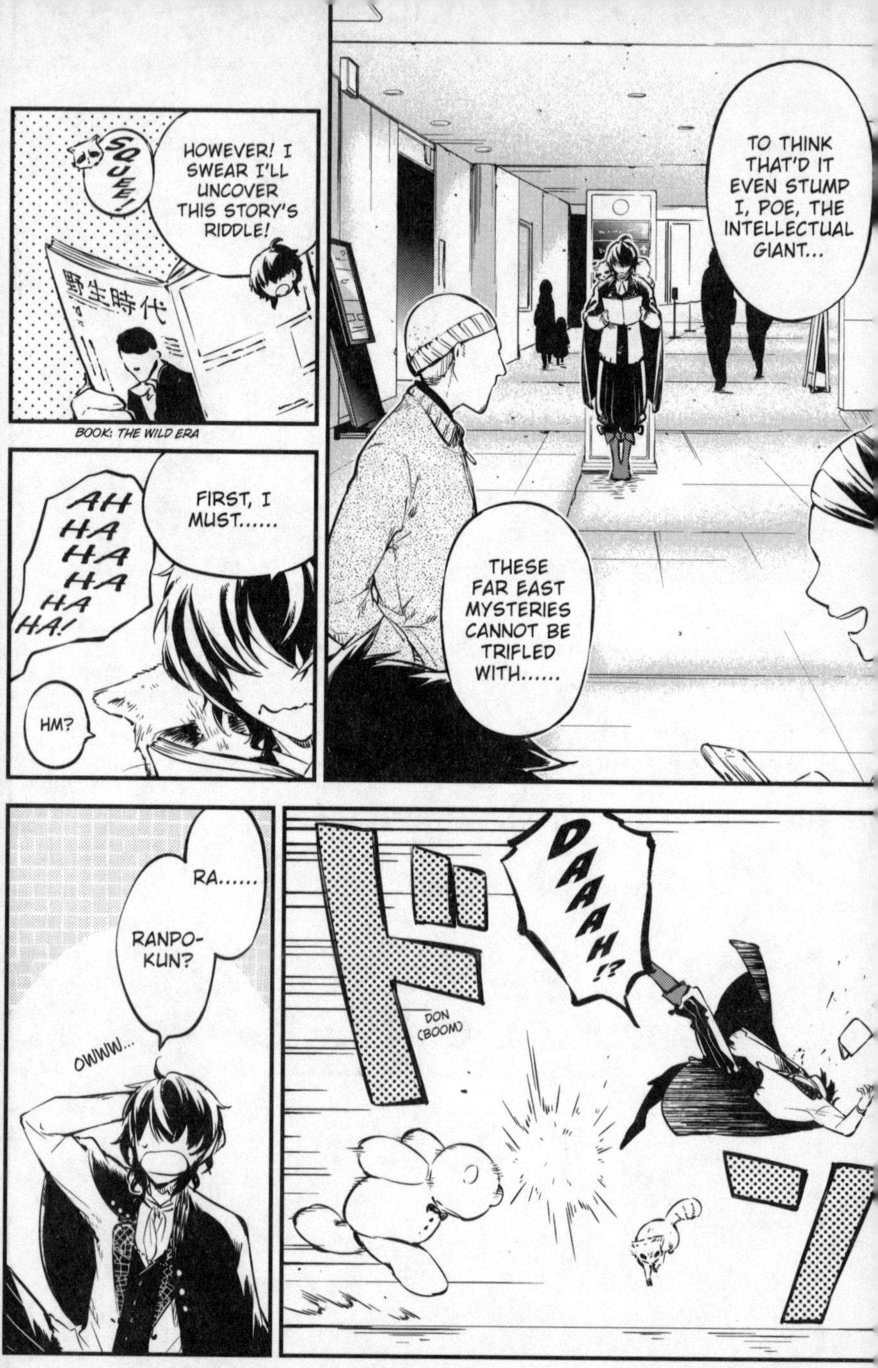
TO THINK THAT'D IT EVEN STUMP I, POE, THE INTELLECTUAL GIANT...
THESE FAR EAST MYSTERIES CANNOT BE TRIFLED WITH......
SQUEE!
HOWEVER! I SWEAR I'LL UNCOVER THIS STORY'S RIDDLE!
野生時代
BOOK: THE WILD ERA
FIRST, I MUST......
AH HA HA HA HA HA!
HM?
DAAAH!?
DON (BOOM)
RA......
RANPO-KUN?
OWWW...

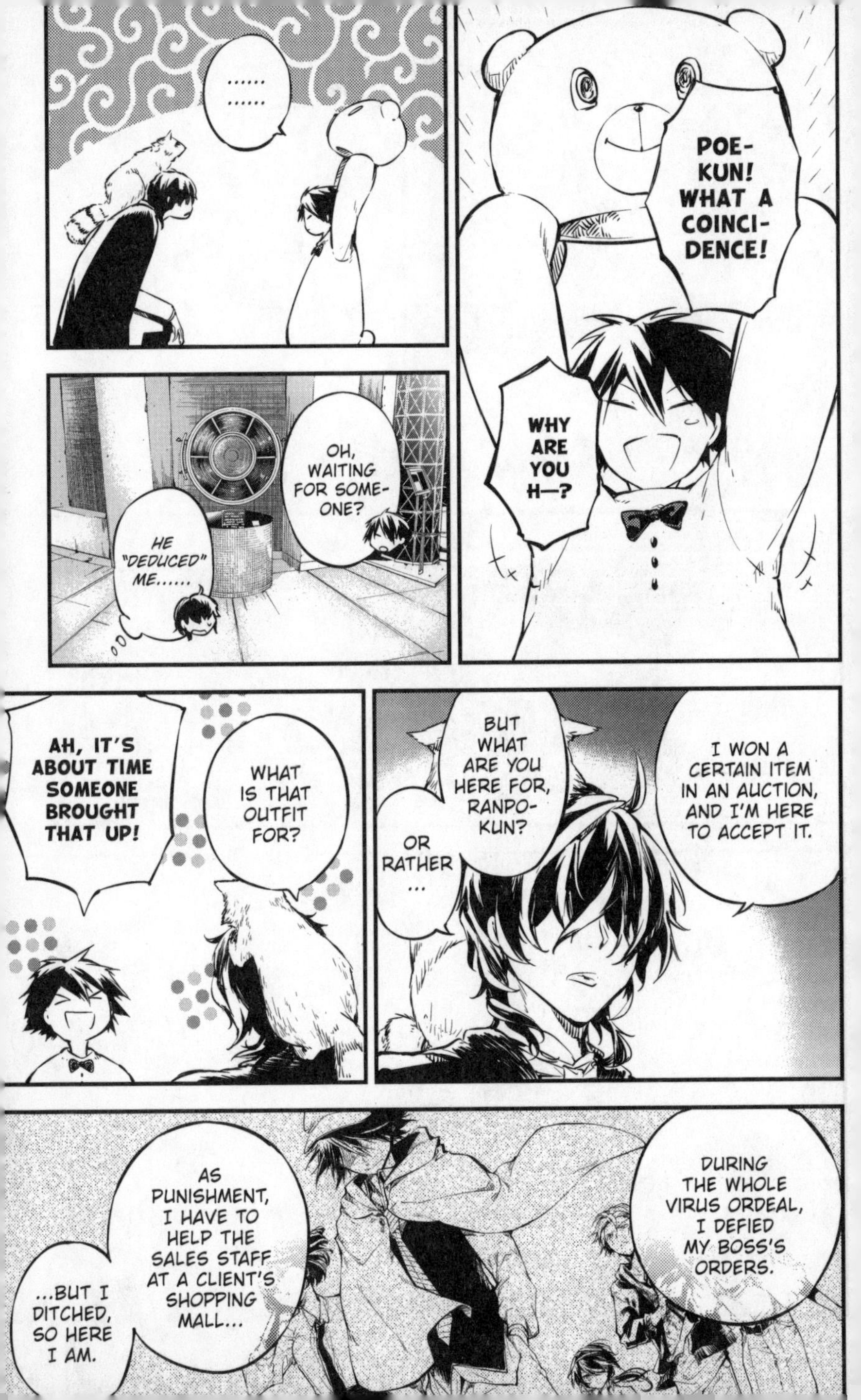
POE-KUN! WHAT A COINCI-DENCE!
WHY ARE YOU H—?
....
OH, WAITING FOR SOME-ONE?
HE "DEDUCED" ME......
BUT WHAT ARE YOU HERE FOR, RANPO-KUN?
I WON A CERTAIN ITEM IN AN AUCTION, AND I'M HERE TO ACCEPT IT.
OR RATHER ...
WHAT IS THAT OUTFIT FOR?
AH, IT'S ABOUT TIME SOMEONE BROUGHT THAT UP!
DURING THE WHOLE VIRUS ORDEAL, I DEFIED MY BOSS'S ORDERS.
AS PUNISHMENT, I HAVE TO HELP THE SALES STAFF AT A CLIENT'S SHOPPING MALL...
...BUT I DITCHED, SO HERE I AM.

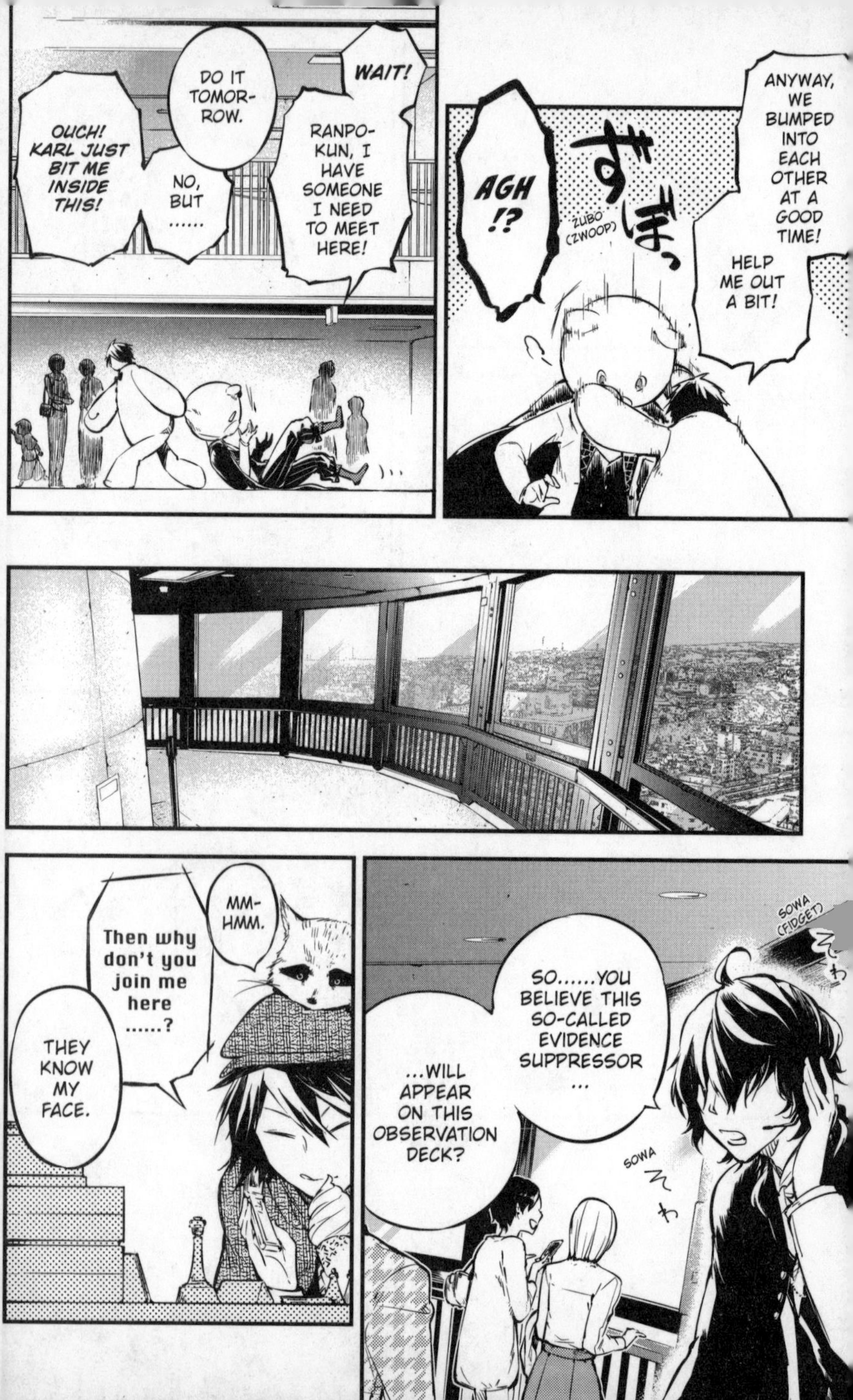
ANYWAY, WE BUMPED INTO EACH OTHER AT A GOOD TIME!
HELP ME OUT A BIT!
ZUBO (ZWOOP)
AGH!?
WAIT!
DO IT TOMORROW.
RANPO-KUN, I HAVE SOMEONE I NEED TO MEET HERE!
NO, BUT ......
OUCH! KARL JUST BIT ME INSIDE THIS!
SOWA (FIDGET)
SO......YOU BELIEVE THIS SO-CALLED EVIDENCE SUPPRESSOR ...
...WILL APPEAR ON THIS OBSERVATION DECK?
SOWA
MM-HMM.
Then why don't you join me here ......?
THEY KNOW MY FACE.

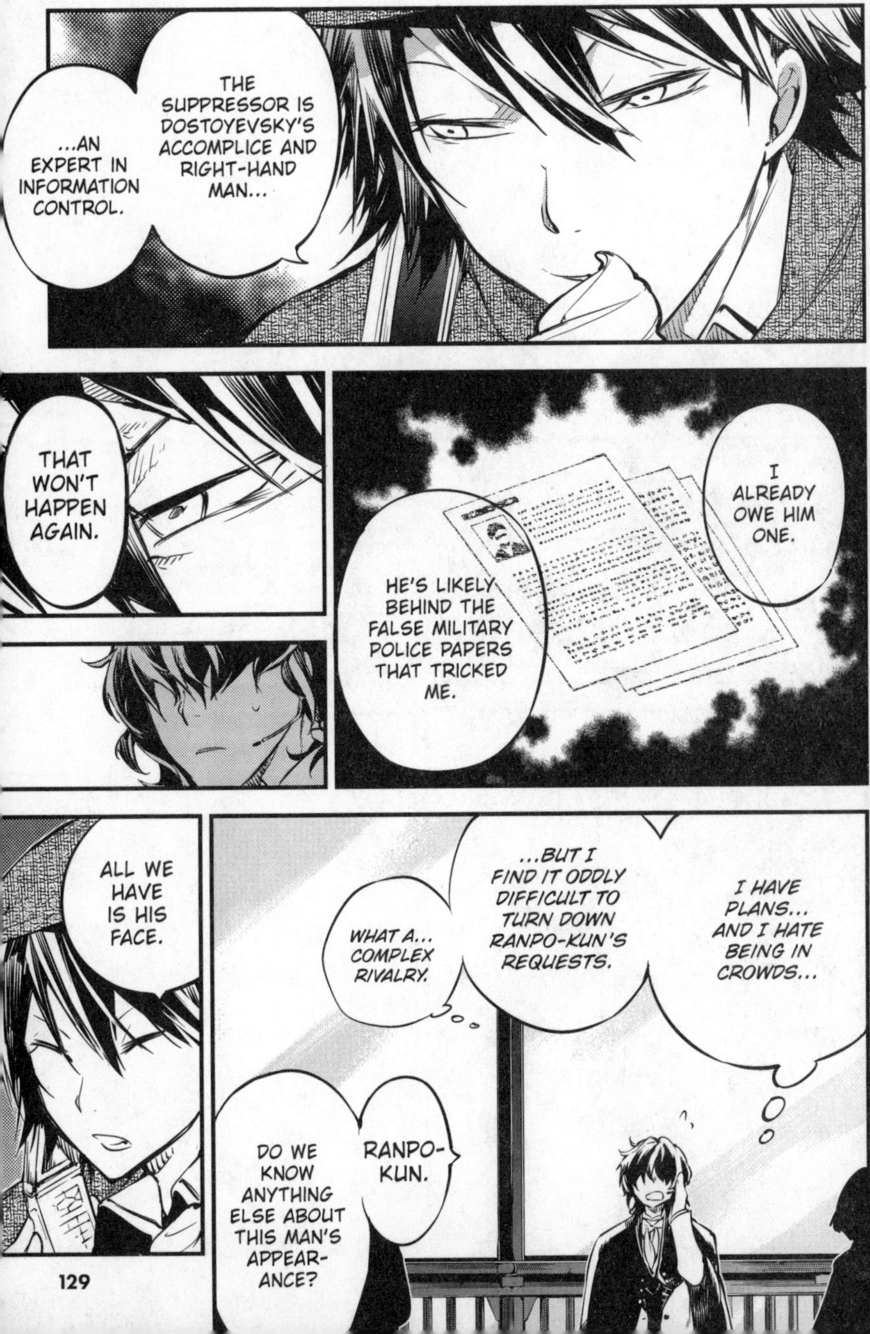
THE SUPPRESSOR IS DOSTOYEVSKY'S ACCOMPLICE AND RIGHT-HAND MAN...
...AN EXPERT IN INFORMATION CONTROL.
I ALREADY OWE HIM ONE.
HE'S LIKELY BEHIND THE FALSE MILITARY POLICE PAPERS THAT TRICKED ME.
THAT WON'T HAPPEN AGAIN.
I HAVE PLANS... AND I HATE BEING IN CROWDS...
...BUT I FIND IT ODDLY DIFFICULT TO TURN DOWN RANPO-KUN'S REQUESTS.
WHAT A... COMPLEX RIVALRY.
RANPO-KUN.
DO WE KNOW ANYTHING ELSE ABOUT THIS MAN'S APPEAR-ANCE?
ALL WE HAVE IS HIS FACE.

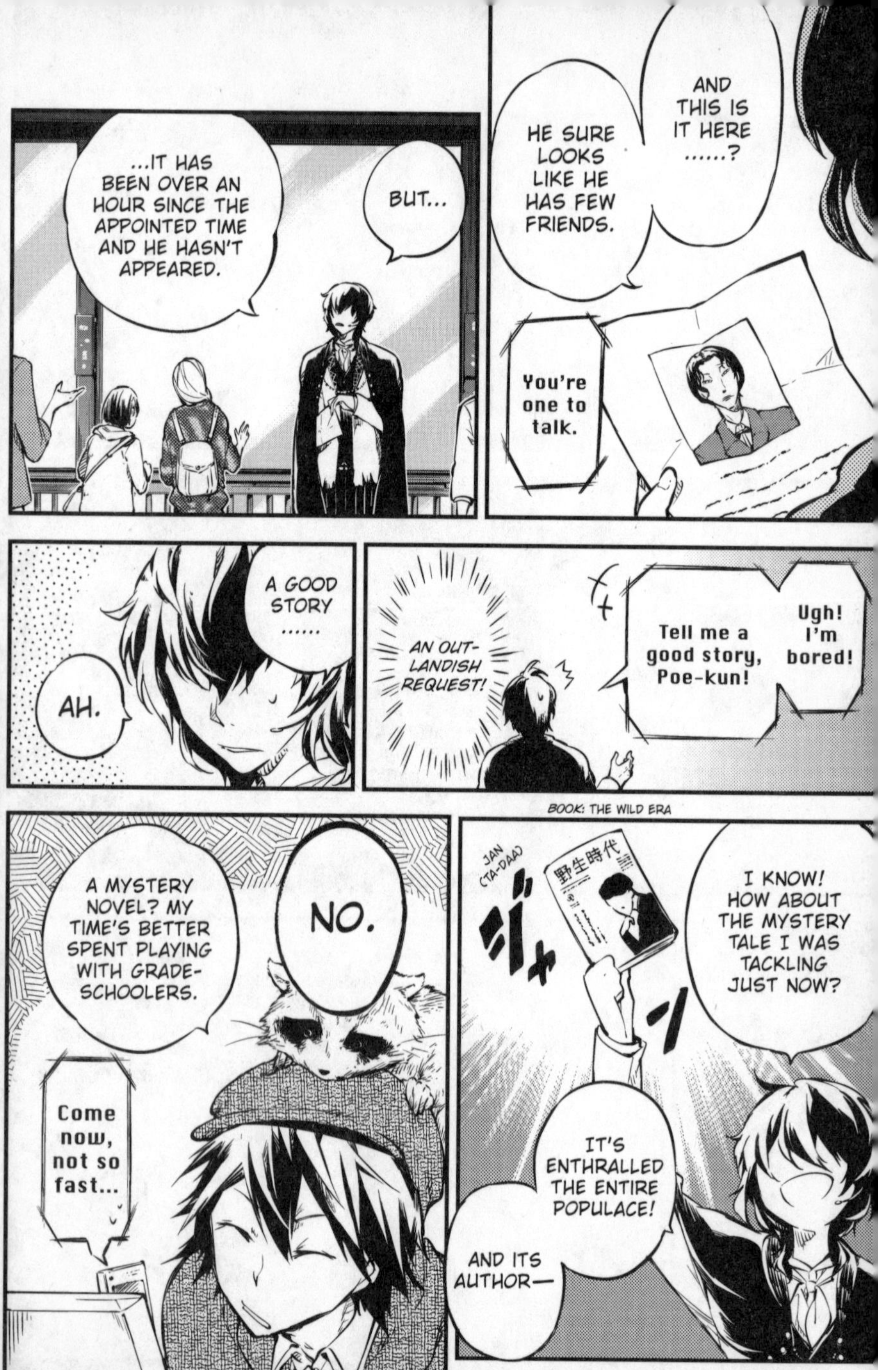
AND THIS IS IT HERE ......?
HE SURE LOOKS LIKE HE HAS FEW FRIENDS.
You're one to talk.
BUT...
...IT HAS BEEN OVER AN HOUR SINCE THE APPOINTED TIME AND HE HASN'T APPEARED.
Ugh! I'm bored!
Tell me a good story, Poe-kun!
AN OUT-LANDISH REQUEST!
A GOOD STORY ......
AH.
BOOK: THE WILD ERA
I KNOW! HOW ABOUT THE MYSTERY TALE I WAS TACKLING JUST NOW?
野生時代
JAN (TA-DAA)
IT'S ENTHRALLED THE ENTIRE POPULACE!
AND ITS AUTHOR—
NO.
A MYSTERY NOVEL? MY TIME'S BETTER SPENT PLAYING WITH GRADE-SCHOOLERS.
Come now, not so fast...

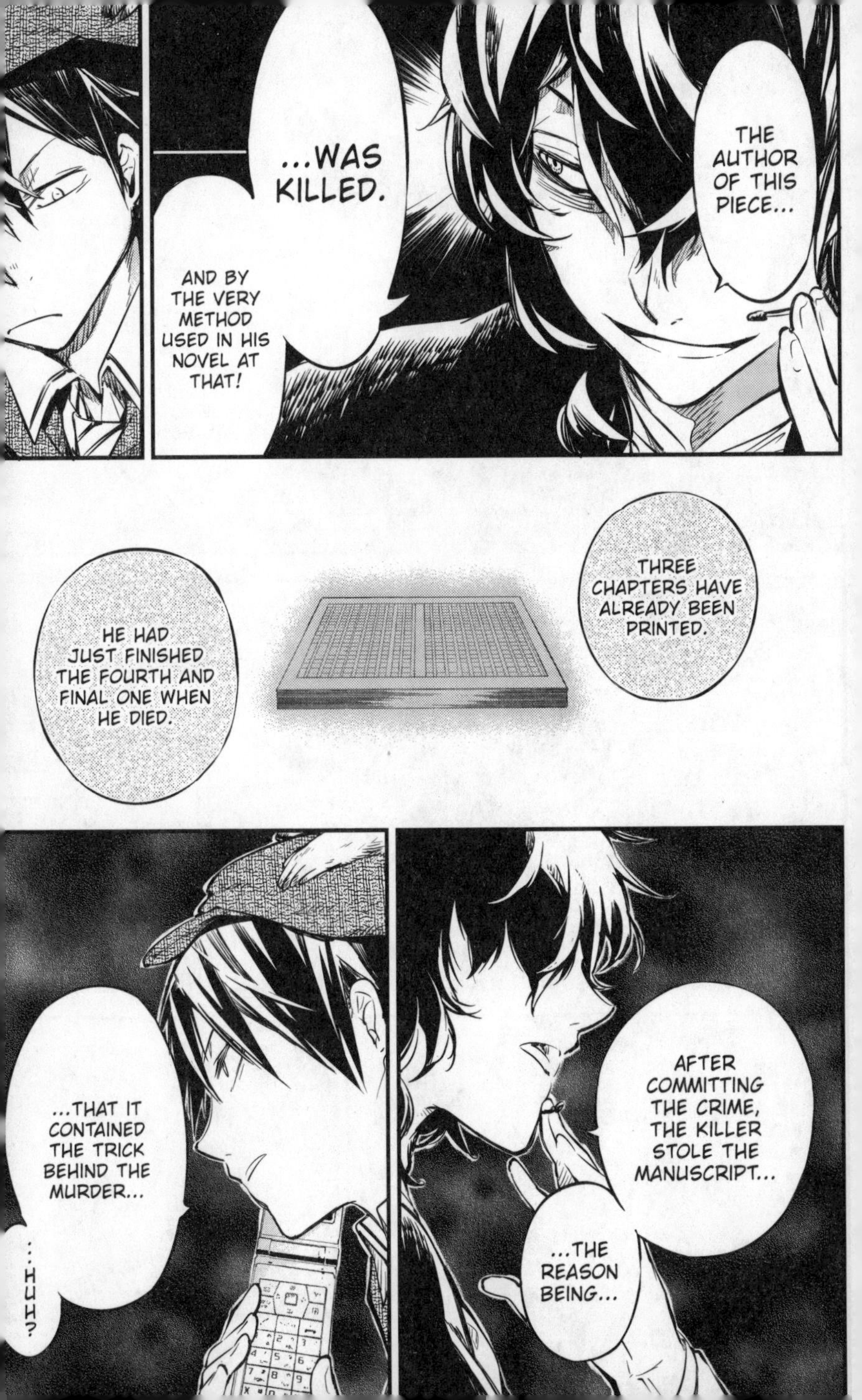
THE AUTHOR OF THIS PIECE...
...WAS KILLED.
AND BY THE VERY METHOD USED IN HIS NOVEL AT THAT!
THREE CHAPTERS HAVE ALREADY BEEN PRINTED.
HE HAD JUST FINISHED THE FOURTH AND FINAL ONE WHEN HE DIED.
AFTER COMMITTING THE CRIME, THE KILLER STOLE THE MANUSCRIPT...
...THE REASON BEING...
...THAT IT CONTAINED THE TRICK BEHIND THE MURDER...
...HUH?

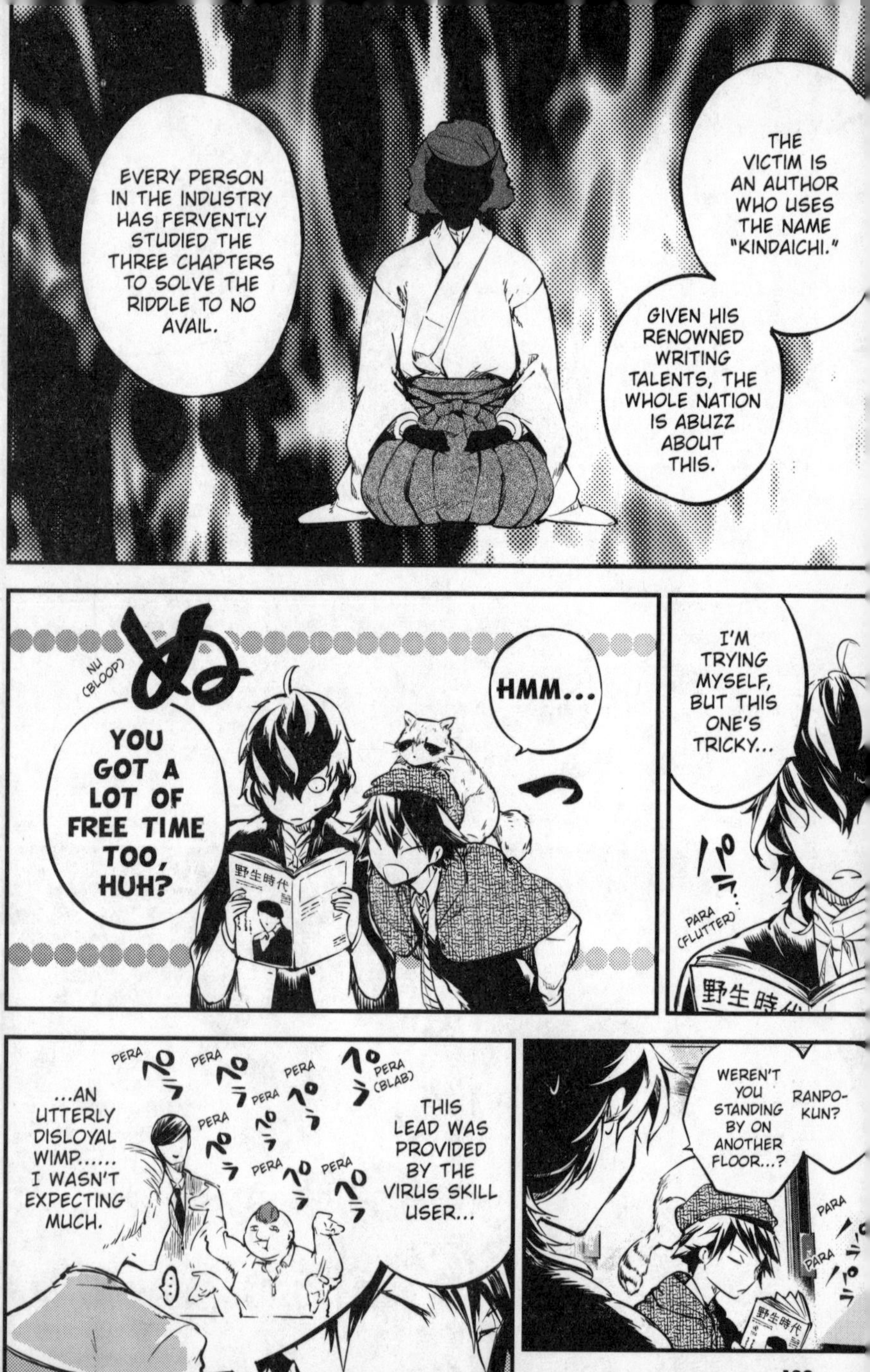
THE VICTIM IS AN AUTHOR WHO USES THE NAME "KINDAICHI."
GIVEN HIS RENOWNED WRITING TALENTS, THE WHOLE NATION IS ABUZZ ABOUT THIS.
EVERY PERSON IN THE INDUSTRY HAS FERVENTLY STUDIED THE THREE CHAPTERS TO SOLVE THE RIDDLE TO NO AVAIL.
I'M TRYING MYSELF, BUT THIS ONE'S TRICKY...
PARA (FLUTTER)
野生時代
HMM...
NU (BLOOP)
YOU GOT A LOT OF FREE TIME TOO, HUH?
野生時代
WEREN'T YOU STANDING BY ON ANOTHER FLOOR...? RANPO-KUN?
PARA
PARA
野生時代
THIS LEAD WAS PROVIDED BY THE VIRUS SKILL USER...
PERA (BLAB)
PERA
PERA
PERA
PERA
PERA
PERA
PERA
...AN UTTERLY DISLOYAL WIMP...... I WASN'T EXPECTING MUCH.

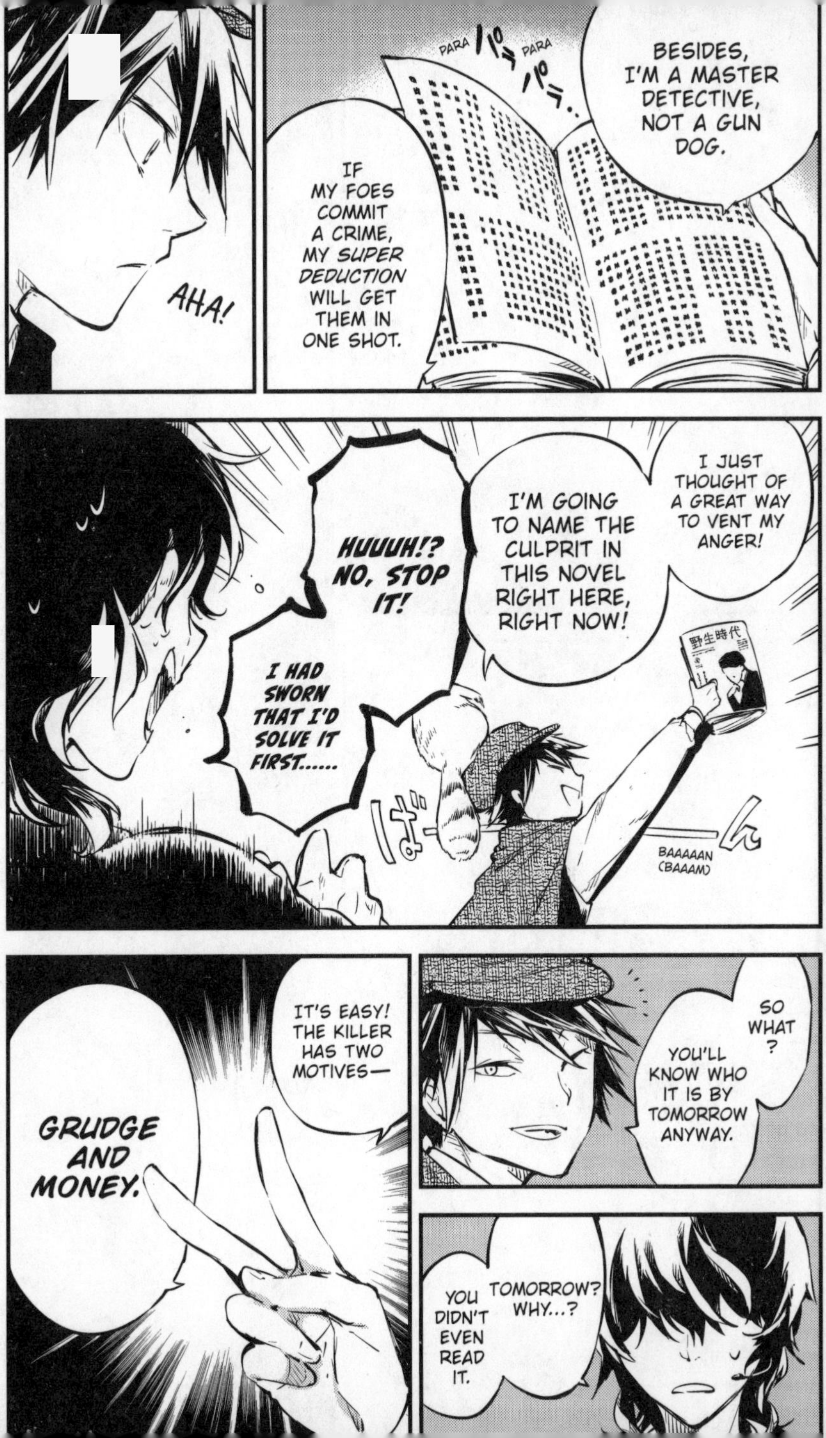
PARA
PARA
BESIDES, I'M A MASTER DETECTIVE, NOT A GUN DOG.
IF MY FOES COMMIT A CRIME, MY SUPER DEDUCTION WILL GET THEM IN ONE SHOT.
AHA!
I JUST THOUGHT OF A GREAT WAY TO VENT MY ANGER!
I'M GOING TO NAME THE CULPRIT IN THIS NOVEL RIGHT HERE, RIGHT NOW!
野生時代
HUUUH!? NO, STOP IT!
I HAD SWORN THAT I'D SOLVE IT FIRST......
BAAAAAN (BAAAM)
SO WHAT?
YOU'LL KNOW WHO IT IS BY TOMORROW ANYWAY.
TOMORROW? WHY...?
YOU DIDN'T EVEN READ IT.
IT'S EASY! THE KILLER HAS TWO MOTIVES—
GRUDGE AND MONEY.

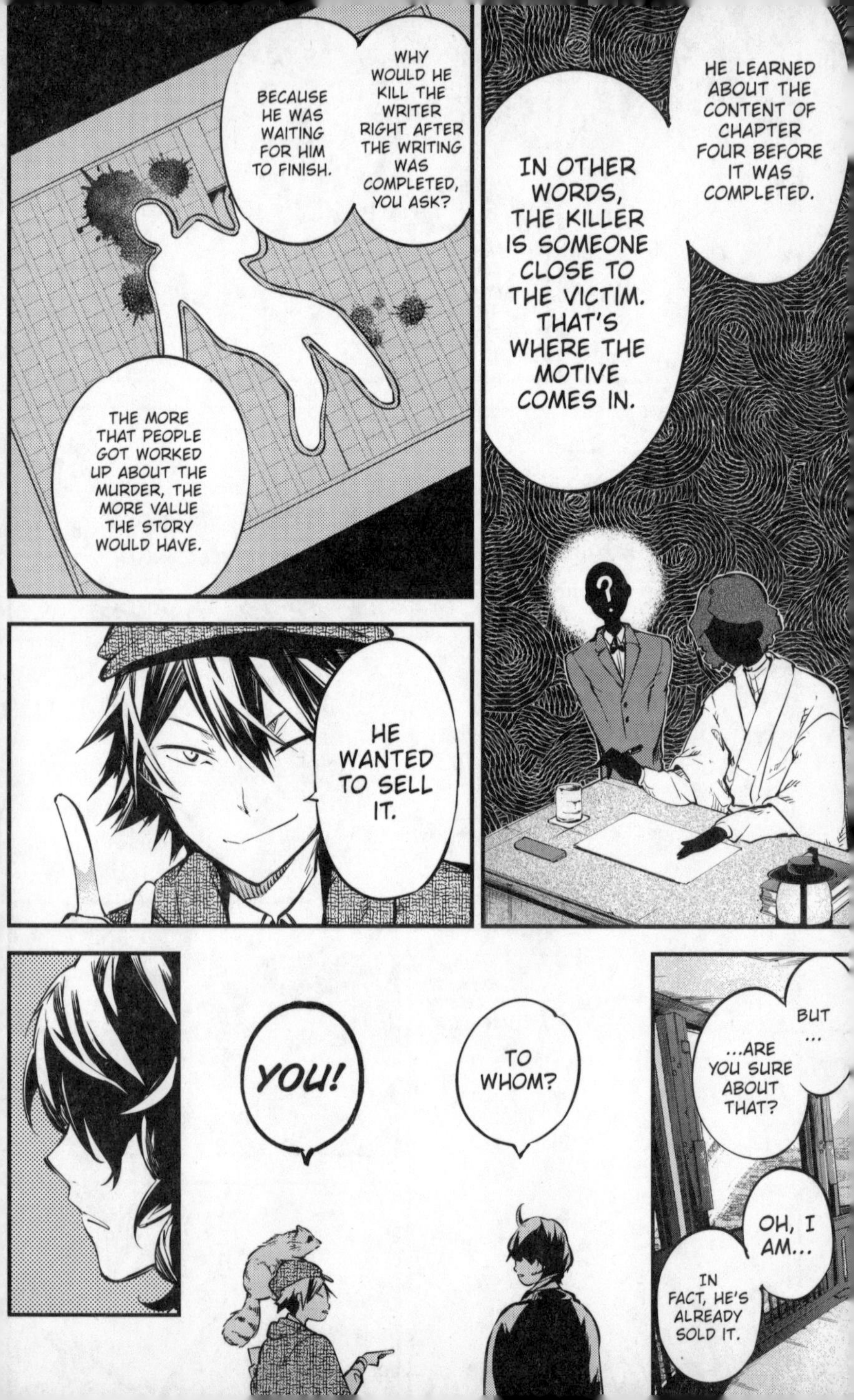
HE LEARNED ABOUT THE CONTENT OF CHAPTER FOUR BEFORE IT WAS COMPLETED.
IN OTHER WORDS, THE KILLER IS SOMEONE CLOSE TO THE VICTIM. THAT'S WHERE THE MOTIVE COMES IN.
WHY WOULD HE KILL THE WRITER RIGHT AFTER THE WRITING WAS COMPLETED, YOU ASK?
BECAUSE HE WAS WAITING FOR HIM TO FINISH.
THE MORE THAT PEOPLE GOT WORKED UP ABOUT THE MURDER, THE MORE VALUE THE STORY WOULD HAVE.
HE WANTED TO SELL IT.
BUT...
...ARE YOU SURE ABOUT THAT?
OH, I AM...
IN FACT, HE'S ALREADY SOLD IT.
TO WHOM?
YOU!

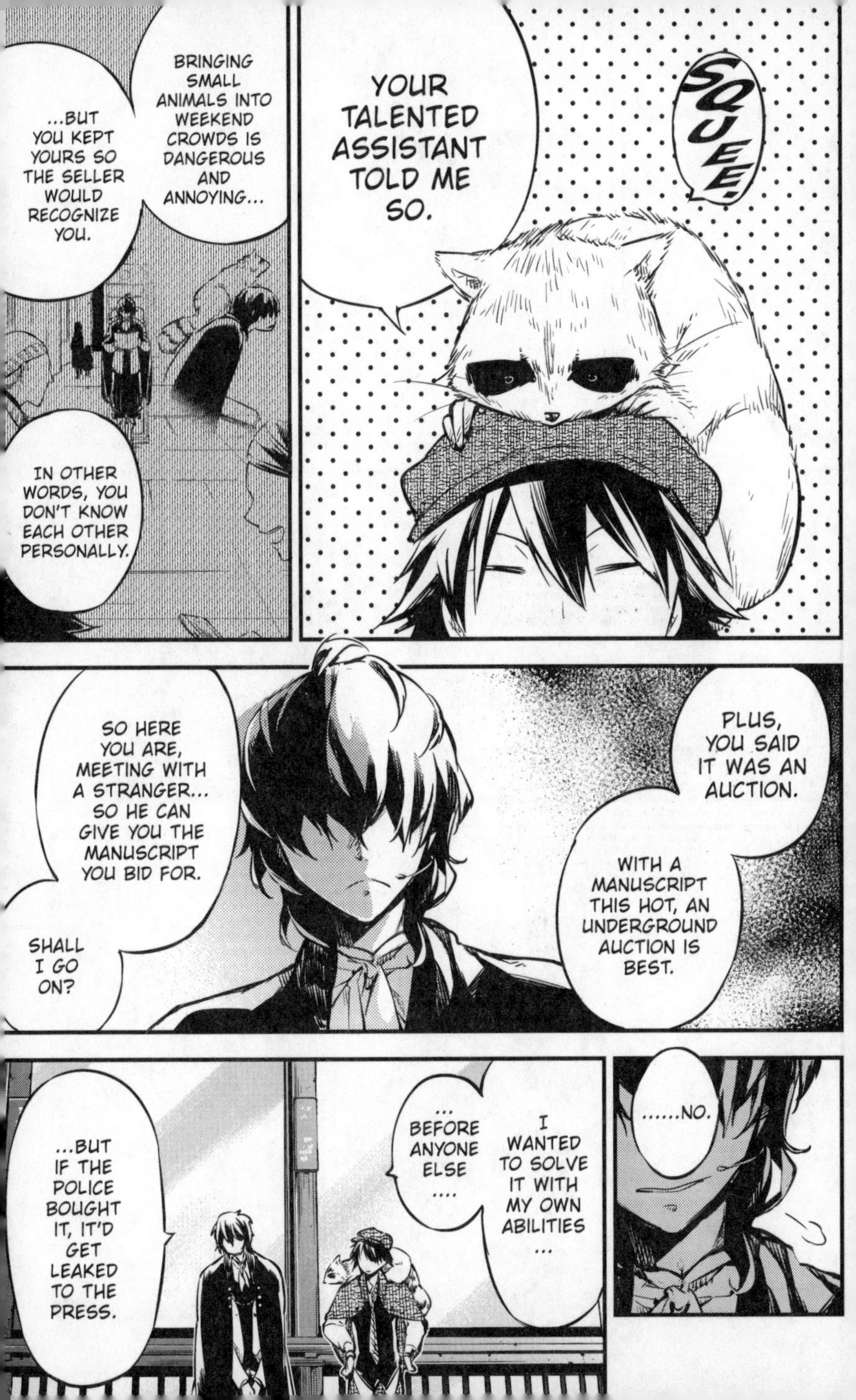
SQUEE.
YOUR TALENTED ASSISTANT TOLD ME SO.
BRINGING SMALL ANIMALS INTO WEEKEND CROWDS IS DANGEROUS AND ANNOYING...
...BUT YOU KEPT YOURS SO THE SELLER WOULD RECOGNIZE YOU.
IN OTHER WORDS, YOU DON'T KNOW EACH OTHER PERSONALLY.
PLUS, YOU SAID IT WAS AN AUCTION.
WITH A MANUSCRIPT THIS HOT, AN UNDERGROUND AUCTION IS BEST.
SO HERE YOU ARE, MEETING WITH A STRANGER... SO HE CAN GIVE YOU THE MANUSCRIPT YOU BID FOR.
SHALL I GO ON?
......NO.
I WANTED TO SOLVE IT WITH MY OWN ABILITIES ...
... BEFORE ANYONE ELSE ....
...BUT IF THE POLICE BOUGHT IT, IT'D GET LEAKED TO THE PRESS.

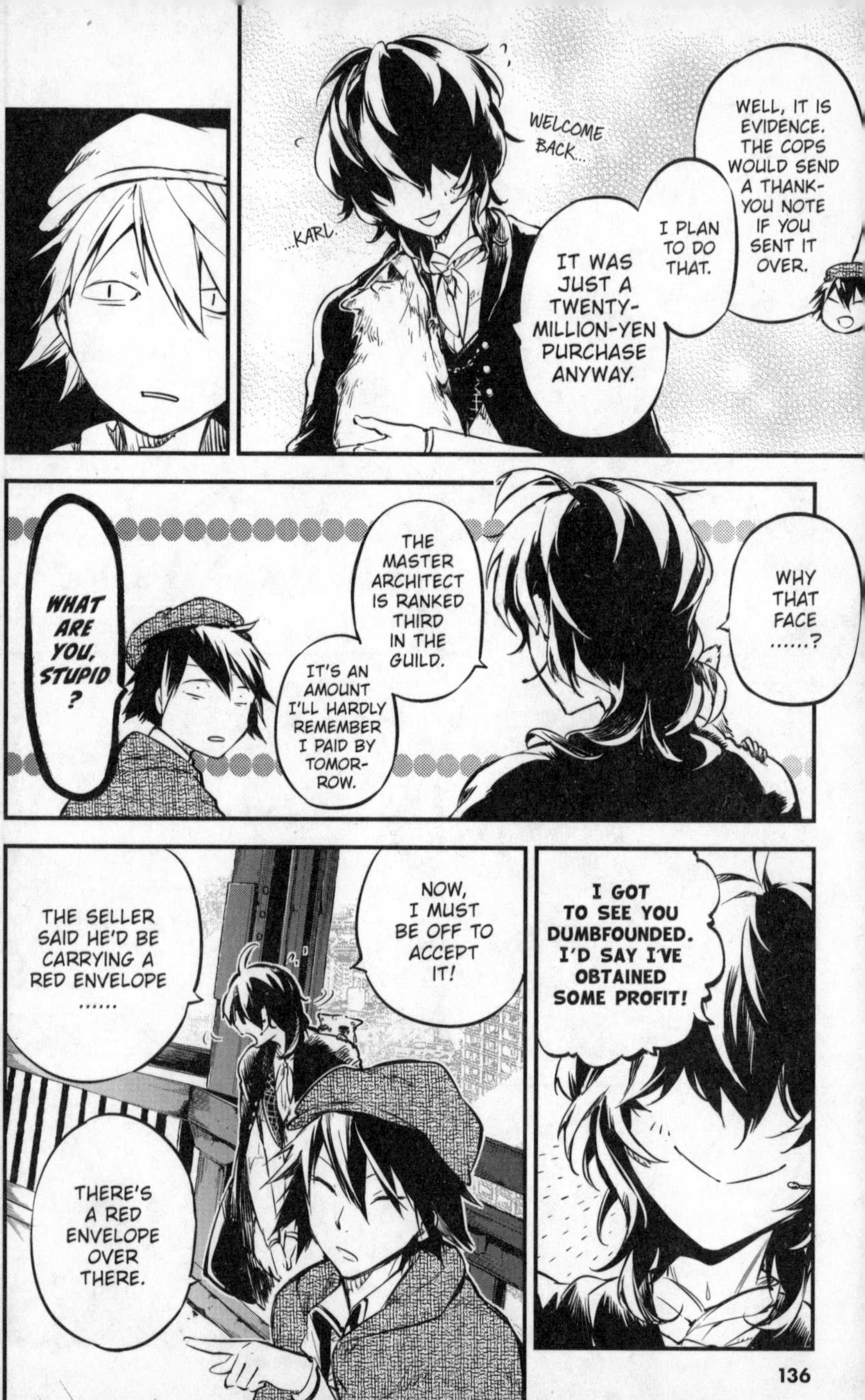
WELL, IT IS EVIDENCE. THE COPS WOULD SEND A THANK-YOU NOTE IF YOU SENT IT OVER.
I PLAN TO DO THAT.
IT WAS JUST A TWENTY-MILLION-YEN PURCHASE ANYWAY.
WELCOME BACK...
...KARL.
WHY THAT FACE......?
THE MASTER ARCHITECT IS RANKED THIRD IN THE GUILD.
IT'S AN AMOUNT I'LL HARDLY REMEMBER I PAID BY TOMOR-ROW.
WHAT ARE YOU, STUPID?
I GOT TO SEE YOU DUMBFOUNDED. I'D SAY I'VE OBTAINED SOME PROFIT!
NOW, I MUST BE OFF TO ACCEPT IT!
THE SELLER SAID HE'D BE CARRYING A RED ENVELOPE ......
THERE'S A RED ENVELOPE OVER THERE.

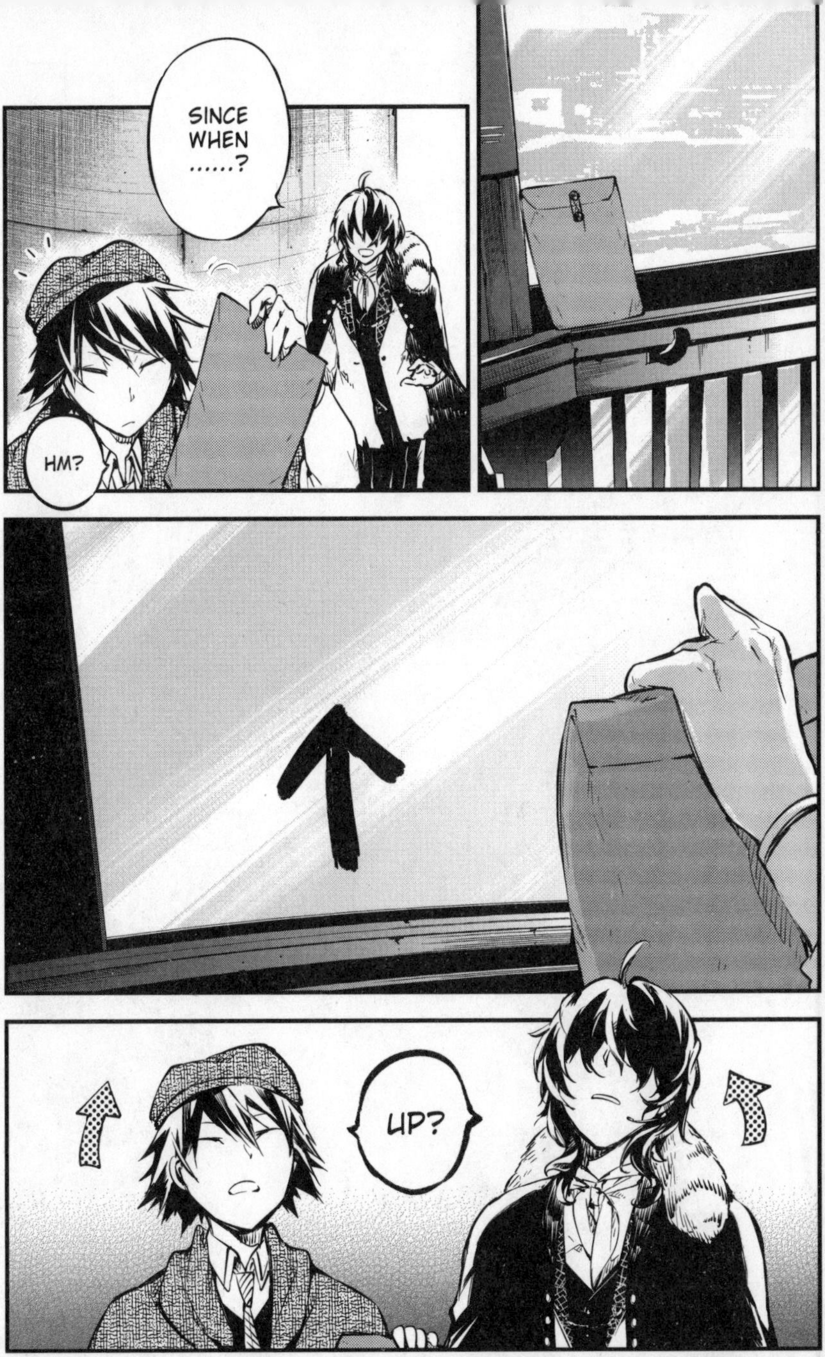
SINCE WHEN ......?
HM?
UP?

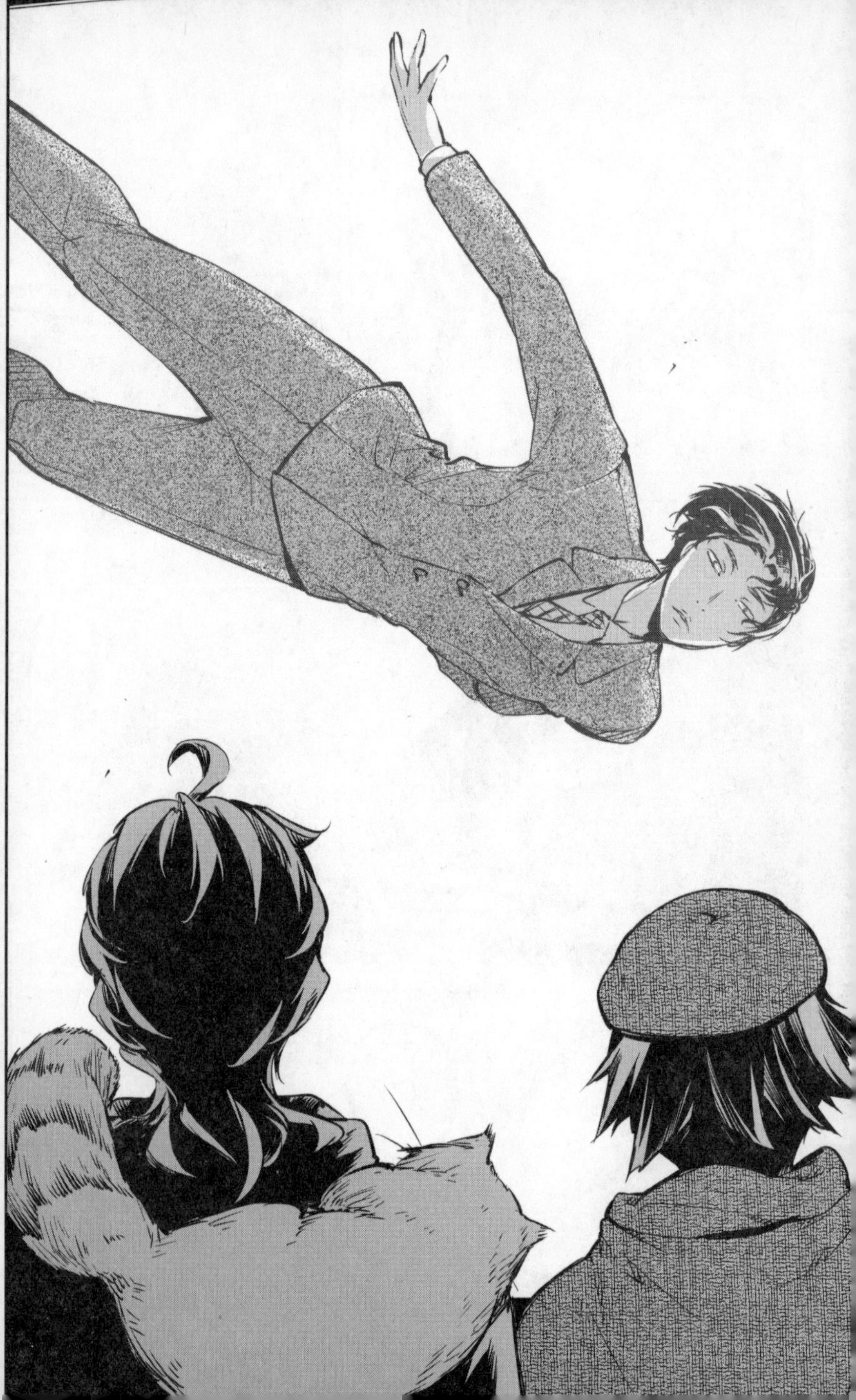

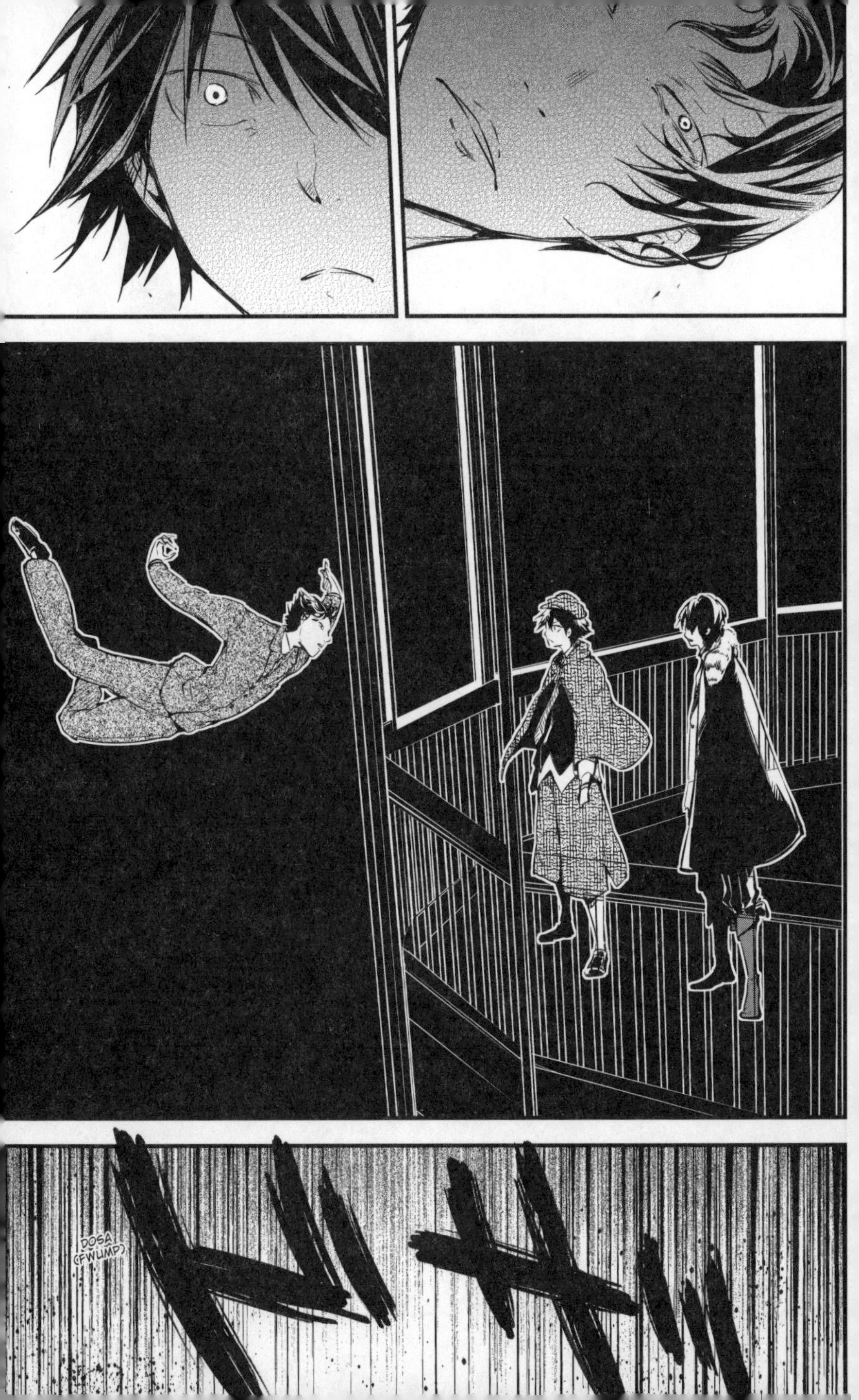
DOSA (FWUMP)

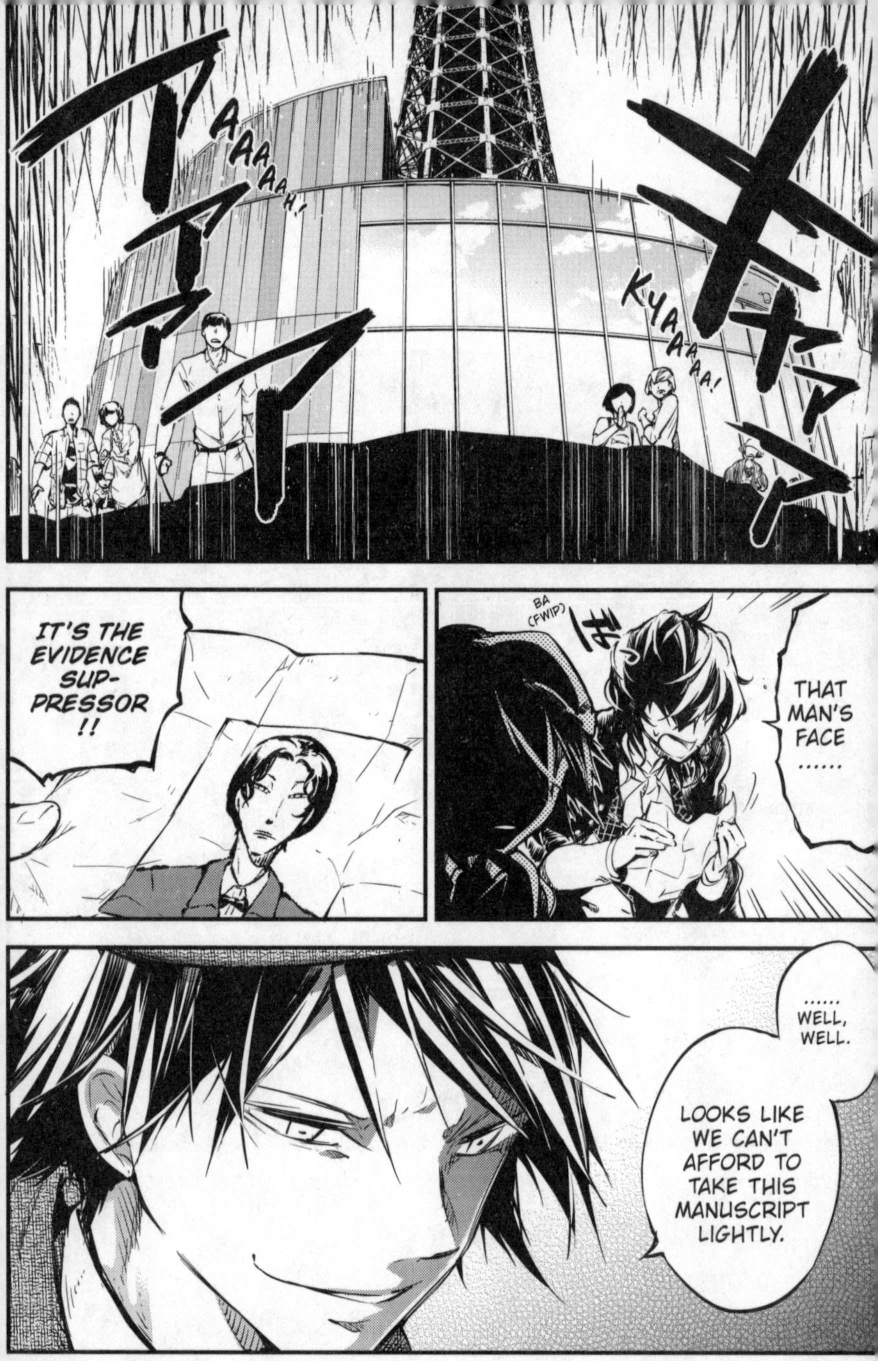
KYAAAAAA!
AAAAAH!
BA (FWIP)
THAT MAN'S FACE ......
IT'S THE EVIDENCE SUP-PRESSOR !!
...... WELL, WELL.
LOOKS LIKE WE CAN'T AFFORD TO TAKE THIS MANUSCRIPT LIGHTLY.

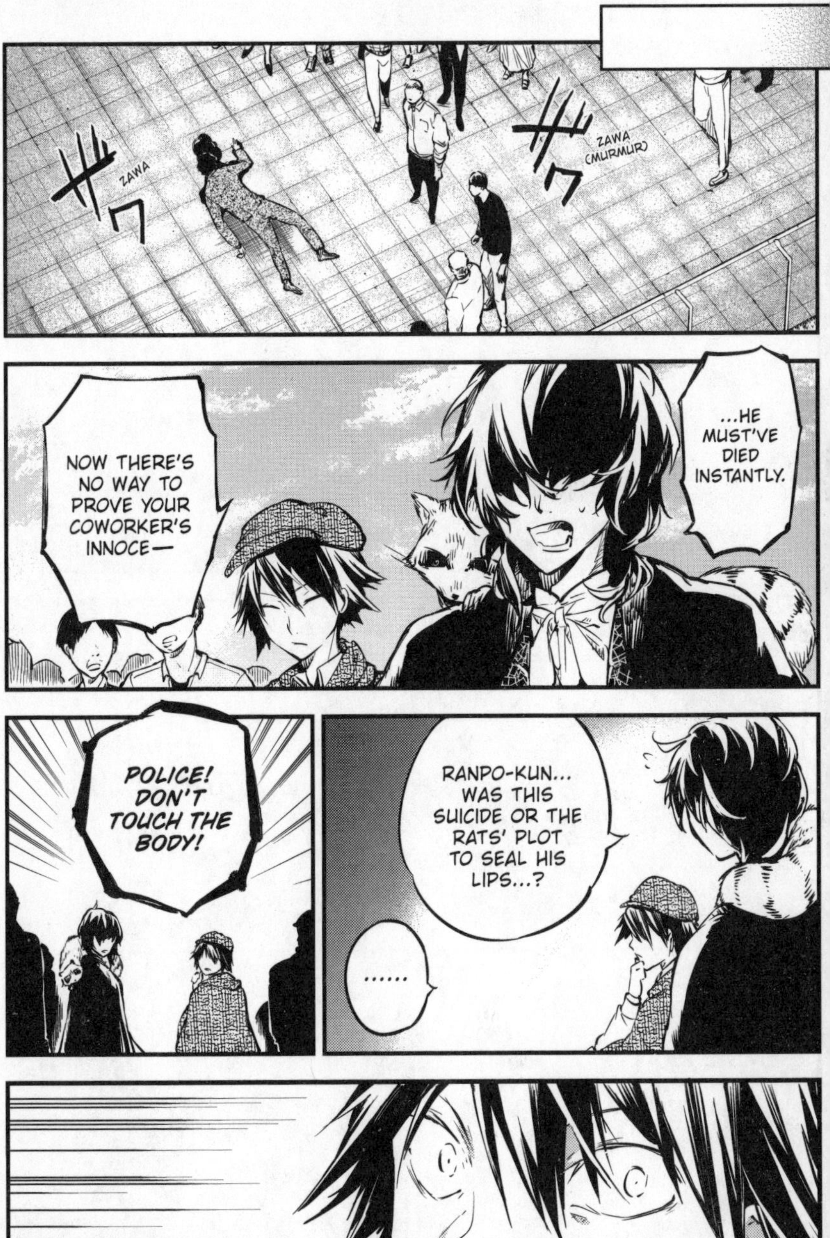
ZAWA (MURMUR)
ZAWA
...HE MUST'VE DIED INSTANTLY.
NOW THERE'S NO WAY TO PROVE YOUR COWORKER'S INNOCE—
RANPO-KUN... WAS THIS SUICIDE OR THE RATS' PLOT TO SEAL HIS LIPS...?
......
POLICE! DON'T TOUCH THE BODY!

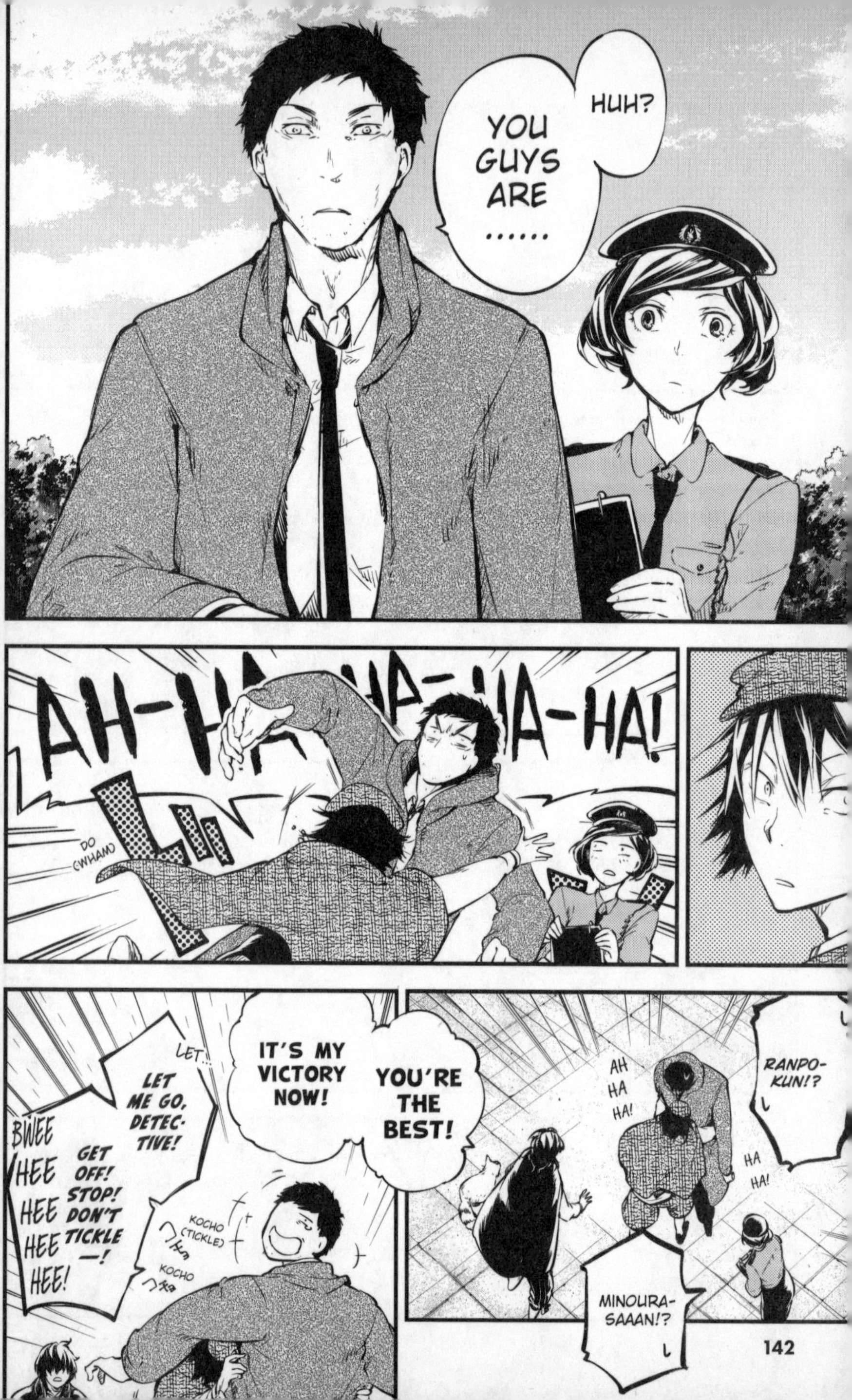

HUH? YOU GUYS ARE ......
AH-HA-HA-HA-HA!
DO (WHAM)
RANPO-KUN!?
HA HA!
AH HA HA!
MINOURA-SAAAN!?
YOU'RE THE BEST!
IT'S MY VICTORY NOW!
LET...
LET ME GO, DETECTIVE!
GET OFF! STOP! DON'T TICKLE—!
BWEE HEE HEE HEE HEE!
KOCHO (TICKLE)
KOCHO

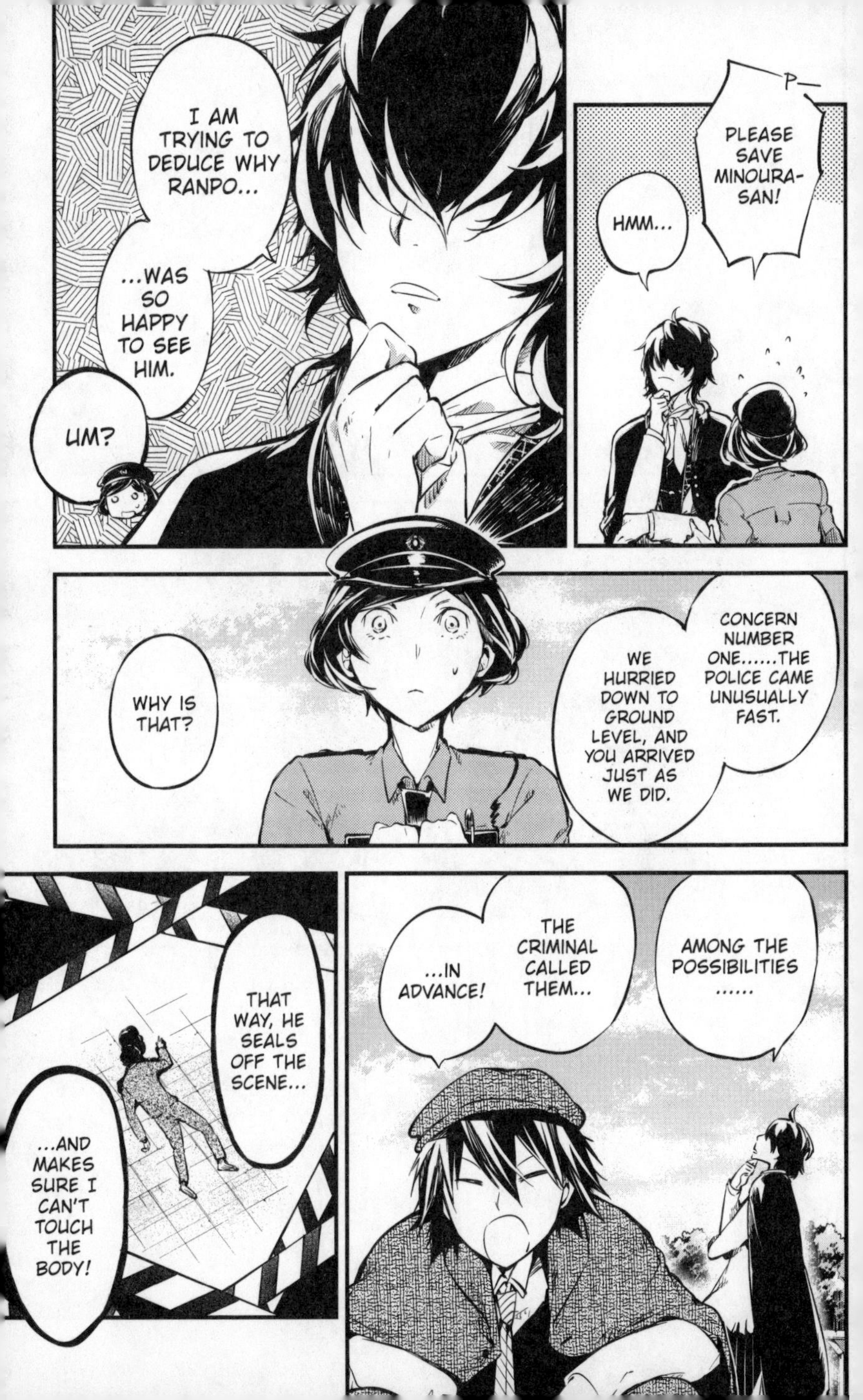
—P—
PLEASE SAVE MINOURA-SAN!
HMM...
I AM TRYING TO DEDUCE WHY RANPO...
...WAS SO HAPPY TO SEE HIM.
UM?
CONCERN NUMBER ONE......THE POLICE CAME UNUSUALLY FAST.
WE HURRIED DOWN TO GROUND LEVEL, AND YOU ARRIVED JUST AS WE DID.
WHY IS THAT?
AMONG THE POSSIBILITIES ......
THE CRIMINAL CALLED THEM...
...IN ADVANCE!
THAT WAY, HE SEALS OFF THE SCENE...
...AND MAKES SURE I CAN'T TOUCH THE BODY!

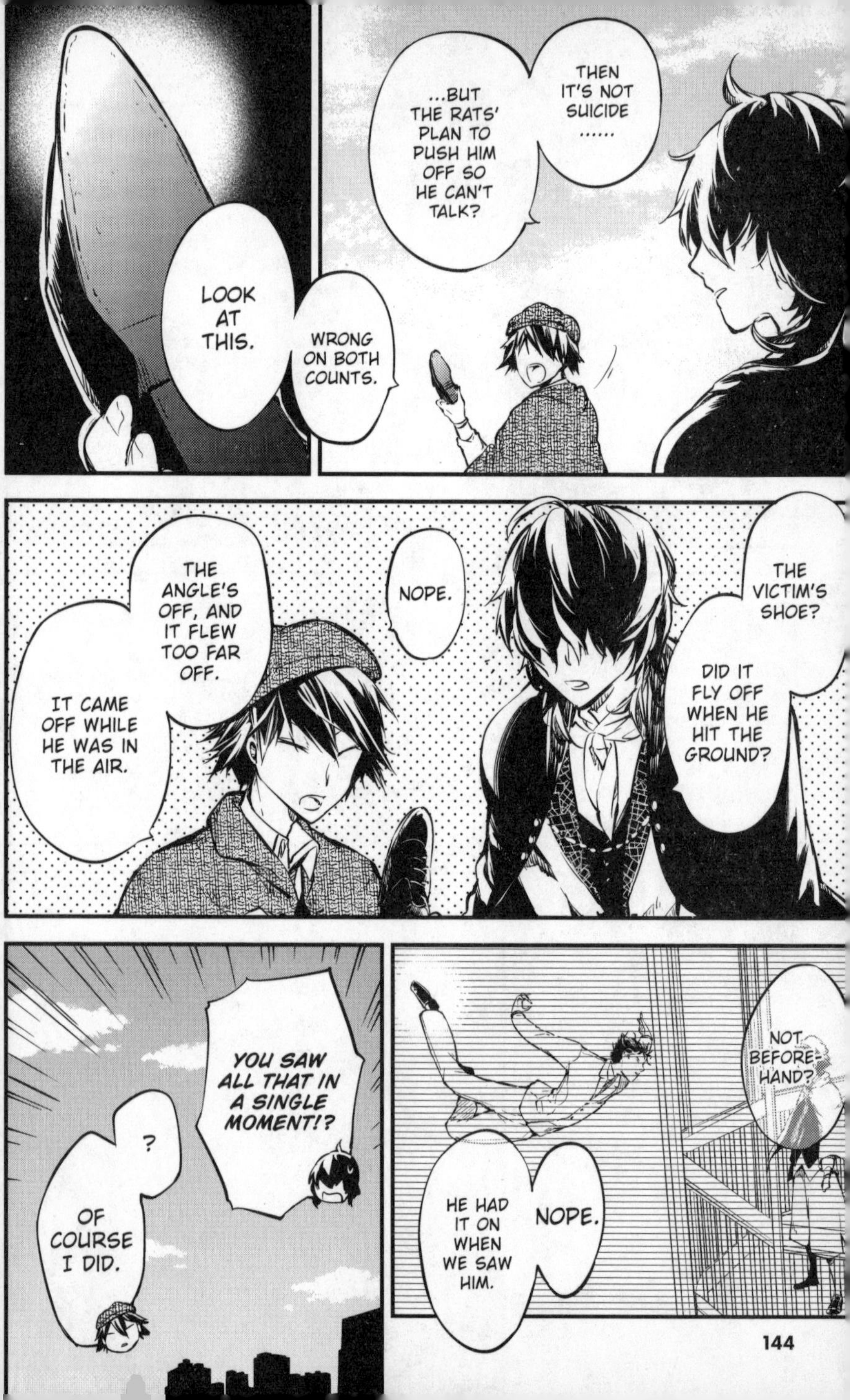

THEN IT'S NOT SUICIDE ......
...BUT THE RATS' PLAN TO PUSH HIM OFF SO HE CAN'T TALK?
WRONG ON BOTH COUNTS.
LOOK AT THIS.
THE VICTIM'S SHOE?
DID IT FLY OFF WHEN HE HIT THE GROUND?
NOPE.
THE ANGLE'S OFF, AND IT FLEW TOO FAR OFF.
IT CAME OFF WHILE HE WAS IN THE AIR.
NOT BEFORE-HAND?
NOPE.
HE HAD IT ON WHEN WE SAW HIM.
YOU SAW ALL THAT IN A SINGLE MOMENT!?
?
OF COURSE I DID.

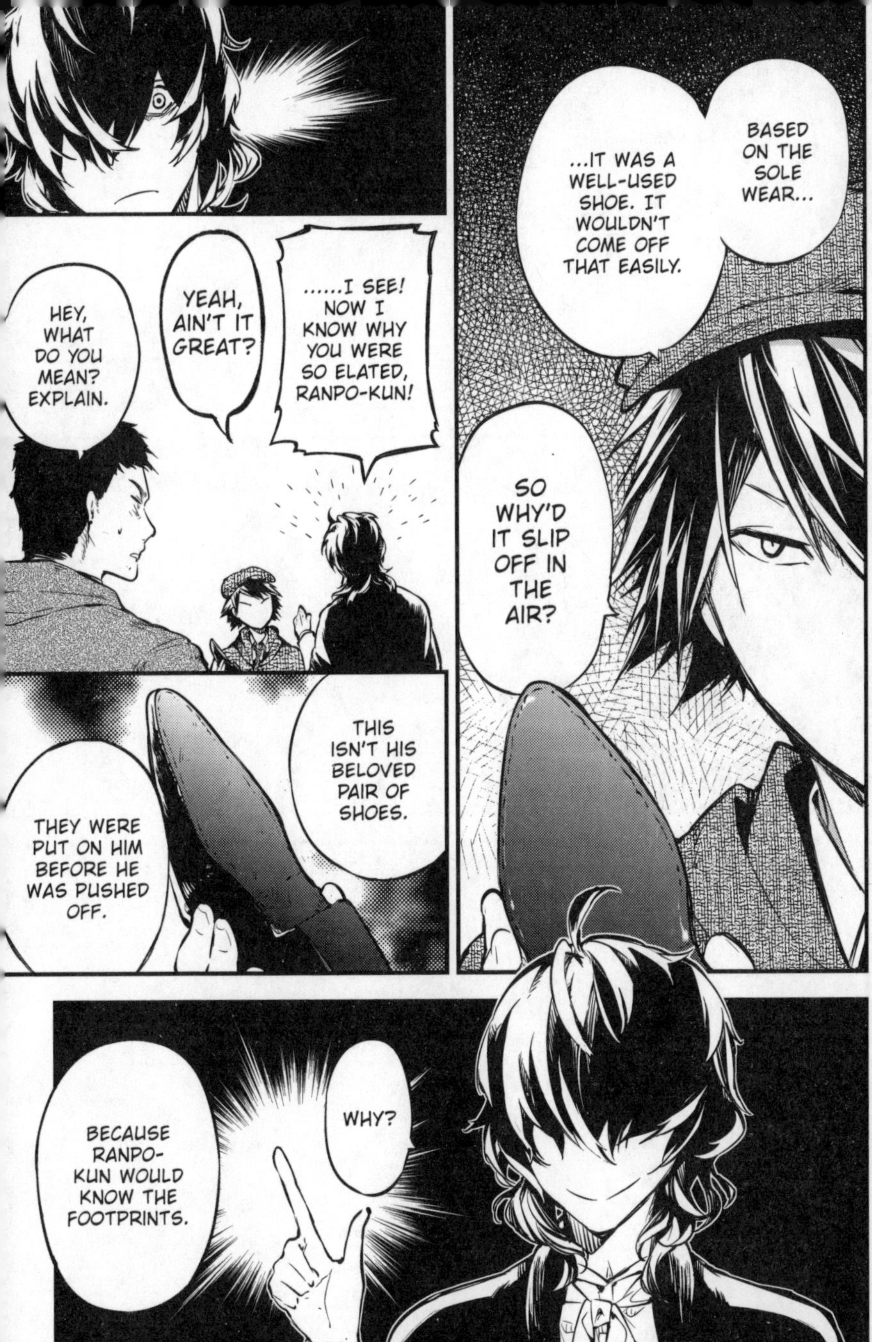
BASED ON THE SOLE WEAR...
...IT WAS A WELL-USED SHOE. IT WOULDN'T COME OFF THAT EASILY.
SO WHY'D IT SLIP OFF IN THE AIR?
......I SEE! NOW I KNOW WHY YOU WERE SO ELATED, RANPO-KUN!
YEAH, AIN'T IT GREAT?
HEY, WHAT DO YOU MEAN? EXPLAIN.
THIS ISN'T HIS BELOVED PAIR OF SHOES.
THEY WERE PUT ON HIM BEFORE HE WAS PUSHED OFF.
WHY?
BECAUSE RANPO-KUN WOULD KNOW THE FOOTPRINTS.

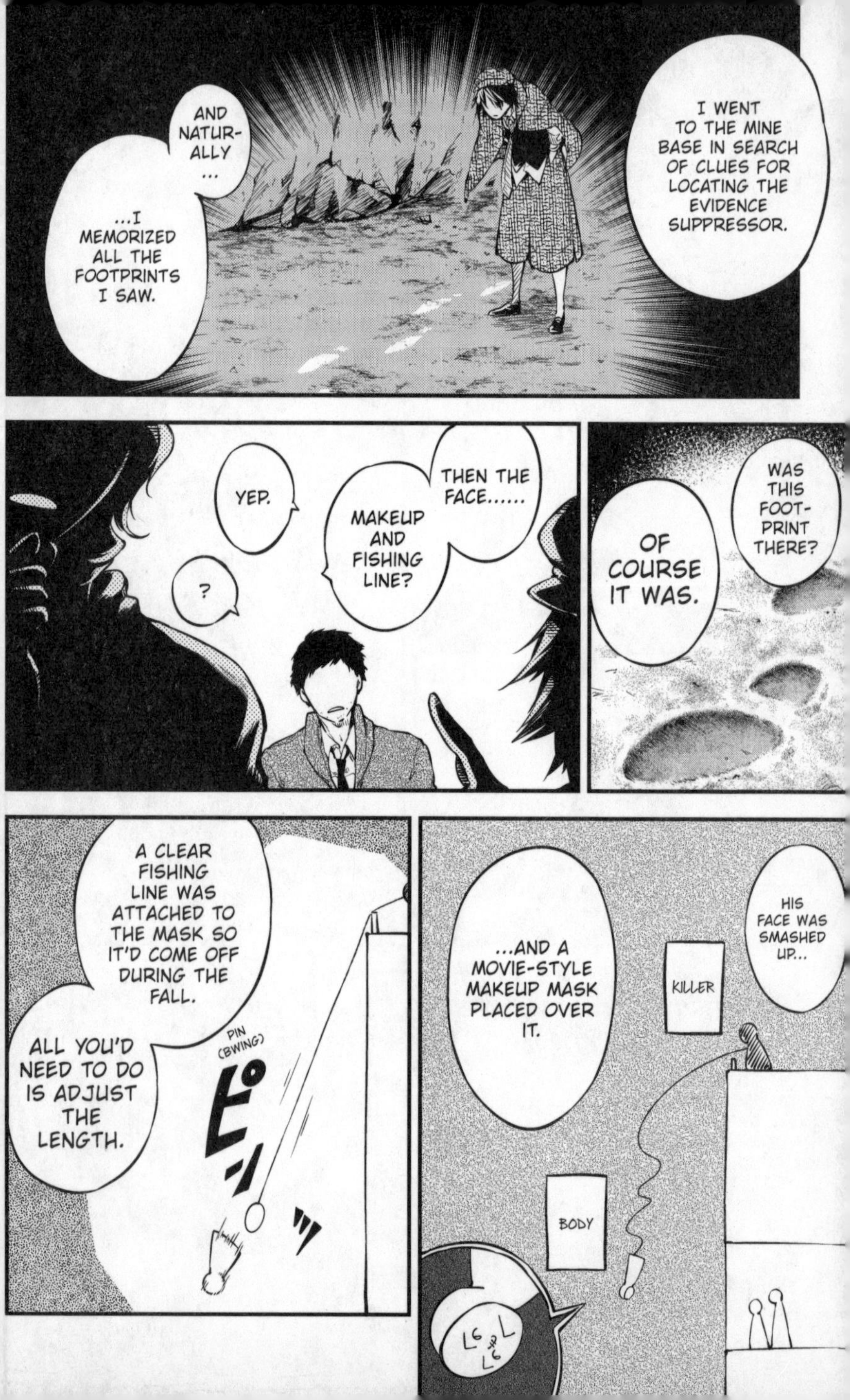
I WENT TO THE MINE BASE IN SEARCH OF CLUES FOR LOCATING THE EVIDENCE SUPPRESSOR.
AND NATURALLY...
...I MEMORIZED ALL THE FOOTPRINTS I SAW.
WAS THIS FOOT-PRINT THERE?
OF COURSE IT WAS.
THEN THE FACE......
MAKEUP AND FISHING LINE?
YEP.
?
HIS FACE WAS SMASHED UP...
...AND A MOVIE-STYLE MAKEUP MASK PLACED OVER IT.
KILLER
BODY
A CLEAR FISHING LINE WAS ATTACHED TO THE MASK SO IT'D COME OFF DURING THE FALL.
ALL YOU'D NEED TO DO IS ADJUST THE LENGTH.
PIN (BWING)

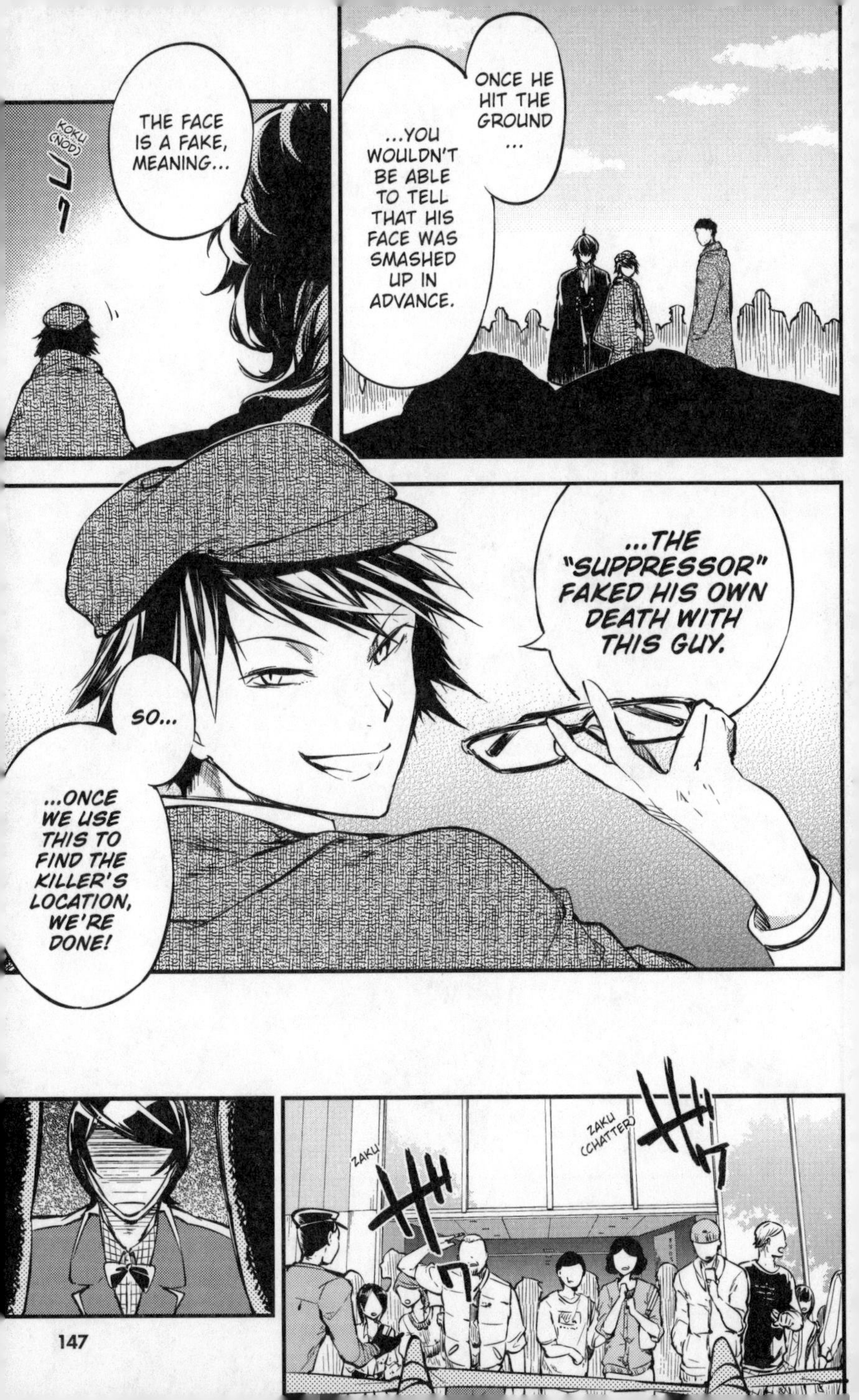
ONCE HE HIT THE GROUND ...
...YOU WOULDN'T BE ABLE TO TELL THAT HIS FACE WAS SMASHED UP IN ADVANCE.
THE FACE IS A FAKE, MEANING...
KOKU (NOD)
...THE "SUPPRESSOR" FAKED HIS OWN DEATH WITH THIS GUY.
SO...
...ONCE WE USE THIS TO FIND THE KILLER'S LOCATION, WE'RE DONE!
ZAKU (CHATTER)
ZAKU

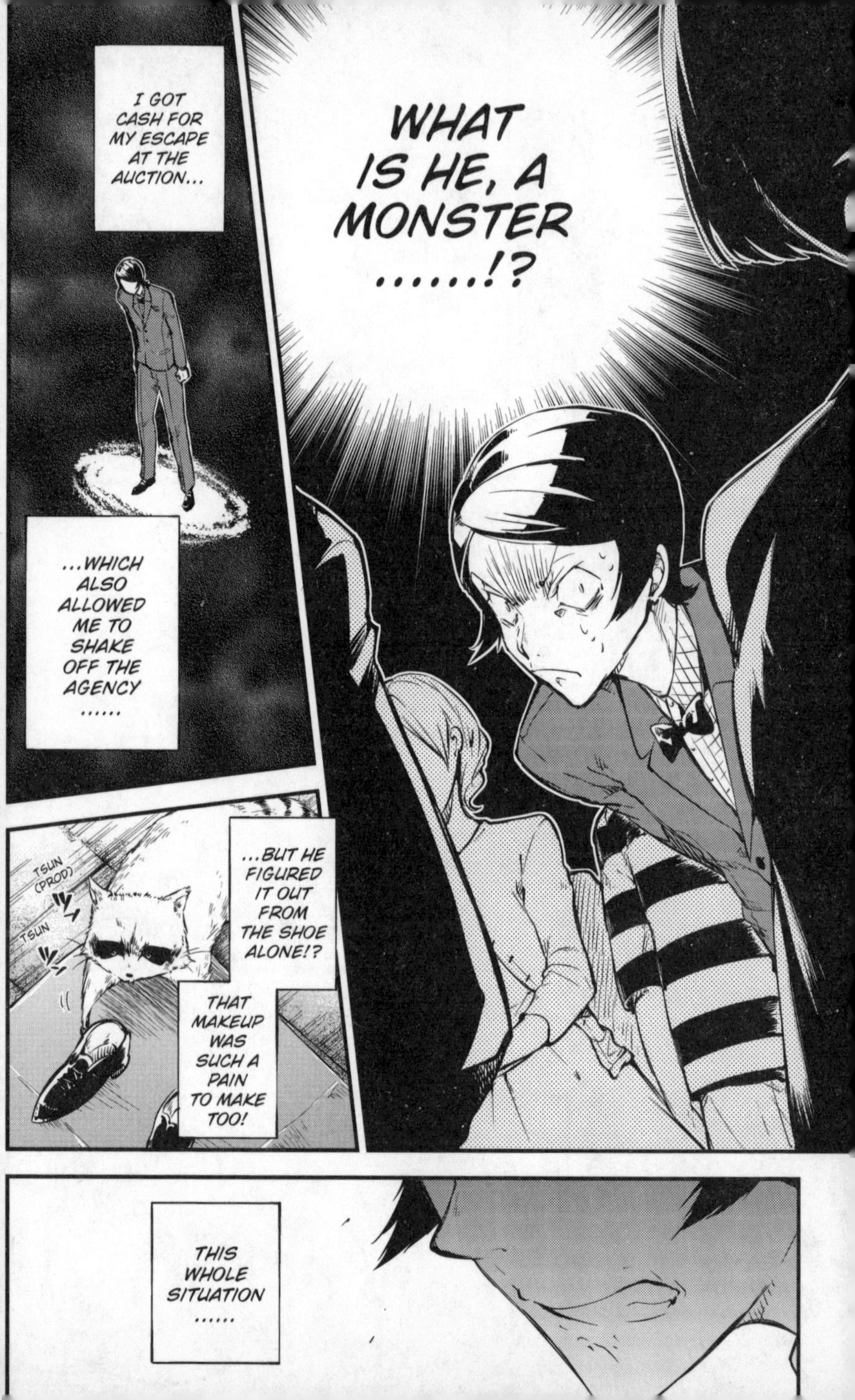
WHAT IS HE, A MONSTER ......!?
I GOT CASH FOR MY ESCAPE AT THE AUCTION...
...WHICH ALSO ALLOWED ME TO SHAKE OFF THE AGENCY ......
...BUT HE FIGURED IT OUT FROM THE SHOE ALONE!?
THAT MAKEUP WAS SUCH A PAIN TO MAKE TOO!
TSUN (PROD)
TSUN
THIS WHOLE SITUATION ......

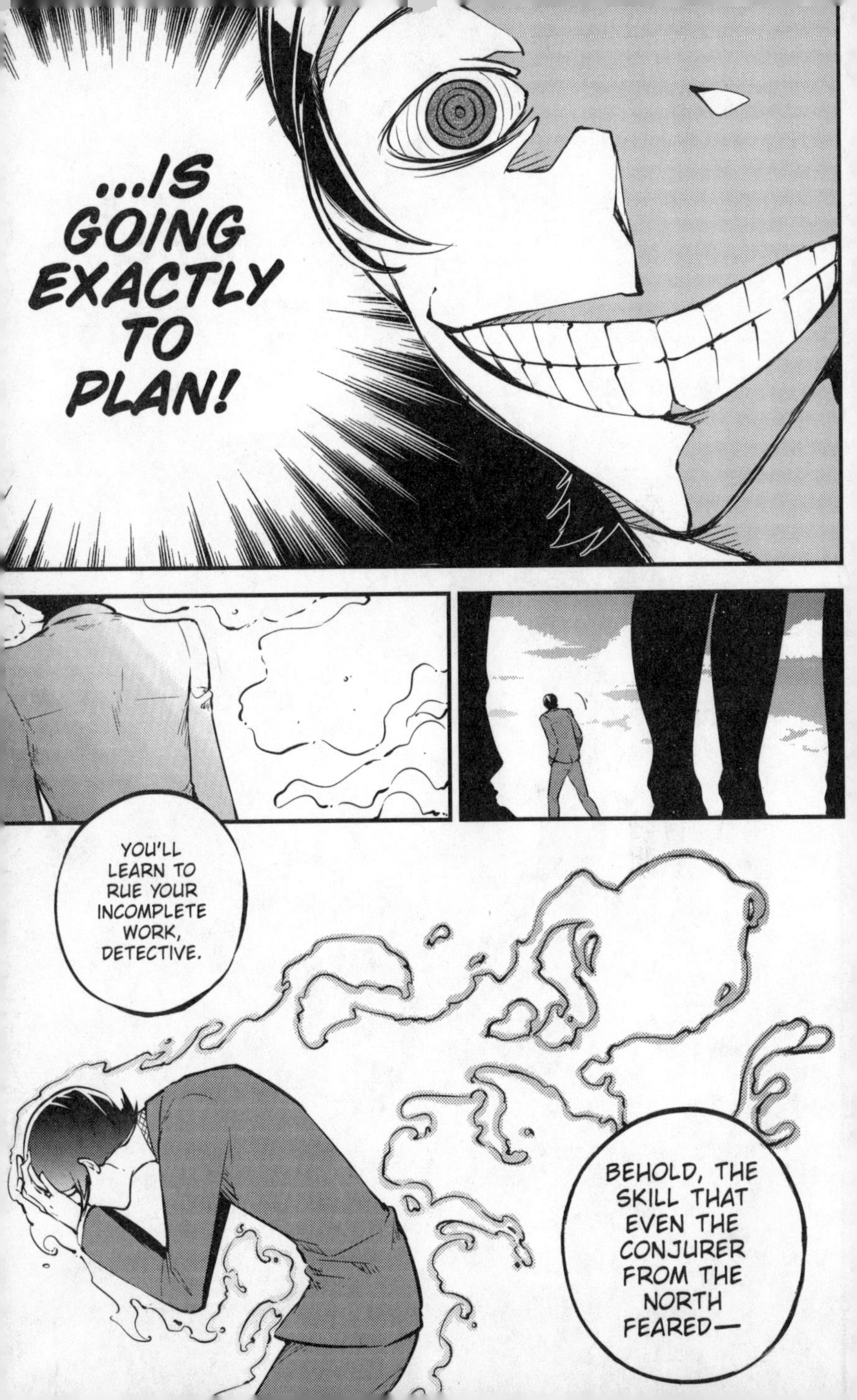
...IS GOING EXACTLY TO PLAN!
YOU'LL LEARN TO RUE YOUR INCOMPLETE WORK, DETECTIVE.
BEHOLD, THE SKILL THAT EVEN THE CONJURER FROM THE NORTH FEARED—

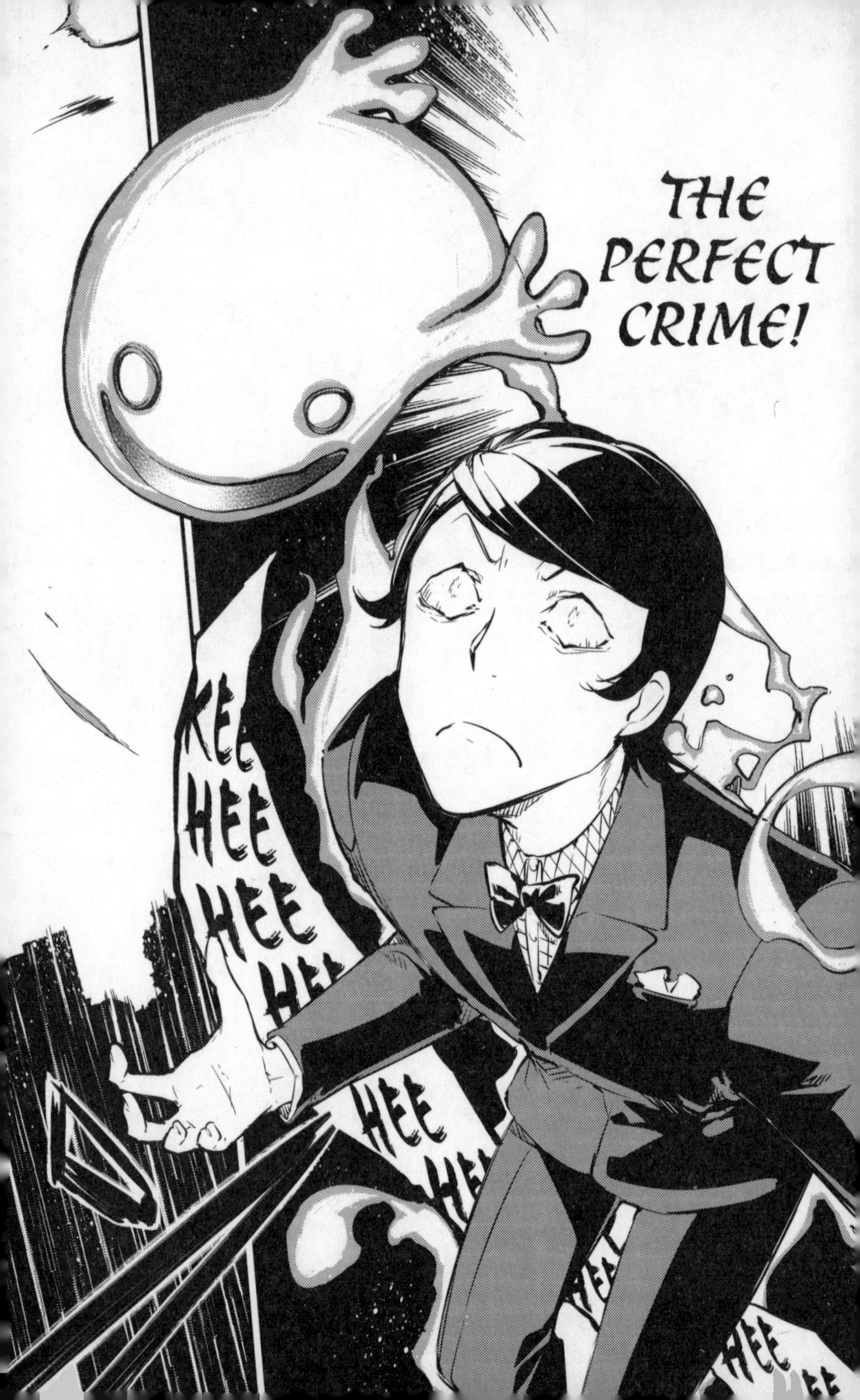
THE PERFECT CRIME!
KEE HEE HEE HEE
HEE
HEE

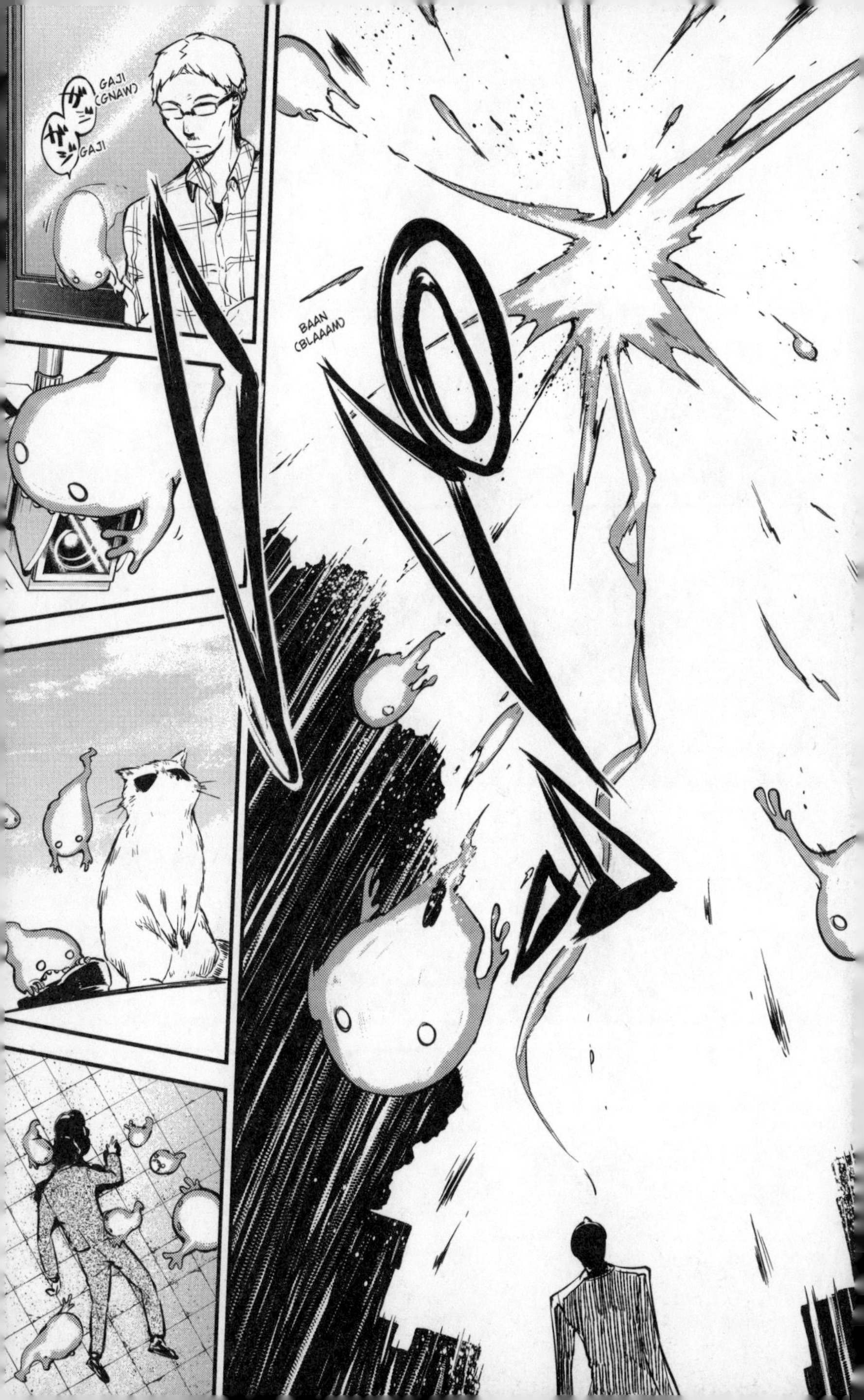
BAAN (BLAAAM)
GAJI (GNAW)
GAJI

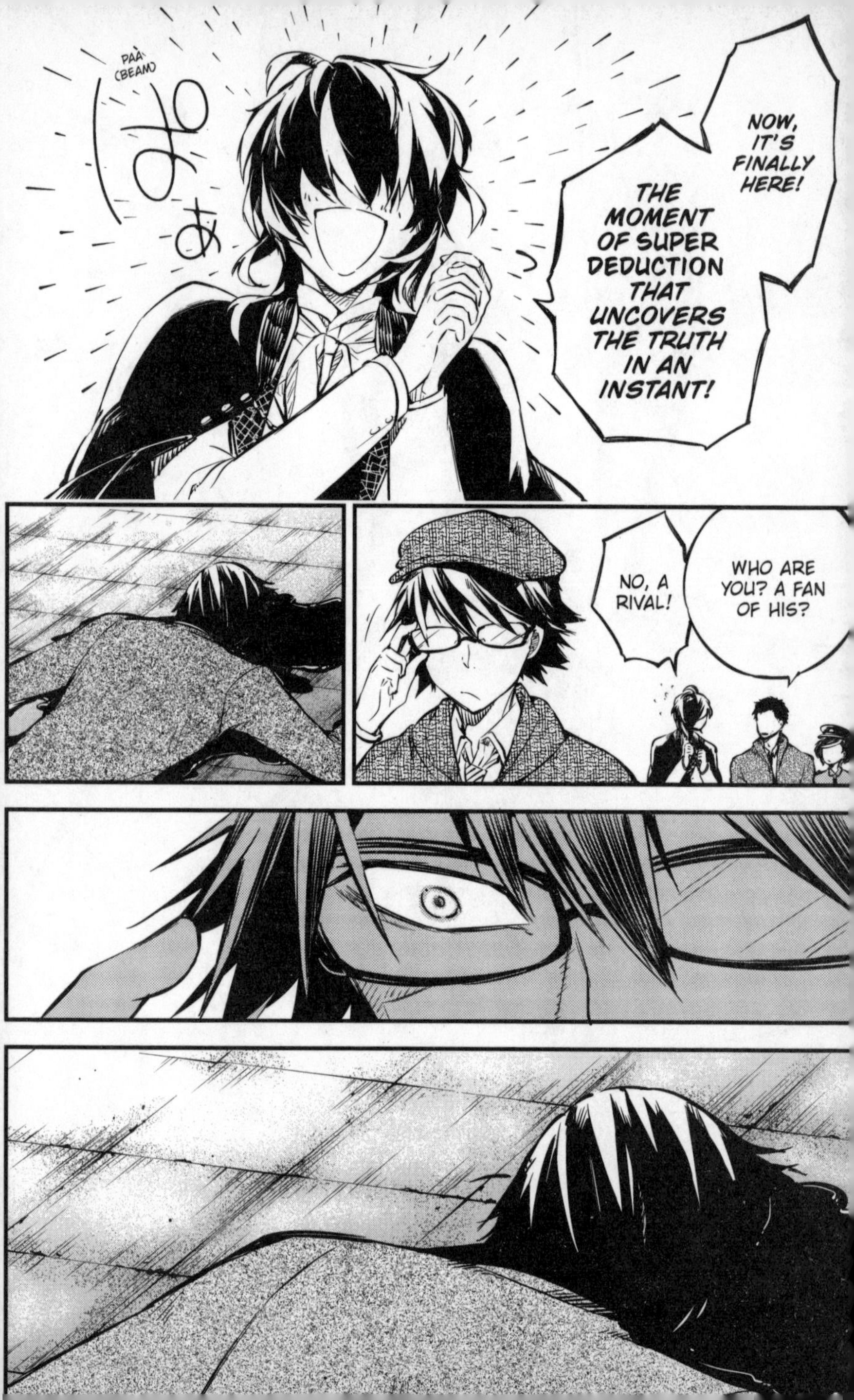
NOW, IT'S FINALLY HERE!
THE MOMENT OF SUPER DEDUCTION THAT UNCOVERS THE TRUTH IN AN INSTANT!
PAA (BEAM)
WHO ARE YOU? A FAN OF HIS?
NO, A RIVAL!

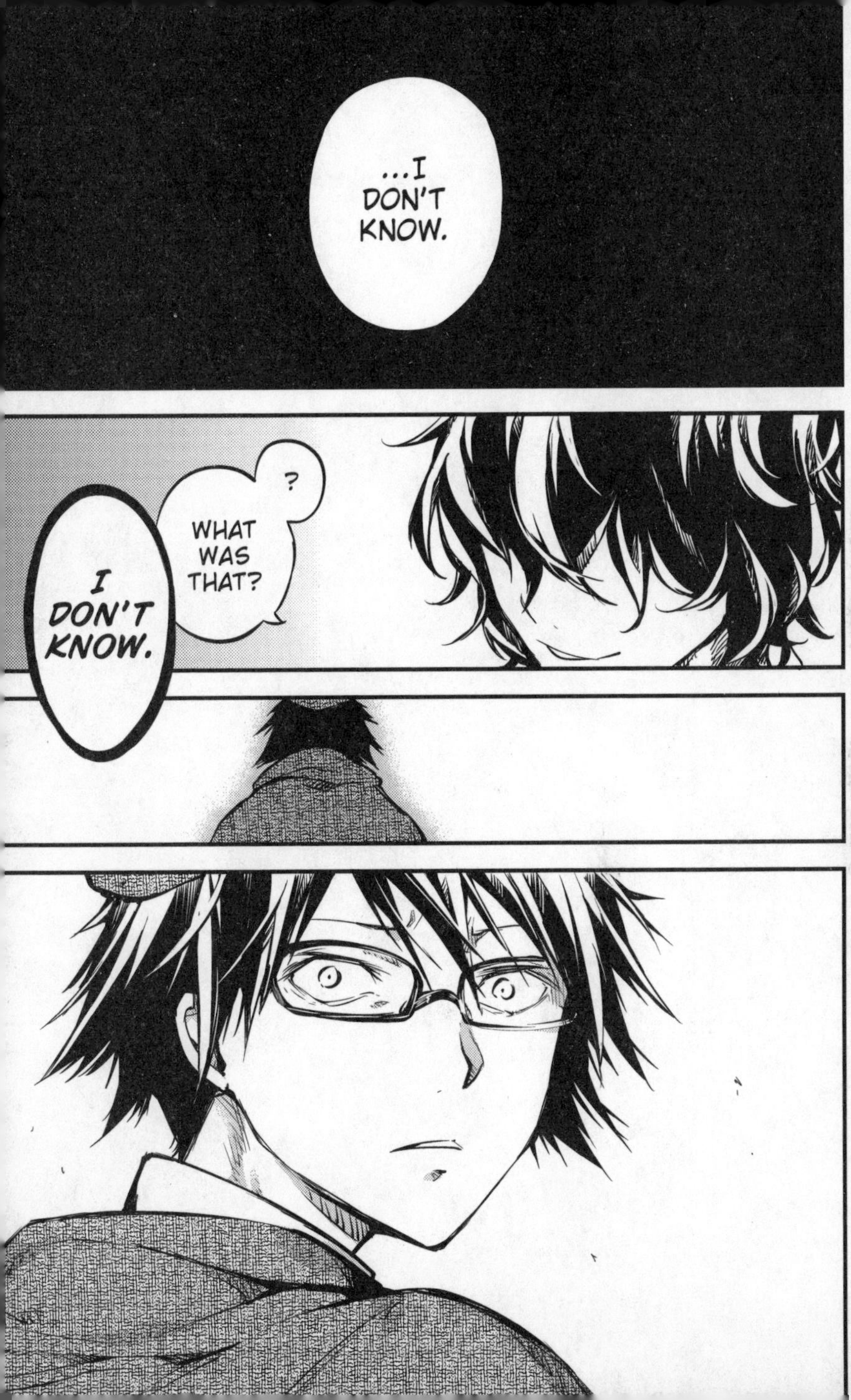
...I DON'T KNOW.
?
WHAT WAS THAT?
I DON'T KNOW.

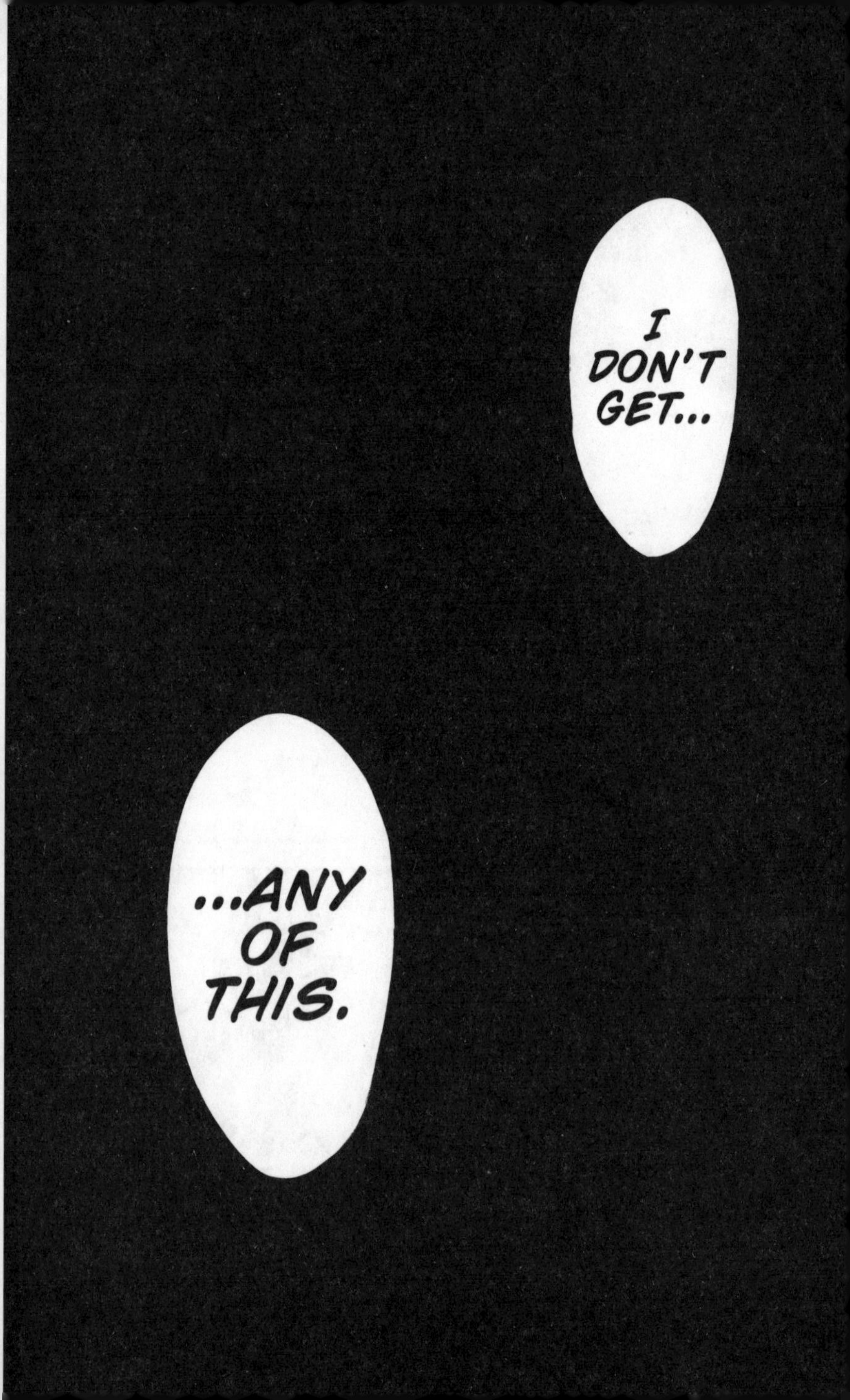
I DON'T GET...
...ANY OF THIS.

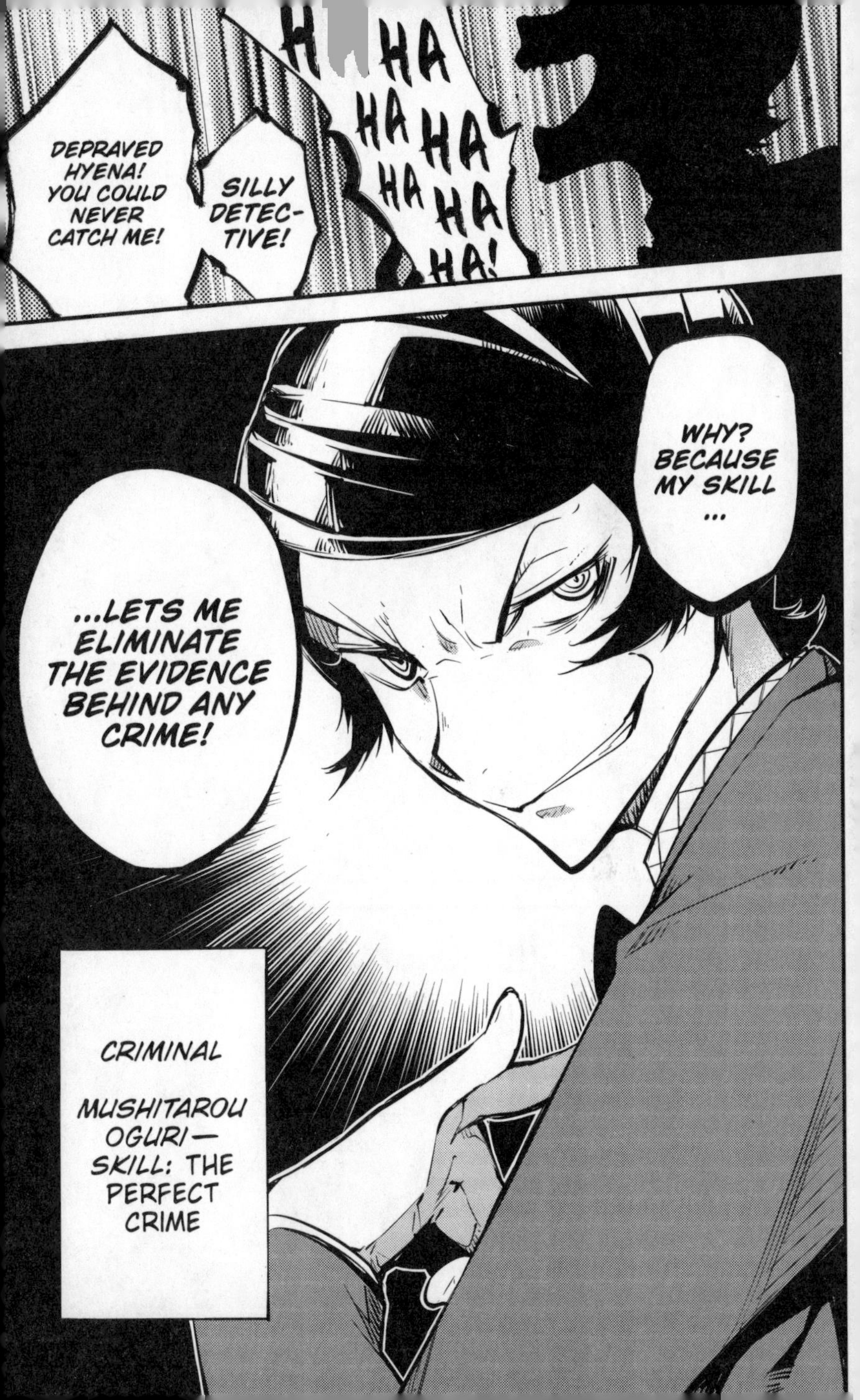
HA HA HA HA HA HA HA HA HA!
SILLY DETECTIVE!
DEPRAVED HYENA! YOU COULD NEVER CATCH ME!
WHY? BECAUSE MY SKILL...
...LETS ME ELIMINATE THE EVIDENCE BEHIND ANY CRIME!
CRIMINAL
MUSHITAROU OGURI—SKILL: THE PERFECT CRIME

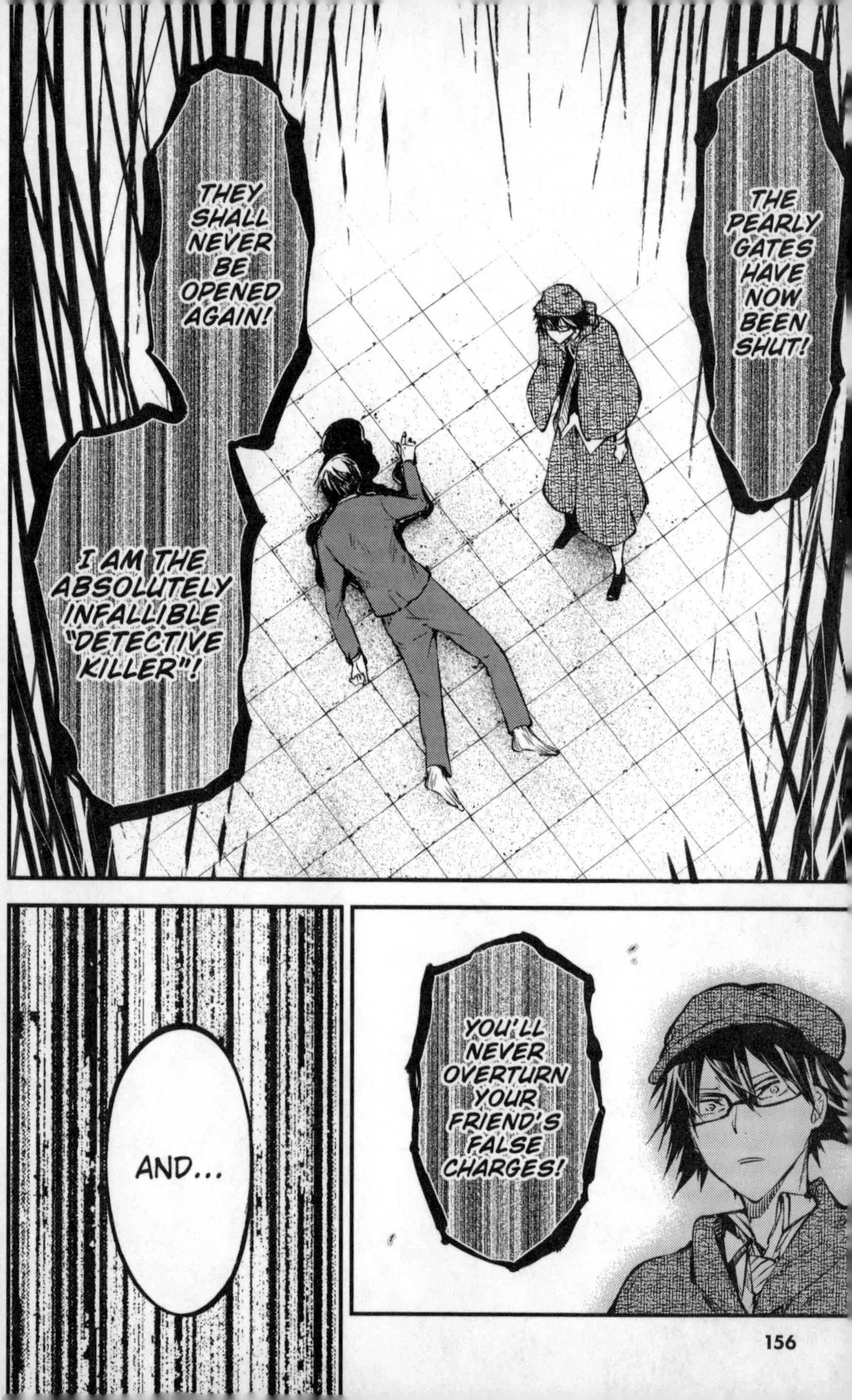
THE PEARLY GATES HAVE NOW BEEN SHUT!
THEY SHALL NEVER BE OPENED AGAIN!
I AM THE ABSOLUTELY INFALLIBLE "DETECTIVE KILLER"!
YOU'LL NEVER OVERTURN YOUR FRIEND'S FALSE CHARGES!
AND...

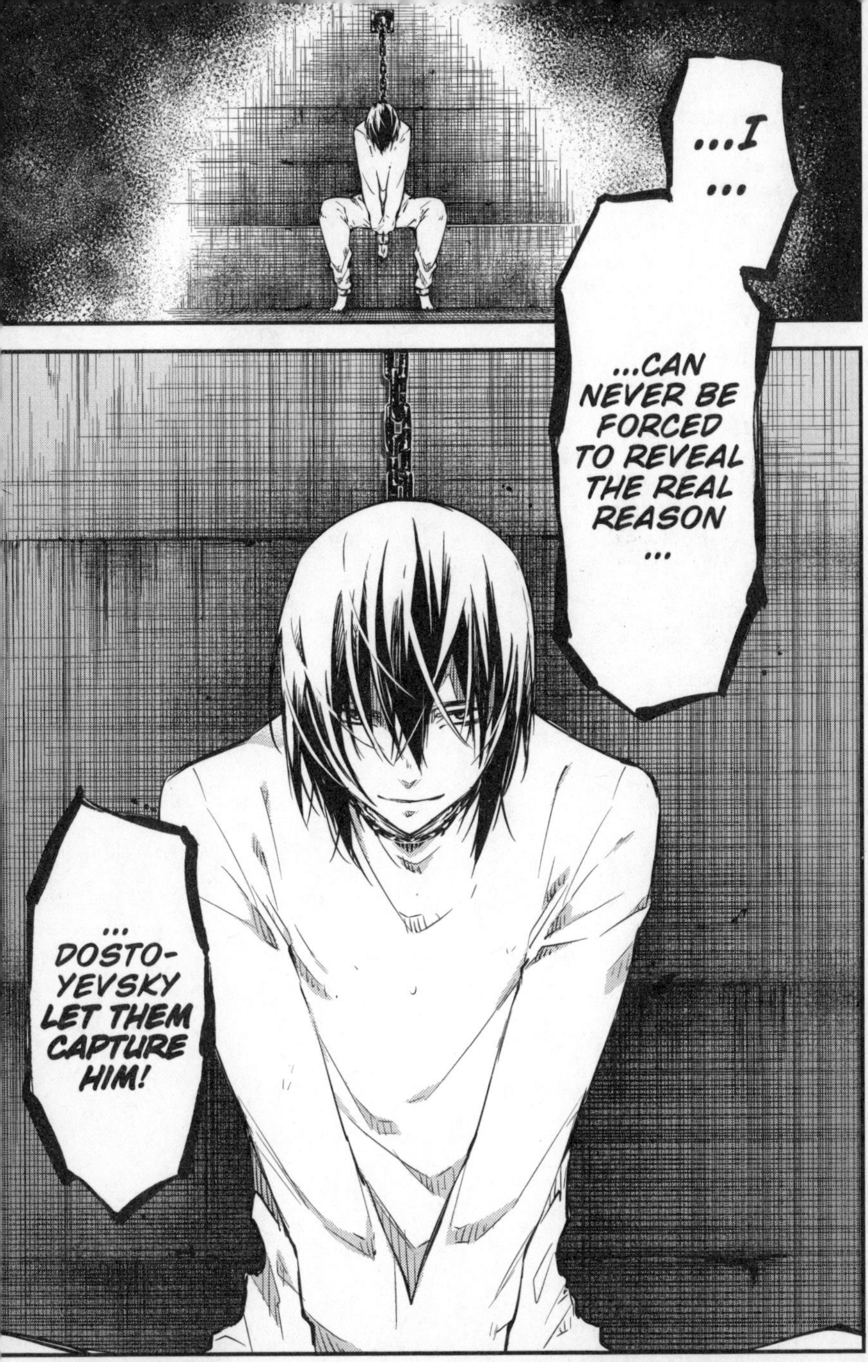
...I ...
...CAN NEVER BE FORCED TO REVEAL THE REAL REASON ...
... DOSTO-YEVSKY LET THEM CAPTURE HIM!

To be continued

Translation Notes

Page 32
In the original Japanese, Dazai is intentionally conflating various word etymologies for similar-sounding terms. For example, this involves mixing up *takenoko* (**bamboo shoots**—literally "child of bamboo") with the fact that *kinoko* ("**mushroom**") kind of sounds like *ki no ko* ("child of wood"). Similarly, *edamame* (young **soybeans** cooked in their pod) literally means "branch beans"), so Dazai implies that **horse beans** (aka fava beans) turn into sky because the Japanese word, *soramame*, literally means "sky beans."

Page 106
Nii-sama is a respectful way of addressing one's older brother.

Page 164
Ukiyo-e are wood-block prints most commonly known for depicting the pleasure quarters and entertainment scene of Edo-period Japan.

Turn to the end of the book for essays by Japanese writer and translator Yuu Ookubo about the author inspirations for the *Bungo Stray Dogs* characters!

BUNGO STRAY DOGS

Story: *Kafka Asagiri* Art: *Sango Harukawa*

Translation: Kevin Gifford   †   Lettering: Bianca Pistillo

BUNGO STRAY DOGS Volume 13
©Kafka ASAGIRI 2017
©Sango HARUKAWA 2017
First published in Japan in 2017 by KADOKAWA CORPORATION, Tokyo.
English translation rights arranged with KADOKAWA CORPORATION, Tokyo through TUTTLE-MORI AGENCY, INC., Tokyo.

English translation © 2019 by Yen Press, LLC

Yen Press
150 West 30th Street, 19th Floor
New York, NY 10001

Visit us at yenpress.com
facebook.com/yenpress
twitter.com/yenpress
yenpress.tumblr.com
instagram.com/yenpress

First Yen Press Edition: December 2019

Yen Press is an imprint of Yen Press, LLC.
The Yen Press name and logo are trademarks of Yen Press, LLC.

Library of Congress Control Number: 2016956681

ISBNs: 978-1-9753-0455-3 (paperback)
      978-1-9753-0456-0 (ebook)

10 9 8 7 6 5 4 3

WOR

Printed in the United States of America

Bungo Episodes

Fyodor Dostoyevsky

By Yuu Ookubo

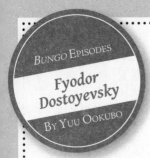

The "King of Garbage," a Pauper Addicted to Gambling, Awakens to His Literary Talent......?!

It's common to see the lives of literary giants fall apart or exist under less than satisfactory conditions. Fyodor Dostoyevsky is perhaps one of the most outstanding examples of this, as he was the type of person whose masterworks were born from pretty terrible situations.

Take, for instance, his famous work *Crime and Punishment*. This major literary work was completed only after the author went overseas while his first wife lay dying, hung out with his lovers, and got addicted to betting on roulette. After her death, Dostoyevsky landed in debt, only to escape it by gambling and womanizing overseas once more. Only when he was deep in the abyss, all but penniless, did the novel get done. And that's not all—near the end of writing *Crime and Punishment*, he signed a contract that handed over the rights to all his previous work if he couldn't complete a new piece. This was all but doomed to happen—he was intent on crafting a masterpiece, which basically meant that he could never muster the courage to touch it. However, as the deadline loomed near, Dostoyevsky hired a stenographer, and after being cornered, made up an entirely new story. This eventually became *The Gambler*, which tells the tale of a man who loses everything to gambling. (The stenographer also became his second wife, funnily enough.)

Despite the fact that *Crime and Punishment* sold a decent amount, he soon went into debt once more, forcing the newlyweds to go on a half-honeymoon, half-mad dash to escape his creditors. In the midst of this, he abandoned his pregnant wife and fell into a roulette addiction once more. Only when they were completely broke did he manage to begin another masterpiece of his, *The Idiot*. His newborn daughter wound up dying at the age of three months, affected by their poverty and grueling travel, putting Dostoyevsky into a deep (albeit rather selfish) sadness and giving him enough force to finish *The Idiot*.

His second wife would later stand at the forefront of honoring him as a great author after his death, but as she herself put it, "He could only write novels after he lost all his money to gambling and was put through despair."

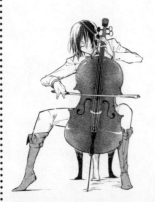

Bungo Episodes

Lucy Maud Montgomery

By Yuu Ookubo

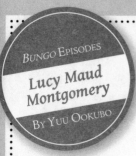

Unassuming in Greatness—a Young Girl's Passionate Diary and Scrapbook!

The story of *Anne of Green Gables*—about the bright young girl who breezily spoke of all the fantasies she came up with—is one many of us have read at a young age. Lots of people can see parallels between Anne and her creator, L. M. Montgomery, who lost her mother young and lived as a de-facto orphan under her strict grandparents. But despite that, Anne's and Lucy's personalities couldn't have been more different.

Being from a strict family, Montgomery had an inability to express her emotions, which led to a passion for reading alone, pouring her heart into her diary, and putting together and showing off her scrapbooks that were full of Anne-esque fantasy and romance.

YAAAAAAAY!

Combine the loquacity of her diaries with the sparkle in her scrapbooks, and you have Anne. However, just before she became an author, Montgomery was actually working for a newspaper—the Canadian *Daily Echo*—where she spent half a year as a proofreader and reporter. In an era where women in the workplace was still a rarity, Montgomery described in her own diary how smitten she was with the ring of the word *newspaperwoman*.

Writing as "Cynthia" (a name just as elegant as "Anne" with an *e*), she mainly wrote filler columns about social events, as well as advertorial pieces where she visited women's hat shops and the like during the Christmas season. Proofreading, to her, was a daily battle against the mischief secretly lurking among the text, to the point that it showed up in her nightmares.

By the time she got used to the work, she was beginning to write fiction on the office clock—and there's no doubt that this reporting experience gave her skills that she leveraged in her life as a writer. At one point, her newspaper received the final chapter of a romance serial from the UK, only to find that the ending had been lost at some point in the process. Who came to the rescue? Montgomery, who by then was well versed enough in literature to write up her own fan fiction–style alternate ending and save the day. That episode wound up providing material for her semiautobiographical series *Emily*—if you're interested in hearing more about it, I'd recommend a read.

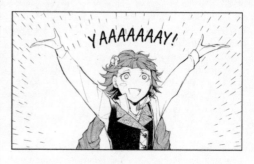

Bungo Episodes

Ougai Mori

By Yuu Ookubo

Well-Mannered Discipline Akin to a Yawn, Backed by Herculean Effort?!

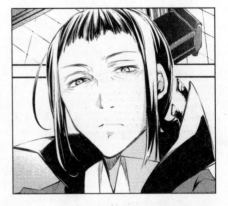

Pictures of Ougai Mori printed in textbooks usually have him wearing a *yukata* or other Japanese garb, but due to his day job as an army doctor, he arguably looked more at home in a crisp military uniform. When fellow authors Ryuunosuke Akutagawa and Touson Shimazaki visited Ougai at Kanchou-ro, his residence, they wrote that they were surprised to see him in a military shirt and white trousers—an outfit considered far too formal for home wear at the time.

Being as tightly wound as that, it's perhaps no surprise that he was a stickler for punctuality. Like German philosopher Immanuel Kant, he kept a rigorous schedule timed down to the last minute, even factoring in his commute and pleasure walks. When a guest would arrive—even one with a formal letter of introduction—he would sit them down, place a clock within their line of sight, and blithely state, "I have plans soon, but we can talk for fifteen minutes."

It goes without saying that his bookshelves were as neatly organized as his day planner. At work, if he needed a book he knew he had back home, he would tell an assistant to run back and pick it up from this or that exact shelf, and they'd bring back the correct one every time. He was also one of the first to translate Poe and Dostoyevsky into Japanese. There's a famous story about an editor visiting to inquire about a translation Ougai had promised him, only to watch the man take the original German volume off the shelf and dictate its contents in Japanese without hesitation, right then and there.

Ougai's home library was well-stocked with all the paper and writing supplies he needed, and not having it all in perfect order was one good way to catch him on his bad side. When it was all there, he was famous for writing out his manuscripts in a refined, elegant hand, with no editing or corrections in the margins—and he'd do this in the most casual of manners while occasionally conversing with people. It made a good friend of his observe once that writing to him seemed to be like yawning—although Ougai's daughter later stated that his handwriting used to be terrible before he made a concerted effort to improve.

He maintained a perfect attendance record at his army job for thirty years, not because he was in good health the whole time, but because he forced himself to report for duty. He may have done this because he was a doctor. This led to a bout of pneumonia once. It just proves that being well-regulated and unhesitant is more the fruit of concerted effort than anything else.

Bungo Episodes

Kenji Miyazawa

By Yuu Ookubo

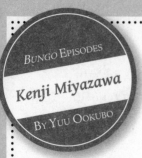

Gotta Catch 'Em All! Kenji, the Unrivaled Collector of Stones, Sounds, and Flowers

Kenji Miyazawa is well-known for his one-of-a-kind poetry and novels, but perhaps because he lived far away from the core of the literary world, little is known about his nature as a person. Did you know, for instance, that he had a penchant for collecting all kinds of items?

When it came to minerals and rocks in particular, he was a cut above the pack, his collecting habits earning him the nickname of "Ken-san the Stone Kid." The sight of him setting off to go hunting for new rocks, a hammer hanging off his hip, left enough of an impression on his friends that they frequently mentioned it in their own recollections later.

Yellow quartz, opals, wavellites, amazonites, rhodonites, malachites…Many stones, precious or not, appear in Kenji's own works, but when it came to real-life stones, he would joyfully show them off by either bringing the real thing or sharing guidebook pictures with his classmates. By the time he became a teacher himself, local jewelers came to visit whenever they needed someone to appraise certain stones. That sort of deep, broad knowledge added a unique accent to his writings.

In addition to his geological hobbies, his upper-class upbringing helped spur him into collecting classical music records. Phonographs and discs were still expensive commodities during his lifetime, so he often held "recitals" of his collection at his house, usually talking over the music to add his own observations and reflections in poetic form.

He also had an interest in insects and plants, building specimen collections and engaging in a little home gardening. He hung reproductions of Western art masterpieces on his walls, and he also boasted a large collection of Japanese *ukiyo-e* (which often included the flowery, otherworldly courtesans that were popular subjects in erotic prints).

It's enough to conjure up the image of a young Kenji (of the *Bungo Stray Dogs* world, at least), Poké Ball in hand, running around the fields and mountains in search of Stone and Grass-type Pokémon. Suits him well, doesn't it?

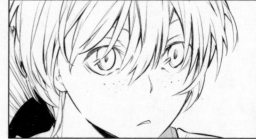

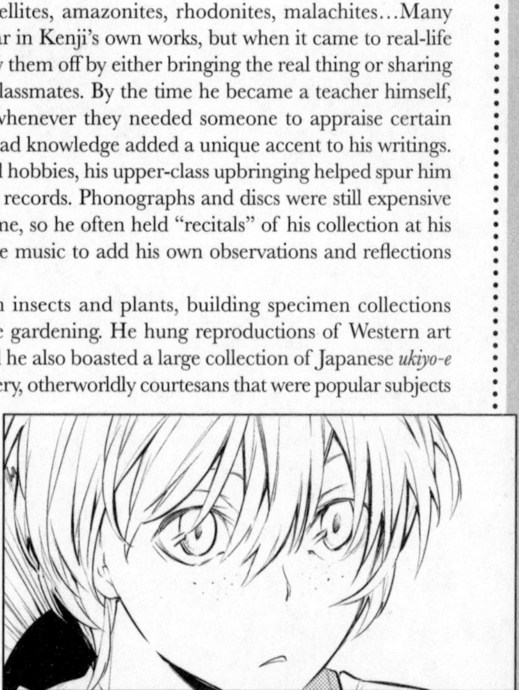